EIGHT PLAYS FOR

THEATRE

EIGHT PLAYS FOR
THEATRE

Edited and with introductions by

Robert Cohen
University of California at Irvine

Mayfield Publishing Company
Mountain View, California

Library of Congress Cataloging-in-Publication Data

Eight plays for theatre.

   Contents: Oedipus Tyrannos / Sophocles—The Plaie Called Corpus Christi, Part I: The Beginnings / Anonymous; modern adaptation by Robert Cohen and Edgar Schell—Romeo and Juliet / by William Shakespeare—[etc.].
   1. Drama—Collections. I. Cohen, Robert, 1938-
II. Title: 8 plays for theatre.
PN6112.E34   1988   808.82   87-31437
ISBN 0-87484-850-4

International Standard Book Number: 0-87484-850-4

Manufactured in the United States of America

10 9 8 7 6 5 4 3 2 1

Mayfield Publishing Company
1240 Villa St.
Mountain View, California 94041

Sponsoring editor, Janet M. Beatty; production editor, Richard Mason; manuscript editor, Richard Mason; text designer, Hal Lockwood; cover designer, Hal Lockwood. The text was set in 9½/11 ITC Zapf International Light by TC Systems and printed on 50 lb. Maple Opaque by the Maple-Vail Book Manufacturing Group.

PREFACE

The eight plays in this edition were selected for three reasons. First, these plays are the full texts of works discussed in my companion volume, *Theatre*. Second, they represent, in combination, the full range of Western Drama since the beginnings of recorded dramatic history. They are not necessarily the greatest plays of all time (although they are all undisputed masterpieces), but they do comprise, as much as any collection can, the broadest possible spectrum of dramatic creativity.

Finally, the plays were selected because they are all wonderful pieces of theatre; each work appearing in this volume is widely read, and regularly translated and staged, throughout the world. For these reasons the versions presented in this text have been selected with a special consideration for their readability and present-day stageworthiness, as well as for their appropriateness to the other demands of this volume.

The plays fall into three general categories: three classic plays from the Greek period through the English Renaissance; three domestic plays from the seventeenth-century "Royal" era to the nineteenth-century Victorian era; and two contemporary plays that strikingly demonstrate, in contrasting fashion, the modern drama's realistic and anti-realistic modes.

Sophocles' *Oedipus Tyrannos* (sometimes known as *Oedipus Rex*, or *Oedipus the King*) is drama's most celebrated tragedy; Aristotle himself considered it the best model of the form when he investigated tragedy in

his monumental work, *The Poetics*. The Ted Brunner-Luci Berkowitz translation was originally commissioned for stage productions in 1967 and 1985. *The Plaie Called Corpus Christi* is a modern (1985–87) consolidation and adaptation of the anonymous mystery plays on Biblical themes that were regularly performed in the streets of York, Wakefield, and other cities and towns in fifteenth-century England; the present adaptation, although collated and modernized for present-day reading and stage production, retains the flavor and the linguistic intricacy of the original Middle English texts. William Shakespeare's *Romeo and Juliet* is perhaps the author's most popular play. It is a work characteristic of England's greatest dramatic writer, of the Elizabethan period in general, and of the romantic spirit, which has its genesis in the sprawling, larger-than-life tragedies and tragicomedies of Elizabethan times.

Molière's *The Bourgeois Gentleman* represents the body of comic entertainments written for the royal courts of Europe in the seventeenth century; this play was initially performed for the French Sun King, Louis XIV, and it exemplifies comic playwriting techniques familiar to the theatre since the days of the Romans and before. August Strindberg's *Miss Julie*, published here together with its author's original preface, is perhaps the epitome of naturalistic drama; even the convention of an intermission is dispensed with by the playwright in his search for a theatre without conventions. And Anton Chekhov's *The Three Sisters* represents the summit of European poetic realism; here is a beautiful study of life in provincial Russia, with characters that live in the audience's mind as people rather than as dramatic integers.

Two plays represent the contemporary, or post–World War II theatre. Samuel Beckett's *Happy Days* is perhaps the clearest expression of the "theatre of the absurd" in the world's dramatic repertoire, and it represents the culmination of the anti-realistic movement that began in Europe about a century ago. And contemporary American supra-realism is arrestingly presented in Sam Shepard's *Fool for Love*, which is both a play about life today in rural America and one that includes dramatic elements that have their roots in virtually all the other plays in this anthology.

I believe that the plays in this volume will be both entertaining and instructive. I hope that they will create, in the reader's mind, a *comprehensive vision of drama*—one that focuses both on the individuality of the theatre's many playwrights and on the common elements of dramatic form and theatrical expression linking Sophocles to Shepard, and Beckett to the Middle Ages.

Robert Cohen
UC Irvine, California

CONTENTS

1 OEDIPUS TYRANNOS

Sophocles

ABOUT 425 B.C.

Translated from the Greek and supplied
with footnotes by Ted Brunner and Luci Berkowitz

Oedipus Tyrannos is more usually known as *Oedipus Rex* or *Oedipus the King*. But "tyrannos" is the more correct title for the mythical ruler of ancient Thebes who is the subject of this play. To the ancient Greeks "tyrannos," from which comes our word "tyrant," designated a leader chosen on the basis of power, not lineage; it designated a leader whose exercise of that power always courted the danger of *hubris*, or excessive pride—the pride that, in tragedy, "goeth before a fall."

Oedipus is such a ruler. Were he real, he would have lived in the Dark Ages of Greece, sometime between the end of the Mycenaean culture (around 1,100 B.C.) and the reappearance of civilization during the emergence of the Greek city-states (around 750 B.C.). His legend has the mythic proportion of its Dark Age origin: a powerful tribal chief who unknowingly murders his father and marries his mother, and who finally discovers his violation of these archetypal taboos and effects his own, horrific self-punishment. It is a legend that would have come down to us even without Sophocles' extraordinary play, for it reveals, just in its retelling, the deepest forces of human nature.

Sophocles' play, however, is an independent masterpiece. Written at the height of the "Golden Age" of Athens—the most brilliant period of An-cient Greek art and culture—it creates a dramatic model that has never been surpassed in its tragic power and sustained emotional force. Aristotle frequently cited the plot of this play as the finest example of the playwright's craft, as exemplified by the combination of reversal and recognition: when the Corinthian messenger comes to cheer Oedipus by relieving him of the fear of marrying his mother, he creates a reversal instead by forcing Oedipus to realize (recognition) that he is the son of Laius, not Polybus, and therefore *is* his mother's husband. The plot of *Oedipus Tyrannos* is constructed with tight precision: it moves with unrelenting intensity towards its predestined end, and it provokes a tragic catharsis that can prove as overwhelming today as it did to Athenian audiences twenty-four hundred years ago.

Sophocles (496–406 B.C.) was the most successful of the ancient Greek tragedians; his plays were immensely popular, and no fewer than eighty of them won the first prize at the Great Dionysia, the Athenian annual springtime festival. Sophocles was revered, both in life and after, for the eloquence and wisdom of his poetic odes, for his dramatic skill and authority, and for his reported personal "gentleness;" still, his popular success and apparent serenity did not prevent him from exploring the depths of

1

his tragic vision. No one can reach the end of *Oedipus Tyrannos* without reflecting deeply, along with the chorus, on our human destiny:

Look at Oedipus—
proof that none of us mortals
can truly be thought of as happy
until he is granted deliverance from life,
until he is dead
and must suffer no more.

A NOTE ON THE TEXT

This translation, by Ted Brunner and Luci Berkowitz, was originally commissioned by the editor of this anthology for stage production; it was subsequently published as the *Norton Critical Edition* of the play, and is here reprinted with the permission of W. W. Norton and Company. The translation employs a modern idiom and, apart from the choruses, is punctuated in the fashion of spoken prose rather than traditional literary verse; this lends the Brunner/Berkowitz translation a power and immediacy comparable to the original Greek, which is not always available in other versions.

OEDIPUS TYRANNOS

CAST OF CHARACTERS

OEDIPUS, *ruler of Thebes*[1]
JOCASTA, *wife of Oedipus*[2]
CREON, *brother of Jocasta*[3]
TEIRESIAS, *a blind prophet*
A PRIEST
MESSENGER 1

MESSENGER 2
A SHEPHERD
AN ATTENDANT
ANTIGONE ⎫ *daughters of Oedipus and Jocasta*
ISMENE ⎭
CHORUS OF THEBAN ELDERS

OEDIPUS: What is it, children, sons of the ancient house of Cadmus?[4] Why do you sit as suppliants crowned with laurel branches? What is the meaning of the incense which fills the city? The pleas to end pain? The cries of sorrow? I chose not to hear it from my messengers, but came myself—I came, Oedipus, Oedipus, whose name is known to all. You, old one—age gives you the right to speak for all of them—you tell me why they sit before my altar. Has something frightened you? What brings you here? Some need? Some want? I'll help you all I can. I would be cruel did I not greet you with compassion when you are gathered here before me.

PRIEST: My Lord and King, we represent the young and old; some are priests and some the best of Theban youth. And I—I am a priest of Zeus.[5]

There are many more who carry laurel boughs like these—in the market-places, at the twin altars of Pallas,[6] by the sacred ashes of Ismenus' oracle.[7] You see yourself how torn our city is, how she craves relief from the waves of death which now crash over her. Death is everywhere—in the harvests of the land, in the flocks that roam the pastures, in the unborn children of our mothers' wombs. A fiery plague is ravaging the city, festering, spreading its pestilence, wasting the house of Cadmus, filling the house of Hades[8] with screams of pain and of fear. This is the reason why we come to you, these children and I. No, we do not think you a god. But we deem you a mortal set apart to face life's common issues and the trials which the gods dispense to men. It was you who once before came to Thebes and freed us from the spell that hypnotized our lives. You did this, and yet you knew no more than we—less even. You had no help from us. God aided you. Yes, you restored our life. And now a second time, great Oedipus, we turn to you for help. Find some relief for us, whether with god or man to guide your way. You helped us then. Yes. And we believe that

---

1. Son of Laius and Jocasta; the meaning of his name is "swollen foot."

The persons, places, and divinities mentioned in the footnotes are identified with reference to their special functions in the *Oedipus Tyrannos*. For example, Hermes is identified as a god of flocks and pastures, even though his divine precincts are far more numerous, *e.g.*, commerce, trickery, music, messenger, guardian of city boundaries, etc.
2. Daughter of Menoeceus, sister of Creon, wife of Laius, mother of Oedipus.
3. Son of Menoeceus. After the death of Laius, he ruled Thebes until the arrival of Oedipus and resumed the rule of the city after Oedipus' fall.
4. Son of Agenor and founder of Cadmea, the citadel that grew to be the city of Thebes (in central Greece), where the drama takes place.
5. Most supreme of the divinities; regarded as the father of gods and men alike. He was often appealed to as a dispenser of justice.

6. Title of the goddess Athena (originally the name of a friend whom she accidentally killed). Athena was goddess of wisdom, but of particular importance as a protectress of cities in Attica and Boeotia.
7. Referring to the shrine of Apollo, located near the river, Ismenus in the vicinity of Thebes. It contained an altar made of ashes supposed to have divining powers.
8. Brother of Zeus; god of the underworld.

you will help us now. O Lord, revive our city; restore her life. Think of your fame, your own repute. The people know you saved us from our past despair. Let no one say you raised us up to let us fall. Save us and keep us safe. You found good omens once to aid you and brought us fortune then. Find them again. If you will rule this land as king and lord, rule over men and not a wall encircling emptiness. No city wall, no ship can justify its claim to strength if it is stripped of men who give it life.

OEDIPUS: O my children, I know well the pain you suffer and understand what brings you here. You suffer—and yet not one among you suffers more than I. Each of you grieves for himself alone, while my heart must bear the strain of sorrow for all—myself and you and all our city's people. No, I am not blind to it. I have wept and in my weeping set my thoughts on countless paths, searching for an answer. I have sent my own wife's brother Creon, son of Menoeceus, to Apollo's Pythian shrine[9] to learn what I might say or do to ease our city's suffering. I am concerned that he is not yet here—he left many days ago. But this I promise: whenever he returns, whatever news he brings, whatever course the god reveals—*that* is the course that I shall take.

PRIEST: Well spoken. Look! They are giving signs that Creon is returning.

OEDIPUS: O God! If only he brings news as welcome as his smiling face.

PRIEST: I think he does. His head is crowned with laurel leaves.

OEDIPUS: We shall know soon enough. There. My Lord Creon, what word do you bring from the god?

(*Enter* CREON)

CREON: Good news. I tell you this: if all goes well, our troubles will be past.

OEDIPUS: But what was the oracle? Right now I'm swaying between hope and fear.

CREON: If you want to hear it in the presence of these people, I shall tell you. If not, let's go inside.

OEDIPUS: Say it before all of us. I sorrow more for them than for myself.

CREON: Then I shall tell you exactly what the god Apollo answered. These are his words: Pollution. A hidden sore is festering in our land. We are to stop its growth before it is too late.

OEDIPUS: Pollution? How are we to save ourselves?

CREON: Blood for blood. To save ourselves we are to banish a man or pay for blood with blood. It is a murder which has led to this despair.

OEDIPUS: Murder? Whose? Did the god say whose . . . ?

CREON: My Lord, before you came to rule our city, we had a king. His name was Laius. . . .

OEDIPUS: I know, although I never saw him.

CREON: He was murdered. And the god's command is clear: we must find the assassin and destroy him.

OEDIPUS: But where? Where is he to be found? How can we find the traces of a crime committed long ago?

CREON: He lives among us. If we seek, we will find; what we do not seek cannot be found.

OEDIPUS: Where was it that Laius met his death? At home? The country? In some foreign land?

CREON: One day he left and told us he would go to Delphi. That was the last we saw of him.

OEDIPUS: And there was no one who could tell what happened? No one who traveled with him? Did no one see? Is there no evidence?

CREON: All perished. All—except one who ran in panic from the scene and could not tell us anything for certain, except . . .

OEDIPUS: Except? What? What was it? One clue might lead to many. We have to grasp the smallest shred of hope.

CREON: He said that robbers—many of them—fell upon Laius and his men and murdered them.

OEDIPUS: Robbers? Who committed *murder?* Why? Unless they were paid assassins?

CREON: We considered that. But the king was dead and we were plagued with trouble. No one came forth as an avenger.

OEDIPUS: Trouble? What could have kept you from investigating the death of your king?

---

9. Apollo was god of light, prophecy, plague and healing, purification, and justice; he was the son of Zeus and Leto and the brother of Artemis. "Pythian" was an epithet of Apollo, also describing the sanctuary, oracle, and attendants at Delphi. The term originated from the belief that Apollo slew the monster Python to gain control of Delphi, the most sacred sanctuary of Apollo in Greece, located on the southern slope of Mt. Parnassus.

CREON: The Sphinx.[1] The Sphinx was confounding us with her riddles, forcing us to abandon our search for the unknown and to tend to what was then before us.

OEDIPUS: Then I—I shall begin again. I shall not cease until I bring the truth to light. Apollo has shown, and you have shown, the duty which we owe the dead. You have my gratitude. You will find me a firm ally, and together we shall exact vengeance for our land and for the god. I shall not rest till I dispel this defilement—not just for another man's sake, but for my own as well. For whoever the assassin—he might turn his hand against me too. Yes, I shall be serving Laius and myself. Now go, my children. Leave the steps of my altar. Go. Take away your laurel branches. Go to the people of Cadmus. Summon them. Tell them that I, their king, will leave nothing untried. And with the help of God, we shall find success—or ruin.

(*Exit* OEDIPUS)

PRIEST: Come, children. We have learned what we came to learn.
Come, Apollo, come yourself, who sent these oracles!
Come as our savior! Come! Deliver us from this plague!

CHORUS: O prophecy of Zeus, sweet is the sound of your words
as they come to our glorious city of Thebes
from Apollo's glittering shrine.
Yet I quake and I dread and I tremble at those words.
Io, Delian Lord![2]

What will you bring to pass? Disaster unknown,
or familiar to us, as the ever recurring seasons?
Tell me, O oracle,
heavenly daughter of blessèd hope.

Foremost I call on you, daughter of Zeus,
Athena, goddess supreme;
and on Artemis,[3] shielding the world,
shielding this land from her circular shrine
graced with renown.
And on you I call, Phoebus,[4] Lord of the unerring bow.

Come to my aid, you averters of doom!
Come to my aid if ever you came!
Come to my aid as once you did, when you quenched
the fires of doom that fell on our soil!
Hear me, and come to my aid!

Boundless the pain, boundless the grief I bear;
sickness pervades this land,
affliction without reprieve.
Barren the soil, barren of fruit;
children are born no longer to light;
all of us flutter in agony
winging our way into darkness and death.

Countless the number of dead in the land;
corpses of children cover the plain,
children dying before they have lived,
no one to pity them,
reeking, and spreading diseases and death.

Moaning and wailing our wives,
moaning and wailing our mothers
stream to the altars this way and that,
scream to the air with helpless cries.
Hear us, golden daughter of Zeus,
hear us! Send us release!

Ares[5] now rages in our midst
brandishing in his hands
the firebrands of disease,
raving, consuming, rousing the screams of death.
Hear us, O goddess!
Help us, and still his rage!

---

1. A mythological monster with a woman's head, the body of a lion, and wings, who tormented the city of Thebes with the following riddle: "What walks on four feet in the morning, two feet at noon, and three feet at night?" Only Oedipus was able to offer the correct answer: "Man" (in his infancy, adulthood, and old age).
2. "Io" (pronounced *ee-oh*) was a cry used in invoking a god or praying for help. "Delian" was an epithet of Apollo who, traditionally, is said to have been born on the island of Delos in the Aegean Sea. Delos was an important center of the god's worship.

3. Daughter of Zeus and Leto; sister of Apollo; goddess of the hunt, but also of childbirth, and protectress of the young. Her shrine was commonly located in the agora, the marketplace, which was often of circular shape.
4. Epithet of Apollo meaning "bright" or "radiant," from his identification with the sun.
5. Son of Zeus and Hera; god of war, whose favorite haunt was Thrace. He was sometimes considered the bringer of plague.

Turn back his assault!
Help us! Banish him from our land!
Drive him into the angry sea,
to the wave-swept border of Thrace![6]

We who escape him tonight
will be struck down at dawn.
Help us, O father Zeus,
Lord of the thunderbolt,
crush him! Destroy him!
Burn him with fires of lightning!

Help us, Apollo, Lycean[7] Lord!
Stand at our side with your golden bow!
Artemis, help us!
Come from the Lycian[8] hills!
Come with your torches aflame!
Dionysus,[9] protector, come to our aid,
come with your revelers' band!
Burn with your torch the god
hated among the gods!

(*Enter* OEDIPUS)

OEDIPUS: I have heard your prayers and answer with
relief and help, if you will heed my words and
tend the sickness with the cure it cries for. My
words are uttered as a stranger to the act, a
stranger to its tale. I cannot trace its path alone,
without a sign. As a citizen newer to Thebes
than you, I make this proclamation: If one
among you knows who murdered Laius, the
son of Labdacus,[1] let him tell us now. If he fears
for his life, let him confess and know a milder
penalty. He will be banished from this land.
Nothing more. Or if you know the assassin to be
an alien, do not protect him with your silence.
You will be rewarded. But if in fear you protect
yourself or any other man and keep your silence, then hear what I say now: Whoever he is,

this assassin must be denied entrance to your
homes. Any man where I rule is forbidden to
receive him or speak to him or share with him
his prayers and sacrifice or offer him the holy
rites of purification. I command you to drive
this hideous curse out of your homes; I command you to obey the will of Pythian Apollo. I
will serve the god and the dead. On the assassin
or assassins, I call down the most vile damnation—for this vicious act, may the brand of
shame be theirs to wear forever. And if I know-
ingly harbor their guilt within my own walls, I
shall not exempt myself from the curse that I
have called upon them. It is for me, for God,
and for this city that staggers toward ruin that
you must fulfill these injunctions. Even if
Heaven gave you no sign, you had the sacred
duty to insure that this act did not go unexam-
ined, unavenged! It was the assassination of a
noble man—your king! Now that I hold the
powers that he once held, his bed, his wife—
had fate been unopposed, his children would
have bound us closer yet—and now on him has
this disaster fallen. I will avenge him as I would
avenge my own father. I will leave nothing untried to expose the murderer of Laius, the son of
Labdacus, heir to the house of Cadmus and
Agenor.[2] On those who deny me obedience, I
utter this curse: May the gods visit them with
barrenness in their harvests, barrenness in their
women, barrenness in their fate. Worse still—
may they be haunted and tormented and never
know the peace that comes with death. But for
you, my people, in sympathy with me—I pray
that Justice and all the gods attend you forever.

CHORUS: You have made me swear an oath, my Lord,
and under oath I speak. I did not kill the king
and cannot name the man who did. The question was Apollo's. He could name the man you
seek.

OEDIPUS: I know. And yet no mortal can compel a god
to speak.

CHORUS: The next-best thing, it seems to me . . .

OEDIPUS: Tell me. Tell me all your thoughts. We must
consider everything.

CHORUS: There is one man, second only to Apollo,
who can see the truth, who can clearly help us
in our search—Teiresias.

6. Region east of Macedonia; a favorite haunt of Ares.
7. Epithet of Apollo; it is related to the Greek word meaning
"wolf" and refers to Apollo's role as patron of flocks and killer
of wolves.
8. Referring to Lycia, a region on the southern coast of Asia
Minor, which was one of the haunts of Apollo and Artemis.
9. Son of Zeus and Semele, the daughter of Cadmus, and
thus closely associated with Thebes; god of vegetation and
fertility; he frequently haunted the countryside and mountains, accompanied by woodland nymphs, satyrs, and mae-
nads.
1. Grandson of Cadmus.

2. Mythological king of Phoenicia, father of Cadmus.

OEDIPUS: I thought of this. On Creon's advice, I sent for him. Twice. He should be here.

CHORUS: There were some rumors once, but no one hears them now.

OEDIPUS: What rumors? I want to look at every tale that is told.

CHORUS: They said that travelers murdered Laius.

OEDIPUS: I have heard that too. And yet there's no one to be found who saw the murderer in the act.

CHORUS: He will come forth himself, once he has heard your curse, if he knows what it means to be afraid.

OEDIPUS: Why? Why should a man now fear words if then he did not fear to kill?

CHORUS: But there is one man who can point him out—the man in whom the truth resides, the god-inspired prophet. And there—they are bringing him now.

(*Enter* TEIRESIAS *guided by a servant*)

OEDIPUS: Teiresias, all things are known to you—the secrets of heaven and earth, the sacred and profane. Though you are blind, you surely see the plague that rakes our city. My Lord Teiresias, we turn to you as our only hope. My messengers may have told you—we have sent to Apollo and he has answered us. We must find Laius' murderers and deal with them. Or drive them out. Then—only then will we find release from our suffering. I ask you not to spare your gifts of prophecy. Look to the voices of prophetic birds or the answers written in the flames. Spare nothing. Save all of us—yourself, your city, your king, and all that is touched by this deathly pollution. We turn to you. My Lord, it is man's most noble role to help his fellow man the best his talents will allow.

TEIRESIAS: O God! How horrible wisdom is! How horrible when it does not help the wise! How could I have forgotten? I should not have come.

OEDIPUS: Why? What's wrong?

TEIRESIAS: Let me go. It will be better if you bear your own distress and I bear mine. It will be better this way.

OEDIPUS: This city gave you life and yet you refuse her an answer! You speak as if you were her enemy.

TEIRESIAS: No! No! It is because I see the danger in your words. And mine would add still more.

OEDIPUS: For God's sake, if you know, don't turn away from us! We are pleading. We are begging you.

TEIRESIAS: Because you are blind! No! I shall not reveal my secrets. I shall not reveal yours.

OEDIPUS: What? You know, and yet you refuse to speak? Would you betray us and watch our city fall helplessly to her death?

TEIRESIAS: I will not cause you further grief. I will not grieve myself. Stop asking me to tell; I will tell you nothing.

OEDIPUS: You will not tell? You monster! You could stir the stones of earth to a burning rage! You will never tell? What will it take?

TEIRESIAS: Know yourself, Oedipus. You denounce me, but you do not yet know yourself.

OEDIPUS: Yes! You disgrace your city. And then you expect us to control our rage!

TEIRESIAS: It does not matter if I speak; the future has already been determined.

OEDIPUS: And if it has, then it is for you to tell me, *prophet!*

TEIRESIAS: I shall say no more. Rage, if you wish.

OEDIPUS: I *am* enraged. And now I will tell you what I think. I think this was *your* doing. *You* plotted the crime, *you* saw it carried out. It was *your* doing. All but the actual killing. And had you not been blind, you would have done *that*, too!

TEIRESIAS: Do you believe what you have said? Then accept your own decree! From this day on, deny yourself the right to speak to anyone. You, Oedipus, are the desecrator, the polluter of this land!

OEDIPUS: You traitor! Do you think that you can get away with this?

TEIRESIAS: The truth is my protection.

OEDIPUS: Who taught you this? It did not come from prophecy!

TEIRESIAS: *You* taught me. *You* drove me, *you* forced me to say it against my will.

OEDIPUS: Say it again. I want to make sure that I understand you.

TEIRESIAS: Understand me? Or are you trying to provoke me?

OEDIPUS: No, I want to be sure, I want to know. Say it again.

TEIRESIAS: I say that you, Oedipus Tyrannos, are the murderer you seek.

OEDIPUS: So! A second time! Now twice you will regret what you have said!

TEIRESIAS: Shall I tell you more? Shall I fan your flames of anger?

OEDIPUS: Yes. Tell me more. Tell me more—whatever suits you. It will be in vain.

TEIRESIAS: I say you live in shame with the woman you love, blind to your own calamity.

OEDIPUS: Do you think you can speak like this forever?

TEIRESIAS: I do, if there is any strength in truth.

OEDIPUS: There is—for everyone but you. You—you cripple! Your ears are deaf, your eyes are blind, your mind—your *mind* is crippled!

TEIRESIAS: You fool! You slander me when one day you will hear the same . . .

OEDIPUS: You live in night, Teiresias, in night that never turns to day. And so, you cannot hurt me—or any man who sees the light.

TEIRESIAS: No—it is not I who will cause your fall. That is Apollo's office—and he will discharge it.

OEDIPUS: Was this *your* trick—or Creon's?

TEIRESIAS: No, not Creon's. No, Oedipus. You are destroying yourself!

OEDIPUS: Ah, wealth and sovereignty and skill surpassing skill in life's contentions, why must envy always attend them? This city *gave* me power; I did not ask for it. And Creon, my friend, my trusted friend, would plot to overthrow me—with this charlatan, this impostor, who auctions off his magic wares! His eyes see profit clearly, but they are blind in prophecy. Tell me, Teiresias, what makes you a prophet? Where were you when the monster was here weaving her spells and taunts? What words of relief did Thebes hear from you? Her riddle would stagger the simple mind; it demanded the mind of a seer. Yet, put to the test, all your birds and god-craft proved useless; you had no answer. Then *I* came—ignorant Oedipus— I came and smothered her, using only my wit. There were no birds to tell me what to do. I am the man you would overthrow so you can stand near Creon's throne. You will regret—you and your conspirator—you will regret your attempt to purify this land. If you were not an old man, I would make you suffer the pain which you deserve for your audacity.

CHORUS: Both of you, my Lord, have spoken in bitter rage. No more—not when we must direct our every thought to obey the god's command.

TEIRESIAS: Though you are king, the right to speak does not belong to you alone. It is *my* right as well and I shall claim it. I am not your servant and Creon is not my patron. I serve only Loxian[3] Apollo. And I tell you this, since you mock my blindness. You have eyes, Oedipus, and do not see your own destruction. You have eyes and do not see what lives with you. Do you know whose son you are? I say that you have sinned and do not know it; you have sinned against your own—the living and the dead. A double scourge, your mother's and your father's curse, will drive you from this land. Then darkness will shroud those eyes that now can see the light. Cithaeron[4]—the whole earth will resound with your mournful cries when you discover the meaning of the wedding-song that brought you to this place you falsely thought a haven. More sorrow still awaits you—more than you can know—to show you what you are and what your children are. Damn Creon, if you will; damn the words I say. No man on earth will ever know the doom that waits for you.

OEDIPUS: How much of this am I to bear? Leave! Now! Leave my house!

TEIRESIAS: I would not be here had you not sent for me.

OEDIPUS: I never would have sent for you had I known the madness I would hear.

TEIRESIAS: To you, I am mad; but not to your parents . . .

OEDIPUS: Wait! My parents? Who are my parents?

TEIRESIAS: This day shall bring you birth *and* death.

OEDIPUS: Why must you persist with riddles?

TEIRESIAS: Are you not the best of men when it comes to riddles?

OEDIPUS: You mock the very skill that proves me great.

TEIRESIAS: A great misfortune—which will destroy you.

OEDIPUS: I don't care. If I have saved this land, I do not care.

TEIRESIAS: Then I shall go. (*to his servant*) Come, take me home.

OEDIPUS: Yes, go home. You won't be missed.

TEIRESIAS: I will go when I've said all that I came to say. I am not afraid of you. You cannot hurt me.

---

3. Epithet of Apollo. The term has been explained to mean "ambiguous" with reference to the nature of the god's oracles.
4. Mountain range southwest of Thebes, on the border of Attica and Boeotia.

And I tell you this: The man you seek—the man whose death or banishment you ordered, the man who murdered Laius—that man is here, passing as an alien, living in our midst. Soon it will be known to all of you—he is a native Theban. And he will find no joy in that discovery. His eyes now see, but soon they will be blind: rich now, but soon a beggar. Holding a scepter now, but soon a cane, he will grope for the earth beneath him—in a foreign land. Both brother and father to the children that he loves. Both son and husband to the woman who bore him. Both heir and spoiler of his father's bed and the one who took his life. Go, think on this. And if you find the words I speak are lies, *then* say that I am blind.

(*Exeunt* OEDIPUS, TEIRESIAS)

CHORUS: Who is he? Who is the man?
  Who is the man whom the voice of the Delphian shrine
  denounced as the killer, the murderer,
  the man who committed the terrible crime?
  Where is he? Where is he now?
  Let him run, let him flee!
  Let him rush with the speed of the wind on his flight!
  For with fire and lightning the god will attack,
  and relentlessly fate will pursue him and haunt him
  and drive him to doom.

  Do you hear? Do you hear the command of the god?
  From Parnassus[5] he orders the hunt.
  In vain will the murderer hide,
  in vain will he run,
  in vain will he lurk in the forests and caves
  like an animal roaming the desolate hills.
  Let him flee to the edge of the world:
  On his heels he will find
  the command of the god!

  Confusion and fear
  have been spread by the prophet's words.
  For I cannot affirm, yet I cannot refute

what he spoke. And I'm lost, I am lost—
What am I to believe?
Now foreboding is gripping my heart.
Was there ever a strife between Laius and Polybus' house?[6]
Can I test? Can I prove?
Can I ever believe that the name of my king
has been soiled by a murder unknown?

It is Zeus and Apollo who know,
who can see the affairs of men.
But the seer and I,
we are mortal, and blind.
Who is right? Who can judge?
We are mortal, our wisdom assigned in degrees.
Does the seer know? Do I?
No, I will not believe in the prophet's charge
till the charge has been proved to my mind.
For I saw how the king
in the test with the Sphinx
proved his wisdom and worth
when he saved this city from doom.
No! I can *never* condemn the king!

(*Enter* CREON)

CREON: My fellow-citizens, anger has impelled me to come because I have heard the accusation which Oedipus has brought against me—and I will not tolerate it. If he thinks that I—in the midst of this torment—I have thought to harm him in any way, I will not spend the rest of my life branded by his charge. Doesn't he see the implications of such slander? To you, to my friends, to my city—I would be a traitor!
CHORUS: He spoke in anger—without thinking.
CREON: Yes—and who was it who said that the prophet lied on my advice?
CHORUS: It was said, but I don't know how it was meant.
CREON: And was this a charge leveled by one whose eyes were clear? Whose head was clear?
CHORUS: I don't know. I do not judge my master's actions. But here he comes.

---

5. Mountain massif in central Greece, at the foot of which Delphi was located; sacred to Apollo.

6. Polybus was king of Corinth and foster-father of Oedipus.

(*Enter* OEDIPUS)

OEDIPUS: Why have you come, Creon? Do you have the audacity to show your face in my presence? Assassin! And now you would steal my throne! What drove you to this plot? Did you see cowardice in me? Stupidity? Did you imagine that I would not see your treachery? Did you expect that I wouldn't act to stop you? You fool! Your plot was mad! You go after a throne without money, without friends! How do you think thrones are won?

CREON: You listen to me! And when you have heard me out, when you have heard the truth, *then* judge for yourself.

OEDIPUS: Ah yes, your oratory! I can learn nothing from that. This is what I have learned—you are my enemy!

CREON: Just let me say . . .

OEDIPUS: Say one thing—say that you are not a traitor.

CREON: If you think that senseless stubbornness is a precious gift, you are a fool.

OEDIPUS: If you think that you can threaten the house of Cadmus—your own house—and not pay for it, you are mad.

CREON: I grant you that. But tell me: just what is this terrible thing you say I have done to you?

OEDIPUS: Did you or did you not tell me to send for that—that—prophet?

CREON: I did. And I would again.

OEDIPUS: Then, how long since Laius . . . ?

CREON: What? I do not follow . . .

OEDIPUS: . . . Disappeared?

CREON: A long time ago.

OEDIPUS: Your Teiresias—was he—was he a prophet then?

CREON: Yes—and just as honored and just as wise.

OEDIPUS: Did he ever mention me—then?

CREON: Not in my presence.

OEDIPUS: But didn't you investigate the murder?

CREON: Of course we did—

OEDIPUS: And why didn't the prophet say anything *then?*

CREON: I do not know. It's not for me to try to understand.

OEDIPUS: You know this much which you will try to tell me . . .

CREON: What is it? I will tell you if I can.

OEDIPUS: Just this: Had he not acted under your instructions, he would not have named *me* killer of Laius.

CREON: If this is what he said, you ought to know. You heard him. But now I claim the right to question you, as you have me.

OEDIPUS: Ask what you wish. I am not the murderer.

CREON: Then answer me. Did you marry my sister?

OEDIPUS: Of course I did.

CREON: And do you rule on equal terms with her?

OEDIPUS: She has all that she wants from me.

CREON: And am I not the third and equal partner?

OEDIPUS: You are—and that is where you have proved yourself a traitor.

CREON: Not true. Consider rationally, as I have done. First ask yourself—would any man prefer a life of fear to one in which the self-same rank, the self-same rights are guaranteed untroubled peace? I have no wish to be a king when I can act as one without a throne. And any man would feel the same, if he were wise. I share with you a king's prerogatives, yet you alone must face the danger lurking around the throne. If *I* were king, I would have to act in many ways against my pleasure. What added benefit could kingship hold when I have rank and rule without the threat of pain? I am not deluded—no, I would not look for honors beyond the ones which profit me. I have the favor of every man; each greets me first when he would hope to have *your* favor. Why should I exchange this for a throne? Only a fool would. No, I am not a traitor nor would I aid an act of treason. You want proof? Go to Delphi; ask if I have brought you the truth. Then, if you find me guilty of conspiracy with the prophet, command my death. I will face that. But do not condemn me without proof. You are wrong to judge the guilty innocent, the innocent guilty— without proof. Casting off a true friend is like casting off your greatest prize—your life. You will know in time that this is true. Time alone reveals the just; a single day condemns the guilty.

CHORUS: He is right, my Lord. Respect his words. A man who plans in haste will gamble the result.

OEDIPUS: This is a plot conceived in rashness. It must be met with quick response. I cannot sit and wait until the plot succeeds.

CREON: What will you do then? Do you intend to banish me?

OEDIPUS: No. No, not banish you. I want to see you *dead*—to make you an example for all aspiring to my throne.

CREON: Then you won't do as I suggest? You won't believe me?

OEDIPUS: You have not shown that you deserve belief.

CREON: No, because I see that you are mad.

OEDIPUS: In my own eyes, I am sane.

CREON: You should be sane in mine as well.

OEDIPUS: No. You are a traitor!

CREON: And what if you are wrong?

OEDIPUS: Still—*I* will rule.

CREON: Not when you rule treacherously.

OEDIPUS: O Thebes! My city! Listen to him!

CREON: *My* city too!

CHORUS: My Lords, no more. Here comes Jocasta. Perhaps the queen can end this bitter clash.

(*Enter* JOCASTA)

JOCASTA: Why do you behave like senseless fools and quarrel without reason? Are you not ashamed to add trouble of your own when your city is sick and dying? Go, Creon. Go and leave us alone. Forget those petty grievances which you exaggerate. How important can they be?

CREON: This important, sister: Oedipus, your husband, in his insanity, has threatened me with banishment or death.

OEDIPUS: Yes, for I have realized his plot—a plot against my person.

CREON: May the gods haunt me forever, if that is true—if I am guilty of that charge.

JOCASTA: In the name of God, believe him, Oedipus! Believe him for the sake of his oath, for my own sake, and for theirs!

CHORUS: Listen to her, my Lord. I beg you to consider and comply.

OEDIPUS: What would you have me do?

CHORUS: Respect the oath that Creon gave you. Respect his past integrity.

OEDIPUS: Do you know what you are asking?

CHORUS: Yes, I know.

OEDIPUS: Then, tell me what you mean.

CHORUS: I mean that you are wrong to charge a friend who has invoked a curse upon his head. You are wrong to slander without proof and be the cause for his dishonor.

OEDIPUS: Then you must know that when you ask for this, you ask for banishment or doom—for *me*.

CHORUS: O God, No!
   O Helios,[7] no!
   May Heaven and Earth exact my doom
   if that is what I thought!
   When our city is torn by sickness
   and my heart is torn with pain—
   do not compound the troubles
   that beset us!

OEDIPUS: Then, let him go, although it surely means my death—or banishment with dishonor. *Your* words—not his—have touched my heart. But Creon—wherever he may be—I will hate him.

CREON: You are hard when you should yield, cruel when you should pity. Such natures deserve the pain they bear.

OEDIPUS: Just go—and leave me in peace.

CREON: I will go—my guilt pronounced by you alone. Behold my judge and jury—Oedipus Tyrannos!

(*Exit* CREON)

CHORUS: My queen, persuade your husband to rest awhile.

JOCASTA: I will—when I have learned the truth.

CHORUS: Blind suspicion has consumed the king. And Creon's passions flared beneath the sting of unjust accusations.

JOCASTA: Are *both* at fault?

CHORUS: Yes, both of them.

JOCASTA: But what is the reason for their rage?

CHORUS: Don't ask again. Our city is weary enough from suffering. Enough. Let the matter rest where it now stands.

OEDIPUS: Do you see what you have done? Do you see where you have come—with your good intentions, your noble efforts to dull the sharpness of my anger?

CHORUS: My Lord, I have said before
   and now I say again:
   I would be mad,
   a reckless fool
   to turn away my king,
   who saved us from a sea of troubles
   and set us on a fairer course,
   and who will lead us once again
   to peace, a haven from our pain.

---

7. As god of the sun, he sees and hears everything and is, thus, often appealed to as a witness of oaths.

JOCASTA: In the name of Heaven, my Lord, tell me the reason for your bitterness.

OEDIPUS: I will—because you mean more to me than anyone. The reason is Creon and his plot against my throne.

JOCASTA: But can you *prove* a plot?

OEDIPUS: He says that I—Oedipus—bear the guilt of Laius' death.

JOCASTA: How does he justify this charge?

OEDIPUS: He does not stain his own lips by saying it. No. He uses that false prophet to speak for him.

JOCASTA: Then, you can exonerate yourself because no mortal has the power of divination. And I can prove it. An oracle came to Laius once from the Pythian priests—I'll not say from Apollo himself—that he would die at the hands of his own child, his child and mine. Yet the story which *we* heard was that robbers murdered Laius in a place where three roads meet. As for the child—when he was three days old, Laius drove pins into his ankles and handed him to someone to cast upon a deserted mountain path—to die. And so, Apollo's prophecy was unfulfilled—the child did not kill his father. And Laius' fears were unfulfilled—he did not die by the hand of his child. Yet, these had been the prophecies. You need not give them any credence. For the god will reveal what he wants.

OEDIPUS: Jocasta—my heart is troubled at your words. Suddenly, my thoughts are wandering, disturbed . . .

JOCASTA: What is it? What makes you so frightened?

OEDIPUS: Your statement—that Laius was murdered in a place where three roads meet. Isn't that what you said?

JOCASTA: Yes. That was the story then; that is the story now.

OEDIPUS: Where is this place where three roads meet?

JOCASTA: In the land called Phocis where the roads from Delphi and from Daulia converge.[8]

OEDIPUS: How long a time has passed since then?

JOCASTA: We heard it shortly before you came.

OEDIPUS: O God, what have you planned for me?

JOCASTA: What is it, Oedipus? What frightens you?

OEDIPUS: Do not ask me. Do not ask. Just tell me—what was Laius like? How old was he?

JOCASTA: He was tall and his hair was lightly cast

with silver tones, the contour of his body much like yours.

OEDIPUS: O God! Am I cursed and cannot see it?

JOCASTA: What is it, Oedipus? You frighten me.

OEDIPUS: It cannot be—that the prophet sees! Tell me one more thing.

JOCASTA: You frighten me, my Lord, but I will try to tell you what I know.

OEDIPUS: Who traveled with the king? Was he alone? Was there a guide? An escort? A few? Many?

JOCASTA: There were five—one of them a herald—and a carriage in which Laius rode.

OEDIPUS: O God! O God! I see it all now! Jocasta, who told you this?

JOCASTA: A servant—the only one who returned alive.

OEDIPUS: Is he here now? In our house?

JOCASTA: No. When he came back and saw you ruling where once his master was, he pleaded with me—begged me—to send him to the fields to tend the flocks, far from the city. And so I did. He was a good servant and I would have granted him more than that, if he had asked.

OEDIPUS: Could we arrange to have him here—now?

JOCASTA: Yes, but what do you want with him?

OEDIPUS: I am afraid, Jocasta. I have said too much and now I have to see him.

JOCASTA: Then he shall be brought. But I, too, must know the cause of your distress. I have the right to know.

OEDIPUS: Yes, you have the right. And I must tell you—now. You, more than anyone, will have to know what I am going through. My father was Polybus of Corinth, my mother a Dorian—Merope.[9] I was held in high regard in Corinth until—until something strange occurred—something uncanny and strange, although I might have given it too much concern. There was a man dining with us one day who had had far too much wine and shouted at me—half-drunk and shouting that I was not rightly called my father's son. I could barely endure the rest of that day and on the next I went to my parents and questioned them. They were enraged at the remark. I felt relieved at their response. But still, this—this thing—kept gnawing at my

---

8. Phocis was a region in central Greece, in which Delphi was located; the city of Daulia was southeast of Mt. Parnassus.

9. Corinth was a city in the northern Peloponnese on the Isthmus of Corinth; it was the name of Polybus and Merope, the foster-parents of Oedipus. "Dorian" denotes association with the inhabitants of the Peloponnese and the Isthmus of Corinth.

heart. And it was spread about in vulgar whispers. And then, without my parents' knowledge, I went to Delphi, but Apollo did not say what I had gone to hear. Instead, he answered questions I had not asked and told of horror and misery beyond belief—how I would know my mother's bed and bring to the world a race of children too terrible for men to see and cause the death of my own father. I trembled at those words and fled from Corinth—as far as I could—to where no star could ever guide me back, where I could never see that infamous prophecy fulfilled. And as I traveled, I came to that place where you say the king was murdered. This is the truth, Jocasta—I was in that place where the three roads meet. There was a herald leading a carriage drawn by horses and a man riding in the carriage—just as you described. The man in front, and the old one, ordered me out of the path. I refused. The driver pushed. In anger, I struck him. The old man saw it, reached for his lash and waited till I had passed. Then he struck me on the head. But he paid—oh yes, he paid. He lost his balance and fell from the carriage and as he lay there helpless—on his back—I killed him. I killed them all. But if this stranger had any tie with Laius—O God—who could be more hated in the eyes of Heaven and Earth? *I* am the one whom strangers and citizens are forbidden to receive! *I* am the one to whom all are forbidden to speak! *I* am the one who must be driven out! *I* am the one for whom my curse was meant! I have touched his bed with the very hands that killed him! O God! The sin! The horror! I am to be banished, never to see my people, never to walk in my fatherland. Or else I must take my mother for a bride and kill my father Polybus, who gave me life and cared for me. What cruel god has sent this torture? Hear me, you gods, you holy gods—I will never see that day! I will die before I ever see the stain of this abominable act!

CHORUS: Your words frighten us, my Lord. But you must have hope until you hear the story from the man who saw.

OEDIPUS: Yes—hope. My only hope is waiting for this shepherd.

JOCASTA: Why? What do you hope to find with him?

OEDIPUS: This—if his story agrees with what you say, then I am safe.

JOCASTA: What did I say that makes you sure of this?

OEDIPUS: You said he told of *robbers*—that *robbers* killed the king. If he still says *robbers*, then I am not the guilty one—because no man can talk of many when he means a single one. But if he names a *single* traveler, there will be no doubt—the guilt is mine.

JOCASTA: You can be sure that this was what he said—and he cannot deny it. The whole city heard him—not I alone. But even if he alters what he said before, he cannot prove that Laius met his death as it was prophesied. For Apollo said that he would die at the hand of a child—of mine. And as it happens, the child is dead. So prophecy is worthless. I wouldn't dignify it with a moment's thought.

OEDIPUS: You are right. But still—send someone for the shepherd. Now.

JOCASTA: I shall—immediately. I shall do what you ask. But now—let us go inside.

(*Exeunt* OEDIPUS, JOCASTA)

CHORUS: I pray, may destiny permit
that honestly I live my life
in word and deed.
That I obey the laws
the heavens have begotten
and prescribed.
Those laws created by Olympus,[1]
laws pure, immortal,
forever lasting, essence of the god
who lives in them.
On arrogance and pride
a tyrant feeds.
The goad of insolence,
of senseless overbearing, blind conceit,
of seeking things unseasonable,
unreasonable,
will prick a man to climb to heights
where he must lose his footing
and tumble to his doom.
Ambition must be used
to benefit the state;
else it is wrong, and God
must strike it from this earth.
Forever, God, I pray,
may you stand at my side!

---

1. The highest mountain on the Greek peninsula, considered by the Greeks to be the home of the gods. By transference the term "Olympus" is applied to the sky or heaven.

A man who goes through life
with insolence in word and deed,
who lacks respect for law and right,
and scorns the shrines and temples of the gods,
may he find evil fate and doom
as his reward for wantonness,
for seeking ill-begotten gains
and reaching after sacred things
with sacrilegious hands.
No! Surely no such man
escapes the wrath, the vengeance of the god!
For if he did, if he could find reward
in actions which are wrong,
why should I trouble to acclaim,
to honor you, God, in my song?

No longer shall my feet
take me to Delphi's sacred shrine;
no longer shall they Abae or Olympia's altars[2]
   seek
unless the oracles are shown to tell the truth
to mortals without fail!
Where are you, Zeus, all-powerful, all-ruling?
You must be told,
you must know in your all-pervading power:
Apollo's oracles now fall into dishonor,
and what the god has spoken about Laius
finds disregard.
Could God be dead?

(*Enter* JOCASTA)

JOCASTA: My Lords, I want to lay these laurel wreaths
and incense offerings at the shrines of Thebes—
for Oedipus is torturing himself, tearing his
heart with grief. His vision to weigh the present
against the past is blurred by fear and terror.
He devours every word of dread, drinks in every
thought of pain, destruction, death. And I no
longer have the power to ease his suffering.
Now I turn to you, Apollo, since you are near-
est, with prayer and suppliant offerings. Find
some way to free us, end our agony! O God of
Light, release us! You see the fear that grips
us—like sailors who watch their captain para-
lyzed by some unknown terror on the seas.

---

2. Abae was a city in central Greece and Olympia a city in
the western Peloponnese where there were important oracles
of Apollo and Zeus, respectively.

(*Enter* MESSENGER 1)

MESSENGER 1: Strangers, would you direct me to the
house of Oedipus? Or if you know where I
might find the king himself, please tell me.
CHORUS: This is his house, stranger. He is inside. But
this is the queen—his wife, and mother of his
children.
MESSENGER 1: Then, blessings on the house of Oedipus—his house, his children, and his wife.
JOCASTA: Blessings on you as well, stranger. Your
words are kind. But why have you come? What
is it?
MESSENGER 1: Good news, my lady—for your husband
and your house.
JOCASTA: What news? Where do you come from?
MESSENGER 1: From Corinth, my lady. My news will
surely bring you joy—but sorrow, too.
JOCASTA: What? How can that be?
MESSENGER 1: Your husband now is ruler of the Isthmus!
JOCASTA: Do you mean that Polybus of Corinth has
been deposed?
MESSENGER 1: Deposed by death, my lady. He has
passed away.
JOCASTA: What! Polybus dead?
MESSENGER 1: I swear on my life that this is true.
JOCASTA: (*to a servant*): Go! Quickly! Tell your master. (*to the heavens*) You prophecies—you di-
vinely-uttered prophecies! Where do you stand
now? The man that Oedipus feared, the man he
dared not face lest he should be his killer—that
man is dead! Time claimed his life—not Oedipus!

(*Enter* OEDIPUS)

OEDIPUS: Why, Jocasta? Why have you sent for me
again?
JOCASTA: I want you to listen to this man. Listen to
him and judge for yourself the worth of those
holy prophecies.
OEDIPUS: Who is he? What news could he have for
me?
JOCASTA: He comes from Corinth with the news
that—that Polybus—is dead.
OEDIPUS: What! Tell me.
MESSENGER 1: If you must know this first, then I shall
tell you—plainly. Polybus has died.
OEDIPUS: How? An act of treason? Sickness? How?
MESSENGER 1: My Lord, only a slight shift in the scales
is required to bring the aged to their rest.

OEDIPUS: Then it was sickness. Poor old man.

MESSENGER 1: Sickness—yes. And the weight of years.

OEDIPUS: Oh, Jocasta! Why? Why should we even look to oracles, the prophetic words delivered at their shrines or the birds that scream above us? They led me to believe that I would kill my father. But he is dead and in his grave, while I stand here—never having touched a weapon. Unless he died of longing for his son. If that is so, then I *was* the instrument of his death. And those oracles! Where are they now? Polybus has taken them to his grave. What worth have they now?

JOCASTA: Have I not been saying this all along?

OEDIPUS: Yes, you have. But I was misled by fear.

JOCASTA: Now you will no longer have to think of it.

OEDIPUS: But—my mother's bed. I still have *that* to fear.

JOCASTA: No. No, mortals have no need to fear when chance reigns supreme. The knowledge of the future is denied to us. It is better to live as you will, live as you can. You need not fear a union with your mother. Men often, in their dreams, approach their mothers' beds, lie with them, possess them. But the man who sees that this is meaningless can live without the threat of fear.

OEDIPUS: You would be right, Jocasta, if my mother were not alive. But she *is* alive. And no matter what you say, I have reason to fear.

JOCASTA: At least your father's death has brought some comfort.

OEDIPUS: Yes—some comfort. But my fear is of *her*— as long as she lives.

MESSENGER 1: Who is *she?* The woman you fear?

OEDIPUS: Queen Merope, old man, the wife of Polybus.

MESSENGER 1: But why does *she* instill fear in you?

OEDIPUS: There was an oracle—a dreadful oracle sent by the gods.

MESSENGER 1: Can you tell me—a stranger—what it is?

OEDIPUS: Yes, it is all right to tell. Once Loxian Apollo said that I would take my mother for my bride and murder my father with my own hands. This is the reason that I left Corinth long ago. Fortunately. And yet, I have often longed to see my parents.

MESSENGER 1: Is this the fear that drove you away from Corinth?

OEDIPUS: Yes. I did not want to kill my father.

MESSENGER 1: But I can free you from this fear, my Lord. My purpose for coming was a good one.

OEDIPUS: And I shall see that you receive a fitting reward.

MESSENGER 1: Yes—that's why I came. To fare well myself by your returning home.

OEDIPUS: Home? To Corinth? To my parents? Never.

MESSENGER 1: My son, you do not realize what you are doing.

OEDIPUS: What do you mean, old man? For God's sake, tell me what you mean.

MESSENGER 1: I mean—the reasons why you dread returning home.

OEDIPUS: I dread Apollo's prophecy—and its fulfillment.

MESSENGER 1: You mean the curse—the stain they say lies with your parents?

OEDIPUS: Yes, old man. That is the fear that lives with me.

MESSENGER 1: Then you must realize that this fear is groundless.

OEDIPUS: How can that be—if I am their son?

MESSENGER 1: Because Polybus was no relative of yours.

OEDIPUS: What are you saying! Polybus was *not* my father?

MESSENGER 1: No more than I.

OEDIPUS: No more than you? But you are nothing to me.

MESSENGER 1: He was not your father any more than I.

OEDIPUS: Then why did he call me his son?

MESSENGER 1: You were a gift to him—from me.

OEDIPUS: A gift? From you? And yet he loved me as his son?

MESSENGER 1: Yes, my Lord. He had been childless.

OEDIPUS: And when you gave me to him—had you bought me? Or found me?

MESSENGER 1: I found you—in the hills of Cithaeron.

OEDIPUS: What were you doing there?

MESSENGER 1: Tending sheep along the mountain side.

OEDIPUS: Then you were a—hired shepherd?

MESSENGER 1: Yes, my son—a hired shepherd who saved you at that time.

OEDIPUS: Saved me? Was I in pain when you found me? Was I in trouble?

MESSENGER 1: Yes, your ankles are the proof of that.

OEDIPUS: Ah, you mean this old trouble. What has that do to with it?

MESSENGER 1: When I found you, your ankles were pierced with rivets. And I freed you.

OEDIPUS: Yes, I have had this horrible stigma since infancy.

MESSENGER 1: And so it was the swelling in your ankles that caused your name: Oedipus—"Clubfoot."

OEDIPUS: Oh! Who did this to me? My father? Or my mother?

MESSENGER 1: I don't know. You will have to ask the man who handed you to me.

OEDIPUS: You mean—*you* did not find me? It was someone else?

MESSENGER 1: Another shepherd.

OEDIPUS: Who? Do you remember who he was?

MESSENGER 1: I think—he was of the house of Laius.

OEDIPUS: The king who ruled this city?

MESSENGER 1: Yes. He was a shepherd in the service of the king.

OEDIPUS: Is he still alive? Can I see him?

MESSENGER 1 (*addressing* THE CHORUS): You—you people here—could answer that.

OEDIPUS: Do any of you know this shepherd? Have you seen him in the fields? Here in Thebes? Tell me now! Now is the time to unravel this mystery—once and for all.

CHORUS: I think it is the shepherd you asked to see before. But the queen will know.

OEDIPUS: Jocasta, is that the man he means? Is it the shepherd we have sent for? Is *he* the one?

JOCASTA: Why? What difference does it make? Don't think about it. Pay no attention to what he said. It makes no difference.

OEDIPUS: No difference? When I must have every clue to untangle the line of mystery surrounding my birth?

JOCASTA: In the name of God, if you care at all for your own life, you must not go on with this. I cannot bear it any longer.

OEDIPUS: Do not worry, Jocasta. Even if I am a slave—a third-generation slave, it is no stain on your nobility.

JOCASTA: Oedipus! I beg you—don't do this!

OEDIPUS: I can't grant you that. I cannot leave the truth unknown.

JOCASTA: It is for *your* sake that I beg you to stop. For your own good.

OEDIPUS: My own good has brought me pain too long.

JOCASTA: God help you! May you never know what you are!

OEDIPUS: Go, someone, and bring the shepherd to me. Leave the queen to exult in her noble birth.

JOCASTA: God help you! This is all that I can say to you—now or ever.

(*Exit* JOCASTA)

CHORUS: Why has the queen left like this—grief-stricken and tortured with pain? My Lord, I fear—I fear that from her silence some horror will burst forth.

OEDIPUS: Let it explode! I will still want to uncover the secret of my birth—no matter how horrible. She—she is a woman with a woman's pride—and she feels shame for my humble birth. But I am the child of Fortune—beneficent Fortune—and I shall not be shamed! She is my mother. My sisters are the months and they have seen me rise and fall. This is my family. I will never deny my birth—and I will learn its secret!

(*Exit* OEDIPUS)

CHORUS: Ah Cithaeron,
  if in my judgment I am right,
  if I interpret what I hear correctly,
  then—by Olympus' boundless majesty!—
  tomorrow's full moon will not pass
  before, Cithaeron, you will find
  that Oedipus will honor you
  as mother and as nurse!
  That we will praise you in our song,
  benevolent and friendly to our king.
  Apollo, our Lord, may you find joy in this!

  Who bore you, Oedipus? A nymph?
  Did Pan[3] beget you in the hills?
  Were you begotten by Apollo?
  Perhaps so, for he likes the mountain glens.
  Could Hermes[4] be your father?
  Or Dionysus? Could it be
  that he received you as a gift
  high in the mountains from a nymph
  with whom he lay?

(*Enter* OEDIPUS)

OEDIPUS: My Lords, I have never met him, but could that be the shepherd we have been waiting for? He seems to be of the same age as the stranger from Corinth. And I can see now—those are my servants who are bringing him here. But, perhaps you know—if you have seen him before. Is he the shepherd?

---

3. A woodland god; patron of shepherds and flocks; usually represented as part man and part goat.
4. Son of Zeus and Maia; god of flocks and pastures.

(*Enter* SHEPHERD)

CHORUS: Yes. I recognize him. He was a shepherd in the service of Laius—as loyal as any man could be.

OEDIPUS: Corinthian, I ask you—is this the man you mean?

MESSENGER 1: Yes, my Lord, This is the man.

OEDIPUS: And you, old man, look at me and answer what I ask. Were you in the service of Laius?

SHEPHERD: I was. But not bought. I was reared in his house.

OEDIPUS: What occupation? What way of life?

SHEPHERD: Tending flocks—for most of my life.

OEDIPUS: And where did you tend those flocks?

SHEPHERD: Sometimes Cithaeron, sometimes the neighboring places.

OEDIPUS: Have you ever seen this man before?

SHEPHERD: What man do you mean? Doing what?

OEDIPUS: This man. Have you ever met him before?

SHEPHERD: Not that I recall, my Lord.

MESSENGER 1: No wonder, my Lord. But I shall help him to recall. I am sure that he'll remember the time we spent on Cithaeron—he with his two flocks and I with one. Six months—spring to autumn—every year—for three years. In the winter I would drive my flocks to my fold in Corinth, and he to the fold of Laius. Isn't that right, sir?

SHEPHERD: That is what happened. But it was a long time ago.

MESSENGER 1: Then tell me this. Do you remember a child you gave me to bring up as my own?

SHEPHERD: What are you saying? Why are you asking me this?

MESSENGER 1: This, my friend, this—is that child.

SHEPHERD: Damn you! Will you keep your mouth shut!

OEDIPUS: Save your reproaches, old man. It is you who deserve them—your words deserve them.

SHEPHERD: But master—how have I offended?

OEDIPUS: By refusing to answer his question about the child.

SHEPHERD: He doesn't know what he's saying. He's crazy.

OEDIPUS: If you don't answer of your own accord, we'll make you talk.

SHEPHERD: No! My Lord, please! Don't hurt an old man.

OEDIPUS (*to* THE CHORUS): One of you—twist his hands behind his back!

SHEPHERD: Why? Why? What do you want to know?

OEDIPUS: Did you or did you not give him that child?

SHEPHERD: I did. I gave it to him—and I wish that I had died that day.

OEDIPUS: You tell the truth, or you'll have your wish now.

SHEPHERD: If I tell, it will be worse.

OEDIPUS: Still he puts it off!

SHEPHERD: I said that I gave him the child!

OEDIPUS: Where did you get it? Your house? Someone else's? Where?

SHEPHERD: Not mine. Someone else's.

OEDIPUS: Whose? One of the citizens? Whose house?

SHEPHERD: O God, master! Don't ask me any more.

OEDIPUS: This is the last time that I ask you.

SHEPHERD: It was a child—of the house of Laius.

OEDIPUS: A slave? Or of his own line?

SHEPHERD: Ah, master, do I *have* to speak?

OEDIPUS: You have to. And I *have* to hear.

SHEPHERD: They said—it was his child. But the queen could tell you best.

OEDIPUS: Why? Did *she* give you the child?

SHEPHERD: Yes, my Lord.

OEDIPUS: Why?

SHEPHERD: To—kill!

OEDIPUS: Her own child!

SHEPHERD: Yes. Because she was terrified of some dreadful prophecy.

OEDIPUS: What prophecy?

SHEPHERD: The child would kill his father.

OEDIPUS: Then why did you give him to this man?

SHEPHERD: I felt sorry for him, master. And I thought that he would take him to his own home. But he saved him from his suffering—for worse suffering yet. My Lord, if you are the man he says you are—O God—you were born to suffering!

OEDIPUS: O God! O no! I see it now! All clear! O Light! I will never look on you again! Sin! Sin in my birth! Sin in my marriage! Sin in blood!

(*Exit* OEDIPUS)

CHORUS: O generations of men, you are nothing!
You are nothing!
And I count you as not having lived at all!
Was there ever a man,
was there ever a man on this earth
who could say he was happy,
who knew happiness, true happiness,
not an image, a dream,
an illusion, a vision, which would disappear?
Your example, Oedipus,

your example, your fate, your disaster,
show that none of us mortals
ever knew, ever felt what happiness truly is.

Here is Oedipus,
fortune and fame and bliss
leading him by the hand,
prodding him on to heights
mortals had never attained.
Zeus, it was he who removed
the scourge of the riddling maid,
of the sharp-clawed, murderous Sphinx!
He restored me to life from the brink
of disaster, of doom and of death.
It was he who was honored and hailed,
who was crowned and acclaimed as our king.

Here is Oedipus:
Anyone on this earth
struck by a harder blow,
stung by a fate more perverse?
Wretched Oedipus!
Father and son alike,
pleasures you took from where
once you were given life.
Furrows your father ploughed
bore you in silence. How, how, oh how could it
    be?

Time found you out,
all-seeing, irrepressible time.
Time sits in judgment on
the union that never could be;
judges you, father and son,
begot and begetter alike.
Would that I never had
laid eyes on Laius' child!
Now I wail and I weep,
and my lips are drenched in lament.
It was you, who offered me life;
is you, who now bring me death.

(*Enter* MESSENGER 2)

MESSENGER 2: O you most honored citizens of Thebes,
    you will mourn for the things you will hear, you
    will mourn for the things you will see, you will
    ache from the burden of sorrow—if you are
    true sons of the house of Labdacus, if you care,

if you feel. The waters of Ister and Phasis[5] can
never cleanse this house of the horrors hidden
within it and soon to be revealed—horrors willfully done! Worst of the sorrows we know are
those that are willfully done!

CHORUS: We have mourned enough for sorrows we
    have known. What more is there that you can
    add?

MESSENGER 2: One more and only one—Jocasta, the
    queen, is dead.

CHORUS: O God—no! How?

MESSENGER 2: By her own hand. But the most dreadful
    pain you have not seen. You have not seen the
    worst. I have seen it and I shall tell you what I
    can of her terrible suffering. She ran in frenzied
    despair through the palace halls and rushed
    straight to her bridal bed—her fingers clutch-
    ing and tearing at her hair. Then, inside the
    bedroom, she flung the doors closed and cried
    out to Laius, long since dead. She cried out to
    him, remembering the son that she had borne
    long ago, the son who killed his father, the son
    who left her to bear a dread curse—the chil-
    dren of her own son! She wept pitifully for that
    bridal bed which she had twice defiled—hus-
    band born of husband, child born of child. I
    didn't see what happened then. I didn't see her
    die. At that moment the king rushed in and
    shrieked in horror. All eyes turned to him as he
    paced in frantic passion and confusion. He
    sprang at each of us and begged to have a
    sword. He begged to know where he could find
    the wife that was no wife to him, the woman
    who had been mother to him and to his chil-
    dren. Some power beyond the scope of man
    held him in its sway and guided him to her. It
    was none of us. Then—as if someone had beck-
    oned to him and bade him follow—he
    screamed in terror and threw himself against
    the doors that she had locked. His body's
    weight and force shattered the bolts and thrust
    them from their sockets and he rushed into the
    room. There we saw the queen hanging from a
    noose of twisted cords. And when the king saw
    her, he cried out and moaned in deep, sorrow-

---

5. The Ister (the lower Danube) was considered by the
Greeks the largest river of Europe; the Phasis is a large river
originating in the Caucasus mountain range and flowing into
the eastern portion of the Black Sea.

ful misery. Then he untied the rope that hung about her neck and laid her body on the ground. But what happened then was even worse. Her gold brooches, her pins—he tore them from her gown and plunged them into his eyes again and again and again and screamed, "No longer shall you see the suffering you have known and caused! You saw what was forbidden to be seen, yet failed to recognize those whom you longed to see! Now you shall see only darkness!" And as he cried out in such desperate misery, he struck his eyes over and over—until a shower of blood and tears splattered down his beard, like a torrent of crimson rain and hail. And now suffering is mingled with pain for man and wife for the sins that both have done. Not one alone. Once—long ago—this house was happy—and rightly so. But now—today—sorrow, destruction, death, shame—all torments that have a name—all, all are theirs to endure.

CHORUS: But the king—does he have any relief from his suffering now?

MESSENGER 2: He calls for someone to unlock the gates and reveal to Thebes his father's killer, his mother's—I can't say it. I cannot say this unholy word. He cries out that he will banish himself from the land to free this house of the curse that he has uttered. But he is weak, drained. There is no one to guide his way. The pain is more than he can bear. You will see for yourselves. The palace gates are opening. You will see a sight so hideous that even his most bitter enemy would pity him.

(*Enter* OEDIPUS)

CHORUS: Ah!
Dread horror for men to see!
Most dreadful of all that I have seen!
Ah!
Wretched one,
what madness has possessed you?
What demon has descended upon you
and bound you to this dire fate?
Ah!
Wretched one,
I cannot bear to look at you.
I want to ask you more
and learn still more
and understand—
but I shudder at the sight of you!

OEDIPUS: Ah! Ah! Where has this misery brought me? Is this my own voice I hear—carried on the wings of the air? O Fate! What have you done to me?

CHORUS: Terrible! Too terrible to hear! Too terrible to see!

OEDIPUS: O cloud of darkness! Cruel! Driven by the winds of fate! Assaulting me! With no defense to hold you back! O God! The pain! The pain! My flesh aches from its wounds! My soul aches from the memory of its horrors!

CHORUS: Body and soul—each suffers and mourns.

OEDIPUS: Ah! You still remain with me—a constant friend. You still remain to care for me—a blind man now. Now there is darkness and I cannot see your face. But I can hear your voice and I know that you are near.

CHORUS: O my Lord, how could you have done this? How could you blind yourself? What demon drove you?

OEDIPUS: Apollo! It was Apollo! *He* brought this pain, this suffering to me. But it was my own hand that struck the blow. Not his. O God! Why should I have sight when all that I would see is ugliness?

CHORUS: It is as you say.

OEDIPUS: What is there for me to see and love? What sight would give me joy? What sound? Take me away! Take me out of this land! I am cursed! Doomed! I am the man most hated by the gods!

CHORUS: You have suffered equally for your fortune and for your disaster. I wish that you had never come to Thebes.

OEDIPUS: Damn the man who set me free! Who loosed the fetters from my feet and let me live! I never will forgive him. If he had let me die, I would never have become the cause—the grief . . .

CHORUS: I wish that it had been this way.

OEDIPUS: If it had been, I would not have come to this—killer of my father, bridegroom of the woman who gave me birth, despised by the gods, child of shame, father and brother to my children. Is there any horror worse than these—any horror that has not fallen upon Oedipus?

CHORUS: My Lord, I cannot condone what you have done. You would have been better dead than alive and blind.

OEDIPUS: I did what I had to. You know I did. No more advice. Could these eyes have looked upon my father in the house of Hades? Could these eyes have faced my mother in her agony? I sinned against them both—a sin no suicide could purge. Could I have joy at the sight of my children—born as they were born? With these eyes? Never! Could I look upon the city of Thebes? The turrets that grace her walls? The sacred statues of her gods? Never! Damned! I—the noblest of the sons of Thebes—I have damned myself. It was I who commanded that Thebes must cast out the one who is guilty, unholy, cursed by the heavenly gods. *I* was the curse of Thebes! Could these eyes look upon the people? Never! And if I could raise a wall to channel the fountain of my hearing, I would spare nothing to build a prison for this defiled body where sight and sound would never penetrate. Then only would I have peace—where grief could not reach my mind. O Cithaeron! Why did you receive me? Why did you not let me die then? Why did you let me live to show the world how I was born? O Polybus! O Corinth! My home that was no home! You raised me, thinking I was fair and never knowing the evil that festered beneath. Now—now see the evil from which I was born, the evil I have become. O God! The three roads! The hidden glen! The thickets! The pathway where three roads meet! The blood you drank from my hands—do you not know—it was the blood of my father! Do you remember? Do you remember what I did then and what I did for Thebes? Wedding-rites! You gave me birth and gave my children birth! Born of the same womb that bore my children! Father! Brother! Child! Incestuous sin! Bride! Wife! Mother! All of one union! All the most heinous sins that man can know! The most horrible shame—I can no longer speak of it. For the love of God, hide me somewhere. Hide me away from this land! Kill me! Cast me into the sea where you will never have to look at me again! I beg you—touch me—in my misery. Touch me. Do not be afraid. My sins are mine alone to bear and touch no other man.

(*Enter* CREON)

CHORUS: My Lord, Creon is here to act or counsel in what you ask. In your stead—he is now our sole protector.

OEDIPUS: What can I say to him? How can I ask for his trust? I have wronged him. I know that now.

CREON: I have not come to mock you, Oedipus, nor to reproach you for the past. But you—if you have no respect for men, at least respect the lord of the sun whose fires give life to men. Hide your naked guilt from his sight. No earth or sacred rain or light can endure its presence. (*to a servant*) Take him inside. It is impious for any but his own family to see and hear his suffering.

OEDIPUS: I ask you in the name of God to grant one favor. You have been kinder to me than I deserved. But one favor. I ask it for you—not for myself.

CREON: What do you ask of me?

OEDIPUS: Cast me out of this land. Cast me out to where no man can see me. Cast me out now.

CREON: I would have done so, you can be sure. But I must wait and do the will of the god.

OEDIPUS: He has signified his will—with clarity. Destroy the parricide! Destroy the unholy one! Destroy Oedipus!

CREON: That was the god's command, I know. But now—with what has happened—I think it better to wait and learn what we must do.

OEDIPUS: You mean that you would ask for guidance for a man so sorrowful as I?

CREON: Surely, you are ready to put your trust in the god—now.

OEDIPUS: Yes, I am ready now. But I ask this of you. Inside—she is lying inside—give her whatever funeral rites you wish. You will do the right thing for her. She is your sister. But for me—do not condemn this city—my father's city—to suffer any longer from my presence as long as I live. Let me go and live upon Cithaeron—O Cithaeron, your name is ever linked with mine! Where my parents chose a grave for me. Where they would have had me die. Where I shall die in answer to their wish. And yet, I know, neither sickness nor anything else will ever bring me death. For I would not have been saved from death that once. No—I was saved for a more dreadful fate. Let it be. Creon, do not worry about my sons. They are boys and will have all they need, no matter where they go. But my daughers—poor creatures! They never ate a single meal without their father. We shared everything together. Creon, take care of them. Creon, let me touch them one last time. And let me weep—one last time. Please, my Lord, please, allow it—you're generous, you're kind. If I could only touch them and feel that they are with me—as I used to—when I could see them. (*enter* ANTIGONE *and* ISMENE) What is that crying? Is it my daughters? Has Creon taken pity on me? Has he sent my daughters to me? Are they here?

CREON: Yes, Oedipus, they are here. I had them brought to you. I know how much you love them, how much you have always loved them.

OEDIPUS: Bless you for this, Creon. Heaven bless you and grant you greater kindness than it has granted me. Ah, children, where are you? Come—come, touch my hands, the hands of your father, the hands of your brother, the hands that blinded these eyes which once were bright—these eyes—your father's eyes which neither saw nor knew what he had done when he became your father. I weep for you, my children. I cannot see you now. But when I think of the bitterness that waits for you in life, what you will have to suffer—the festivals, the holidays—the sadness you will know when you should share in gaiety! And when you are old enough to marry—who will there be, who will be the man strong enough to bear the slander that will haunt you—because you are *my* children? What disgrace will you now know? Your father killed his father. And lay with the woman that bore him and his children. These are the taunts that will follow you. And what man will marry you? No man, my children. You will spend your lives unwed—without children of your own—barren and wasted. Ah, Creon, you are the only father left to them. We—their parents—are lost. We gave them life. And we are lost to them. Take care of them. See that they do not wander poor and lonely. Do not let them suffer for what I have done. Pity them. They are so young. So lost. They have no one but

you. Take my hand and promise me. And oh, my children, if you were older, I could make you understand. But now, make this your prayer—to find some place where you can live and have a better life than what your father knew.

CREON: Enough, my Lord. Go inside now.

OEDIPUS: Yes. I do not want to, but I will go.

CREON: All things have their time and their place.

OEDIPUS: I shall go—on this condition.

CREON: What condition? I am listening.

OEDIPUS: That you will send me away.

CREON: That is the god's decision, not mine.

OEDIPUS: The gods will not care where I go.

CREON: Then you shall have your wish.

OEDIPUS: Then—you consent?

CREON: It has nothing to do with my consent.

OEDIPUS: Let me go away from here.

CREON: Go then—but leave the children.

OEDIPUS: No! Do not take them away from me!

CREON: Do not presume that you are still in power. Your power has not survived with you.

CHORUS: There goes Oedipus—
he was the man who was able
to answer the riddle proposed by the Sphinx.
Mighty Oedipus—
he was an object of envy
to all for his fortune and fame.
There goes Oedipus—
now he is drowning in waves of dread and
despair.
Look at Oedipus—
proof that none of us mortals
can truly be thought of as happy
until he is granted deliverance from life,
until he is dead
and must suffer no more.

CURTAIN

2

THE PLAIE CALLED CORPUS CHRISTI

PART ONE: THE BEGINNINGS

Anonymous, 14th–16th Century

Adapted by Robert Cohen and Edgar Schell

Reading a medieval play, even in a modern adaptation, may at first seem a daunting prospect, for the language appears ancient and the pious references seem wholly unsuited to our more skeptical and secular age. On closer examination, however, or in an out-loud reading, the language will reveal itself to be as vigorous and engaging as anything we might find today, and the seeming pieties of the Middle Ages will prove to be fraught with brilliant political satire, theological debate, bawdy earthiness, and biting social commentary. In recent years, the English Cycle Plays—those series of medieval plays in our language that treated the cycle of biblical history from the creation of the universe to Doomsday—have enjoyed a popular renaissance, and have been played to public acclaim in London, Toronto, Hartford, and Irvine, California.

The Plaie Called Corpus Christi is not itself an original Cycle Play, but rather a sequence of several such plays, drawn from various medieval cycles (mainly those of York and Wakefield), and adapted for modern staging by the Focused Research Program in Medieval Drama at the University of California, Irvine. *The Plaie Called Corpus Christi* is divided, for production purposes, into three separate sections, each comprising a full evening's performance. *The Beginnings*, which is included in this

volume, includes the York plays titled *The Creation of the Universe and the Fall of Lucifer*, *The Creation of Adam and Eve*, *The Fall of Man*, and *The Explusion*; the Wakefield plays titled *The Murder of Abel* and *Noah*; and the play of *Abraham and Isaac* (Wakefield, with some interpolations from the Brome manuscript).[1]

The Beginnings tells the stories of the Old Testament—but through New Testament eyes. Indeed, the Old Testament stories are told here mainly inasmuch as they foreshadow key elements of Christian theology; Adam's sin makes necessary Christian redemption; and Abel's lamb and Isaac's ass prefigure the innocence and humility of Jesus. Anachronisms abound in these plays—for example, Noah speaks of the Trinity—but to the medieval mind the past and

---

1. The rest of *The Plaie Called Corpus Christi* includes *Nativity: The Annunciation, The Nativity, The Second Shepherd's Play, The Magi, The Flight Into Egypt, The Massacre of the Innocents,* and *The Death of Herod*; and *Doomsday: The Passion, The Resurrection,* and *The Judgement*. The translations/adaptations of these plays from Middle English were executed under the overall supervision of Edgar Schell, with the participation of Schell, Robert Cohen, Linda Giorgianna, and Stephen Barney. Robert Cohen directed the play's production and served also as the translator/adaptor of *The Beginnings*, which is the text included in this anthology.

the future were combined in Godhead, and the Cycle Plays were not created in order to present a view of history but to exemplify morality and the proper way of life.

Each play has its distinct dramatic values. *The Creation of the Universe and the Fall of Lucifer* is a musical spectacular, with angels singing in heaven and devils fighting in hell: Lucifer's Fall was probably a stunning stage effect. *Adam and Eve* (really three plays combined here as one) is an affecting play, exploring man's first sensory experiences (breathing, speaking, eating, and seeing) together with the sudden horror of guilt and shame. *The Murder of Abel* is a rough-textured play, depicting the first human murder (astonishingly, the murderer does not understand death for it did not yet exist) amidst a general theatrical wash of barnyard humor, impious jesting, and scatalogical sibling badinage. *Noah*, which is by the so-called "Wakefield Master" and is *The Beginnings'* literary gem, creates the prototype for marital banter and abuse, to be perfected later by Shakespeare in *The Taming of the Shrew* and Molière in *The Bourgeois Gentleman*. And *Abraham and Isaac*, often regarded as the most emotionally powerful of all medieval plays, caps the performance of *The Beginnings* with its searing exploration of paternal love versus divine obedience.

A NOTE ON THE TEXT

The text is slightly adapted for modern audiences and readers, but much of the medieval vocabulary is retained, particularly when it continues as the root of modern English; the casual reader will soon come to recognize "take tent" (for "pay attention"), "seldseen" (for "seldom seen"), and "ay" (for "always" or "forever"). As in all medieval drama, meter, alliteration, and rhyme are aggressively pursued by the (anonymous) authors, and often the language is tortured into tight verse structures to the apparent detriment of sense. But the rhymes and rhythms of medieval verse conveyed meanings of their own to the original audiences—offering the implicit suggestion that the words were magical, extraterrestrial, and divinely inspired. We do not have to entertain such theological considerations today in order to feel similar otherworldly qualities in these texts.

Some cuts have been made in the original texts,

and the plays are blended together in ways not originally intended; the *Abraham and Isaac* play, which is from the Wakefield (Towneley) cycle, is provided with an ending from the Brome play because the ending of the Wakefield is lost. Also, the concluding speech of the *Abraham and Isaac* play (beginning "Lo, now sovereigns and sirs, . . ."), which was originally spoken by a "Doctor" who came forward at the play's end, is here divided among the members of the acting ensemble so as to create a more fitting closure to the entire sequence of *The Beginnings*.

Finally, some archaic words remaining in the adapted text are noted by degree signs, and the reader is provided with modern meanings in the margin; these meanings are not meant to be precise definitions, but rather to convey the general sense of the word in its particular context. In performance, most of these archaic words can be made meaningful by the actors through expressive intonation and gesture, and their retention in the text preserves the play's medieval linguistic texture.

A NOTE ON THE STAGING

It is not clear how these medieval Cycle Plays were originally staged; some perhaps were performed on mobile pageant wagons, some perhaps were staged in great halls, or on scaffolds set up in city squares or open fields. Stage directions in the present text are those created for the 1985 Irvine production of *The Beginnings*, and are included with the text in order to make the play easy to follow. At Irvine, *The Plaie Called Corpus Christi* was adapted to be performed by a company of twelve to sixteen actors who play, in alternation, all of the roles (human, divine, and animal). The stage, designed by Douglas Scott Goheen, consisted of a long, narrow platform with various trap doors, and towers on either side; for *The Beginnings*, the tops of the towers were connected by a footbridge to represent Heaven. A hill and a tree rose from the platform floor, and a hand-operated elevator was used to hoist Adam and Eve through a platform trapdoor. Noah's ship was created by detaching and lowering the footbridge that had represented Heaven, and Hell was entered through a Hellmouth that swung open on hinges from the platform. Other than electric lighting, no staging effect was employed that could not have been used in medieval times.

THE PLAIE CALLED CORPUS CHRISTI: THE BEGINNINGS

CAST OF CHARACTERS

GOD

SERAPH

LUCIFER (SATAN)

ADAM

EVE

GARCIO

CAIN

ABEL

NOAH

NOAH'S WIFE

SHEM

JAPHET

HAM

SHEM'S WIFE

JAPHET'S WIFE

HAM'S WIFE

ABRAHAM

ISAAC

ANGELS, DEVILS, and SERVANTS

PART ONE

(*The stage setting is a platform and two towers; one tower represents* GOD's *tower, the other* LUCIFER'S. *The tops of the towers are connected by a footbridge (heaven) and a diagonal cable extends from* LUCIFER's *tower to the platform. The platform is Middle Earth—but Earth has not yet been created.*)

(*Music: angels can be heard singing "Ego Sum Alpha and Omega. Primus et novissimus." [I am the beginning and the end, the first and last.] Lights come up on* GOD's *tower;* GOD *and the angels,* CHERUBIM *and* SERAPHIM, *appear in Heaven.*)

GOD: *Ego sum Alpha et Omega: vita, via, veritas, primus et novissimus.* [I am the beginning and the end: life, the way, the truth; first, last, and always.]

> I am gracious and great, God without beginning
> I am maker unmade, all might is in me;
> I am life, and way unto wealth-winning
> I am foremost and first, as I bid shall it be.
> My blessing on all shall be blending
> And shielding, from harm to be hiding.
> My body in bliss e're-abiding,
> Unending, without any ending.

(*The Choir of Angels sings "Ego sum via, Veritas et Vita. Alleluia, Alleluia." [I am the way, the truth, and the life.]*)

Since I am maker unmade, and most am of might,
And e're shall be endless, and nought is but I,
Unto my dignity dear should duly be dight°   ° built
A place full of plenty, to my pleasing I'll ply.°   ° work
And therewith right well I have wrought
Many diverse doings fast,
Which work shall ever last
And all shall be made—even from nought.

But only the worthy work of my will
In my spirit shall inspire the might of me;
And in the first, faithly, my thought to fulfil,
Now in my blessing I bid that there be
A bliss all-befriending around me,
In the which bliss I bid to be here:
Nine orders of angels full clear,
In loving e're lasting to sound me.

(*Lights come up on the bridge, and angels enter and surround* GOD,
singing "Te deum laudamus," [We praise thee, O God]. GOD *continues
to the angels*).

Here 'neath me now a new isle I neven°,   ° name
The island of Earth. And see, now, it starts:

(*The platform is dimly illuminated below him.*)

Earth, wholly; and Hell. This highest be Heaven,
And those wielding wealth shall dwell in these parts.
This grant I ye, ministers mine
To-whiles° ye are stable in thought.   ° while
But to them that are nought,
Be put to my prison—and pine°.   ° suffer

(GOD *turns to an angel, who steps forward and kneels.*)

Of all the mights I have made, most next after me
I make thee as master and mirror of my might
I build thee here boonly°, in bliss for to be,   ° happily
I name thee for Lucifer, bearer of light.

No one here shall be thee daring
In this bliss shall be your building,
And have all wealth at your wielding
Ay-whiles° ye are dutifully bearing.   ° as long as

(*Then the angels sing as* LUCIFER *moves apart, basking in his new glory.
An angel, one of the* SERAPHIM, *approaches* GOD.)

SERAPH: Ah, merciful Maker, full mickle° is Thy might,   ° powerful
That all this work at a word worthily hast wrought,
Ay° loved be that lovely Lord for his light,   ° forever
That us mighty has made that till now was right nought,
In bliss for to bide in His blessing

E'relasting in love let us lout° Him,   ° praise
And set us thus freely about Him
Of mirth nevermore to be missing.

LUCIFER (*exulting, he moves away from the angels*):
All the mirth that is made is marked in me!
The beams of my brighthood are burning so bright,
And I, so seemly in sight, myself now I see,
For, like a lord, am I left to live in this light.
More fairer by far than my feres°,   ° brothers
In me is no point to repair,
I feel me in fashion and fair,
My power surpasses my peers!

SERAPH (*speaking to* GOD):
Lord, with a lasting love we proffer Thee praise,
Thou mightyful maker that marked us and made us,
And wrought us thus worthy to live in this place,
Here no feeling of filth may be-foul us nor fade us.
All bliss is here building about us,
To-whiles we are stable in thought,
In the worship of Him that us wrought,
Of harm never fear us nor doubt us.

LUCIFER (*dancing about on his tower, with other bad angels*):
Oh, how I am featured, and fair, and figured full fit!
The form of all fairhead upon me is fest°,   ° festooned
All wealth in my world is—I wot° by my wit;   ° know
The beams of my brighthead are as big as the best.
My showing is shimmering and shining,
So bigly to bliss am I brought,
My needs to annoy me are nought,
Here shall never pain me be pining!

SERAPH (*to* GOD):
With all the wit that we wield, we worship Thy will
Thou glorious God that is ground of all grace,
Ay° with steadfast resounding let us stand still   ° always
Lord, to be fed with the food of Thy fair face.
In life that is loy'lly e'relasting
Thy dole°, Lord, is e're-daintily dealing,   ° punishment
And who so that food may be feeling,
To see Thy fair face is not fasting.

LUCIFER: Oh, certes°, how I am worthily wrought° with worship, iwis°!   ° certainly ° made
For in glorious glee, my glittering gleams;   ° indeed
I am so mightily made, my mirth may not miss—
E'er shall I bide in this bliss through brightness of beams.
Me needs no annouyance to neven,
All wealth in my world am I wielding.
Above yet shall I make my building
On high in the highest of heaven.

There shall I set myself full seemly to sight
To receive my reverence through right of renown

I shall be like unto him that is highest in height

Oh, how I'm dear-worth and deft—

(LUCIFER *falls, descending the diagonal "slide" to the platform, and shedding his angel robes; he is now a devil.*)

Ow! Deuce! All goes down!

My might and my main is all marring.

Help, fellows! In faith, I am falling!

(*Other angels fall down after him, and, now transformed into devils, are crawling around on the platform attacking him.*)

FIRST DEVIL: From heaven on hands we are crawling

To woe are we wending, I warrant.

LUCIFER: Out! Out! Harrow! Helpless, such heat is there here.

This is a dungeon of dole in which I can't delight.

What has my kind become, so comely° and clear?   ° pretty

Now I am loathsome, alas who was light.

My brightness is blackest and blue now,

My bale° is e'er beating and burning.   ° torment

I hie me a-howling and churning.

Out! Ay, welaway!° I wallow in woe now.   ° alas

SECOND DEVIL: Out! Out! I go wild with woe, my wit is all went now.

All our food is but filth, we find us fore-tossed,

We that were bathed in bliss, in bale are we burnt now.

Out on thee Lucifer, lurdan°, our light has thou lost.   ° scoundrel

Thy deeds to this dole now has damned us,

To spill us thou was our speeder,

For thou was our light and our leader,

To highest of heaven had thou aimed us.

LUCIFER: Welaway! Woe is me now, now is it worse than it was.

Unthrivingly threap ye! I said but a thought.

FIRST DEVIL: We! Lurdan, thou lost us.

(*Hellfire and smoke cover the stage. A Giant hellmouth opens on the platform, and more devils come out of it, dragging LUCIFER and the others into its maw.*)

LUCIFER: Ye lie! Out, alas!

I wished not this woe should be wrought.

Out on you, lurdens, ye smore° me in smoke!   ° smother

SECOND DEVIL (*kicking LUCIFER*): This woe has thou wrought us!

LUCIFER: Ye lie! Ye Lie!

FIRST DEVIL (*striking LUCIFER*):

Thou liest, and that shall thou buy!

You lurdan, have at you, go choke!

(*He and the other devils strangle LUCIFER and drag him into Hell. Hell closes over and the smoke dissipates. Light returns to heaven above.*)

CHERUB: Ah, Lord, loved be Thy name that us this light lent,

Since Lucifer our leader has alighted so low

For his disobedience, in bale to be burnt,

Thy righteousness rewards all a-row
Each work rightly as wrought.
Through grace of thy merciful might
The cause I see it in sight,
Wherefore to bale he is brought.

GOD: Those fools from their fairhead in fantasies fell,
And made moan of my might that marked them and made them.
For that, and their works, well in woe shall they dwell,
For some are fallen into filth that evermore shall fade them,
And never shall have grace for to guard them.
So surpassing of power they thought them,
They would not me worship that wrought them,
Therefore shall my wrath ever go with them.

And all that me worship shall dwell here, iwis!
Wherefore, forth my work! Work now I will.
Since their might is all marred, that meant all amiss.
Even to mine own figure, this bliss to fulfil,
Mankind of mould° shall I make!   ° earth
But e're I will form him—before—
I'll make all things that shall him restore.
To which that his talent will take.

And in my first making, to muster my might,
Since earth is vain and void, and murky as well
I bid in my blessing ye angels give light
To the earth, for it faded when the fiends fell.

(*Stars appear.*)

In Hell shall murkiness never be missing,
The murkiness thus name I night.

(*Daylight arrives.*)

The day, that call I this light—
My afterworks shall it be guiding.

(*Singing is heard.*)

And now in my blessing I twin them in two,
The night even from the day, so that they meet never.
But either, in a kindly course, their trails running true.
Both the night and the day, go duly forever.
In all I shall work without cessing.
This day's work is done—I can tell—
And all this work likes me right well,
And freely I give it my blessing.

(GOD *retires. The singing suddenly becomes the sounds of animals, and
the ensemble, now dressed as animals, clambers upon the platform. It
is dawn, and the morning sounds of wild and domestic animals fill the
theatre. The play of* ADAM AND EVE *begins.*)

28   ANONYMOUS

GOD (*as daylight breaks on the animals below*):
    In heaven and earth, duly be seen
    My five days' work, with no relent.
    All's made complete, by courses clean;
    Methinks the space of them well spent.

    In heaven are angels, fair and bright
    Stars and planets, their courses go.
    The moon serves unto the night,
    The sun to light the day also.

    In earth are trees and grass to spring;
    Beasts and fowls, both great and small,

(*Animal cries answer his words.*)

    Fishes in flood, all other thing,
    Thrive and have my blessings all.

(GOD *descends to the platform, and walks about the animals, who nuzzle him affectionately.*)

    This work is wrought now at my will,
    But yet can I here no beast see
    That accords by kind and skill,
    And for my work might worship me.

    To keep this world, both more and less
    A skillful beast then will I make
    After my shape and my likeness,
    The which shall worship to me take.

(GOD *reaches down and takes some sand from the platform floor.*)

    Of the simplest part of earth that is here
    I shall make man, and for this skill:
    For to abate his haughty cheer,
    Both his great pride and other ill,

    And also for to have in mind
    How simple he is at his making,
    For all this—*feeble* I shall him find,
    When he is dead, at his ending.

    For this reason and skill alone
    I shall make man like unto me.
    Rise up, thou earth, in blood and bone,
    In shape of man, I command thee!

(ADAM *rises through the platform. He is naked and unseeing.*)

    A female shall thou have as mate,
    Her shall I make of thy left rib.

(GOD *pulls a rib from* ADAM's *side;* ADAM *groans.*)

So shalt thou not live in lonely state,
Without a faithful friend and sib.

(EVE *rises from the platform.* GOD *takes each by the hand.*)

Take now here the ghost of life

(GOD *blows air into each of them, "inspiring" them with life. They inhale
briskly; their eyes open, they see* GOD *and then each other, and then the
animals. Amazed, they look about as* GOD *places* EVE'S *hand in* ADAM'S.)

And receive both your souls of me,
This female take thou to thy wife,
Adam and Eve your names shall be.
ADAM: Ah . . .
    Ah . . . (*he is learning how to speak*)
    Lor . . .
    Lorrrrrr . . . (*he begins to get the knack of it*)
    Lord, . . . full mickle° is Thy might.   ° powerful
    And that is seen on every side;
    For now is here a joyful sight
    To see this world so long and wide.

(*The animals cavort around him.*)

    Many diverse things now here is,
    Of beasts and fowls both wild and tame;
    Yet is none made to Thy likness,
    But we alone—Ah, loved be Thy name!
EVE (*in great wonderment at her condition*):
    To such a Lord in all degree
    Be evermore lasting loving,
    That to us such a dignity
    Has given above all other thing.

    And seld-seen things may we see here
    Of this same world so long and broad,
    With beasts and fowls so many and fair,
    Blessed be He that has us made.
ADAM: Ah, blessed Lord, now at Thy will
    Since we are wrought, vouchsafe to tell—
    And also say us two until—
    What we shall do, and where to dwell?
GOD: For this skill made I you this day:
    My name to worship evermore.
    Love me, therefore, and praise me ay°   ° always
    For your making: I ask no more.

    Both wise and witty° shalt thou be,   ° intelligent
    As man that I have made of nought;
    Lordship on earth then grant I thee,
    All thing to serve thee that is wrought.

To paradise shall ye both go.
Of earthly thing you'll have no need.
Ill and good both shall ye two know,
I shall you learn° your life to lead.   ° teach

(ADAM *and* EVE *study* GOD *in wonder and reverence.*)

ADAM: Ah, Lord since we shall do no thing
　　　But love Thee for Thy great goodness,
　　　We shall obey to Thy bidding,
　　　And fulfil it both more and less.
EVE (to ADAM):
　　　His sign since He has on us set
　　　Before all other things that reign,
　　　For Him to love we shall nought let,
　　　And worship Him with might and main.

(ADAM *and* EVE *wander about the platform, discovering the animals.* EVE
*sits backwards on an ox, who moans plaintively until she corrects
herself.* GOD *speaks to the audience.*)

GOD: At heaven and earth first I began
　　　And six days wrought ere I would rest;
　　　My work is ended now at man:
　　　All likes me well, but this the best.

　　　My blessing have they ever and ay;
　　　The seventh day shall my resting be.
　　　Thus will I cease, soothly° to say,   ° truly
　　　Of my doing in this degree.

(GOD *turns back to* ADAM *and* EVE.)

　　　To bliss I shall you bring;
　　　Come forth, you two, with me.
　　　Ye shall live in liking;
　　　My blessing with you be.

(GOD *leads* ADAM, EVE, *and the animals to Paradise. The hill and tree rise
up through the platform.*)

GOD: Adam and Eve, this is the place
　　　That I shall grant you of my grace
　　　To have your dwelling in.
　　　Herbs, spice, fruit on tree,
　　　Beasts, fowls, all that you see
　　　Shall bow to you, more and min°.   ° less
　　　This place is Paradise,
　　　Here shall your joys begin;
　　　And if that ye be wise,
　　　From this it needs you never twin.

　　　All your will here shall ye have,
　　　Liking for to eat or save,
　　　Fish, fowl, or fee;

And for to take at your own will
All other creatures thereuntil
Your subjects shall they be.
Adam, of more and less
Lordship in earth, here grant I thee:
This place that worthy is—
Keep it honestly.

(GOD *climbs the stairs to heaven, and* ADAM *calls after him.*)

ADAM: O lord, loved be Thy name,
    For now is this a joyful home
    That Thou hast brought us to.
    Full of mirth and solace nigh,
    Herbs and trees, fruit on high,
    A hill with many spices, too.

(*To* EVE)

    Look, Eve, now are we brought
    To rest and peace, both I and you,
    We need to take no thought
    But look e'er well to do.

EVE: Loving be always to such a Lord
    To us has given so great reward,
    To govern both great and small,
    And made us after His own advice
    To serve Him here in Paradise,
    Among these mirths with all.
    Here is a joyful sight—
    Here where we dwell in thrall;
    We love Thee, most of might,
    Great God, that we on call.

GOD (*speaking now from Heaven, with a more distant authority than
    before*):
    Love my name with good intent
    And hark to my commanding-ment,
    And do my bidding buxomly°:   ° heartily
    Of all the fruit in paradise,
    Take ye thereof what you most prize,
    And make you right merry.
    But the tree of good and ill,

(*An apple appears on the tree.*)

    What time you eat of this
    Thou speeds thyself to spill°   ° fall
    And be brought out of bliss.

    All things is made, man, for thy prow°.   ° overseeing
    All creatures shall to thee all bow
    That here is made earth by.
    On earth I make thee lord of all,
    And beast unto thee shall be thrall°,   ° obedience

Thy kind shall multiply.
Therefore this tree alone,
Adam, this out-take I;
The fruit of it, near shall you none,
For if you do, then shall ye die.

ADAM: Alas, Lord, that we should do so ill,
Thy blessed bidding we shall fulfill,
Both in thought and deed.
We shall not near this tree nor its boughs,
Nor yet the fruit that thereon grows,
Therewith our flesh to feed.

EVE: We shall do Thy bidding,
We have none other need:
This fruit full still shall hang,
Lord, that Thou has us forbade.

GOD (commandingly): Look that you do as ye have said,
Of all that there hold you a-dread.
For here is wealth at will;
This tree that bears the Fruit of Life
Look neither thou nor Eve thy wife,
Lay you no hands theretill.
Because it is knowing
Both of good and ill,
Unless you let this fruit but hang
You speed yourself to spill.

Thefore, this tree that I out-take,
Now keep it rightly for my sake.
That nothing shall go near;
All other at your will shall be,
I out-take nothing but this tree.
To feed you—never fear:
Here shall ye lead your life
With dainties that are dear.
Adam, and Eve thy wife,
My blessings have ye here.

(GOD *departs. Angels sing* "Quam Pulcra Es" [*how beautiful it is.*] ADAM
and EVE *begin to explore and enjoy Paradise.* ADAM *approaches* EVE; *he
would like to kiss her, but doesn't know how. Confused, she approaches
him affectionately, and bites him. That wasn't quite it.* ADAM *sits on the
hill and sleeps.* EVE *gazes at the tree, and sleeps too.* SATAN—LUCIFER—
enters slitheringly from below, and the animals, frightened, depart.)

SATAN: For woe my wit is in a weir°   ° quandry
That moves me mickle in my mind!
The Godhead that I saw so clear—
I perceived that He should take his kind
From a degree
That He had wrought, but He designed
That angel kind should it not be!

But we were fair and bright,
Therefore me thought that He
The kind of us take might,
But he disdained me!

The kind of *man* he thought to take.
And there-at had I great envy,
But he has made to him a make°,   ° mate
And hard to *her* I will me hie
That ready way;
His purposed prowess to put by,
And fend to pick from him that prey.
My travail were well set.
Might I Him so betray!
His liking for to let,
And soon I shall assay.

(SATAN *falls to the floor, and assumes a serpentine manner.*)

In a worm's likeness will I wend,
And fend to feign a loud lying.
Eve! Eve!
EVE (*waking*): Who is there?
SATAN: I, a friend.
And for the good is to thee coming
I hither sought.
Of all the fruit ye see hanging
In Paradise, why eat ye nought?
EVE: We may of all about
Take all that us good thought
Save one tree taken out,
Which would us harm to nigh it ought.
SATAN: And why that tree, that would I wit,
Any more than all other by?
EVE: For our Lord God forbids us it,
The fruit thereof, Adam nor I
To nigh it near;
And if we did we both should die,
He said, and cease our solace here.
SATAN: Hah! Eve, to me take tent°.   ° attention
Take heed, and thou shalt hear:
What that the matter meant
He moved in that manner?

(SATAN *slithers around the tree, and around* EVE.)

To eat thereof he bade you not do—
I know it well, this was his skill—
Because he would none other knew
These great virtues that belong theretill.
For will thou see,
Who eats the fruit of good and ill,
Shall have knowing as well as he.

34   ANONYMOUS

(SATAN *licks* EVE, *who recoils.*)

EVE: Why, what kind thing art thou
    That tells this tale to me?
SATAN: A worm, that wotteth° well how   ° knows
    That ye may worshipped be.
EVE: What worship should we win thereby?
    To eat therof us needeth it nought.
    We have lordship to make mastery
    Of all thing that on earth is wrought.
SATAN: Woman, do way°!   ° be quiet!
    To *greater* state ye may be brought.
    If ye will do as I shall say.
EVE: To do is us full loath
    That should our God displease.
SATAN: Nay, certes, He'll not be wroth°.   ° angry
    Now eat it at your ease!

    For peril right there none in lies.
    But worship and a great winning—
    For right as God ye shall be wise,
    And peer to him—in everything!
    Aye—Gods shall *ye* be,
    Of ill and good to have knowing,
    For to be as wise as He.

(*He holds the apple under* EVE's *nose, tauntingly.*)

EVE: Is this sooth° that thou says?   ° truth
SATAN: Yea. Why trustest thou not me?
    I would in no ways
    Tell nought but truth to thee.
EVE: Then will I to thy teaching trust,
    And find this fruit unto our food.

(EVE *accepts the apple.*)

SATAN: Bite on boldly. Be not abashed.
    And bear Adam to amend his mood,
    And eke° his bliss.   ° increase

(EVE *eats.* SATAN *hisses and departs.* EVE, *thrilled, goes to* ADAM *and wakes him.*)

EVE: Adam, have here of fruit full good!
ADAM (*sees the plucked apple, horrified*):
    Alas, woman, why took thou this?
    Our Lord commanded us both
    T'attend this tree of his.
    Thy work will make Him wroth.
    Alas, thou'st done amiss.
EVE: Nay, Adam, grieve thee not at it,
    And I shall say the reason why:
    A worm has done me for to wit

We shall be as gods—*we*—thou and I!
If that we eat
Here of this tree! Adam, deny
Us not that worship for to get.
For we shall be as wise
As God that is so great,
And as mickle of price,
Therefore eat of this meat!

ADAM: To eat it would I not eschew°   ° avoid
    Might I be sure in thy saying.

EVE: Bite on boldly, for it is true:
    We shall be gods and know all thing!

ADAM: To win that name
    I shall it taste at thy teaching.

(*He eats, and immediately spits it out.*)

Alas, what have I done, for shame!
Ill counsel! Woe worth thee!
Ah, Eve, thou art to blame,
To this enticed thou me—
Me shames with my frame,

(*He suddenly stares at his body.*)

For I am *naked* as methink!

EVE (*looks at herself, and is suddenly horrified*):
    Alas, Adam, right so am I!

ADAM: And for sorrow sore might we now sink
    For we have grieved God almighty
    That made me man—
    Broken his bidding bitterly.
    Alas that ever we it began.
    (*blindly accusing her*)
    This work, Eve, hast thou wrought,
    And made this bad bargain!

EVE: Nay, Adam, twit me not!

ADAM: Away, dear Eve! Whom then?

EVE: The worm to twit well worthy were,
    With tales untrue he me betrayed.
    (*sobs*)

ADAM: Alas, that I allowed thy lore°   ° story
    Or trusted the trifles that thou did beseech,
    So may I bid,
    For I may ban that bitter breach,
    And dreary deed, that I it did.
    (*again suddenly self-conscious*)
    Our shapes! In dole, me grieves!
    Wherewith shall they be hid?

EVE (*finding the fig leaves, she makes loincloths*):
    Let us take there fig leaves,
    Since it is thus betid.

ADAM: Just as thou says, so it shall be.
   For we are naked and all bare;
   Full wonder fain I would hide me
   From my Lord's sight, But where? But where?
   Were I seen not!
GOD (*calling down from Heaven*): Adam! Adam!
ADAM (*trying to hide*): Lord?
GOD (*appearing in Heaven with a* CHERUB):
   Where art thou? Yare!
ADAM: I hear thee Lord, and see thee not.
GOD: Say! Whereon does this belong?
   This work? What has thou wrought?
ADAM: Lord, Eve made me do wrong!
   And to that breach me brought!
GOD: Say Eve, why hast thou made thy make°   ° mate
   Eat fruit I bade thee should hang still,
   And commanded none of it to take?
EVE: A worm, Lord, enticed me theretill:
   So welaway°,   ° alas
   That ever I did that deed so dill.

(SATAN *climbs out of hell and laughs.* GOD *curses him.*)

GOD: Ah, wicked worm, woe worth thee ay°!   ° forever
   For thou on this manner
   Hast made them such a fray:
   My curses have thou here
   With all the might I may.

   And on thy womb then shall thou glide
   And be e'er full of enmity.
   To all mankind on every side,
   And earth it shall thy sustenance be
   To eat and drink.

(SATAN *collapses on his stomach and slithers back to Hell.*)

   Adam and Eve also, ye
   On earth then shall sweat and swink,
   And travail for your food.

(*The tree and the hill begin to sink. Paradise is disappearing.*)

ADAM: Alas, when might we sink?
   We that have had all world's good,
   Full dolefully may us think.
GOD (*to the* CHERUB):
   Now, Cherubyn, mine angel bright,
   To middle-earth go drive these two.
ANGEL: All ready, Lord, as it is right,
   Since thy will is that it be so,
   And thy liking,
   Adam and Eve, do you two go,

For here may ye make no dwelling;
Go ye forth fast to fare,
Of sorrow may ye sing.

(*The* CHERUB *descends, drawing his sword, and chases* ADAM *and* EVE *off the platform.*)

ADAM: Alas for sorrow and care
Our hands may we wring.

(ADAM *and* EVE *are driven offstage, followed by the* ANGEL. GOD *disappears. From the other side of the stage, horses and oxen are heard.* GARCIO, *young servant of* CAIN, *enters at a fast clip. The play of* ABEL'S MURDER *begins.*)

GARCIO (*bolting on, he scans the audience, and calls out to them*):
All hail! All hail! Both blithe and glad,
For here come I, a merry lad!

(*Members of the ensemble have joined the audience, and begin to heckle him.*)

Be peace your din, my master heed
Or else the devil you speed!
(*derisive laughter from the "audience"*)
Know ye not whom I come before?
(*cries of "No, who? Not Cain!!"*)
He that jangles any more,
He must blow my black-holed bore
Both behind and before
Till his teeth bleed!
(*derisive sarcastic cries: "Oh, I'm afraid of you!"* CAIN *pleads with the audience.*)
Fellows, here I you forbid
To make neither noise nor cry
Whoso is so hardy to do that deed,
The devil hang him up to dry! (*he makes a gallows gesture; everyone laughs*)

Goodlings°, I am a full great guy.   ° good people
That good yeoman°, my master's nigh,   ° farmer
Full well ye all him ken°.   ° understand
Begin he with you to strive°,   ° do battle
Be sure that ye will never thrive.
But I trow°, by God alive,   ° believe
Some of you are his men.
But let your lips cover your grin,
Harlots°, everyone!   ° rascals
And if my master come, welcome him then.
Farewell, for I am gone.

(GARCIO *flees as* CAIN *enters, driving his ornery plow-team of horses and oxen, whom he calls by name. The plow-team stops, suddenly, causing him to lose balance.*)

CAIN: Yo! Forth, Grayhorn! War-out° Gryme!   ° move it
    Draw on! God give you ill this time.
    Ye stand as ye were fallen in slime!

(The animals murmer and refuse to budge. CAIN *addresses Gryme.)*

    What, will ye no farther, mare?
    (Gryme collapses.)
    War: Woah! Let me see how Down will draw!
    (beating his animals)
    Yit! Schew! Yit! Pull on a thraw!
    (Grayhorne relieves himself on CAIN's *foot.)*
    What? It seems of me none stand in awe!
    I say, Donnying, go fare!
    Aha! God give thee sorrow and care!
    Lo, now heard she what I said!
    Now, Yit, art thou the worst mare
    In plough that ever I bred.
    (crying for GARCIO, *also called Pickharness ["saddle-thief"])*
    How, Pickharness, how! Come hither, by'r life!
    (Re-enter GARCIO*)*
GARCIO: I forfend°, God so bid, that ever thou thrive.   ° hope not
CAIN: What, boy, shall I both hold and drive?
    Hearest thou not how I cry?
GARCIO *(trying to move the team)*:
    Say, Mall and Stott, will ye not go?
    Lemyng, Morell, Whitehorn, Yo!

(They do not move. GARCIO *continues to* CAIN *sarcastically.)*

    Now will ye not see how they hie?
CAIN: Gog° give thee sorrow, boy! Your feeding's a farce.   ° God
GARCIO: Their provisions, sir, I put back of their arse!
    And tied them fast by the necks,
    With many stones in their sacks.
CAIN: That shall thee buy on thy false cheeks! *(strikes him)*
GARCIO: And have back again! Right? *(strikes him back)*
CAIN: I am thy master. Wilt thou fight?
GARCIO: Yea, with the same measure and might!
    What I take I'll requite.

(They fight, running around the stage.)

CAIN: Away! Now nothing will make things right,
    But that we shall have plowed this land.
GARCIO *(a last try)*: Up, Morrell! Yo! Forth! Giddye-Hyte!
    (the animals run away, leaving the plow)
    (forlornly) And let the plow stand.
ABEL *(enters, carrying a lamb over his shoulders)*:
    God, as He both may and can,
    Speed thee, brother, and this man.
CAIN: Come kiss mine arse!—*(changes his tone)* But I'll not banter;
    Welcome stands the route!

(ABEL *smiles, refusing to take the hint and leave.*)

Thou should have stayed till thou were called!
Come near, and either drive or hold—
Or kiss the devil's toute°!   ° end
(*glancing disapprovingly at* ABEL'S *lamb*)
Go grease thy sheep under thy roof.
For that would be most lief°.   ° proper

ABEL: Brother, there is none heareabouts,
That would'st thee any grief.
But, dear brother, hear my saw°:   ° saying
It is the custom of our law,
All that work as they are wise
Shall worship God with sacrifice.
Our Father us bade, from him have we learned
That our tenth° should be burned.   ° tithe
Come forth, brother, and let us go
To worship God. (CAIN *doesn't move*)
We dwell too long.
Give we Him part of our fee°,   ° property
Corn or cattle, whichever it be.
And therefore, brother, let us wend,
But first cleanse us from the fiend
E'er we make sacrifice.
Then bliss without an end
Get we for our service
To Him that is our bad blood's leech°.   ° medicine

CAIN: How! Let forth your geese: the fox will preach!
How long wilt thou me impeach
With thy sermoning?
Hold thy tongue, yet I say,
Even where the good wife stroked the hay.
Or sit down in the devil's way,
With thy vain carping.
Should I leave my plow and everything.
And go with thee to make offering?
Nay, thou finds me not so mad!
Go to the devil, and say I so bade!
What gave God thee, to praise him so?
Me gives He nought but sorrow and woe.

ABEL: Cain, leave this vain carping,
For God gives thee all thy living.

CAIN: Yet borrowed I never a farthing
Of him—(*raising his hand to swear*) On that here's my hand.

ABEL: Brother, as our elders gave command,
A tenth should we offer with our hand,
And to His glory that tithe burn.

CAIN: My farthing is in the priest's hand
From the last time I offered.

ABEL: Dear brother, let us walk o'er the land.
I would our tenth were proffered.

CAIN: What? Whereof should I "tenth," dear brother?
    For I am each year worse than other—
    (*picks up a few wheat sheaves from his plough*)
    Here my troth—it is none other:
    My winnings° are but mean,   ° crops
    No wonder if I be so lean,
    Full long to Him° I may complain!   ° God
    For by Him° that me dearly bought,   ° Christ
    I swear that He° will lend me nought.   ° God
ABEL: Yes, but all the goods that thou do own
    From God's good grace is but a loan.
CAIN: Lends He to me? As come thrift upon thee so!
    For He has ever yet been my foe;
    For had He my friend been,
    In other ways it had been seen.
    When all men's corn was fair in field,
    Then was mine not worth a needle.
    When I should sow and wanted seed,
    And of corn had full great need,
    Then gave He me none of His,
    No more will I give Him of this!
    Hardly hold me to blame
    If I but serve him just the same.
ABEL: Dear brother, say not so,
    But let us forth together go.
    Good brother, let us wend our way;
    No longer here can we delay.
CAIN: Yea! Yea! Thou jangles waste!
    The devil speed me if I have haste
    As long as I may live
    To deal my goods, or give,
    Either to God or yet to man,
    Of any good that ever I won.
ABEL: Dear brother, it were great wonder
    That I and thou should go asunder;
    Then would our father amazed be:
    Are we not brothers, I and thee?
CAIN: No, but cry on, cry, whilst thee thinks good!
    Hear my troth: (*tapping* ABEL'*s head*) I hold thee wood!
    Whether that He be blithe or wroth,
    To share my goods makes me full loath.
    I have gone oft in softer wise,
    When'ere I saw a profit rise!
    But, well I see, go must I need;
    Now wend before—ill might thou speed!
    Since that we shall at any rate go.
ABEL: Dear brother, why says thou so?
    But go we forth both together.
    Blessed be God, we have fair weather.
(CAIN *and* ABEL *pick up a "trussel," or bundle of wheat sheaves for
sacrifice, and walk around the stage. The hill rises and they mount it.*)

CAIN: Lay down thy trussel upon this hill.
ABEL: Forsooth, brother, so I will;
    Gog of heaven! Take it for good.
CAIN: Thou shalt tenth first, if thou would.
ABEL (*kneels and prays*): God that shaped both earth and sky,
    I pray to Thee, Thou hear my cry.
    And take in thanks, if Thy will be,
    The tenth that here I offer thee.
    For I give it in good intent,
    To Thee, my Lord, that all has sent.
    (ABEL *ignites his trussel*)
    I burn it now with steadfast thought,
    In worship of Him that all has wrought.
    (*the sheaves burn brightly*)
CAIN: Rise! Let me now, since thou has done.
    (*kneels*) Lord of heaven, hear *my* plea!
    For God forbid that Thou to me
    Should show Your thanks, or courtesy.
    For, as bent as I these two shanks°,   ° as I kneel
    It is I am full sore with mine *un*thanks,
    For this tenth that I here give to thee—
    Of corn or things that grow for me!
    But now will I begin my turn,
    Since I must needs my tenth to burn.
    (CAIN *begins to count out ten sheaves*)
    One sheaf, one, and this makes two;
    (*sets them aside to retain for himself*)
    But neither shall I give to You.
    Two, two, now this is three:
    (*sets them aside*)
    Yet this also shall I keep with me.
    For I will choose which to retain,
    This one for thrift, and this good grain.
    Woah! Woah! Four, lo, here!
    (*pauses to complain to* GOD)
    Better grew me none this year
    At planting time I sowed fair corn,
    Yet was it such when it was shorn,
    Thistles and briars—in great plenty—
    And all the kinds of weeds there could be—
    (*resuming his count*) Four sheaves, four, lo, this makes five:
    Deal I thus fast, I'll never thrive.
    Five and six, now this is seven,
    (*sets these aside*)
    But this gets not to God in heaven.
    (*sets all the others aside*)
    Nor none of these four, by my might,
    Shall never come in God's own sight.
    Seven, seven, now this is eight—
ABEL: Cain, brother, you'll make God irate.
CAIN: Why? Therefore is it that I say

I will not deal my goods away!
Well! eight, eight, and nine, and ten is this:
(*comes up with a pathetic little sheaf*)
Well! This may be best miss.
(*pulls all the others aside*)
Give that one lying there o'er?
It goes against mine heart full sore.

ABEL: Cain! Your tenth right now. And quickly seen.

CAIN: Way lo! (*rushing through it, grabbing all the tiny ones*)
Twelve, fifteen, sixteen—

ABEL: Cain! you're tenthing wrong, with all the worst!

CAIN: Thou wouldst I gave him this sheaf? Or this sheaf?
No, neither of these two will I leave.
But take this. (*holds up the two tiniest sheaves*)
Now has He two,
And for my soul now this will do.
But it goes sore against my will,
Even shall He like full ill.

ABEL: Cain, I beg you so tend,
That God of heaven be thy friend.

CAIN: My friend? Naw, not unless He will!
I never did him any ill.
If He be ever so my foe
I am advised give Him no mo.
But change thy conscience, as I do mine,
Have you not tithed thy measly swine?

ABEL: If thou tenth right thou shalt good find.

CAIN: Yea, kiss the devil's arse behind!
The devil hang thee by the neck!
Just how I tenth, never thou reck°!   ° reckon
Will thou not yet hold thy peace?
Of this jangling, I advise you cease;
And tenth I well, or tenth I ill,
Bear thee even, and speak with skill.
But now, since thou has tendered thine,
Now will I set fire to mine.

(CAIN *tries to burn his tithe but it does not ignite. He begins to blow on it.*)

Out! Harrow! Help me blow!
It will not burn for me, I trow.

(ABEL *tries to help, but it refuses to burn, and instead it begins to smoke. He withdraws.*)

Puff! This smoke does me much shame—
Now burn in the devil's name!

(CAIN *blows again, but the smoke overcomes him, and he and* ABEL *are forced off the hill, choking.*)

Ah! What devil of Hell is it?
Almost had mine breath gone quit!

Had I blown out one blast more,
I had been chocked right sore.
It stank like the devil in Hell,
That longer there might I not dwell.

ABEL: Cain, this is not a joke!
Thy tenth should burn without this smoke!

CAIN: Come kiss the devil right in the arse!
Because of *thee* it burns the worse!
I would that it were up thy throat,
Fire, and sheaf, and every mote!

(GOD *suddenly appears above.*)

GOD: Cain, why art thou a rebel
Against thy brother Abel?

(CAIN *cowers under the tower and tries to hide.*)

Thou needs neither chide nor fight.
If thou tenth well, thou gets thy right.
And, be thou sure, if thou tenth false,
Thou be'est condemned forever als.

(GOD *disappears.* ABEL *looks about in wonderment,* CAIN *in angry confusion.*)

CAIN: Why, who is that hob over the wall?
Way! Who was that that piped so small?
Come, go we hence, from perils all;
God is out of his wit!
Come forth, Abel, and let us wend.
Me thinks that God is not my friend.
On land then will I flit!°   ° fly

(CAIN *tries to lead* ABEL *away, but* ABEL *moves off in the opposite direction.*)

ABEL: Ah, Cain, brother, this is ill done.

CAIN: No, but go we hence soon.
And if I may, I shall be
There where God shall not me see.

ABEL: Dear brother, I will fare
To field where our beasts are,
To look as if they be hungry or full.
(*starts off away from* CAIN, *who pulls him back*)

CAIN: Naw, naw! Abide. We have a craw to pull°!   ° bone to pick
Hark, speak with me 'ere thou go.
What, thinkst thou to 'scape so?
Way! Naw! I owe thee some foul spite;
A blow that now I thee requite!
(CAIN *strikes* ABEL, *who recoils in puzzlement.*)

ABEL: Brother, why art thou so to me in ire?

CAIN: Way! Thief! Why burned thy tenth in such bright fire
When mine but smoked?
Right as it would us both have choked?

ABEL: God's will I trow° it were   ° believe
    That mine burned so clear;
    If thine smoked, am I to blame?
CAIN: Way! Yea! That shall I proclaim!

(CAIN *picks up the jawbone of an ass.*)

    With cheekbone, whilst I still abide,
    I shall thy life and thee divide!

(CAIN *strikes* ABEL *with the jawbone;* ABEL *falls.*)

    So, lie down there and take thy rest;
    Thus shall shrews be chastised best.
ABEL: Vengeance, vengeance, Lord, I cry!
    For I am slain, and not guilty! (*dies*)
CAIN: Yea, lie there, old shrew! Lie there, lie!
    (*turns to audience, threatening them with the jawbone*)
    And if any of *you* think I did amiss,
    I shall amend it worse than it is.
    That all men may it see:
    Well worse than it is,
    Right so shall it be.

(*He turns back to* ABEL, *trying to find out what has happened to his brother; he does not understand what death is, never having heard of it.*)

    But now, since he is brought to . . . sleep,
    Into some hole fain would I creep.
    For fear I quake; I've lost my head.
    If be I taken, I be but dead.
    (*lies down on the stage*) Here will I lie these forty days,
    And I curse him that me first shall raise.
GOD (*from heaven*): Cain! Cain!
CAIN: Who is it that calls me?
    I am yonder, may thou not see?
GOD: Cain, where is thy brother Abel?
CAIN: What asks thou me? I trow in Hell,
    In Hell I think he be—
    Whoso were there then might he see—
    Or somewhere he may be sleeping.
    Since when was he in *my* keeping?
GOD: Cain, Cain, thy head is wood!
    The voice of thy dear brother's blood,
    That thou hast slain in falsest wise,
    From earth to heaven "Vengeance" cries.
    And, for thou hast brought thy brother down,
    Thou shalt hear My curses sound!
CAIN: Yea! Deal them out, for I'll have none,
    Or take it Thee when I am gone.
    Since I have done so great a sin,
    That I may not thy mercy win,
    And Thou thus sends me from Thy grace

I shall hide me from Thy face.
(*rises, speaks to the audience*)
And whereso any man may find me,
Let him slay me hardily—
Wherever any man me meet,
In the sty° or in the street.   ° animal pen
And surely when that I am dead,
Bury me in Gudeborn's° quarry head;   ° place near Wakefield
For, as from this world I'll part,
By all men set I not a fart.

(*He starts to leave, but* GOD *speaks again, and* CAIN *collapses at the sound of His voice.*)

GOD: Nay, Cain, it be not that way.
I will no man another slay,
For he that slays thee, young or old,
He shall be punished sevenfold.

(GOD *disappears.*)

CAIN: No force! I know where I am headed:
In Hell, I guess, will I be bedded.
It is no use, mercy to crave,
For though I do, I must none have.
(*looking at* ABEL'*s body*)
But this . . . corpse . . . I would were hid,
For some man might come here again:
"Flee, false shrew," would he me bid,
Knowing I had my brother slain.
But were Pickharness, my knave here,
We should both bury him to ease our fear.
How, Pickharness! Scapethrift! How, Pickharness, How!

(GARCIO *reenters and* CAIN *hits him.*)

GARCIO: Master, Master!
CAIN: Hear boy? There is a pudding in the pot.
(*hits him again*) Take thee that, boy take thee that!
GARCIO: I beshrew thy head under thy hood;
Though thou were my sire in flesh and blood.
(*to the audience*)
All the day I run and trot
Ever to be struck! My lot
Is all this buffetting I stand!
CAIN: Peace, man! I did it but to use my hand.
But hark, boy, I have a counsel to thee to say—
I slew my brother this same day;
I pray thee, good boy, and thou may,
To take away the body plain.
GARCIO (*terrified, starts to run away*): Way! Out upon thee, thief!
Hast thou thy brother slain?

CAIN: Peace, man, for God's pain!
    I said it just by chance.
GARCIO: Yea, but for fear of grievance,
    Here I thee forsake;
    We will have mickle° mischance,   ° awful
    And the baillifs shall us take.
CAIN: Ah, sir, I cry you mercy! Cease,
    And I shall make you a release.
GARCIO: What, wilt thou cry my peace
    Throughout this land?
CAIN: Yea, I swear to God alive.
GARCIO: How will thou do that? May you not thrive!
CAIN: Hey! Come down in twenty devil's way!
    The devil keep you watch!
    For but it were Abel, my brother,

(ABEL's *body begins to sink below the platform.*)

    Yet knew I never thy match.

(*He becomes pensive, watching his brother descend. The lights of hell begin to glow on the platform.*)

GARCIO (*to the audience*): Now old and young, ere that ye wend,
    The same blessing without an end,
    Together shall ye have,
    That God of heaven to my master did give.
    Enjoy it well, whiles that ye live,
    I vouch it will you save.
CAIN: Come down yet in the devil's way,
    And anger me no more!

(*The lights of Hell glow more menacingly, and* SATAN's *laugh is heard.*)

    And take yon plow I say,
    And wend thee forth fast before;
    And I shall, if I may,
    Teach thee another lore°.   ° story
    I warn thee, lad, beyond today,
    From henceforth evermore,
    That thou grieve me not;
    For, by God's sides, if thou do,
    I shall hang thee upon this plow,
    With this rope, lo, lad, lo.
    By Him that me dear bought!

(GARCIO *runs off.* CAIN *is alone. He looks for someone to hit, but finds no one. Hell mouth cracks open and smoke floods the stage.* CAIN *addresses the audience.*)

    Now fare well, fellows all, for I must wend
    And to the devil be in thrall, world without an end;
    Ordained there is my stall, with Satan as my friend.
    Forever ill might him befall that thither me commend

This tide—
Farewell less and farewell more!
For now and evermore
I will go me to hide.

(CAIN *disappears in smoke.*)

INTERMISSION

PART TWO

(*The lights come up on a bare platform for the play of* NOAH. NOAH *enters,
whistling. Laboriously, he kneels to pray.*)

NOAH: Mightyfull God, truly I say, maker of all that is,
  Three persons—without a nay, one God in endless bliss:
  They made both night and day; beast, fowl and fish;
  All creatures that live may, wrought Thou at Thy wish,
  As Thou well might.
  The sun, the moon, all that was meant
  Thou made: the firmament;
  The stars also—full fervent
  To shine, Thou made full bright.

  Angels Thou made full even, all order that is,
  To have the bliss in heaven: this did Thou more and less,
  Full marvellous to neven°. Yet was their unkindness   ° name
  More by six times seven than I can well express,
  For why?
  (*turns to audience*)
  Of all angels in brightness,
  God gave Lucifer most lightness,
  Yet proudly he fled his dais,
  To set him even Him by.

  He thought himself as worthy as Him that him made
  In brightness, in beauty; therefore He him did degrade,
  Put him in a low degree soon after, who disobeyed,
  Him and all his minions, where he may be unglad
  Forever!
  They shall never get away
  From hence until doomsday,
  But shall burn in bale° for ay°,   ° discomfort   ° forever
  They shall never dissever°!   ° escape

  Soon after, that gracious Lord to his likeness made man,
  That place to be restored, even as He began.
  Of the Trinity by accord, Adam, and Eve that woman,
  To multiply without discord—in Paradise, He put them,
  And thenceforth to both
  Gave His commandment:

On the Tree of Life to lay no hand.
But yet the false fiend
Made Him with man wroth.

Enticed man to gluttony, stirred him to sin in pride.
But in Paradise, surely, might no sin abide;
And therefore man full hastily was put out in that tide
In woe and wandering. Where to be? In paid did he bide,
To know:
You're first on earth, and then in Hell,
With fiends with whom to live,
Unless God will mercy give
To those that will Him trow!°   ° believe

Oil of mercy He us hight°, as I have heard read,   ° gave
To every living wight° that would Him love and dread.   ° child
But now before his sight, why every living head,
Most part of day and night—do Sin in word and deed!
Full bold!
Some in pride, ire and envy,
Some in covetousness and gluttony,
Some in sloth and lechery,
And all of them manyfold.

Therefore I dread lest God on us will take vengeance;
For sin is now abroad, without any repentance.
Six hundred years and odd have lived I—without distance,
On earth, as any sod, lived with great grievance,
Allway;
And now I wax old,
Sick, sorry, and cold;
As muck upon mould°,   ° earth
I wither away.

But yet will I cry for mercy, and call:
Noah, Thy servant, am I, Lord over all!
Therefore me, and my fry°, who with me fall,   ° children
Save from villainy, and bring to Thy hall
On high.
And keep me from sin,
This world within.
Comely° king of man's kin,   ° beautiful
I pray thee hear my cry!

(NOAH *lies down and sleeps.* GOD *appears in heaven and watches him.*)

GOD: Since I have made all thing that is living,
    Duke, emperor, and king, with mine own hand,
    For to have their likings, by sea and by sand,
    Every man to My bidding should be bowing
    Full fervent—
    I, that made man such a creature,

Fairest of favor—
Man must love Me paramour°,   ° over all
By reason, and repent.

Me thought I showed man love when I made him to be
All angels above, like to the Trinity;
And now in great reproof, full low lies he,
On earth, himself to stuff with sins that displease me
Most of all.
Vengeance will I take
On earth for sin's sake;
My wrath thus will I wake
On both great and small.
I repent full sore that ever made I man;
By me he sets no store, 'though I am his sovereign.
I will destroy, therefore, both beast, man, and woman:
All shall perish, less and more. Their bargain may they ban
That ill have done
On earth. (*looks around*) I see right nought
But sin that is unsought,
Of those that well have wrought
Find I but one.

Therefore shall I fordo all this middle earth
With floods that shall flow and run with hideous wrath.
I have good cause thereto; for of Me, no man's afeard.
As I say, so shall I do—in vengeance draw my sword,
And make end
Of all that does bear life (NOAH *snores*)
Save Noah and his wife,
For they have never strife
With Me nor Me offend.

Him to mickle win, hastily will I go
To Noah my servant, before I begin, to warn him of his woe.
On earth I see but sin, reigning to and fro,
Among both more and min°, each one th'other's foe,   ° less
With all their intent.
All shall I fordo,
With floods that shall flow,
Work shall I them woe
That will not repent.

(GOD *addresses* NOAH.)

Noah, my friend,

(NOAH *bolts up, astounded, and sees* GOD.)

I thee command, from cares thee to quell,
A ship shall thou ordain, of nail and board full well.
Thou was always well-working, to me true as steel,
To my bidding obedient; My friendship shall thou feel

As reward.
Of length thy ship be
Three hundred cubits.

(NOAH *nods, bewildered.* GOD *cries to him.*)

Warn I thee!

(NOAH *takes out a notepad and pen;* GOD *continues as* NOAH *writes down his instructions.*)

Of height even thirty,
And fifty also broad.

Anoint thy ship with pitch and tar, without and als within,
The water out to spar; this is a noble gin°.   ° piece of work
Look no man thee mar!° Three tiers of rooms begin;   ° stop
Thou must spend many a spar, this work, 'ere thou win
To end it fully.
Make in thy ship also
Parlors one or two,
And houses of office mo°   ° more
For beasts that there must be.

One cubit in height a window thou shall make;
On the side a door, with sleight, beneath shall thou take.
With thee shall no man fight, nor do thee any wrake°.   ° harm
When all is done thus right, thy wife, that is thy make°,   ° mate
Take in to thee;
And thy sons of good fame,
Shem, Japhet, and Ham,
Take in also them,
And their wives three.

For all shall be foredone, that lives on land, but ye;
With floods that from above shall fall, and that plenty.
It shall begin full soon to rain incessantly,
After days seven be done, and endure for days forty,
Without it fail.
Take to thy ship also
Of each kind beasts two,
Male and female, but no mo,
Ere thou pull up thy sail.

For they may thee avail when all this thing is wrought.
Stuff thy ship with victuals, so of hunger ye perish not.
Of beasts, fowl, and cattle, for them have thou in thought
For them it is My counsel, that some succor be sought
In haste.
They must have corn and hay
And other meat alway.
Do now as I thee say,
In the name of the Holy Ghost.

NOAH (*suddenly skeptical at all these instructions and the strange man giving them*):
    Ah, Benedicite! What art Thou that thus
    Tells afore what shall be? Thou art full marvellous!
    Tell me, for charity, Thy name so gracious.
GOD: My name is of dignity, and also full glorious
    To know:
    I am GOD most mighty,
    One God in Trinity,
    I made thee and each man to be,
    To love Me well thou owe.
NOAH (*collapsing to his knees in reverence*):
    I thank Thee Lord, so dear, that would vouchsafe
    Thus low to appear to a simple knave.
    Bless us Lord, here, for charity I it crave,
    The better may we steer the ship that we shall have,
    Certain.
GOD: Noah, to thee and to thy fry
    My blessing grant I;
    Ye shall wax and multiply
    And fill the earth again,
    When all these floods are past, and fully gone away.

(GOD *disappears.*)

NOAH: Lord, homeward will I haste as fast as that I may;
    My wife will I ask what she will say
    And I am aghast that we get some fray°   ° fight
    Betwixt us both.
    For she is full touchy,
    for little—oft angry,
    If anything wrong be,
    Soon is she wroth°   ° angry

(NOAH *goes to his wife and speaks to her.*)

    God speed, dear wife! How fare ye?
NOAH'S WIFE: Now, as ever might I thrive, the worse I thee see.
    Do tell me belief, where has thou thus long be?
    To death may we drive, for all it means to thee,
    For want.
    When I sweat and swink°,   ° work
    Thou does what thou think,
    Yet of meat and of drink,
    Have we very skant°.   ° little
NOAH: Wife, we are hard bestead with tidings new.
NOAH'S WIFE: But thou were worthy be clad in Stafford blue,°   ° a fine local cloth
    For thou are always a-dread, be it false or true.
    But God knows I am led—and this I may rue—
    Full ill;
    For I dare thy blows borrow—
    From evening til morrow

Thou speaks only of sorrow—
God send thee once thy fill!

(*She speaks to the women in the audience.*)

We women may be-wary all ill husbands;
I have one, by Mary, that loosed me of my bands!
If he fumes, I must tarry, howsoever it stands,
In seemly full sorry, wringing both my hands,
For dread:
But yet otherwhile,
What with gaming and guile,
I shall smite him and smile,
And quit him his head!

(*She swings at him and misses; he threatens her in return.*)

NOAH: Woah! Hold thy tongue, ram-shit, or I shall thee still!
NOAH'S WIFE: By my troth, if thou smite, turn on thee I will.
NOAH: We shall try it a mite. Have at thee, Jill!
  Upon the bone shall it bite.

(*He strikes at her and misses; she falls to the floor and begins tying his shoelaces together.*)

NOAH'S WIFE: Ah, so! Marry, thou smitest ill!
  But I suppose
  I shall not for thy grace
  Fly from this place
  Take thee there a shoelace
  To tie up thy hose!
NOAH (*she moves away, he falls trying to follow her*):
  Ah! Wilt thou so? (*he rises*) Marry, have thine

(*He strikes her twice.*)

NOAH'S WIFE (*she strikes him three times*):
  Thou shall three for two, I swear by God's pine!°   ° pain
NOAH: And I shall quite thee those, in faith here is mine!

(*He swings at her and misses.*)

NOAH'S WIFE: Out upon thee, ho!
NOAH: Thou can both bite and whine—
  with a roar!
  (*to the audience*)
  For all, if she strike,
  Yet fast will she shriek,
  In faith, I hold none like
  In all middle earth!

(*Thunder.* NOAH *looks up.*)

But I will keep charity, for I have things to do.
NOAH'S WIFE: Here shall no man tarry thee; I pray thee, go to!

Full well may we miss thee, as ever I do!
To spin will I 'dress me. (*she sits on the hill and spins*)
NOAH: Well! Farewell! Lo!
But wife
Pray for me busily,
Till back I come unto thee.
NOAH'S WIFE: Even as thou pray'st for me,
As ever might I thrive.
NOAH: I tarry full long from my work, I trow;
Now my gear will I get and thitherward go.

(NOAH *gets his tools and starts building the ship.*)

I may full ill gang, in truth I don't know,
Unless if God help me along, I will have to eat crow
Before men.
Now assay will I
How I can of carpentry,
In nominis patris, et filii,
Et spiritus sancti. Amen.
[In the name of the father, the son, and the Holy Ghost, Amen]

(*He mimes chopping down a tree; the footbridge that represented heaven begins to descend; it will become the ark.*)

To begin with this tree, my bones will I bend;
I trust that the Trinity succor will send.

(*As* NOAH *begins to build, he is helped by mysterious forces, which amazes him.*)

It fares full fair, thinks me, this work to my hand!
Now blessed be He that my work does amend!

(*The ark is complete;* NOAH *takes its measurements.*)

Lo, here, the length,
Three hundred cubits evenly;
Of breadth, lo, is it fifty;
The height is even thirty
Cubits, full strength.

(*He takes off his cloak and climbs onto the ark.*)

Now my gown will I cast, and work in my coat;
Make will I the mast ere I go further a foot.
Ah! My back, I trow, will burst! This is a sorry note!
It is wonder that I last, I'm such an old dote,
All dold!°   ° stupid
I'll work for His sake,
My bones close to break,
No wonder that they ache,
For I am full old.

The top and the sail both will I make;
The helm and the fo'c'sle also will I take;

To drive every nail will I not forsake.
This gear may never fail, that I dare undertake,
From here on.
This is a noble gin;
These nails are hard in.
Through, more and min,
These boards, every one.

Window and door, even as He said;
Three tiers of rooms, they are well made;
Pitch and tar full sure thereupon laid.
This will ever endure, thereof am I well paid.
For why?
It is better wrought
Than I could have thought.
Him that made all from naught
I thank hereby.

(NOAH *goes to his family—wife, three sons, three daughters-in-law—
who enter, staring at the ark in complete bewilderment.*)

Now will I hie me, and nought can I dither,
My wife and my family to bring even hither.
(*to his wife*) Attend hither tidely, wife, and consider;
Hence must we flee, and all us together,
In haste.
NOAH'S WIFE: Why, sir, what ails you?
Who is that assails you?
To flee it avails you
And ye be disgraced?
NOAH (*pointing to her spinning reel*):
There is yarn on the reel other, my dame.
NOAH'S WIFE: Tell me the deal, else get ye my blame.
NOAH: He that our cares doth feel—blessed be His name—
He has behest, for our weal°, to shield us from shame;   ° good fortune
And said,
All this world about,
By floods—so stout
That they run in a rout—
Shall be overlaid.

He said all shall be slain, except only we,
Our boys that obey, and their wives three.
A ship he bade me ordain, to save us and our fee;
Therefore with all our main, thank we that great He;
Our Helper we hail!
Hie us fast, go we thither.
NOAH'S WIFE: I know never whither;
I'm dazed and I dither
For fear of that tale.
NOAH: Be not afeard. Have done, truss up our gear,
That we be there ere noon, and all without fear.

SHEM (*a tremendous thunderclap, the children begin helping load the ship.*): It shall be done full soon.
    Brother, help to bear.
JAPHET: I'll not long linger to do my duty here.
    Brother Ham?
HAM: Without any yelp
    With my might I shall help.
NOAH'S WIFE (*grabbing* HAM *and holding him back*):
    Yet, for dread of a skelp°   ° slap
    Help well thy dam!

(*More thunder. They cross to the Ark, and all but* NOAH'S WIFE *prepare to board.*)

NOAH: Now are we there as we should be.
    Do get in our gear, our cattle and fee°,   ° possessions
    Into this vessel here, my children free.

(NOAH, *his sons, and daughters-in-law enter the ark. Rain is heard.* NOAH'S WIFE *remains outside, petulant.*)

NOAH'S WIFE: I was ne'er barred up before—as ever might I thee—
    In such an hostelry as this!
    (*studying the ark*) In faith, I cannot find
    Which is the front, which the behind.
    But shall we here be impined°,   ° imprisoned
    Noah, as thou have bliss?
NOAH: Dame, if we have skill, here must we abide grace.
    Therefore, wife, with good will come into this place.
NOAH'S WIFE: Sir, for Jack nor for Jill will I turn my face
    Till I have on this hill spun a space
    On my rock°.   ° spinning distaff
    Well were he that might get me!
    Now will I down set me;

(*She sits down on the hill and starts spinning. Thunder. The ark begins to rise.*)

    And reck° I no man stop me   ° reckon
    For dread of a knock!
NOAH (*more thunder,* NOAH *calls from the rapidly rising Ark.*):
    Behold to the heavens! The cateracts all,
    They are open full even, great and small,
    And the planets all seven have left their stall.
    (*thunder and lightning*)
    These thunders and lightings down here fall
    Full stout
    On both halls and bowers,
    Castles and towers.
    Full sharp are these showers
    That rain hereabout.

    Therefore, wife, have done; come into ship fast.

NOAH'S WIFE: Yea, Noah—Go clout thy shoon!°   ° fix your shoes
>The better will they last.
SHEM'S WIFE: Good mother, come in soon, for all is overcast.
>Both the sun and the moon.
JAPHET'S WIFE: And many a wind-blast
>Full sharp.
>These floods, so they run;
>Therefore, mother, come in.
NOAH'S WIFE: In faith, yet will I spin,
>All in vain ye carp.
HAM'S WIFE: If ye like ye may spin, mother, in the ship!
NOAH: Now is this twice: Come in, dame, on my friendship!
NOAH'S WIFE: Whether I lose or I win, in faith, thy fellowship
>Set I not at a pin. This spindle will I slip
>Upon this hill,
>Ere I stir one foot.
NOAH (*more thunder*):
>Peter! I trow we dote.
>Without any more note,
>Come in if ye will.

(*A giant thunderclap, and intense rain. The hill begins to sink under the waters.*)

NOAH'S WIFE: Yipes! Water nighs so near that I sit not dry!
>Into ship with my gear, therefore will I hie
>For dread that I drown here!

(*She struggles onto the ark.*)

NOAH: Dame, surely
>It be'est brought full dear ye abode so long by
>Out of ship.
NOAH'S WIFE: I will not for thy bidding
>Go from door to the midding°   ° amidships
NOAH: In faith, and for your long tarrying,
>Ye shall have a lick of the whip.
NOAH'S WIFE: Spare me not, I pray thee, but e'en as thou think;
>These great words shall not flay me.
NOAH: Abide, dame, and drink:
>For beaten shall thou be with this staff till thou stink.

(*He strikes her with his staff.*)

>Are my strokes good? Say me.
NOAH'S WIFE (*she has tucked the spinning "rock" and "spindle" into her
>costume as protection, and feels little*):
>What say ye, Fred Fink?
NOAH: Speak! (*they fight*) Cry me mercy, I say!
NOAH'S WIFE: Thereto say I, *nay*!
NOAH: If thou don't, by this day,
>Thy head shall I break!

NOAH'S WIFE: Lord, I were at ease, and heartily I'd heal,
    Might I once have a mess of honest widow's meal,
    For thy soul, no less, a mass penny should I deal
    (*pointing to the women in the audience*)
    And so would all of these, here in the commonweal,
    These wives that are here,
    For the lives they have led,
    Wish their husbands dead.
    For, as ever ate I bread,
    So wish I our sire were.
NOAH (*addressing the men in the audience*):
    Ye men that have wives, while they are young,
    If ye love your lives, chastise their tongue.
    Me thinks my heart rives°, both liver and lung,   ° breaks
    To see such strives°, wed-men among.   ° arguments
    But I,
    As have I bliss,
    Shall chastise this.

(*He strikes at her; she deftly dodges away.*)

NOAH'S WIFE: Yet may ye miss,
    Simple Si!
NOAH: I shall make thee still as stone, beginner of blunder!
    I shall beat thy back and bone, and break all in sunder.

(*They resume their fight.*)

NOAH'S WIFE: Out, alas, I am gone! Out upon thee, man's wonder!

(*She climbs on top of him as his strength gives out.*)

NOAH: See how she can groan, and I lie under!
    But wife,
    Let us halt this ado,
    For my back is near in two.
NOAH'S WIFE: And I'm so black and blue
    That I may lose my life.
SHEM: Ah! Why fare ye thus, father and mother both?
HAM: Ye should not be so spiteful, with danger so close.
JAPHET: These weathers are hideous, to freeze we are loath.

(*The rain has stopped, but a great wind is seen and heard.*)

NOAH: We will do as ye bid us; we will no more be wroth.
    Dear bairns.°   ° children

(*He goes to the tiller.*)

    Now to the helm will I hend,
    And my steering attend.
NOAH'S WIFE: I see on the firmament,
    Me thinks, the seven stars.
NOAH: This is a great flood, wife, take heed.

(*The ark sways madly in the wind;* NOAH's *family grabs for the rails, and* NOAH *steers as best he can.*)

NOAH'S WIFE: So me thought, as I stood. We are in great dread;
  These waves are so wide!
NOAH: Help, God, in this need!
  As Thou art steer-man good, and best, as I reed,
  Of all,
  Thou rule us in this race,
  As Thou said face to face.
NOAH'S WIFE: This is a perilous case.
  Help, God, when we call!

(*Screaming, they all cry their prayers. The storm begins to abate.*)

NOAH: Wife, attend the steer-tree, and I shall assay
  The deepness of the sea that we bear if I may.
NOAH'S WIFE: That shall I do full wisely. Now go thy way.

(*Daylight returns. The sea is calm.*)

  For upon this flood have we floated many a day
  In pain.
NOAH: Now the water will I sound:

(*He lowers a plummet.*)

  Ah! It is far to the ground,
  This travail I expound
  I've done in vain.

  Above all hills be seen, the water is risen of late
  Cubits fifteen. But in a higher state
  It may not be, I ween°, for this well I wit°:   ° think ° know
  This forty days has rain been; it will therefore abate,
  I feel.
  This water at last,
  Again will I test.

(*He again lowers a plummet.*)

  Now I am aghast!
  It has waned a great deal!

  Now are the weathers ceased, and cateracts knit,
  Both the most and the least.
NOAH'S WIFE: Me thinks, by my wit,
  The sun shines in the East. (*points*) Lo, is not yond it?
  We should have a good feast, would these floods flit°,   ° go
  So pitiless.
NOAH: We have been here, all we,
  Three hundred days and fifty.
NOAH'S WIFE: Aye, now wanes the sea:
  Lord, well is us.
NOAH (*preparing to lower the plummet a third time*):
  The third time I'll demand what deepness we bear.

(*But he puts down the plummet and reaches with his hand. The ark
begins to descend, the hill rises.*)

NOAH'S WIFE: How long shalt thou stand? Lay in thy line
   there.
NOAH (*touching the hill*):
   I may touch with my hand the ground even here!
NOAH'S WIFE: Then begins to expand to us merry cheer!
   But husband,
   What ground may this be?
NOAH: The hills of Armonie!
NOAH'S WIFE: Now blessed be He
   That thus for us ordained.
NOAH: I see tops of hills high, many at a sight;
   Nothing to stop me, the weather is so bright.
NOAH'S WIFE: These are of mercy tokens full right.
NOAH: Dame, then counsel me what fowl best might
   Go forth
   With flight of wing
   Bring without tarrying
   Of mercy some tokening
   Either by south or north.
NOAH'S WIFE: The raven, durst I lay, will come back again soon.
   As fast as thou may, cast him forth—and have done!

(NOAH *sends out a raven.*)

   He may happen today—(*to the raven*) Come again ere noon
   With speed!
NOAH: I will cast out also
   Doves one or two,

(*He does, and then calls after the doves.*)

   Go your way, go!
   God grant what we need.

   Now are these fowls flown into each country.
   Pray we fast each one, kneeling on our knee,
   To Him that is alone, worthiest of degree,
   That he would send or loan our fowls some fee
   To glad us.

(*The family kneels in a silent prayer.*)

NOAH'S WIFE: They may not fail of land,
   The water is so waned.
NOAH: Thank we God well deigned,
   That Lord that made us!
   It is a wonder thing, me thinks truly,
   They are so long tarrying, the fowls that we
   Cast out in the morning.
NOAH'S WIFE: Sir, it may be
   They tarry til they bring.
NOAH: The raven is a-hungry
   Allway.
   He is without any reason;

If he find any carrion,
As peraventure may be found,
He will not away.

The dove is more gentle, her trust I unto,
Like to the turtle°, she always is true.   ° turtledove
NOAH'S WIFE: Hence but a little—she comes! Lew! Lew!

(*The dove returns.* NOAH'S WIFE *catches it.*)

She brings in her bill some novelties new.
Behold.
It is of an olive tree
A branch, thinks me!
NOAH: It is sooth°, perdy°,   ° truth   ° by God
Right so it is called.

Dove, bird full blest, fair tidings thee befall!
Thou art true to thy tryst as stone in the wall.
Full well I it wist thou would come to thy hall.
NOAH'S WIFE: A true token is't we shall be saved all,
For why?
The water, since she come,
Of deepness plumbed,
Is fallen a fathom
And more, hereby.
HAM: These floods are gone, father, behold!
SHEM: There is left right none, and that be ye bold.
JAPHET: As still as a stone our ship is stold°.   ° landed
NOAH: Upon land, here, alone are we now, so be told.
My children dear,
Shem, Japhet, and Ham,
With glee and with game,
Come go we all same;
We will no longer abide here.

(*They all leave the ark.*)

NOAH'S WIFE: Here have we been, Noah, long enough
With trouble and teen, and seas very rough.
NOAH: Behold on this green! Neither cart nor plough
Is left, as I ween, neither tree nor bough.
No other thing,
But all is away;
Many castles, I say,
Great towns of array,
Fled from this flooding.
NOAH'S WIFE: These floods, not afright, all this world so wide
Have moved with might on sea and by side.
NOAH: To death are they dight, those proudest of pride
Every such wight that ever was spied
With sin:

All are they slain,
And put into pain.

NOAH'S WIFE: From thence again
    May they never win?

NOAH: Win? No, iwis°. 'Lest He that might has   ° certainly
    Would take mind of their miss, and admit them to grace.
    (*making the sign of the cross*)
    As He in pain is bliss, I pray Him in this space,
    In heaven high, with His, to purvey us a place
    That we,
    With His saints in sight,
    And His angels bright,
    May come to His light.
    Amen, for charity.

(*They gather and sing "Quam Pulcra Es," and then depart separately for the three continents.*)

(*The hill sinks and the lights change.* ABRAHAM, *an aged man, enters the stage platform. He looks around, and prays* GOD *for mercy after death.*)

ABRAHAM: Adonai°, Thou God I say,   ° Lord
    Thou hear us when we to Thee call,
    As thou art He that bestest may,
    Thou giv'st most succor and help of all;
    Mightyfull Lord! To Thee I pray,
    Let once the oil of mercy fall,
    Shall I never abide that day°—   ° (of death)
    Yet truly I hope I shall.

(*faces* GOD'*s tower*) Mercy, Lord omnipotent!
(*faces audience*)
Long since He this world has wrought°;   ° made
Whither° have all our elders went?   ° where
I muse thus mickle° in my thought: ° intensely
Since Adam, all with Eve's assent,
Ate of that apple, spared God nought,
And for the wisdom he was sent,
Full dear that bargain Adam bought.

From Paradise God bade him gang°;   ° go
He mourning went, with simple cheer,
And after lived he here full long,
More than three hundred year,
In sorrow and in travail° strong,   ° hard work
And every day in wary fear;
His children angered him among;
Cain slew Abel, to Adam dear.

Then Noah, that was true and good,
He and his children three,

Were saved when all was flood:
That was a wonder thing to see.
And Lot from Sodom, when he strode,
Three cities burned, escape did he;
Thus, for they moved my Lord's mood,
He venged their sin most mightily.

When I think of our elders all,
And of the marvels that have been,
No gladness in my heart may fall,
My comfort goes away full clean.
Lord, when shall Death make me his thrall?
An hundred years, certes° have I seen.   ° surely
In fay°, soon I hope he shall,   ° faith
For it were right high time I ween°.   ° believe

(*broods in anguish*)
Yet Adam is to Hellfire gone!
And there has lain many a day!
And all our elders, everyone,
They are gone the same way,
Until God will hear their moan;
(*looks up for* GOD, *imploringly*)
Now help, Lord, Adonai!
For, certes, I can no better own°,   ° explain
And there is none that better may.

(GOD *appears in heaven, unseen by* ABRAHAM.)

GOD: I will help Adam and his kind,
If I might love and loyalty find.
So they to me be true—begin
To cease their pride and then their sin—
My servant will I prove and test.
Abraham, if he be best,
In certain wise I will him prove
If he to me be true in love.

(ABRAHAM *moves about, looking for the voice. Suddenly he hears his name called.*)

    Abraham! Abraham!
ABRAHAM (*stopping*): Who is that? where? Let me see!
    I heard one call my name.

(*Turning, he sees* GOD *in heaven and falls to his knees.*)

GOD: It is I, take tent° to me,   ° pay attention
That formed thy father Adam,
And every thing in its degree.
ABRAHAM: To hear Thy will, ready I am,
And to fulfill what ever it be.
GOD: Of mercy have I heard thy cry,
Thy devout prayers are Me upon.

If thou Me love, look that thou hie°   ° go
Unto the land of Visyon;
And the third day be there, bid I,
And take with thee Isaac, thy son,
As a beast to sacrify°.   ° sacrifice
To slay him, look thou not shun,
And burn him there in offering.

ABRAHAM (*gradually understanding* GOD's *instruction, he moans horribly*): Ahhhhhhhhhhhhh!
(*resolving himself to the deed*)
Loved be Thou, Lord in throne.
Hold over me, Lord, Thy holy hand,
For certes Thy bidding shall be done.
Blessed be that Lord in every land,
To visit his servant in this way.
Fain do I this thing on command,
For it profits not to delay.

(GOD *holds his hand in benediction over* ABRAHAM, *and then disappears.*
ABRAHAM *looks after him, then recognizes he is alone.*)

This commandment must I needs fulfil,
E'en though my heart wax° heavy as lead;   ° grows
Should I offend my Lord's will?
Nay, yet were I liefer° my child were dead.   ° to prefer
What so he bids me, good or ill
That shall be done in every stead;
Both wife and child, if he bid kill
I will not 'gainst his wishes tread.

Would Isaac, whereso he were,
He would be abashed now,
To know how he is in danger.
(*calls to his son*) Isaac! Son! Where art thou?

ISAAC (*entering briskly*): All ready, father. Lo, me here;
Now was I coming unto you:
I love you so much, father dear.

ABRAHAM: And doest thou so? I would know how
Lovest thou me, son, as thou hast said.

ISAAC: Yea, father, with all mine heart,
More than all that ever was made;
God to you long life impart!

ABRAHAM: Now, who would not be glad that had
A child so loving as thou art?
Thy lovely cheer makes my heart glad,
And many a time so has it gart°.   ° pleased

Go home, son, come soon again,
And tell thy mother I come full fast.

(ISAAC *exits.*)

So now, God bless thee safe from pain!
Now well is me that he is past.
Alone, right here in this plain,
Might I speak to mine heart brast°.   ° broken
I would that all were well full fain°,   ° I wish
But it must needs be done at last.

And it is good that I be ware°—   ° aware
To be advised full good it were.
The land of Visyon is full far,
The third day's end must I be there.
Mine ass shall with us; it shall bear
Our wood and harness, less and more,
For my son must be slain not near,
A sword must with us yet therefore.

And I shall start to make me yare°;   ° ready
This night will I begin my way,
Though Isaac be never so fair,
And mine own son, the sooth° to say,   ° truth
For though he be mine own right heir,
And all should wield° after my day,   ° control
God's bidding shall I nothing spare;
Should I that gainsay°? Why nay, in fay°!   ° argue ° faith
Isaac!

ISAAC (*reenters*): Sir?
ABRAHAM: Look thou be bound
    For certain, son, thyself and I,
    We two must now wend forth from town,

(*Two servants enter, with an ass, harnessed.*)

    In far country to sacrify,
    For certain reasons and causes sound.
    Take wood and fire with thee, we'll hie
    By hills and dales, both up and down,
    Son, thou shall ride, and I'll walk by.

(ISAAC *mounts the ass,* ABRAHAM *takes the lead.*)

    Look thou miss nought that thou should need;
    Do make thee ready, my darling!
ISAAC: I am ready to do this deed,
    And ever to fulfil your calling.
ABRAHAM: My dear son, look thou have no dread,
    We shall come home with great loving;
    Both to and fro I shall us lead;
    Come now, son, in my blessing.

(*They all walk about the platform,* ISAAC *on the ass; the hill rises and
they approach it.* ABRAHAM *motions for* ISAAC *to dismount.*)

    (*to the servants*) Ye two here with this ass abide,
    For Isaac and I will to yond hill;

It is so high we may not ride,
Therefore ye two shall abide here still.
FIRST SERVANT: Sir, ye ought not to be denied:
We are ready your bidding to fulfill.
SECOND SERVANT: What so ever to us betide°,   ° shall happen
To do your bidding aye we will.
ABRAHAM: God's blessing to you both appear.
I shall not tarry long you fro°.   ° from
FIRST SERVANT: Sir, we shall abide you here,
Out of this place shall we not go.
ABRAHAM: Children, you are ever to me full dear.
I pray God keep you ever from woe.
SECOND SERVANT: We will do sir, as you've taught us here.

(*The servants leave the stage, leading the ass.*)

ABRAHAM: Isaac, now alone we go.

(ABRAHAM *and* ISAAC *walk up the hill.*)

We must go a full good pace,
For it is farther than I learned.
We shall have mirth and great solace,
When this thing an end has earned.

(*They arrive at the hilltop.*)

Lo, my son, here is the place.
ISAAC: With wood and fire am I concerned:
(*looking around*) Tell me now, in all this space,
Where is the beast that should be burned?
ABRAHAM: Now, son, I may no longer hide,
Such will° is into mine heart went   ° thoughts
Thou wast ever to me tied,
Ever to fulfil mine intent.
But certainly thou must be slain,
And it may be as I have willed.
ISAAC: I am heavy and nothing fain°,   ° wishing
Thus hastily that shall be killed.

(ISAAC *starts down the hill.*)

ABRAHAM: Isaac!
ISAAC (*stopping, in obedient terror*): Sir?
ABRAHAM: Come hither, bid I;
Thou shall be dead what so ever betide°.   ° shall happen
ISAAC (*dutifully returning, kneels*): Ah, father! Mercy! Mercy!
ABRAHAM: That I say may not be denied;
Take thy death therefore meekly.

(ABRAHAM *places* ISAAC *down on the ground, and draws his sword.*)

ISAAC: Ah, good sir, abide;
Father!
ABRAHAM (*stops, anguished*): What, son?

ISAAC: To do your will I am ready,
    Where so ever ye go or ride,
    If I may ought overtake your will
    For I do trespass, let me be beat!
    (*starts beating himself*)

ABRAHAM: Isaac!

ISAAC: What, sir?

ABRAHAM: Good son, be still.

ISAAC: Father!

ABRAHAM: What, son?

ISAAC: Think on thy get°!
    What have I done?   ° begotten child

ABRAHAM: Truly, none ill.

ISAAC: And shall I be slain?

ABRAHAM: So am I set.

ISAAC: Sir, what may help?

ABRAHAM: There's no such skill.

ISAAC: I ask mercy.

ABRAHAM: That may not let.

ISAAC: When I am dead and closed in clay,
    Who shall then be your son?

ABRAHAM: Ah, Lord, that I should abide this day!

ISAAC: Sir, who shall do what I have done?

ABRAHAM: Speak no such words son, I thee pray.

ISAAC: Shall ye me slay?

ABRAHAM: I must, good son.
    (*raising his sword*) Lie still! I smite!

ISAAC: Sir, let me say . . .

ABRAHAM: My sword, dear child, thou may not shun.

ISAAC: The shining of your bright blade,
    It makes me quake for fear of thee.

ABRAHAM (*turning* ISAAC *over facedown*):
    Therefore downface thou shall be laid,
    Then when I strike thou shall not see.

ISAAC: What have I done, father, what have I said?

ABRAHAM: Truly, no kind of ill to me.

ISAAC: And thus guiltless shall be dead.

ABRAHAM: Now good son, let such words be.

ISAAC: I love you ay°.   ° always

ABRAHAM: So do I thee.

ISAAC: Father!

ABRAHAM: What, son?

ISAAC: Let not this be seen
    For my mother's love.

ABRAHAM: Let be! Let be!
    It will not help what thou would mean;

(*Rising, unable to complete the act*)

    But lie still till I come to thee,
    I miss a little thing, I ween.

(ABRAHAM *runs down the hill in tears, and speaks apart.*)

    He speaks so ruefully to me,
    That water shoots in both mine eeyn°.   ° eyes

(*He drops his sword on the ground.*)

    I would rather than all worldly win°   ° goods
    That I had found him once unkind,
    But no default I found him in;
    I would be dead for him, or pined°;   ° suffering
    To slay him thus, I think great sin,
    So rueful words I with him find;
    I am full woe that we should twin°,   ° separate
    For he will never out of my mind.

    What shall I to his mother say?
    When "Where is he?" will she inquire.
    If I tell her: "Ran away,"
    Her answer, best believe: "Nay, sire!"
    And I am feared her for to slay;
    I know not what I shall say to her,
    He lies full still there as he lay,
    For till I come, dare he not stir.

GOD (*appearing in heaven, with an angel at his side*):
    Angel, hie with all thy main!
    To Abraham thou shall be sent;
    Say: "Isaac shall not be slain;
    He shall live, not burned or bent.
    My bidding stands he not again.
    Go, put him out of his intent,
    Bid him go home again,
    I know how well he meant.

ANGEL: Gladly, Lord, I am ready;
    Thy bidding shall be magnified;
    I shall me speed full hastily,
    Thee to obey at every tide;
    Thy will, Thy name, to glorify,
    Over all this world so wide;
    And to thy servant now from high
    To good, true, Abraham will I glide.

ABRAHAM (*slowly picks up his sword*):
    But might I yet of weeping cease,
    Till I had done this sacrifice;
    It must needs be, with no more lease,
    Though all I carp on this kind wise,
    The more my sorrow will increase;
    And though I shudder at his sighs,
    I will run and release
    And slay him here—right as he lies!

(ABRAHAM *runs up the hill to complete the sacrifice, but the angel slides down the cable and intercepts him.*)

ANGEL: Abraham! Abraham!

ABRAHAM: Who is there now?

Way! Let me go.

ANGEL: Stand up, now, stand;

Thy good will come I to allow.

Therefore I bid thee hold thy hand.

ABRAHAM: Say, who bade so: Any but thou?

ANGEL: Yea, God; and sends this beast for thine offering.

(*He points to a sheep which appears on the edge of the stage.*)

ABRAHAM: I spoke with God lately, I trow,

And to do this He made a command.

ANGEL: He has perceived thy meekness

And thy good will also in this.

He wills thou do thy son no distress,

For he has granted to thee his bliss.

ABRAHAM: But knowst thou well that it is

As you has said?

ANGEL: I say thee yes.

(*The* ANGEL *ascends to heaven, and* ABRAHAM *addresses* GOD.)

ABRAHAM: I thank Thee, Lord, well of goodness,

That all thus has released me this.

To speak with thee have I no space,

Till with my dear son I have spoken.

(*to* ISAAC) My good son, thou shalt have grace,

On thee now will I not be wroken;

Rise up now, with thy favored face.

ISAAC (*rising*): Sir, shall I live?

ABRAHAM (*kisses him*): Yea, this to token.

Son, thou has scaped a full hard grace,

Thou should have been both burnt and broken.

ISAAC: But, father, shall I not be slain?

ABRAHAM: No, certain, son.

ISAAC: Then am I glad;

(*still a bit wary*) Good sir, put up your sword again.

ABRAHAM: Nay, son, be thou not adread.

ISAAC: Is all forga'yn?

ABRAHAM: Yea, son, certain.

ISAAC: For fear, sir, was I near-hand mad.

[*Note: it is at this point that the Wakefield manuscript breaks off. What concludes the play is taken from the Brome manuscript version. See the note on the text.*]

ABRAHAM: Yon beast shall die here in thy stead,

In the worship of our Lord. Be gone,

And fetch him hither, my child; God speed!

ISAAC: Father, I will go seize him by the head,

And bring yon beast with me anon.

(ISAAC *brings the sheep over.*)

Ah, sheep, sheep, blessed may thou be,
That ever thou wert sent down hither.
Thou shalt die this day for me,
In worship of the Holy Trinity.
Now come fast and go we together,
To my father of Heaven.
Though thou be never so gentle and good,
Yet I had liefer° thou sheddest thy blood   ° rather
In truth, sheep, than I.

(ISAAC *presents the sheep to his father.*)

Lo, father, I have brought here, full smart,
This gentle sheep, and him to you I give.
But, Lord God, I thank thee with all my heart,
For I am glad that I shall live
And kiss once more my dear mother!
ABRAHAM: Now be right merry, my sweet child,
For this quick beast, that is so mild,
Here I shall present before all other.
ISAAC (*lighting a fire*): And I will fast begin to blow;
This fire shall burn a full good speed.
(*hesitating*) But, father, if I stoop down low,
Ye will not kill me with your sword, I trow?
ABRAHAM: No, hardly, sweet son; have no dread.
My mourning is past!
ISAAC: Yea, but would that sword were burned instead,
For, in truth, father, it make me full ill aghast.

(ABRAHAM *kneels and makes his offering.*)

Ah, Lord God of Heaven in Trinity,
Almighty God omnipotent,
My offering I make in the worship of Thee,
And this quick beast I Thee present.
(*sacrifices sheep*)
Lord, receive Thou mine intent,
As thou art God and ground of our grace.
GOD (*appears in heaven*):
Abraham, Abraham, well mayest thou speed,
And Isaac, thy young son, thee by!
Truly, Abraham, for this deed,
I shall multiply your and your son's seed
As thick as stars be in the sky.
Both of bigger and less.
And as thick as gravel in the sea,
So thick multiplied your seed shall be;
This grant I you for your goodness.

Of you shall come fruit son on son,
And ever be in bliss without end.

For as ye dread God's will be done,
And keep my commandments, every one,
My blessing I give wheresoever ye wend!

ABRAHAM: Yea, come on with me, my own sweet son,
And homeward fast let us be gone.

ISAAC: By my faith, father, thereto I grant!
I had never such good will to go home,
And to speak with my dear mother.

ABRAHAM: Ah, Lord of Heaven, I thank thee,
For now may I lead home with me
Isaac, my yong son so free.
The gentlest child above all other—
This may I well avow-ee.
Now, go we forth, my blessed son.

(They start to leave. The lights change, however, and all the members of the acting ensemble come forth. Actors in animal costumes take off their masks. The lines of this last speech are assigned to the actors at random.)

THE ACTING ENSEMBLE: —Lo, now sovereigns and sirs, now have we
        showed,
—This solemn story to great and small.
—It is a good lesson for both learned and lowed,
—And the wisest of us all,
—With none away crouching.
—For this story showeth you here,
—How we should keep without fear,
—God's commandments without grouching.

—Think ye, sirs, if God sent an angel,
And commanded you your child be slain,
—By your truth, is there any of you
That neither would grudge or strive there-again?
How think ye now, sirs, thereby?
—I think there be three or four or mo,
—And those women that weep so sorrowfully
When that their children die them fro,
As nature takes from our kind,
—It is folly, as I may well avow,
To grudge against God, or to grieve you.
—For ye shall never see Him mischiefed, well I know,
By land nor water—have this in mind!

THE ACTOR PLAYING GOD: And grudge not against our Lord God,
In wealth or woe, whatever He you send,
Though ye be never so hard bestead;
For when He willeth, He may it amend,
His commandments truly if ye keep with good heart,
As this story hath now showed you beforn,

And faithfully serve him, while ye be smart,
That ye may please God both evening and morn.
Now Jesu, that wore The crown of Thorn,
Bring us all to heaven's bliss!

(*The play concludes with the acting ensemble singing "Light and Origin of Light."*)

CURTAIN

3 THE TRAGEDY OF ROMEO AND JULIET

William Shakespeare
ABOUT 1595

The poet William Shakespeare (1564–1616) hardly needs introducing; he is universally considered the greatest dramatic author in the English-speaking theatre, and is often accounted the greatest writer in all of literary history. His works are dense in evocative imagery, brilliant in rhetorical craftsmanship, profound in thought and poetry—and they are also magnificently funny, rich in suspense, and hugely entertaining. No writer in history has ever succeeded in so many genres of literary art, and none has retained such massive and virtually uninterrupted public acclaim for so many centuries.

Romeo and Juliet is one of Shakespeare's early plays. As with the other two plays in this section, it was adapted from a popular story, thought to be based on a true event; more than a dozen versions of the tragic tale—poems, novellas, and at least one play—had been written by the time Shakespeare turned his attention to it. Shakespeare's achievement, however, went far beyond good storytelling; in this play he managed to create a language of lyrical, almost spiritual eroticism, and a plot of such stunning reversals and dramatic momentum that the play virtually leaps off the page and into the reality of life itself. Surely there are few other plays in literary history that develop such sympathy for their principal characters; in Verona today, tens of thousands of tourists visit "Juliet's house" every year.

Romeo and Juliet has a rich stage history; few great actresses pass up the opportunity to test themselves in the role of Juliet, and modern audiences attend, with astonishing regularity, not only productions of Shakespeare's play, but the many balletic and operatic versions that have been derived from it. Still, the stage history of *Romeo and Juliet* has not been without its problems, chief of which is the age of the two main characters: Juliet, who is thirteen, and Romeo, who is apparently not much older. Veteran actors cannot easily portray the youthful intensity and innocence of these teenagers. Yet it is precisely their youthful intensity and innocence with which Shakespeare is primarily concerned—their discovery of romance, love, and their emergence into adulthood. Actors with the potential to perform these roles are often too far removed from their own first-time experiences to recreate them "from the inside," as great actors must do. The vaunted skepticism of the modern age, and the current distrust of lyrical infatuation and verbal lovemaking, sometimes also hinders a successful performance of the play.

Romeo and Juliet is not a play that speaks easily to the present world; more than most Shakespearean tragedies, it is very much tied to its early Renaissance setting, to a world of masqued balls, arranged marriages, and lovers exchanging sonnets rather than telephone calls. Nonetheless, despite these potential drawbacks to performances of *Romeo and Juliet*, it ranks as one of his most theatrical works, and one of his most popular. Romeo and Juliet remain today the purest examples of passionate young lovers—lovers so in love with loving that they would die rather than sacrifice their mutual devotion.

A NOTE ON THE TEXT

Romeo and Juliet was first published in a "bad quarto" edition in 1597, which was apparently tran-scribed or reconstructed (with numerous mistakes) from a stage production. A "good quarto" edition, probably based primarily on Shakespeare's own manuscript, appeared two years later, and two other quartos were published before the First Folio edition of Shakespeare's plays in 1623. None of these published versions included act and scene divisions, which have been added by later editors.

The present version has been edited by Marilyn F. Moriarty, who has provided footnotes, word glosses, and some indications of stage action for the reader's benefit.

THE TRAGEDY OF ROMEO AND JULIET

CAST OF CHARACTERS

CHORUS
ESCALES, *Prince of Verona*
PARIS, *a young nobleman, kinsman to the Prince*
MONTAGUE } *heads of two houses at variance*
CAPULET } *with each other*
COUSIN CAPULET, *kinsman to Capulet*
ROMEO, *son to Montague*
MERCUTIO, *kinsman to the Prince, and friend to Romeo*
BENVOLIO, *nephew to Montague, and friend to Romeo*
TYBALT, *nephew to Lady Capulet*
PETRUCHIO, *a (mute) follower of Tybalt*
FRIAR LAWRENCE } *Franciscans*
FRIAR JOHN }
BALTHASAR, *servant to Romeo*
ABRAM, *servant to Montague*

SAMPSON }
GREGORY } *servants to Capulet*
CLOWN }
PETER, *servant to Juliet's Nurse*
PAGE *to Paris*
APOTHECARY
Three MUSICIANS

LADY MONTAGUE, *wife to Montague*
LADY CAPULET, *wife to Capulet*
JULIET, *daughter to Capulet*
NURSE *to Juliet*

GENTLEMEN *and* GENTLEWOMEN, MASKERS, TORCH-BEARERS, OFFICERS *of the Watch, other* CITIZENS, SERVINGMEN *and* ATTENDANTS

SCENE: *Verona, Mantua*

ACT ONE

The Prologue[1]

(*Enter* CHORUS)

CHORUS: Two households, both alike in dignity°,   ° rank
    In fair Verona (where we lay our scene),
    From ancient grudge° break to new mutiny°,   ° old feud ° revolt

---

1. The Prologue, spoken by one person, takes the form of a Shakespearean sonnet (three quatrains and a couplet). Two causes are given for the lovers' deaths: they are the victims of an unfortunate destiny—"star-crossed" and "misadventured"—and their deaths atone for "their parents' rage." Shakespeare drew his story and all his principal characters except Mercutio from Arthur Brooke's poem *The Tragicall Historye of Romeus and Juliet* (1562).

Where civil blood° makes civil hands° unclean.   ° blood of civil strife ° citizens'
From forth the fatal loins of these two foes
A pair of star-crossed lovers take their life;
Whose misadventured piteous overthrows
Doth with their death bury their parents' strife.
The fearful passage of their death-marked love,
And the continuance of their parents' rage,
Which but their children's end nought could remove,
Is now the two hours' traffic° of our stage;   ° business
The which if you with patient ears attend,
What here shall miss°, our toil shall strive to mend.   ° seem inadequate

(*Exit*)

Act One, Scene One. Verona: a street.

(*Enter* SAMPSON *and* GREGORY, *with swords and bucklers, of the house of Capulet*)

SAMPSON: Gregory, on my word, we'll not carry coals.°   ° submit to insult
GREGORY: No, for then we should be colliers.°   ° coal carriers, abusive term
SAMPSON: I mean, and we be in choler°, we'll draw.   ° anger
GREGORY: Ay, while you live, draw your neck out of collar°.   ° slip out of hangman's noose
SAMPSON: I strike quickly, being moved°.   ° react emotionally
GREGORY: But thou art not quickly moved to strike.
SAMPSON: A dog of the house of Montague moves me.
GREGORY: To move is to stir, and to be valiant is to stand: therefore if thou art moved thou runn'st away.
SAMPSON: A dog of that house shall move me to stand.[2] I will take the wall[3] of any man or maid of Montague's.
GREGORY: That shows thee a weak slave, for the weakest goes to the wall.
SAMPSON: 'Tis true, and therefore women being the weaker vessels are ever thrust to the wall: therefore I will push Montague's men from the wall, and thrust his maids to the wall.
GREGORY: The quarrel is between our masters, and us their men.
SAMPSON: 'Tis all one, I will show myself a tyrant: when I have fought with the men, I will be civil with the maids; I will cut off their heads.
GREGORY: The heads of the maids?
SAMPSON: Ay, the heads of the maids, or their maidenheads, take it in what sense thou wilt.
GREGORY: They must take it in sense that feel it.
SAMPSON: Me they shall feel while I am able to stand, and 'tis known I am a pretty piece of flesh.

---

2. "Move to stand" indicates an emotional reaction, a forced retreat, and a position taken under threat of attack.
3. "To take the wall" was to occupy the cleanest part of the walk; to yield the wall thus demonstrated courtesy. The weak, backed into a corner with no place to run, also took the wall.

GREGORY: 'Tis well thou art not fish°; if thou hadst, thou hadst been poor-John°. Draw thy tool,[4] here comes of the house of Montagues.

° woman; prostitute
° salted hake; cheap Lenten fare

(*Enter two other* SERVINGMEN)

SAMPSON: My naked weapon is out. Quarrel, I will back thee.
GREGORY: How, turn thy back and run?
SAMPSON: Fear me not.
GREGORY: No, marry°, I fear thee!
SAMPSON: Let us take the law of our sides, let them begin.
GREGORY: I will frown as I pass by, and let them take it as they list°.
SAMPSON: Nay, as they dare. I will bite my thumb at them°, which is disgrace to them if they bear it.

° indeed (mild oath using name of the Virgin Mary)
° like
° provocative gesture

ABRAM: Do you bite your thumb at us, sir?
SAMPSON: I do bite my thumb, sir.
ABRAM: Do you bite your thumb at us, sir?
SAMPSON (*aside to* GREGORY): Is the law of our side if I say ay?
GREGORY (*aside to* SAMPSON): No.
SAMPSON: No, sir, I do not bite my thumb at you, sir, but I bite my thumb, sir.
GREGORY: Do you quarrel, sir?
ABRAM: Quarrel, sir? No, sir.
SAMPSON: But if you do, sir, I am for you. I serve as good a man as you.
ABRAM: No better.
SAMPSON: Well, sir.

(*Enter* BENVOLIO)

GREGORY (*aside to* SAMPSON): Say 'better', here comes one of my master's kinsmen.
SAMPSON: Yes, better, sir.
ABRAM: You lie.
SAMPSON: Draw, if you be men. Gregory, remember thy washing° blow.
　　(*They fight.*)

° slashing

BENVOLIO: Part, fools!
　　Put up your swords, you know not what you do.
　　(*beats down their swords*)

(*Enter* TYBALT)

TYBALT: What, art thou drawn among these heartless hinds?[5]
　　Turn thee, Benvolio, look upon thy death.
BENVOLIO: I do but keep the peace. Put up thy sword,
　　Or manage it to part these men with me.

---

4. "Thrust," "maidenhead," "stand," "flesh," "fish," "tool," and "naked weapon" are a series of *double entendres*.
5. "Heartless hinds" are female deer without a stag (hart). Tybalt demeans Benvolio by accusing him of fighting with lowly servants. Notice how the violence intensifies as men of higher rank enter the fray.

TYBALT: What, drawn and talk of peace? I hate the word,
    As I hate hell, all Montagues, and thee.
    Have at thee, coward°.   ° here I come at you
    (*they fight*)

(*Enter several of both houses, who join the fray and three or four
Citizens, as* OFFICERS *of the Watch, with clubs or partisans*)

OFFICERS: Clubs, bills, and partisans![6] Strike! Beat them down!
    Down with the Capulets! Down with the Montagues!

(*Enter old* CAPULET *in his gown, and his wife,* LADY CAPULET)

CAPULET: What noise is this? Give me my long sword, ho!
LADY CAPULET: A crutch, a crutch! why call you for a sword?
CAPULET: My sword, I say! old Montague is come,
    And flourishes his blade in spite of me.

(*Enter old* MONTAGUE *and his wife* LADY MONTAGUE)

MONTAGUE: Thou villain° Capulet!—Hold me not, let me go.   ° base
LADY MONTAGUE: Thou shalt not stir one foot to seek a foe.

(*Enter* PRINCE ESCALES *with his train*)

PRINCE: Rebellious subjects, enemies to peace,
    Profaners of this neighbour-stainèd steel—
    Will they not hear?—What ho, you men, you beasts!
    That quench the fire of your pernicious rage
    With purple fountains issuing from your veins:
    On pain of torture, from those bloody hands
    Throw your mistempered weapons to the ground[7],
    And hear the sentence of your movèd prince.
    Three civil brawls, bred of an airy word,
    By thee, old Capulet, and Montague,
    Have thrice disturbed the quiet of our streets,
    And made Verona's ancient citizens
    Cast by their grave beseeming ornaments°   ° ornaments appropriate to the grave
    To wield old partisans, in hands as old,
    Cankered° with peace, to part your cankered hate;   ° corrupted
    If ever you disturb our streets again,
    Your lives shall pay the forfeit° of the peace.   ° penalty
    For this time all the rest depart away:
    You, Capulet, shall go along with me,
    And, Montague, come you this afternoon,
    To know our farther pleasure in this case,
    To old Free-town[8], our common judgement-place.

---

6. Both forms of halberds, a bill is a staff topped with a curved blade; a partisan is
topped with an axe head.
7. Because neighbors' blood stains steel, those weapons are "mistempered," both
wielded by angry adversaries and made hard by hot blood rather than cold water.
8. "Freetown," the name of Capulet's castle, is Shakespeare's translation of the
Italian *Villa Franca* from Brooke's poem.

Once more, on pain of death, all men depart.

(*Exeunt all but* MONTAGUE, LADY MONTAGUE, *and* BENVOLIO)

MONTAGUE: Who set this ancient quarrel new abroach?°   ° open, flowing (as of a barrel with liquid)
    Speak, nephew, were you by when it began?
BENVOLIO: Here were the servants of your adversary,
    And yours, close fighting ere I did approach:
    I drew to part them; in the instant came
    The fiery Tybalt, with his sword prepared,
    Which, as he breathed defiance to my ears,
    He swung about his head and cut the winds,
    Who, nothing° hurt withal,° hissed him in scorn;   ° not at all   ° therewith
    While we were interchanging thrusts and blows,
    Came more and more, and fought on part and part,
    Till the Prince came, who parted either part°.   ° both sides
LADY MONTAGUE: O where is Romeo? saw you him today?
    Right glad I am he was not at this fray.
BENVOLIO: Madam, an hour before the worshipped sun
    Peered forth the golden window of the east,
    A troubled mind drive° me to walk abroad,   ° drove (pronounced *driv*)
    Where underneath the grove of sycamore,
    That westward rooteth from this city side°,   ° this side of the city
    So early walking did I see your son;
    Towards him I made, but he was ware° of me,   ° unaware, wary
    And stole into the covert of the wood;
    I, measuring his affections° by my own,   ° inclinations
    Which then most sought where most might not be found°,   ° desiring solitude
    Being one too many by my weary self,
    Pursued my humour°, not pursuing his,   ° mood
    And gladly shunned who gladly fled from me.
MONTAGUE: Many a morning hath he there been seen,
    With tears augmenting the fresh morning's dew,
    Adding to clouds more clouds with his deep sighs,
    But all so soon as the all-cheering sun
    Should in the farthest east begin to draw
    The shady curtains from Aurora's° bed,   ° goddess of the dawn
    Away from light steals home my heavy son,
    And private in his chamber pens himself,
    Shuts up his windows, locks fair daylight out,
    And makes himself an artificial night:
    Black and portentous must his humour prove°,   ° This mood portends ill.
    Unless good counsel may the cause remove.
BENVOLIO: My noble uncle, do you know the cause?
MONTAGUE: I neither know it, not can learn of him.
BENVOLIO: Have you importuned him by any means?
MONTAGUE: Both by myself and many other friends,
    But he, his own affections' counsellor°,   ° confidante

Is to himself (I will not say how true°)
But to himself so secret and so close,
So far from sounding and discovery,
As is the bud bit with an envious° worm
Ere he can spread his sweet leaves to the air,
Or dedicate his beauty to the sun.
Could we but learn from whence his sorrows grow,
We would as willingly give cure as know.

(Enter ROMEO)

BENVOLIO: See where he comes. So please you° step aside,
    I'll know his grievance or be much denied.
MONTAGUE: I would thou wert so happy by thy stay
    To hear true shrift°. Come, madam, let's away.

(Exeunt MONTAGUE *and* LADY MONTAGUE)

BENVOLIO: Good morrow, cousin°.
ROMEO: Is the day so young?
BENVOLIO: But new struck nine.
ROMEO: Ay me, sad hours seem long.
    Was that my father that went hence so fast?
BENVOLIO: It was. What sadness lengthens Romeo's hours?
ROMEO: Not having that, which, having, makes them short.
BENVOLIO: In love?
ROMEO: Out—
BENVOLIO: Of love?
ROMEO: Out of her favour where I am in love.
BENVOLIO: Alas that Love, so gentle in his view,
    Should be so tyrannous and rough in proof!°
ROMEO: Alas that Love, whose view is muffled still°,
    Should, without eyes, see pathways to his will!
    Where shall we dine? O me! what fray was here?
    Yet tell me not, for I have heard it all:
    Here's much to do with hate, but more with love:
    Why then, O brawling love, O loving hate,
    O any thing of nothing first create!
    O heavy lightness, serious vanity,
    Misshapen chaos of well-seeming forms,
    Feather of lead, bright smoke, cold fire, sick health,
    Still-waking sleep, that is not what it is!
    This love feel I, that feel no love in this.
    Dost thou not laugh?
BENVOLIO: No, coz°, I rather weep.
ROMEO: Good heart, at what?
BENVOLIO: At thy good heart's oppression.
ROMEO: Why, such is love's transgression:
    Griefs of mine own lie heavy in my breast,
    Which thou wilt propagate° to have it pressed°
    With more of thine; this love that thou hast shown
    Doth add more grief to too much of mine own.
    Love is a smoke made with the fume of sighs,

° wise

° malicious

° please

° confession

° kinsman

° experience
° always blindfolded

° cousin, kinsman

° increase ° oppressed; weighted down
    with a lover

Being purged°, a fire sparkling in lovers' eyes,   ° cleared of smoke
Being vexed, a sea nourished with loving tears.
What is it else? a madness most discreet,
A choking gall, and a preserving sweet.
Farewell, my coz.
BENVOLIO: Soft°, I will go along;   ° Not so fast
And if you leave me so, you do me wrong.
ROMEO: Tut, I have lost myself, I am not here,
This is not Romeo, he's some other where.
BENVOLIO: Tell me in sadness, who is that you love?
ROMEO: What, shall I groan and tell thee?
BENVOLIO: Groan? why, no;
But sadly tell me, who?
ROMEO: Bid a sick man in sadness make his will—
A word ill urged to one that is so ill:
In sadness, cousin, I do love a woman.
BENVOLIO: I aimed so near, when I supposed you loved.
ROMEO: A right good mark-man! and she's fair I love.
BENVOLIO: A right fair mark, fair coz, is soonest hit.
ROMEO: Well, in that hit you miss: she'll not be hit
With Cupid's arrow, she hath Dian's° wit;   ° goddess of chastity
And in strong proof° of chastity well armed,   ° tested armor
From Love's weak childish bow she lives uncharmed.
She will not stay the siege of loving terms,
Nor bide th'encounter of assailing eyes,
Nor ope her lap to saint-seducing gold.⁹
O, she is rich in beauty, only poor
That when she dies, with beauty dies her store°.   ° capital
BENVOLIO: Then she hath sworn that she will still° live chaste?   ° always
ROMEO: She hath, and in that sparing° makes huge waste;   ° frugality
For beauty starved with her severity
Cuts beauty off from all posterity.
She is too fair, too wise, wisely too fair,
To merit bliss by making me despair.
She hath forsworn to love, and in that vow
Do I live dead, that live to tell it now.
BENVOLIO: Be ruled by me, forget to think of her.
ROMEO: O teach me how I should forget to think.
BENVOLIO: By giving liberty unto thine eyes,
Examine other beauties.
ROMEO: 'Tis the way
To call hers (exquisite) in question more:
These happy masks that kiss fair ladies' brows,
Being black, puts us in mind they hide the fair¹;
He that is strucken blind cannot forget
The precious treasure of his eyesight lost;

---

9. An allusion to Danae who yielded to Zeus when he appeared to her as a shower
of gold.
1. Black masks remind one of the beauty that they conceal.

Show me a mistress that is passing° fair,   ° surpassing
What doth her beauty serve but as a note
Where I may read who passed° that passing fair?[2]   ° surpassed
Farewell, thou canst not teach me to forget.
BENVOLIO: I'll pay that doctrine, or else die in debt.

(*Exeunt*)

Act One, Scene Two. Verona: a street.

(*Enter* CAPULET, COUNTY PARIS, *and the Clown*, SERVANT *to Capulet*)

CAPULET: But Montague is bound° as well as I,   ° obligated
    In penalty alike, and 'tis not hard, I think,
    For men so old as we to keep the peace.
PARIS: Of honourable reckoning are you both,
    And pity 'tis, you lived at odds so long.
    But now, my lord, what say you to my suit?°   ° petition for Juliet's hand
CAPULET: But saying o'er what I have said before:
    My child is yet a stranger in the world,
    She hath not seen the change of fourteen years;°   ° not yet fourteen
    Let two more summers wither in their pride,
    Ere we may think her ripe to be a bride.
PARIS: Younger than she are happy mothers made.
CAPULET: And too soon marred are those so early made.
    Earth hath swallowed all my hopes but she;
    She's the hopeful lady of my earth.
    But woo her, gentle Paris, get her heart,
    My will to her consent is but a part;
    And she agreed, within her scope of choice
    Lies my consent and fair according voice.
    This night I hold an old accustomed° feast,   ° regularly held for years past
    Whereto I have invited many a guest,
    Such as I love, and you among the store,
    One more, most welcome, makes my number more.
    At my poor house look to behold this night
    Earth-treading stars that make dark heaven light.
    Such comfort as do lusty young men feel
    When well-apparelled April on the heel
    Of limping winter treads, even such delight
    Among fresh fennel buds shall you this night
    Inherit° at my house; hear all, all see;   ° possess
    And like her most whose merit most shall be;
    Which on more view of many, mine, being one,
    May stand in number, though in reck'ning none.
    Come go with me. (*to* SERVANT) Go, sirrah°, trudge about   ° term of address to inferiors

---

2. Rosaline, Capulet's niece, remains the reference by which other beauties are measured.

Through fair Verona, find those persons out
Whose names are written there (*gives a paper*), and to them say,
My house and welcome on their pleasure stay°.   ° wait

(*Exit with* PARIS)

SERVANT: Find them out whose names are written here! It is written that
the shoemaker should meddle with his yard and the tailor with
his last, the fisher with his pencil and the painter with his nets;
but I am sent to find those persons whose names are here writ,
and can never find what names the writing person hath here
writ³. I must to the learnèd. In good time!

(*Enter* BENVOLIO *and* ROMEO)

BENVOLIO: Tut, man, one fire burns out another's burning,
One pain is lessened by another's anguish°;   ° the pain of another pain
Turn giddy, and be holp by backward turning°,   ° helped by turning in the reverse direc-
One desperate grief cures with another's languish: tion
Take thou some new infection to thy eye,
And the rank poison of the old will die.
ROMEO: Your plantain leaf is excellent for that⁴.
BENVOLIO: For what, I pray thee?
ROMEO: For your broken shin°.   ° broken skin on the shin
BENVOLIO: Why, Romeo, art thou mad?
ROMEO: Not mad, but bound more than a madman is:
Shut up in prison, kept without my food,
Whipt and tormented, and—God-den°, good fellow.   ° Good evening (afternoon)
SERVANT: God gi' god-den° I pray, sir, can you read?   ° God give you a good evening
ROMEO: Ay, mine own fortune in my misery.
SERVANT: Perhaps you have learned it without book°; but I pray, can you   ° by heart
read any thing you see?
ROMEO: Ay, if I know the letters and the language.
SERVANT: Ye say honestly, rest you merry.
ROMEO: Stay, fellow, I can read.
(*He reads the letter.*)
   'Signior Martino and his wife and daughters,
   County Anselme and his beauteous sisters,
   The lady widow of Vitruvio,
   Signior Placentio and his lovely nieces,
   Mercutio and his brother Valentine,
   Mine uncle Capulet, his wife and daughters,
   My fair niece Rosaline, and Livia,
   Signior Valentio and his cousin Tybalt,
   Lucio and the lively Helena.'
   A fair assembly: whither should they come?
SERVANT: Up.
ROMEO: Whither? to supper?

---

3. The servant mixes up the attributes he assigns to each profession. The fisher-
man, not the painter, should meddle with nets.
4. Plantain leaves were routinely used as poultices for scrapes. Romeo comments
ironically on Benvolio's pat remedies for love sickness.

SERVANT: To our house.
ROMEO: Whose house?
SERVANT: My master's.
ROMEO: Indeed I should have asked thee that before.
SERVANT: Now I'll tell you without asking. My master is the great rich
Capulet, and if you be not of the house of Montagues, I pray come
and crush a cup of wine. Rest you merry.

(*Exit*)

BENVOLIO: At this same ancient feast of Capulet's
Sups the fair Rosaline whom thou so loves,
With all the admirèd beauties of Verona:
Go thither, and with unattainted° eye   ° pure
Compare her face with some that I shall show,
And I will make thee think thy swan a crow.
ROMEO: When the devout religion of mine eye
Maintains such falsehood, then turn tears to fires;
And these who, often drowned, could never die,
Transparent° heretics, be burnt for liars.   ° manifest
One fairer than my love? the all-seeing sun
Ne'er saw her match since first the world begun.
BENVOLIO: Tut, you saw her fair, none else being by,
Herself poised° with herself in either eye;   ° balanced
But in that crystal scales let there be weighed
You lady's love against some other maid
That I will show you shining at this feast,
And she shall scant show well that now seems best.
ROMEO: I'll go along no such sight to be shown,
But to rejoice in splendour of mine own.

(*Exeunt*)

Act One, Scene Three. Verona: Capulet's
house

(*Enter* CAPULET'S WIFE *and* NURSE)

LADY CAPULET: Nurse, where's my daughter? call her forth to me.
NURSE: Now by my maidenhead at twelve year old,
I bade her come. What, lamb! What, ladybird!
God forbid, where's this girl! What, Juliet!

(*Enter* JULIET)

JULIET: How now, who calls?
NURSE: Your mother.
JULIET: Madam, I am here, what is your will?
LADY CAPULET: This is the matter. Nurse, give leave a while,
We must talk in secret. Nurse, come back again,
I have remembered me, thou s'° hear our counsel.   ° thou shalt
Thou knowest my daughter's of a pretty age.

NURSE: Faith, I can tell her age unto an hour.

LADY CAPULET: She's not fourteen.

NURSE: I'll lay fourteen of my teeth—
    And yet to my teen be it spoken, I have but four—
    She's not fourteen. How long is it now
    To Lammas-tide?°   *° August 1*

LADY CAPULET: A fortnight° and odd days.   *° two weeks*

NURSE: Even or odd, of all days in the year,
    Come Lammas-eve° at night shall she be fourteen.   *° July 31*
    Susan and she—God rest all Christian souls!—
    Were of an age. Well, Susan is with God,
    She was too good for me. But as I said,
    On Lammas-eve at night shall she be fourteen,
    That shall she, marry, I remember it well.
    'Tis since the earthquake now aleven° years,   *° eleven*
    And she was weaned—I never shall forget it—
    Of all the days of the year, upon that day;
    For I had then laid wormwood° to my dug,   *° bitter tasting plant*
    Sitting in the sun under the dove-house wall.
    My lord and you were then at Mantua—
    Nay, I do bear a brain°—but as I said,   *° have a good memory*
    When it° did taste the wormwood on the nipple   *° she*
    Of my dug, and felt it bitter, pretty fool.
    To see it tetchy° and fall out wi'th'dug!   *° fretful*
    'Shake!' quoth the dove-house[5]; 'twas no need, I trow°,   *° I think*
    To bid me trudge.
    And since that time it is aleven years,
    For then she could stand high-lone; nay, by th'rood,°   *° Christ's cross*
    She could have run and waddled all about;
    For even the day before, she broke her brow,
    And then my husband—God be with his soul,
    'A° was a merry man—took up the child.   *° He*
    'Yea', quoth he, 'dost thou fall upon thy face?
    Thou wilt fall backward when thou hast more wit°,   *° with sexual undertones*
    Wilt thou not, Jule?' And by my holidam°,   *° holiness*
    The pretty wretch left crying, and said 'Ay'.
    To see now how a jest shall come about!
    I warrant, and I should live a thousand years,
    I never should forget it: 'Wilt thou not, Jule?' quoth he,
    And, pretty fool, it stinted°, and said 'Ay'.   *° stopped crying*

LADY CAPULET: Enough of this, I pray thee hold thy peace.°   *° be quiet*

NURSE: Yes, madam, yet I cannot choose but laugh,
    To think it should leave crying, and say 'Ay':
    And yet I warrant it had upon it brow
    A bump as big as a young cock'rel's stone°,   *° young cock's testicle*
    A perilous knock, and it cried bitterly.
    'Yea', quoth my husband, 'fall'st upon thy face?

---

5. The dovehouse, shaking, suggested it was time for her to leave.

Thou wilt fall backward when thou comest to age,
Wilt thou not, Jule?' It stinted, and said 'Ay'.
JULIET: And stint thou too, I pray thee, Nurse, say I.
NURSE: Peace, I have done. God mark thee to his grace,
Thou wast the prettiest babe that e'er I nursed.
And I might live to see thee married once,
I have my wish.
LADY CAPULET: Marry, that 'marry' is the very theme
I came to talk of. Tell me, daughter Juliet,
How stands your dispositions° to be married?　　　　　　　° inclination
JULIET: It is an honour that I dream not of.
NURSE: An honour! were not I thine only nurse,
I would say thou hadst sucked wisdom from thy teat°.　　　° the Nurse's
LADY CAPULET: Well, think of marriage now; younger than you,
Here in Verona, ladies of esteem,
Are made already mothers. By my count,
I was your mother much upon these years
That you are now a maid. Thus then in brief:
The valiant Paris seeks you for his love.
NURSE: A man, young lady! lady, such a man
As all the world—Why, he's a man of wax°.　　　　　　　° an ideal man
LADY CAPULET: Verona's summer hath not such a flower.
NURSE: Nay, he's a flower, in faith, a very flower.
LADY CAPULET: What say you, can you love the gentleman?
This night you shall behold him at our feast;
Read o'er the volume of young Paris' face,
And find delight writ there with beauty's pen;
Examine every married° lineament,　　　　　　　　　　　° harmonious
And see how one another lends content;
And what obscured in this fair volume lies
Find written in the margent° of his eyes.　　　　　　　　° margin
This precious book of love, this unbound lover,
To beautify him, only lacks a cover.
The fish lives in the sea, and 'tis much pride
For fair without the fair within to hide;
That book in many's eyes doth share the glory
That in gold clasps locks in the golden story[6]:
So shall you share all that he doth possess,
By having him, making yourself no less.
NURSE: No less! nay, bigger women grow by men.
LADY CAPULET: Speak briefly, can you like° of Paris' love?　　° be pleased
JULIET: I'll look to like, if looking liking move°.　　　　　　° conduce
But no more deep will I endart° mine eye　　　　　　　　° shoot as a dart
Than your consent gives strength to make it fly.

---

6. Through an elaborate comparison of Paris with a manuscript book—"volume,"
"writ," "pen," "content," "margent," "book," "unbound," "cover," "clasps,"
"story"—Lady Capulet maintains that a wife would complete Paris by binding him
like a book.

(*Enter* SERVINGMAN)

SERVINGMAN: Madam, the guests are come, supper served up, you called,
  my young lady asked for, the Nurse cursed in the pantry, and
  every thing in extremity. I must hence to wait, I beseech you
  follow straight.°   ° straightaway

(*Exit*)

LADY CAPULET: We follow thee. Juliet, the County stays.°   ° the Count waits
NURSE: Go, girl, seek happy nights to happy days.

(*Exeunt*)

Act One, Scene Four. Verona: a street.

(*Enter* ROMEO, MERCUTIO, BENVOLIO, *with five or six other* MASKERS, TORCH-
BEARERS)

ROMEO: What, shall this speech be spoke for our excuse?
  Or shall we on without apology?[7]
BENVOLIO: The date is out of such prolixity°:   ° long winded verbiage is out of date
  We'll have no Cupid hoodwinked° with a scarf,   ° blindfolded
  Bearing a Tartar's painted bow of lath°,   ° a Cupid's miniature bow
  Scaring the ladies like a crow-keeper°,   ° scare-crow
  Nor no without-book° prologue, faintly spoke   ° memorized
  After the prompter, for our entrance;
  But let them measure° us by what they will,   ° assess
  We'll measure them a measure° and be gone.   ° mete them out a dance
ROMEO: Give me a torch, I am not for this ambling[8];
  Being but heavy°, I will bear the light.   ° melancholy
MERCUTIO: Nay, gentle Romeo, we must have you dance.
ROMEO: Not I, believe me. You have dancing shoes
  With nimble soles, I have a soul of lead
  So stakes me to the ground I cannot move.
MERCUTIO: You are a lover, borrow Cupid's wings,
  And soar with them above a common bound°.   ° ordinary limit; leap (in dancing)
ROMEO: I am too sore enpiercèd with his shaft
  To soar with his light feathers, and so bound°   ° restricted
  I cannot bound a pitch° above dull woe: ° the upper limit of a falcon's flight
  Under love's heavy burden° do I sink°.   ° of woe ° yield
MERCUTIO: And to sink° in it should you burden° love,   ° penetrate ° weigh down a woman
  Too great oppression for a tender thing.
ROMEO: Is love a tender thing? It is too rough,
  Too rude°, too boist'rous, and it pricks like thorn.   ° rough

---

7. The mask was a musical dance-drama performed by a combination of professional actors and talented courtiers. Maskers often offered a prepared speech
("apology") to explain their excuse for the visit.
8. As a torch-bearer, Romeo is exempted from dancing.

MERCUTIO: If love be rough with you, be rough with love:
    Prick love for pricking, and you beat love down[9].
    Give me a case° to put my visage° in,   ° mask   ° face
    A visor for a visor!° what care I   ° mask for an ugly face
    What curious eye doth cote deformities?°   ° notice blemishes
    Here are the beetle brows shall blush for me.
BENVOLIO: Come knock and enter, and no sooner in,
    But every man betake him to his legs.°   ° join the dancing
ROMEO: A torch for me: let wantons light of heart
    Tickle the senseless° rushes° with their heels; ° without feeling ° floor covering
    For I am proverbed with a grandsire phrase°,   ° old proverb
    I'll be a candle-holder and look on:
    The game was ne'er so fair, and I am done.
MERCUTIO: Tut, dun's the mouse°, the constable's own word. ° proverb: "be silent"
    If thou art Dun, we'll draw thee from the mire,[1]
    Or (save your reverence)° love, wherein thou stickest ° without apology
    Up to the ears. Come, we burn daylight°, ho!   ° waste time
ROMEO: Nay, that's not so.
MERCUTIO: I mean, sir, in delay
    We waste our lights in vain, like lights by day.
    Take our good meaning, for our judgement sits
    Five times in that ere once in our five wits.[2]
ROMEO: And we mean well in going to this mask,
    But 'tis no wit° to go.   ° wisdom
MERCUTIO: Why, may one ask?
ROMEO: I dreamt a dream tonight.
MERCUTIO: And so did I.
ROMEO: Well, what was yours?
MERCUTIO: That dreamers often lie.
ROMEO: In bed asleep, while they do dream things true.
MERCUTIO: O then I see Queen Mab hath been with you:
    She is the fairies' midwife[3], and she comes
    In shape no bigger than an agate-stone°   ° engraved figure on an agate seal-ring
    On the forefinger of an alderman
    Drawn with a team of little atomi°   ° atom-sized creatures
    Over men's noses as they lie asleep.
    Her waggon-spokes made of long spinners'° legs, ° spiders'
    The cover of the wings of grasshoppers,
    Her traces° of the smallest spider web,   ° harness
    Her collars of the moonshine's wat'ry beams,
    Her whip of cricket's bone, the lash of film,
    Her waggoner a small grey-coated gnat,

---

9. Ease (masculine) sexual desire by satisfying and, hence, deflating it.
1. Mercutio refers to a Christmas game when he compares Romeo to a log, symbolizing a horse (Dun) pulled out of the mud by group effort.
2. Take the intended, not the literal, meaning.
3. Queen Mab is one of those fairies who delivers men of their dreams, those "children of an idle brain."

Not half so big as a round little worm
Pricked from the lazy finger of a maid.[4]
Her chariot is an empty hazel-nut,
Made by the joiner squirrel or old grub,
Time out a'mind the fairies' coachmakers:
And in this state she gallops night by night
Through lovers' brains, and then they dream of love,
O'er courtiers' knees, that dream on cur'sies straight°,   ° straightaway
O'er lawyers' fingers, who straight dream on fees,
O'er ladies' lips, who straight on kisses dream,
Which oft the angry Mab with blisters plagues,
Because their breaths with sweetmeats tainted are.
Sometime she gallops o'er a courtier's nose,
And then dreams he of smelling out a suit°;   ° furthering a petition for his own reward
And sometime comes she with a tithe-pig's° tail   ° pig paid as parish dues
Tickling a parson's nose as 'a lies asleep,
Then he dreams of another benefice.
Sometime she driveth o'er a soldier's neck,
And then dreams he of cutting foreign throats,   ° breaking down fortifications   ° am-
Of breaches°, ambuscadoes°, Spanish blades,   bushes
Of healths five fathom deep°; and then anon   ° drinking deeply
Drums in his ear, at which he starts and wakes,
And being thus frighted, swears a prayer or two,
And sleeps again. This is that very Mab
That plats the manes of horses in the night,
And bakes the elf-locks in foul sluttish hairs,
Which, once untangled, much misfortune bodes.
This is the hag, when maids lie on their backs,
That presses them and learns° them first to bear°,   ° teaches   ° children; lover's weight
Making them women of good carriage°.   ° deportment; carrying a burden
This is she—
ROMEO: Peace, peace, Mercutio, peace!
Thou talk'st of nothing.
MERCUTIO: True, I talk of dreams,
Which are the children of an idle brain,
Begot of nothing but vain fantasy,
Which is as thin of substance as the air
And more inconstant than the wind, who woos
Even now the frozen bosom of the north,
And being angered puffs away from thence,
Turning his side to the dew-dropping south.
BENVOLIO: This wind you talk of blows us from ourselves:
Supper is done, and we shall come too late.
ROMEO: I fear too early, for my mind misgives°   ° has misgivings
Some consequence yet hanging in the stars
Shall bitterly begin his fearful date
With this night's revels, and expire the term°   ° terminate a leasehold

---

4. An old wives' tale maintained that worms grew in the fingers of idle girls.

Of a despisèd life closed in my breast,
By some vile forfeit of untimely° death.   ° premature
But He that hath the steerage of my course
Direct my sail! On, lusty gentlemen.
BENVOLIO: Strike, drum.

(*They march about the stage and stand to one side.*)

Act One Scene Five. Verona: Capulet's house.

(SERVINGMEN *come forth with napkins.*)

FIRST SERVINGMAN: Where's Potpan, that he helps not to take away? He
shift a trencher? he scrape a trencher?°   ° wooden plate
SECOND SERVINGMAN: When good manners shall lie all in one or two men's
hands, and they unwashed too, 'tis a foul thing.
FIRST SERVINGMAN: Away with the join-stools, remove the courtcupboard°,   ° sideboard
look to the plate°. Good thou, save me a piece of marchpane°, and   ° silverware   ° marzipan
as thou loves me, let the porter let in Susan Grindstone and Nell.

(*Exit* SECOND SERVINGMAN)

   Anthony and Potpan!

(*Enter two more* SERVINGMEN)

THIRD SERVINGMAN: Ay, boy, ready.
FIRST SERVINGMAN: You are looked for and called for, asked for and sought
for, in the great chamber.
FOURTH SERVINGMAN: We cannot be here and there too. Cheerly°, boys, be   ° Heartily
brisk a while, and the longer liver take all.

(*Exeunt*)

(*Enter* CAPULET, LADY CAPULET, JULIET, TYBALT *and his* PAGE, NURSE, *and all the*
GUESTS *and* GENTLEWOMEN *to the Maskers.*)

CAPULET: Welcome, gentlemen! Ladies that have their toes
Unplagued with corns will walk a bout° with you.   ° dance
Ah, my mistresses, which of you all
Will now deny to dance? She that makes dainty°,   ° seems reluctant
She I'll swear hath corns. Am I come near ye now?
Welcome, gentlemen! I have seen the day
That I have worn a visor and could tell
A whispering tale in a fair lady's ear,
Such as would please; 'tis gone, 'tis gone, 'tis gone.
You are welcome, gentlemen. Come, musicians, play.
(*music plays*)
A hall, a hall, give room!° and foot it, girls.   ° clear the floor
(*and they dance*)
More light, you knaves, and turn the tables up;
And quench the fire, the room is grown too hot.

Ah, sirrah, this unlooked-for sport comes well.
Nay, sit, nay, sit, good Cousin Capulet,
For you and I are past our dancing days.
How long is't now since last yourself and I
Were in a mask?

COUSIN CAPULET: Berlady°, thirty years.   ° By Our Lady

CAPULET: What, man, 'tis not so much, 'tis not so much:
'Tis since the nuptial of Lucentio,
Come Pentecost as quickly as it will,
Some five and twenty years, and then we masked.

COUSIN CAPULET: 'Tis more, 'tis more, his son is elder, sir;
His son is thirty.

CAPULET: Will you tell me that?
His son was but a ward° two years ago.   ° minor

ROMEO (to a SERVINGMAN): What lady's that which doth enrich the
hand
Of yonder knight?

SERVINGMAN: I know not, sir.

ROMEO: O she doth teach the torches to burn bright!
It seems she hangs upon the cheek of night
As a rich jewel in an Ethiop's° ear—   ° black African's
Beauty too rich for use°, for earth too dear°:   ° interest   ° expensive
So shows a snowy dove trooping with crows,
As yonder lady o'er her fellows shows°.   ° appears
The measure° done, I'll watch her place of stand,   ° dance
And touching hers, make blessèd my rude° hand.   ° coarse
Did my heart love till now? forswear it°, sight!   ° deny previous love for Rosaline
For I ne'er saw true beauty till this night.

TYBALT: This, by his voice, should be a Montague.
Fetch me my rapier, boy.

(Exit PAGE)

                    What dares the slave
Come hither, covered with an antic face°,   ° grotesque mask
To fleer° and scorn at our solemnity?   ° sneer
Now by the stock and honour of my kin,
To strike him dead I hold it not a sin.

CAPULET: Why, how now, kinsman, wherefore storm you so?

TYBALT: Uncle, this is a Montague, our foe:
A villain that is hither come in spite,
To scorn at our solemnity° this night.   ° festivity

CAPULET: Young Romeo is it?

TYBALT: 'Tis he, that villain° Romeo.   ° base fellow

CAPULET: Content thee, gentle coz°, let him alone,   ° Calm down, cousin
'A° bears him like a portly° gentleman;   ° He   ° well-mannered
And to say truth, Verona brags of him
To be a virtuous and well-governed youth.
I would not for the wealth of all this town
Here in my house do him disparagement°;   ° indignity
Therefore be patient, take no note of him;
It is my will, the which if thou respect,

Show a fair presence, and put off these frowns°,   ° be civil
    An ill-beseeming semblance° for a feast.   ° facial expression
TYBALT: It fits when such a villain is a guest:
    I'll not endure him.
CAPULET: He shall be endured.
    What, goodman boy°, I say he shall, go to!   ° double insult of yeoman and youngster
    Am I the master here, or you? go to!
    You'll not endure him? God shall mend my soul,
    You'll make a mutiny among my guests!
    You will set cock-a-hoop°! you'll be the man!   ° abandon all restraint
TYBALT: Why, uncle, 'tis a shame.
CAPULET: Go to, go to°,   ° expression of indignation
    You are a saucy° boy. Is't so indeed?   ° insolent
    This trick may chance to scathe° you, I know what. ° injure your financial expectation
    You must contrary me°! Marry, 'tis time—   ° oppose my will
    Well said, my hearts!—You are a princox°, go,   ° conceited youth
    Be quiet, or—More light, more light!—For shame,
    I'll make you quiet, what!—Cheerly°, my hearts!   ° Heartily
TYBALT: Patience perforce° with wilful choler meeting ° Enforced forbearance
    Makes my flesh tremble in their different greeting:
    I will withdraw, but this intrusion shall,
    Now seeming sweet, convert to bitt'rest gall.

(*Exit*)

ROMEO (*to* JULIET): If I profane with my unworthiest hand
    This holy shrine°, the gentle sin is this,   ° her hand
    My lips, two blushing pilgrims, ready stand
    To smooth that rough touch with a tender kiss.
JULIET: Good pilgrim[5], you do wrong your hand too much,
    Which mannerly° devotion shows in this,   ° proper
    For saints have hands that pilgrims' hands do touch,
    And palm to palm is holy palmers'° kiss.   ° pilgrims'
ROMEO: Have not saints lips, and holy palmers too?
JULIET: Ay, pilgrim, lips that they must use in prayer.
ROMEO: O then, dear saint, let lips do what hands do:
    They pray, grant thou, lest faith turn to despair.
JULIET: Saints do not move, though grant for prayers' sake.
ROMEO: Then move not while my prayer's effect I take[6].
    (*kissing her*)
    Thus from my lips, by thine, my sin is purged.
JULIET: Then have my lips the sin that they have took.
ROMEO: Sin from my lips? O trespass sweetly urged!
    Give me my sin again.
    (*kissing her again*)
JULIET: You kiss by th'book°. ° expertly, as if by instruction

---

5. "Romeo" means "pilgrim" (a traveller to Rome) in Italian.
6. The preceding fourteen lines take the form of a Shakespearean sonnet. As the lovers move closer in space, they move closer in language: each speaks one quatrain; they share a quatrain; each contributes a line to the couplet.

NURSE: Madam, your mother craves a word with you.
ROMEO: What° is her mother?   ° Who
NURSE: Marry, bachelor°,   ° Good gracious, young man
    Her mother is the lady of the house,
    And a good lady, and a wise and virtuous.
    I nursed her daughter that you talked withal°;   ° with
    I tell you, he that can lay hold of her
    Shall have the chinks°.   ° money
ROMEO: Is she a Capulet?
    O dear account°! my life is my foe's debt.   ° terrible reckoning
BENVOLIO: Away, be gone, the sport is at the best.
ROMEO: Ay, so I fear, the more is my unrest°.   ° uneasiness
CAPULET: Nay, gentlemen, prepare not to be gone,
    We have a trifling foolish banquet towards°.   ° refreshments on the way
    (they whisper in his ear)
    Is it e'en so? Why then I thank you all.
    I thank you, honest gentlemen, good night.
    More torches here, come on! then let's to bed.
    Ah, sirrah, by my fay°, it waxes late,   ° faith
    I'll to my rest.

(Exeunt all but JULIET and NURSE)

JULIET: Come hither, Nurse. What° is yond gentleman?   ° Who
NURSE: The son and heir of old Tiberio.
JULIET: What's he that now is going out of door?
NURSE: Marry, that I think be young Petruchio.
JULIET: What's he that follows here, that would not dance?
NURSE: I know not.
JULIET: Go ask his name.—If he be marrièd,
    My grave is like to be my wedding bed.
NURSE: His name is Romeo, and a Montague,
    The only son of your great enemy.
JULIET: My only love sprung from my only hate!
    Too early seen unknown, and known too late!
    Prodigious° birth of love it is to me,   ° Ominous
    That I must love a loathèd enemy.
NURSE: What's tis? what's tis°?   ° this
JULIET: A rhyme I learnt even now
    Of one I danced withal°.   ° with
    (One calls within, 'Juliet!')
NURSE: Anon, anon°!   ° At once
    Come let's away, the strangers all are gone.

(Exeunt)

ACT TWO

(Enter CHORUS)

CHORUS: Now old desire doth in his death-bed lie,
    And young affection gapes° to be his heir;   ° longs

That fair° for which love° groaned for and would die, ° Rosaline ° Romeo
With tender Juliet matched is now not fair.
Now Romeo is beloved, and loves again,
Alike bewitchèd by the charm of looks;
But to his foe° supposed he must complain, ° Juliet
And she steal love's sweet bait from fearful hooks.
Being held a foe, he may not have access
To breathe such vows as lovers use to swear,
And she as much in love, her means much less
To meet her new-belovèd any where:
But passion lends them power, time means, to meet,
Temp'ring° extremities with extreme sweet. ° Moderating

(*Exit*)

Act Two, Scene One. Verona: Capulet's orchard.

(*Enter* ROMEO *alone*)

ROMEO: Can I go forward when my heart is here?
    Turn back, dull earth°, and find thy centre° out. ° his body ° Juliet

(ROMEO *withdraws*)

(*Enter* BENVOLIO *with* MERCUTIO)

BENVOLIO: Romeo! my cousin Romeo! Romeo!
MERCUTIO: He is wise,
    And on my life hath stol'n him home to bed.
BENVOLIO: He ran this way and lept this orchard wall.
    Call, good Mercutio.
MERCUTIO: Nay, I'll conjure° too. ° raise him up like a spirit
    Romeo! humours°! madman! passion! lover! ° caprices
    Appear thou in the likeness of a sigh,
    Speak but one rhyme, and I am satisfied;
    Cry but 'Ay me!,' pronounce but 'love' and 'dove,'
    Speak to my gossip Venus one fair word,
    One nickname for her purblind son° and heir, ° totally blind
    Young Abraham° Cupid, he that shot so trim ° rogue
    When King Cophetua loved the beggar-maid[7].
    He heareth not, he stirreth not, he moveth not,
    The ape° is dead, and I must conjure him. ° performing monkey
    I conjure thee by Rosaline's bright eyes,
    By her high forehead and her scarlet lip,
    By her fine foot, straight leg, and quivering thigh,
    And the demesnes° that there adjacent lie, ° estates
    That in thy likeness thou appear to us.

---

7. In the ballad of King Cophetua and the Beggar Maid, Cupid is called "The blinded boy that shoots so trim."

BENVOLIO: And if° he hear thee, thou wilt anger him.   ° If

MERCUTIO: This cannot anger him; 'twould anger him
    To raise a spirit in his mistress' circle,
    Of some strange nature, letting it there stand
    Till she had laid it and conjured it down:
    That were some spite. My invocation
    Is fair and honest°: in his mistress' name   ° inoffensive
    I conjure only but to raise up him.

BENVOLIO: Come, he hath hid himself among these trees
    To be consorted° with the humorous° night: ° associated ° humid
    Blind is his love, and best befits the dark.

MERCUTIO: If love be blind, love cannot hit the mark.
    Now will he sit under a medlar tree,
    And wish his mistress were that kind of fruit
    As maids call medlars, when they laugh alone.
    O Romeo, that she were, O that she were
    An open-arse, thou a pop'rin pear![8]
    Romeo, good night, I'll to my truckle-bed°,   ° trundle bed
    This field-bed° is too cold for me to sleep.   ° bed on the ground
    Come, shall we go!

BENVOLIO: Go then, for 'tis in vain
    To seek him here that means not to be found.

(*Exit with* MERCUTIO)

Act Two, Scene Two. Capulet's orchard.

(ROMEO *advances*)

ROMEO: He° jests at scars that never felt a wound[9].   ° Mercutio

(JULIET *appears aloft as at a window.*)

    But soft, what light through yonder window breaks?
    It is the east, and Juliet is the sun.
    Arise, fair sun, and kill the envious moon,
    Who is already sick and pale with grief
    That thou, her maid, art far more fair than she.
    Be not her maid, since she is envious;
    Her vestal° livery is but sick and green[1]   ° virginal
    And none but fools do wear it; cast it off.

---

8. A medlar is a small brown-skinned apple with a large cup-shaped eye. "Medlar" is also a vulgarism for female genitalia, and "to meddle" was a common expression for sexual activity. Owing to its phallic shape, the pop'rin pear, named for Pop-eringhe in West Flanders, was used as a vulgar term for penis. "Pop'rin" puns on "pop 'er in."
9. The couplet (Romeo's "wound" rhymes with Benvolio's "found") indicates the scene is continuous.
1. "Sick" and "green" allude to the green-sickness, an anemia found in unmarried girls.

It is my lady, O it is my love:
O that she knew she were!
She speaks, yet she says nothing; what of that?
Her eye discourses, I will answer it.
I am too bold, 'tis not to me she speaks:
Two of the fairest stars in all the heaven,
Having some business, do entreat her eyes
To twinkle in their spheres[2] till they return.
What if her eyes were there°, they in her head?   ° in the spheres
The brightness of her cheek would shame those stars,
As daylight doth a lamp; her eyes in heaven
Would through the airy region stream° so bright   ° shine
That birds would sing and think it were not night.
See how she leans her cheek upon her hand!
O that I were a glove upon that hand,
That I might touch that cheek!

JULIET: Ay me!

ROMEO: She speaks.
O speak again, bright angel, for thou art
As glorious to this night, being o'er my head,
As is a wingèd messenger of heaven
Unto the white-upturnèd wond'ring eyes
Of mortals that fall back to gaze on him,
When he bestrides the lazy puffing clouds,
And sails upon the bosom of the air.

JULIET: O Romeo, Romeo, wherefore° art thou Romeo?   ° why
Deny thy father and refuse thy name;
Or if thou wilt not, be but sworn my love,
And I'll no longer be a Capulet.

ROMEO: Shall I hear more, or shall I speak at this?

JULIET: 'Tis but thy name that is my enemy;
Thou art thyself, though not a Montague.
What's Montague? It is nor hand nor foot,
Nor arm nor face, nor any other part
Belonging to a man. O be some other name!
What's in a name? That which we call a rose
By any other word would smell as sweet;
So Romeo would, were he not Romeo called,
Retain that dear perfection which he owes°   ° possesses
Without that title. Romeo, doff° thy name,   ° put off
And for thy name, which is no part of thee,
Take all myself.

ROMEO: I take thee at thy word:
Call me but love, and I'll be new baptised;
Henceforth I never will be Romeo.

JULIET: What man art thou that thus bescreened° in night   ° concealed
So stumblest on my counsel°?   ° private thoughts

---

2. In the Ptolemaic cosmology, the seven planets were thought to be fixed in
hollow, crystalline spheres, which, as they rotated, produced music.

ROMEO: By a name
I know not how to tell thee who I am.
My name, dear saint, is hateful to myself,
Because it is an enemy to thee;
Had I it written, I would tear the word.

JULIET: My ears have yet not drunk a hundred words
Of thy tongue's uttering, yet I know the sound.
Art thou not Romeo, and a Montague?

ROMEO: Neither, fair maid, if either thee dislike°.   ° displease

JULIET: How cam'st thou hither, tell me, and wherefore?
The orchard walls are high and hard to climb,
And the place death, considering who thou art,
If any of my kinsmen find thee here.

ROMEO: With love's light wings did I o'erperch° these walls,   ° fly over
For stony limits cannot hold love out,
And what love can do, that dares love attempt:
Therefore thy kinsmen are no stop to me.

JULIET: If they do see thee, they will murder thee.

ROMEO: Alack, there lies more peril in thine eye
Than twenty of their swords. Look thou but sweet,
And I am proof° against their enmity.   ° armored

JULIET: I would not for the world they saw thee here.

ROMEO: I have night's cloak to hide me from their eyes,
And but° thou love me, let them find me here;   ° unless
My life were better ended by their hate,
Than death proroguèd°, wanting° of thy love.   ° put off   ° lacking

JULIET: By whose direction found'st thou out this place?

ROMEO: By Love, that first did prompt me to enquire:
He lent me counsel, and I lent him eyes.
I am no pilot, yet wert thou as far
As that vast shore washed with the farthest sea,
I should adventure° for such merchandise.   ° venture

JULIET: Thou knowest the mask of night is on my face,
Else would a maiden blush bepaint my cheek
For that which thou hast heard me speak tonight.
Fain° would I dwell on form°, fain, fain deny   ° Gladly   ° observe decorum
What I have spoke, but farewell compliment°.   ° social convention
Dost thou love me? I know thou wilt say 'Ay';
And I will take thy word; yet if thou swear'st,
Thou mayst prove false: at lovers' perjuries
They say Jove laughs. O gentle Romeo,
If thou dost love, pronounce it faithfully;
Or if thou think'st I am too quickly won,
I'll frown and be perverse, and say thee nay,
So thou wilt woo, but else not for the world.
In truth, fair Montague, I am too fond,
And therefore thou mayst think my behaviour light:
But trust me, gentleman, I'll prove more true
Than those that have more coying° to be strange°.   ° coquetry   ° aloof
I should have been more strange, I must confess,

But that thou overheard'st, ere I was ware,
My true-love passion; therefore pardon me,
And not impute this yielding to light° love,   ° easy
Which the dark night hath so discoverèd°.   ° revealed
ROMEO: Lady, by yonder blessèd moon I vow,
    That tips with silver all these fruit-tree tops—
JULIET: O swear not by the moon, th'inconstant moon,
    That monthly changes in her circled orb,
    Lest that thy love prove likewise variable.
ROMEO: What shall I swear by?
JULIET: Do not swear at all;
    Or if thou wilt, swear by thy gracious° self,   ° endowed with graces
    Which is the god of my idolatry,
    And I'll believe thee.
ROMEO: If my heart's dear love—
JULIET: Well, do not swear. Although I joy in thee,
    I have no joy of this contract° tonight,   ° exchange of promises
    It is too rash°, too unadvised°, too sudden,   ° hasty °ill-considered
    Too like the lightning, which doth cease to be
    Ere° one can say 'It lightens.' Sweet, good night: ° Before
    This bud of love, by summer's ripening breath,
    May prove a beauteous flower when next we meet.
    Good night, good night! as sweet repose and rest
    Come to thy heart as that within my breast.
ROMEO: O wilt thou leave me so unsatisfied?
JULIET: What satisfaction canst thou have tonight?
ROMEO: Th'exchange of thy love's faithful vow for mine.
JULIET: I gave thee mine before thou didst request it;
    And yet I would it were to give again.
ROMEO: Wouldst thou withdraw it? for what purpose, love?
JULIET: But to be frank° and give it thee again,   ° generous, out-spoken
    And yet I wish but for the thing I have:
    My bounty is as boundless as the sea,
    My love as deep; the more I give to thee
    The more I have, for both are infinite.
    I hear some noise within; dear love, adieu!—
    Anon°, good Nurse!—Sweet Montague, be true.   ° Presently
    Stay but a little, I will come again.

(*Exit above*)

ROMEO: O blessèd, blessèd night! I am afeard,
    Being in night, all this is but a dream,
    Too flattering-sweet to be substantial.

(*Enter* JULIET *above*)

JULIET: Three words, dear Romeo, and good night indeed.
    If that thy bent° of love be honourable,   ° intention
    Thy purpose marriage, send me word tomorrow,
    By one that I'll procure° to come to thee,   ° arrange

Where and what time thou wilt perform the rite,
And all my fortunes at thy foot I'll lay,
And follow thee my lord throughout the world.

NURSE (*within*): Madam!

JULIET: I come, anon°.—But if thou meanest not well,
    I do beseech thee—   ° soon

NURSE (*within*):   Madam!

JULIET: By and by° I come—   ° immediately
    To cease thy strife°, and leave me to my grief.   ° endeavor
    Tomorrow will I send.

ROMEO: So thrive my soul—

JULIET: A thousand times good night!

(*Exit above*)

ROMEO: A thousand times the worse, to want thy light.
    Love goes toward love as schoolboys from their books,
    But love from love, toward school with heavy looks.

(*Retiring slowly*)

(*Enter* JULIET *again above*)

JULIET: Hist, Romeo, hist! O for a falc'ner's voice°,   ° as a falconer lures a hawk
    To lure this tassel-gentle° back again: ° male falcon
    Bondage is hoarse, and may not speak aloud,
    Else would I tear° the cave where Echo lies,   ° rend
    And make her airy tongue more hoarse than mine
    With repetition of my Romeo's name.

ROMEO: It is my soul that calls upon my name.
    How silver-sweet sound lovers' tongues by night,
    Like softest music to attending ears!

JULIET: Romeo!

ROMEO: My niësse?°   ° young nestling hawk

JULIET: What a'clock tomorrow
    Shall I send to thee?

ROMEO: By the hour of nine.

JULIET: I will not fail, 'tis twenty year till then.°   ° though it seems
    I have forgot why I did call thee back.

ROMEO: Let me stand here till thou remember it.

JULIET: I shall forget, to have thee still° stand there,   ° always
    Rememb'ring how I love thy company.

ROMEO: And I'll still stay, to have thee still forget,
    Forgetting any other home but this.

JULIET: 'Tis almost morning, I would have thee gone:
    And yet no farther than a wanton's° bird,   ° spoiled child's
    That lets it hop a little from his hand,
    Like a poor prisoner in his twisted gyves,°   ° fetters
    And with a silken thread plucks it back again,
    So loving-jealous of his liberty.

ROMEO: I would I were thy bird.

JULIET: Sweet, so would I,
    Yet I should kill thee with much cherishing.
    Good night, good night! Parting is such sweet sorrow,
    That I shall say good night till it be morrow.

(*Exit above*)

ROMEO: Sleep dwell upon thine eyes, peace in thy breast!
    Would I were sleep and peace, so sweet to rest!
    Hence will I to my ghostly° sire's close° cell,   ° spiritual ° secluded, narrow
    His help to crave, and my dear hap° to tell.   ° good fortune

(*Exit*)

Act Two, Scene Three. Verona: Friar Lawrence's cell.

(*Enter* FRIAR LAWRENCE *alone, with a basket*)

FRIAR LAWRENCE: The grey-eyed morn smiles on the frowning night,
    Check'ring the eastern clouds with streaks of light;
    And fleckled° darkness like a drunkard reels   ° dappled
    From forth day's path and Titan's fiery wheels°:   ° the sun-god's chariot wheels
    Now ere the sun advance his burning eye,
    The day to cheer, and night's dank dew to dry,
    I must upfill this osier° cage of ours   ° willow
    With baleful° weeds and precious-juicèd flowers.   ° poisonous
    The earth that's nature's mother is her tomb;
    What is her burying grave, that is her womb;
    And from her womb children of divers kind
    We sucking on her natural bosom find:
    Many for many virtues excellent,
    None but for° some, and yet all different.   ° without
    O mickle° is the powerful grace° that lies   ° great   ° healing power
    In plants, herbs, stones, and their true° qualities: ° inherent
    For nought so vile, that on the earth doth live,
    But to the earth some special good doth give;
    Nor ought so good but, strained° from that fair use,   ° perverted
    Revolts from true birth°, stumbling on abuse.   ° proper nature
    Virtue itself turns vice, being misapplied,
    And vice sometime by action dignified.

(*Enter* ROMEO)

    Within the infant rind of this weak flower
    Poison hath residence, and medicine power:
    For this, being smelt, with that part° cheers each part,   ° odor (of the body)
    Being tasted, stays° all senses with the heart.   ° halts
    Two such opposèd kings encamp them still
    In man as well as herbs, grace and rude will;
    And where the worser is predominant,
    Full soon the canker° death eats up that plant.   ° plant-destroying worm
ROMEO: Good morrow, father.
FRIAR LAWRENCE: Benedicite°!   ° Bless you!
    What early tongue so sweet saluteth me?

Young son, it argues a distempered° head
So soon to bid good morrow° to thy bed:
Care keeps his watch in every old man's eye,
And where care lodges, sleep will never lie;
But where unbruisèd youth will unstuffed° brain
Doth couch his limbs, there golden sleep doth reign.
Therefore thy earliness doth me assure
Thou art uproused with some distemp'rature°;
Or if not so, then here I hit it right,
Our Romeo hath not been in bed tonight.

ROMEO: That last is true, the sweeter rest was mine.

FRIAR LAWRENCE: God pardon sin! wast thou with Rosaline?

ROMEO: With Rosaline, my ghostly° father? no;
I have forgot that name, and that name's woe.

FRIAR LAWRENCE: That's my good son, but where hast thou been then?

ROMEO: I'll tell thee ere thou ask it me again:
I have been feasting with mine enemy,
Where on a sudden one hath wounded me
That's by me wounded; both our remedies
Within thy help and holy physic° lies.
I bear no hatred, blessèd man; for lo,
My intercession° likewise steads° my foe.

FRIAR LAWRENCE: Be plain, good son, and homely° in thy drift,
Riddling° confession finds but riddling shrift.°

ROMEO: Then plainly know, my heart's dear love is set
On the fair daughter of rich Capulet;
As mine on hers, so hers is set on mine,
And all combined, save what thou must combine
By holy marriage. When and where and how
We met, we wooed, and made exchange of vow,
I'll tell thee as we pass°, but this I pray,
That thou consent to marry us today.

FRIAR LAWRENCE: Holy Saint Francis, what a change is here!
Is Rosaline, that thou didst love so dear,
So soon forsaken? Young men's love then lies
Not truly in their hearts, but in their eyes.
Jesu Maria, what a deal of brine°
Hath washed thy sallow° cheeks for Rosaline!
How much salt water thrown away in waste,
To season° love, that of it doth not taste!
The sun not yet thy sighs from heaven clears,
Thy old groans yet ringing in mine ancient ears;
Lo here upon thy cheek the stain doth sit
Of an old tear that is not washed off yet.
If e'er thou wast thyself, and these woes thine,
Thou and these woes were all for Rosaline.
And art thou changed? Pronounce this sentence° then:
Women may fall, when there's no strength in men.

ROMEO: Thou chid'st° me oft for loving Rosaline.

FRIAR LAWRENCE: For doting, not for loving, pupil mine.

ROMEO: And bad'st me bury love.

° disordered
° farewell

° unburdened

° disturbance

° spiritual

° spiritual remedy

° request ° helps
° simple
° ambiguous ° absolution

° go along

° salty tears
° yellow

° flavor and preserve

° moral saying

° criticized

FRIAR LAWRENCE: Not in a grave,
　　To lay one in, another out to have.
ROMEO: I pray thee chide me not. Her I love now
　　Doth grace for grace and love for love allow;
　　The other did not so.
FRIAR LAWRENCE: O she knew well
　　Thy love did read by rote, that could not spell.
　　But come, young waverer, come go with me,
　　In one respect° I'll thy assistant be:　　　　　　　　　° For one reason
　　For this alliance may so happy prove
　　To turn your households' rancour to pure love.
ROMEO: O let us hence, I stand° on sudden haste.　　　° insist
FRIAR LAWRENCE: Wisely and slow, they stumble that run fast.

(*Exeunt*)

Act Two, Scene Four. Verona: a street.

(*Enter* BENVOLIO *and* MERCUTIO)

MERCUTIO: Where the dev'l should this Romeo be?
　　Came he not home tonight°?　　　　　　　　　　　° last night
BENVOLIO: Not to his father's, I spoke with his man.
MERCUTIO: Why, that same pale hard-hearted wench, that Rosaline,
　　Torments him so, that he will sure run mad.
BENVOLIO: Tybalt, the kinsman to old Capulet,
　　Hath sent a letter to his father's house.
MERCUTIO: A challenge, on my life.
BENVOLIO: Romeo will answer° it.　　　　　　　　　　° accept
MERCUTIO: Any man that can write may answer a letter.
BENVOLIO: Nay, he will answer the letter's master, how he dares, being
　　dared.
MERCUTIO: Alas, poor Romeo, he is already dead, stabbed with a white
　　wench's black eye, run through the ear with a love-song, the very
　　pin° of his heart cleft with the blind bow-boy's butt-shaft; and is　　° bull's eye
　　he a man to encounter Tybalt?
BENVOLIO: Why, what is Tybalt?
MERCUTIO: More than Prince of Cats.[3] O, he's the courageous captain of
　　compliments°: he fights as you sing prick-song°, keeps time, dis-　　° fencing ceremony　° printed music
　　tance, and proportion°; he rests his minim rests, one, two, and　　° rhythm
　　the third in your bosom; the very butcher of a silk button, a
　　duellist°, a duellist; a gentleman of the very first house°, of the　　° word newly introduced in England
　　first and second cause. Ah, the immortal 'passado,' the 'punto　　° best duelling school
　　reverso,' the 'hay'[4].

---

3. In *Reynard the Fox* the Prince of Cats is named Tibalt.
4. Mercutio describes Tybalt as a fashionable Italian duellist who fights as precisely as one follows printed music in singing. A skilled fencer "of the very first
house" could pink (hit) any of an opponent's "silk button[s]" and would know the
technicalities of the duel: the steps that lead to it ("cause") and the moves ("pa-
sado" is a forward thrust, "punto reverso" a backhanded thrust, and "hay" a home
thrust).

BENVOLIO: The what?

MERCUTIO: The pox° of such antic, lisping, affecting phantasimes°, these
    new tuners of accent! 'By Jesu, a very good blade! a very tall man!
    a very good whore!' Why, is not this a lamentable thing, grand-
    sire, that we should be thus afflicted with these strange flies°,
    these fashion-mongers°, these pardon-me's, who stand so much
    on the new form°, that they cannot sit at ease on the old bench?⁵
    O their bones, their bones°!

° plague   ° affected gallants

° parasites
° Frenchified gallants
° fashion
° pun on French bons (good)

(*Enter* ROMEO)

BENVOLIO: Here comes Romeo, here comes Romeo.

MERCUTIO: Without his roe, like a dried herring⁶: O flesh, flesh, how art
    thou fishified! Now is he for the numbers that Petrarch flowed in.
    Laura to his lady was a kitchen wench (marry, she had a better
    love to berhyme her), Dido a dowdy, Cleopatra a gipsy, Helen and
    Hero hildings and harlots, Thisbe a grey eye or so, but not to the
    purpose⁷ Signior Romeo, 'bon jour'! there's a French salutation to
    your French slop°. You gave us the counterfeit° fairly last night.

° loose breeches   ° played a trick

ROMEO: Good morrow to you both. What counterfeit did I give you?

MERCUTIO: The slip, sir, the slip°, can you not conceive?

° counterfeit coin; evasion

ROMEO: Pardon, good Mercutio, my business was great, and in such a
    case° as mine a man may strain courtesy.

° situation; pudenda

MERCUTIO: That's as much as to say, such a case as yours constrains a
    man to bow in the hams.

ROMEO: Meaning to cur'sy°.

° curtsy

MERCUTIO: Thou hast most kindly hit it.⁸

ROMEO: A most courteous exposition.

MERCUTIO: Nay, I am the very pink° of courtesy.

° acme; flower; to cut out designs

ROMEO: Pink for flower.

MERCUTIO: Right.

ROMEO: Why then is my pump° well flowered.°

° light shoe   ° pinked

MERCUTIO: Sure wit! Follow me this jest now, till thou hast worn out thy
    pump, that when the single sole of it is worn, the jest may re-
    main, after the wearing, solely singular.

ROMEO: O single-soled° jest, solely singular° for the singleness!

° trivial   ° quite alone

MERCUTIO: Come between us, good Benvolio, my wits faints°.

° faint

ROMEO: Swits and spurs, swits and spurs⁹, or I'll cry a match.

---

5.   Mercutio addresses Benvolio as if they were old men lamenting the folly of
youth.
6.   Half himself without his "roe" (fish-spawn), Romeo is like a depleted rake from
a bawdy house.
7.   Rosaline far outshines those celebrated beauties of myth and history; thus
Romeo would seem to favor the love poetry ("numbers") that made Petrarch famous. Mercutio never learns that Romeo loves Juliet.
8.   "Case" (genitals), "bowed hams" (the effect of venereal disease), and "hit it"
("score" sexually) are bawdy puns.
9.   In calling for switches ("swits") and spurs, Romeo wants to keep the game
going.

MERCUTIO: Nay, if our wits run the wild-goose chase, I am done; for thou hast more of the wild goose[1] in one of thy wits than, I am sure, I have in my whole five. Was I with you there for the goose?

ROMEO: Thou wast never with me for any thing when thou wast not there for the goose.

MERCUTIO: I will bite thee by the ear° for that jest.   ° fond gesture

ROMEO: Nay, good goose, bite not.

MERCUTIO: Thy wit is a very bitter sweeting, it is a most sharp sauce.

ROMEO: And is it not then well served in to a sweet goose?

MERCUTIO: O here's a wit of cheverel° that stretches from an inch narrow   ° kid leather
to an ell° broad!   ° ell: 45 inches

ROMEO: I stretch it out for that word 'broad'°, which, added to the   ° obvious, with pun on indecent
goose, proves thee far and wide a broad goose.

MERCUTIO: Why, is not this better now than groaning for love? Now art thou sociable, now art thou Romeo; now art thou what thou art, by art as well as by nature, for this drivelling love is like a great   ° idiot   ° sticking out his tongue
natural° that runs lolling° up and down to hide his bauble° in a   ° fool's stick; penis
hole.

BENVOLIO: Stop there, stop there.

MERCUTIO: Thou desirest me to stop in my tale against the hair°.   ° against my desire

BENVOLIO: Thou wouldst else have made thy tale large.

MERCUTIO: O thou art deceived; I would have made it short, for I was come to the whole depth of my tale, and meant indeed to occupy the argument no longer[2].

ROMEO: Here's goodly gear!

(*Enter* NURSE *and her man* PETER)

A sail, a sail!

MERCUTIO: Two, two: a shirt and a smock.

NURSE: Peter!

PETER: Anon.

NURSE: My fan, Peter.

MERCUTIO: Good Peter, to hide her face, for her fan's the fairer face.

NURSE: God ye good morrow°, gentlemen.   ° Good morning

MERCUTIO: God ye good den°, fair gentlewoman.   ° Good evening (afternoon)

NURSE: Is it good den°?   ° afternoon

MERCUTIO: 'Tis no less, I tell ye, for the bawdy hand of the dial is now upon the prick° of noon.   ° mark on sundial or clock (with bawdy pun)

NURSE: Out upon you, what a man are you?

ROMEO: One, gentlewoman, that God hath made, himself to mar.

NURSE: By my troth°, it is well said: 'for himself to mar', quoth'a°?   ° faith   ° said he
Gentlemen, can any of you tell me where I may find the young Romeo?

---

1. A fowl proverbially known for its stupidity, "goose" may also refer to a nitwit or a prostitute.
2. These lines turn on a series of bawdy puns. The secondary meaning of "tale" and "gear" is "genitals." "Large" means "long" and "tumescent," and contrasts with "short" or "flaccid." "To occupy" also means " to have sexual intercourse."

ROMEO: I can tell you, but young Romeo will be older when you have found him than he was when you sought him: I am the youngest of that name, for fault of a worse.

NURSE: You say well.

MERCUTIO: Yea, is the worst well? Very well took° i'faith, wisely, wisely.   ° understood

NURSE: If you be he, sir, I desire some confidence° with you.   ° malapropism for "conference"

BENVOLIO: She will indite° him to some supper.   ° invite (mocks Nurse)

MERCUTIO: A bawd, a bawd, a bawd°! So ho!°   ° procurer   ° hunter's cry

ROMEO: What hast thou found?

MERCUTIO: No hare, sir, unless a hare, sir, in a lenten pie, that is something stale and hoar³ ere it be spent°.   ° used up

(*He walks by them and sings*)

> An old hare hoar,
> And an old hare hoar,
> Is very good meat in Lent;
> But a hare that is hoar
> Is too much for a score,
> When it hoars ere it be spent.

Romeo, will you come to your father's? We'll to dinner thither.

ROMEO: I will follow you.

MERCUTIO: Farewell, ancient lady, farewell, lady, (*singing*) 'lady, lady'°.   ° refrain from well-known ballad

(*Exeunt* MERCUTIO *and* BENVOLIO)

NURSE: I pray you, sir, what saucy merchant° was this that was so full of his ropery°?   ° fellow   ° knavery

ROMEO: A gentleman, Nurse, that loves to hear himself talk, and will speak more in a minute than he will stand to in a month.

NURSE: And' a speak any thing against me, I'll take him down°, and 'a were lustier than he is, and twenty such Jacks°; and if I cannot, I'll find those that shall. Scurvy knave, I am none of his flirt-gills°, I am none of his skains-mates°. (*she turns to Peter, her man*) And thou must stand by too and suffer every knave to use° me at his pleasure!   ° humble him   ° knaves   ° loose women   ° cut-throat companions   ° treat as he wished

PETER: I saw no man use you at his pleasure; if I had, my weapon should quickly have been out. I warrant you, I dare draw as soon as another man, if I see occasion in a good quarrel, and the law on my side.

NURSE: Now afore God, I am so vexed that every part about me quivers. Scurvy knave! Pray you, sir, a word: and as I told you, my young lady bid me enquire you out; what she bid me say, I will keep to myself. But first let me tell ye, if ye should lead her in a fool's paradise°, as they say, it were a very gross kind of behaviour, as   ° seduce her
they say; for the gentlewoman is young; and therefore, if you should deal double with her, truly it were an ill thing to be offered to any gentlewoman; and very weak° dealing.   ° mean

---

3. The lines play on "hare" (whore), "hoar" (moldy), and "stale" (whore). The nurse is no hare, unless (unlikely but welcome in a meatless Lenten pie) she is a hoar hare. The song that follows continues this word play.

ROMEO: Nurse, commend me to thy lady and mistress. I protest° unto   ° declare
     thee—
NURSE: Good heart, and i'faith I will tell her as much. Lord, Lord, she
     will be a joyful woman.
ROMEO: What wilt thou tell her, Nurse? thou dost not mark me.
NURSE: I will tell her, sir, that you do protest°, which, as I take it, is a   ° vow
     gentleman-like offer.
ROMEO: Bid her devise
     Some means to come to shrift° this afternoon,   ° confession
     And there she shall at Friar Lawrence's cell
     Be shrived° and married. Here is for thy pains.   ° given absolution
NURSE: No truly, sir, not a penny.
ROMEO: Go to, I say you shall.
NURSE: This afternoon, sir? Well, she shall be there.
ROMEO: And stay, good Nurse, behind the abbey wall:
     Within this hour my man shall be with thee,
     And bring thee cords made like a tackled stair°,   ° rope ladder
     Which to the high top-gallant° of my joy   ° highest mast of a ship
     Must be my convoy° in the secret night.   ° means of passage
     Farewell, be trusty, and I'll quit° thy pains.   ° reward
     Farewell, commend me to thy mistress.
NURSE: Now God in heaven bless thee! Hark you, sir.
ROMEO: What say'st thou, my dear Nurse?
NURSE: Is your man secret°? Did you ne'er hear say,   ° trustworthy
     'Two may keep counsel°, putting one away'?   ° keep a secret
ROMEO: 'Warrant thee, my man's as true as steel.
NURSE: Well, sir, my mistress is the sweetest lady—Lord, Lord! when
     'twas a little prating thing—O, there is a nobleman in town, one
     Paris, that would fain lay knife aboard°, but she, good soul, had   ° press his claim
     as lieve° see a toad, a very toad, as see him. I anger her sometimes,   ° willingly
     and tell her that Paris is the properer man°, but I'll warrant you,   ° more handsome
     when I say so, she looks as pale as any clout° in the versal° world.   ° washed-out rag   ° entire
     Doth not rosemary and Romeo begin both with a letter?
ROMEO: Ay, Nurse, what of that? Both with an R.
NURSE: Ah, mocker, that's the dog-name[4]. R is for the—no, I know it
     begins with some other letter—and she hath the prettiest senten-
     tious° of it, of you and rosemary, that it would do you good to   ° malapropism for "sentence"
     hear it.
ROMEO: Commend me to thy lady.
NURSE: Ay, a thousand times.

(*Exit* ROMEO)

                 Peter!
PETER: Anon.
NURSE: Before and apace.

(*Exit after* PETER)

---

4. The sound of *r* resembles a dog's growl.

Act Two, Scene Five. Verona: Capulet's Orchard.

(*Enter* JULIET)

JULIET: The clock struck nine when I did send the Nurse;
    In half an hour she promised to return.
    Perchance she cannot meet him: that's not so.
    O, she is lame°! Love's heralds should be thoughts,   ° slow
    Which ten times faster glides than the sun's beams,
    Driving back shadows over low'ring hills;
    Therefore do nimble-pinioned° doves draw Love,   ° swift-winged
    And therefore hath the wind-swift Cupid wings.
    Now is the sun upon the highmost hill°   ° the meridian
    Of this day's journey, and from nine till twelve
    Is three long hours, yet she is not come.
    Had she affections and warm youthful blood,
    She would be as swift in motion as a ball;
    My words would bandy° her to my sweet love,   ° toss
    And his to me.
    But old folks, many feign° as they were dead,   ° act like
    Unwieldy, slow, heavy, and pale as lead.

(*Enter* NURSE *with* PETER)

    O God, she comes! O honey Nurse, what news?
    Hast thou met with him? Send thy man away.
NURSE: Peter, stay° at the gate.   ° wait

(*Exit* PETER)

JULIET: Now, good sweet Nurse—O Lord, why look'st thou sad?
    Though news be sad, yet tell them merrily;
    If good, thou shamest the music of sweet news
    By playing it° to me with so sour a face.   ° the news
NURSE: I am a-weary, give me leave a while.
    Fie, how my bones ache! What a jaunce° have I!   ° tiring journey
JULIET: I would thou hadst my bones, and I thy news.
    Nay, come, I pray thee speak, good, good Nurse, speak.
NURSE: Jesu, what haste! can you not stay° a while?   ° wait a moment
    Do you not see that I am out of breath?
JULIET: How art thou out of breath, when thou hast breath
    To say to me that thou art out of breath?
    The excuse that thou dost make in this delay
    Is longer than the tale thou dost excuse.
    Is thy news good or bad? Answer to that.
    Say either, and I'll stay the circumstance°:   ° wait for the details
    Let me be satisfied, is't good or bad?
NURSE: Well, you have made a simple° choice, you know not how to   ° foolish
    choose a man: Romeo? no, not he; though his face be better than
    any man's, yet his leg excels all men's, and for a hand and a foot
    and a body, though they be not to be talked on, yet they are past
    compare. He is not the flower° of courtesy, but I'll warrant him,   ° height

as gentle as a lamb. Go thy ways, wench, serve God. What, have
you dined at home?

JULIET: No, no! But all this did I know before.
What says he of our marriage, what of that?

NURSE: Lord, how my head aches! what a head have I!
It beats as it would fall in twenty pieces.
My back a't'other side—ah, my back, my back!
Beshrew° your heart for sending me about   ° Curse (mild oath)
To catch my death with jauncing° up and down!   ° trudging

JULIET: I'faith, I am sorry that thou art not well.
Sweet, sweet, sweet Nurse, tell me, what says my love?

NURSE: Your love says, like an honest° gentleman,   ° honorable
And a courteous, and a kind, and a handsome,
And I warrant a virtuous—Where is your mother?

JULIET: Where is my mother? why, she is within,
Where should she be? How oddly thou repliest:
'Your love says, like an honest gentleman,
"Where is your mother?"'

NURSE: O God's lady dear,
Are you so hot°? Marry come up°, I trow;   ° impatient   ° behave yourself
Is this the poultice for my aching bones?
Henceforward do your messages yourself.

JULIET: Here's such a coil°! Come, what says Romeo?   ° fuss

NURSE: Have you got leave to go to shrift° today?   ° confession

JULIET: I have.

NURSE: Then hie you hence to Friar Lawrence' cell,
There stays a husband to make you a wife.
Now comes the wanton° blood up in your cheeks,   ° undisciplined
They'll be in scarlet straight at any news.
Hie you to church, I must another way.
To fetch a ladder, by the which your love
Must climb a bird's nest soon when it is dark.
I am the drudge, and toil in your delight;
But you shall bear the burden° soon at night.   ° responsibility; lover's weight
Go, I'll to dinner, hie you to the cell.

JULIET: Hie to high fortune! Honest Nurse, farewell.

(*Exeunt*)

Act Two, Scene Six. Verona: Friar Lawrence's cell.

(*Enter* FRIAR LAWRENCE *and* ROMEO)

FRIAR LAWRENCE: So smile the heavens upon this holy act,
That after-hours with sorrow chide us not.

ROMEO: Amen, amen! but come what sorrow can,
It cannot countervail° the exchange of joy   ° equal
That one short minute gives me in her sight.
Do thou but close° our hands with holy words,   ° join

Then love-devouring Death do what he dare,
It is enough I may but call her mine.
FRIAR LAWRENCE: These violent delights have violent ends,
And in their triumph die like fire and powder,
Which as they kiss consume. The sweetest honey
Is loathsome in his own deliciousness,
And in the taste confounds° the appetite.   ° destroys
Therefore love moderately, long love doth so;
Too swift arrives as tardy as too slow.

(*Enter* JULIET)

Here comes the lady. O, so light a foot
Will ne'er wear out the everlasting flint;
A lover may bestride the gossamers°   ° spiders' threads
That idles in the wanton° summer air,   ° playful
And yet not fall[5], so light is vanity°.   ° transitory earthly joy
JULIET: Good even to my ghostly° confessor.   ° spiritual
FRIAR LAWRENCE: Romeo shall thank thee, daughter, for us both.
JULIET: As much to him, else is his thanks too much.
ROMEO: Ah, Juliet, if the measure of thy joy
Be heaped like mine, and that thy skill be more
To blazon° it, then sweeten with thy breath   ° describe
This neighbour air, and let rich music's tongue
Unfold the imagined° happiness that both   ° felt within but unexpressed
Receive in either by this dear encounter.
JULIET: Conceit°, more rich in matter than in words, ° Understanding
Brags° of his substance°, not of ornament;   ° Takes pride in   ° matter
They are but beggars that can count their worth,
But my true love is grown to such excess
I cannot sum up sum° of half my wealth.   ° calculate the total
FRIAR LAWRENCE: Come, come with me, and we will make short work,
For by your leaves, you shall not stay alone
Till Holy Church incorporate two in one.

(*Exeunt*)

ACT THREE

Act Three, Scene One. Verona: a public place.

(*Enter* MERCUTIO *and his* PAGE, BENVOLIO, *and* MEN)

BENVOLIO: I pray thee, good Mercutio, let's retire:
The day is hot, the Capels are abroad,
And if we meet we shall not scape a brawl,
For now, these hot days, is the mad blood stirring.
MERCUTIO: Thou art like one of these fellows that, when the enters the
confines of a tavern, claps° me his sword upon the table, and says   ° places

---

5. Juliet appears to walk on air.

'God send me no need of thee!'; and by the operation° of the second cup draws him° on the drawer°, when indeed there is no need.

BENVOLIO: Am I like such a fellow?

MERCUTIO: Come, come, thou art as hot a Jack in thy mood° as any in Italy, and as soon moved to be moody, and as soon moody to be moved.

BENVOLIO: And what to?

MERCUTIO: Nay, an there were two such, we should have none shortly, for one would kill the other. Thou! Why, thou wilt quarrel with a man that hath a hair more, or a hair less, in his beard than thou hast. Thou wilt quarrel with a man for cracking nuts, having no other reason but because thou hast hazel eyes. What eye but such an eye would spy out such a quarrel? Thy head is as full of quarrels as an egg is full of meat°, and yet thy head hath been beaten as addle as an egg for quarrelling. Thou hast quarrelled with a man for coughing in the street, because he hath wakened thy dog that hath lain asleep in the sun. Didst thou not fall out with a tailor for wearing his new doublet° before Easter? with another for tying his new shoes with old riband? and yet thou wilt tutor me from quarrelling?

BENVOLIO: And I were so apt to quarrel as thou art, any man should buy the fee-simple° of my life for an hour and a quarter.

MERCUTIO: The fee-simple? O simple°!

(*Enter* TYBALT, PETRUCHIO *and others*)

BENVOLIO: By my head, here comes the Capulets.

MERCUTIO: By my heel°, I care not.

TYBALT: Follow me close, for I will speak to them.
Gentlemen, good den, a word with one of you.

MERCUTIO: And but one word with one of us? Couple it with something, make it a word and a blow.

TYBALT: You shall find me apt enough to that, sir, and you will give me occasion.

MERCUTIO: Could you not take some occasion° without giving?

TYBALT: Mercutio, thou consortest with Romeo.

MERCUTIO: Consort? what, dost thou make us minstrels⁶? And thou make minstrels of us, look to hear nothing but discords. Here's my fiddlestick°, here's that shall make you dance. 'Zounds°, consort!

BENVOLIO: We talk here in the public haunt of men:
Either withdraw unto some private place,
Or reason coldly of your grievances,
Or else depart°; here all eyes gaze on us.

MERCUTIO: Men's eyes were made to look, and let them gaze;
I will not budge for no man's pleasure, I.

(*Enter* ROMEO)

° effect

° his sword   ° tapster

° anger

° edible substance

° jacket

° complete ownership
° simple-minded

° disparaging remark

° excuse

° rapier   ° "By God's wounds".

° part company

6. Mercutio deliberately takes "consort," "keep company with," for the insulting "perform with minstrels."

TYBALT: Well, peace be with you, sir, here comes my man.

MERCUTIO: But I'll be hanged, sir, if he wear your livery°.
    Marry, go before° to field°, he'll be your follower;
    Your worship in that sense may call him man.

TYBALT: Romeo, the love I bear thee can afford
    No better term than this: thou art a villain°.

ROMEO: Tybalt, the reason that I have to love thee
    Doth much excuse the appertaining rage
    To such a greeting. Villain am I none;
    Therefore farewell, I see thou knowest me not.

TYBALT: Boy°, this shall not excuse the injuries
    That thou hast done me, therefore turn and draw.

ROMEO: I do protest I never injuried thee,
    But love thee better than thou canst devise°,
    Till thou shalt know the reason of my love:
    And so, good Capulet, which name I tender
    As dearly as mine own, be satisfied.

MERCUTIO: O calm, dishonourable, vile submission!
    'Alla stoccata' carries it away. (draws)[7]
    Tybalt, you rat-catcher, will you walk°?

TYBALT: What wouldst thou have with me?

MERCUTIO: Good King of Cats, nothing but one of your nine lives that I
    mean to make bold withal, and as you shall use me hereafter,
    dry-beat° the rest of the eight. Will you pluck your sword out of
    his pilcher° by the ears? Make haste, lest mine be about your ears
    ere it be out.

TYBALT: I am for you. (drawing)

ROMEO: Gentle Mercutio, put thy rapier up.

MERCUTIO: Come, sir, your 'passado'°.
    (They fight.)

ROMEO: Draw, Benvolio, beat down their weapons.
    Gentlemen, for shame forbear this outrage!
    Tybalt, Mercutio, the Prince expressly hath
    Forbid this bandying° in Verona streets.
    (ROMEO steps between them)
    Hold, Tybalt! Good Mercutio!
    (TYBALT under ROMEO's arm thrusts into MERCUTIO.
    Away TYBALT with his followers.)

MERCUTIO: I am hurt.
    A plague a'both houses! I am sped°.
    Is he gone and hath nothing?

BENVOLIO: What, art thou hurt?

MERCUTIO: Ay, ay, a scratch, a scratch, marry, 'tis enough.
    Where is my page? Go, villain°, fetch a surgeon.°

(Exit PAGE)

ROMEO: Courage, man, the hurt cannot be much.

---

7. Tybalt, nicknamed "Alla stoccata" (literally, at the thrust) by Mercutio, bests
Romeo.

Marginal glosses
° uniform
° lead the way   ° dueling place
° serious insult
° term of contempt
° imagine
° allusion to King of Cats
° thrash
° its scabbard
° thrust
° strife
° dispatched
° fellow   ° doctor

MERCUTIO: No, 'tis not so deep as a well, nor so wide as a church-door,
but 'tis enough, 'twill serve. Ask for me tomorrow, and you shall
find me a grave° man. I am peppered, I warrant, for this world. A   ° dead and buried
plague a' both your houses! 'Zounds, a dog, a rat, a mouse, a cat,
to scratch a man to death! a braggart, a rogue, a villain, that
fights by the book of arithmetic°. Why the dev'l came you between   ° textbook fencer
us? I was hurt under your arm.
ROMEO: I thought all for the best.
MERCUTIO: Help me into some house, Benvolio,
Or I shall faint. A plague a'both your houses!
They have made worms' meat of me. I have it,
And soundly too. Your houses!

(*Exit with* BENVOLIO)

ROMEO: This gentleman, the Prince's near ally°,   ° relative
My very° friend, hath got this mortal hurt   ° true
In my behalf; my reputation stained
With Tybalt's slander—Tybalt, that an hour
Hath been my cousin. O sweet Juliet,
Thy beauty hath made me effeminate,
And in my temper° softened valour's steel!   ° natural disposition

(*Enter* BENVOLIO)

BENVOLIO: O Romeo, Romeo, brave Mercutio is dead.
That gallant spirit hath aspired° the clouds,   ° mounted to
Which too untimely° here did scorn the earth.   ° prematurely
ROMEO: This day's black fate on moe days doth depend,
This but begins the woe others must end.

(*Enter* TYBALT)

BENVOLIO: Here comes the furious Tybalt back again.
ROMEO: Again, in triumph, and Mercutio slain?
Away to heaven, respective lenity°,   ° considered mildness
And fire-eyed fury be my conduct° now!   ° guide
Now, Tybalt, take the 'villain' back again
That late thou gavest me, for Mercutio's soul
Is but a little way above our heads,
Staying for thine to keep him company:
Either thou or I, or both, must go with him.
TYBALT: Thou wretched boy, that didst consort° him here,   ° associate
Shalt with him hence.
ROMEO: This° shall determine that°.   ° weapon   ° who accompanies Mercutio
(*They fight;* TYBALT *falls*)
BENVOLIO: Romeo, away, be gone!
The citizens are up°, and Tybalt slain.   ° in arms
Stand not amazed°, the Prince will doom thee death   ° filled with consternation
If thou art taken. Hence be gone, away!
ROMEO: O, I am fortune's fool.
BENVOLIO: Why dost thou stay?

(*Exit* ROMEO)

(*Enter citizens as* OFFICERS *of the Watch*)

OFFICER: Which way ran he that killed Mercutio?
    Tybalt, that murderer, which way ran he?
BENVOLIO: There lies that Tybalt.
OFFICER: Up, sir, go with me;
    I charge thee in the Prince's name obey.

(*Enter* PRINCE, *old* MONTAGUE, CAPULET, *their* WIVES, *and all.*)

PRINCE: Where are the vile beginners of this fray?
BENVOLIO: O noble prince, I can discover° all   ° reveal
    The unlucky manage° of this fatal brawl;   ° conduct
    There lies the man, slain by young Romeo,
    That slew thy kinsman, brave Mercutio.
LADY CAPULET: Tybalt, my cousin! O my brother's child!
    O Prince! O husband! O, the blood is spilled
    Of my dear kinsman. Prince, as thou art true,
    For blood of ours, shed blood of Montague.
    O cousin, cousin!
PRINCE: Benvolio, who began this bloody fray?
BENVOLIO: Tybalt, here slain, whom Romeo's hand did slay.
    Romeo, that spoke him fair, bid him bethink°   ° consider
    How nice° the quarrel was, and urgèd withal   ° trivial
    Your high displeasure; all this utterèd
    With gentle breath, calm look, knees humbly bowed,
    Could not take truce with the unruly spleen°   ° fiery anger
    Of Tybalt deaf to peace, but that he tilts
    With piercing steel at bold Mercutio's breast,
    Who, all as hot, turns deadly point to point,
    And with a martial scorn, with one hand beats
    Cold death aside, and with the other sends
    It back to Tybalt, whose dexterity
    Retorts it°. Romeo he cries aloud,   ° Returns the thrust
    'Hold, friends! friends, part!' and swifter than his tongue,
    His agile arm beats down their fatal points,
    And 'twixt them rushes; underneath whose arm
    An envious° thrust from Tybalt hit the life   ° malicious
    Of stout Mercutio, and then Tybalt fled;
    But by and by comes back to Romeo,
    Who had but newly entertained° revenge,   ° considered
    And to't they go like lightning, for ere I
    Could draw to part them, was stout° Tybalt slain;   ° strong
    And as he fell, did Romeo turn and fly.
    This is the truth, or let Benvolio die.
LADY CAPULET: He is a kinsman to the Montague,
    Affection° makes him false, he speaks not true[8]:   ° Partiality

---

8. Although Lady Capulet exaggerates the numbers—twenty needed to kill Tybalt—she rightly indicates some bias in Benvolio's account: he represents Romeo and Mercutio as defensive fighters and stresses Mercutio's kinship with the Prince.

Some twenty of them fought in this black strife,
And all those twenty could but kill one life.
I beg for justice, which thou, Prince, must give:
Romeo slew Tybalt, Romeo must not live.

PRINCE: Romeo slew him, he slew Mercutio;
Who now the price of his dear blood doth owe?

MONTAGUE: Not Romeo, Prince, he was Mercutio's friend;
His fault concludes but what the law should end,
The life of Tybalt.

PRINCE: And for that offence
Immediately we do exhile him hence.
I have an interest° in your hearts' proceeding: ° personal concern
My blood° for your rude brawls doth lie a-bleeding; ° Mercutio
But I'll amerce° you with so strong a fine   ° punish
That you shall all repent the loss of mine.
I will be deaf to pleading and excuses,
Nor tears nor prayers shall purchase° out abuses: ° make amends for
Therefore use none. Let Romeo hence in haste,
Else, when he is found, that hour is his last.
Bear hence° this body, and attend our will: ° Carry out
Mercy but murders, pardoning those that kill.

(*Exeunt*)

Act Three, Scene Two. Verona: Capulet's
house.

(*Enter* JULIET *alone*)

JULIET: Gallop apace, you fiery-footed steeds,
Towards Phoebus'° lodging; such a waggoner   ° sun-god's
As Phaëton° would whip you to the west[9],   ° sun god's son
And bring in cloudy night immediately.
Spread thy close° curtain, love-performing Night,   ° concealing
That runaways' eyes may wink, and Romeo
Leap to these arms, untalked of and unseen:
Lovers can see to do their amorous rites
By their own beauties, or if love be blind,
It best agrees with night. Come, civil° Night,   ° serious
Thou sober-suited matron all in black,
And learn° me how to lose a winning match,   ° teach
Played for a pair of stainless maidenhoods.
Hood my unmanned blood, bating in my cheeks,
With thy black mantle, till strange° love grow bold, ° unfamiliar, shy
Think true love acted simple modesty°.   ° chastity

---

9. Zeus was forced to kill Phaëton, son of Phoebus, when Phaëton lost control of
the sun-bearing chariot.

Come, Night, come, Romeo, come, thou day in night,
For thou wilt lie upon the wings of night,
Whiter than new snow upon a raven's back.
Come, gentle Night, come, loving, black-browed Night,
Give me my Romeo, and when I shall die,
Take him and cut him out in little stars,
And he will make the face of heaven so fine
That all the world will be in love with night,
And pay no worship to the garish° sun.　　　　　　　　　　　° showy
O, I have bought the mansion of a love,
But not possessed it, and though I am sold,
Not yet enjoyed. So tedious is this day
As is the night before some festival
To an impatient child that hath new robes
And may not wear them. O, here comes my Nurse,

(*Enter* NURSE, *with the ladder of cords in her lap*)

And she brings news, and every tongue that speaks
But Romeo's name speaks heavenly eloquence.
Now, Nurse, what news? What hast thou there? the cords
That Romeo bid thee fetch?
NURSE:　　　　　　　　　　　　　　Ay, ay, the cords.
　　(*throws them down*)
JULIET: Ay me, what news? Why dost thou wring thy hands?
NURSE: Ah weraday°, he's dead, he's dead, he's dead!　　　　° alas
　　We are undone, lady, we are undone.
　　Alack the day, he's gone, he's killed, he's dead!
JULIET: Can heaven be so envious°?　　　　　　　　　　° malicious
NURSE:　　　　　　　　　Romeo can,
　　Though heaven cannot. O Romeo, Romeo!
　　Who ever would have thought it? Romeo!
JULIET: What devil art thou that dost torment me thus?
　　This torture should be roared in dismal hell.
　　Hath Romeo slain himself? Say thou but 'ay',
　　And that bare vowel 'I' shall poison more
　　Than the death-darting eye of cockatrice°.　　　　　° basilisk
　　I am not I, if there be such an 'ay',
　　Or those eyes shut, that makes thee answer 'ay'.
　　If he be slain, say 'ay', or if not, 'no':
　　Brief sounds determine my weal or woe.
NURSE: I saw the wound, I saw it with mine eyes
　　(God save the mark!), here on his manly breast:
　　A piteous corse, a bloody piteous corse°,　　　　　° corpse
　　Pale, pale as ashes, all bedaubed in blood,
　　All in gore° blood; I sounded° at the sight.　　° thickened　° swooned
JULIET: O break, my heart, poor bankrout°, break at once!　° bankrupt
　　To prison, eyes, ne'er look on liberty!
　　Vile earth°, to earth resign°, end motion here,　° her body　° surrender
　　And thou and Romeo press one heavy bier!

NURSE: O Tybalt, Tybalt, the best friend I had!
    O courteous Tybalt, honest gentleman,
    That ever I should live to see thee dead!
JULIET: What storm is this that blows so contrary?
    Is Romeo slaughtered? and is Tybalt dead?
    My dearest cousin, and my dearer lord?
    Then, dreadful trumpet, sound the general doom°,   ° of the Last Judgment
    For who is living, if those two are gone?
NURSE: Tybalt is gone and Romeo banishèd,
    Romeo that killed him, he is banishèd.
JULIET: O God, did Romeo's hand shed Tybalt's blood?
NURSE: It did, it did, alas the day, it did!
JULIET: O serpent heart, hid with a flow'ring face!
    Did ever dragon keep° so fair a cave?   ° inhabit
    Beautiful tyrant, fiend angelical!
    Dove-feathered raven, wolvish-ravening lamb°!   ° wolf in sheep's clothing
    Despisèd substance of divinest show!
    Just opposite to what thou justly seem'st,
    A damnèd saint, an honourable villain!
    O nature, what hadst thou to do in hell
    When thou didst bower° the spirit of a fiend   ° lodge
    In mortal paradise of such sweet flesh?
    Was ever book containing such vile matter
    So fairly bound? O that deceit should dwell
    In such a gorgeous palace!
NURSE: There's no trust,
    No faith, no honesty in men, all perjured,
    All forsworn, all naught°, all dissemblers.   ° wicked
    Ah, where's my man? Give me some aqua-vitae°;   ° strong liquor
    These griefs, these woes, these sorrows make me old.
    Shame come to Romeo!
JULIET: Blistered be thy tongue
    For such a wish! he was not born to shame:
    Upon his brow shame is ashamed to sit;
    For 'tis a throne where honour may be crowned
    Sole monarch of the universal earth.
    O what a beast was I to chide at him!
NURSE: Will you speak well of him that killed your cousin?
JULIET: Shall I speak ill of him that is my husband?
    Ah, poor my lord, what tongue shall smooth° thy name,   ° make whole
    When I, thy three-hours wife, have mangled it?
    But wherefore, villain, didst thou kill my cousin?
    That villain cousin would have killed my husband.
    Back, foolish tears, back to your native spring,
    Your tributary drops° belong to woe,   ° tears paid as tribute
    Which you mistaking offer up to joy.
    My husband lives that Tybalt would have slain,
    And Tybalt's dead that would have slain my husband:
    All this is comfort, wherefore weep I then?
    Some word there was, worser than Tybalt's death,
    That murdered me; I would forget it fain,

But O, it presses to my memory,
Like damnèd guilty deeds to sinners' minds:
'Tybalt is dead, and Romeo banishèd.'
That 'banishèd', that one word 'banishèd',
Hath slain ten thousand Tybalts. Tybalt's death
Was woe enough if it had ended there;
Or if sour woe delights in fellowship,
And needly° will be ranked with other griefs,   ° necessarily
Why followed not, when she said 'Tybalt's dead',
'Thy father' or 'thy mother', nay, or both,
Which modern° lamentation might have moved?   ° ordinary
But with a rear-ward° following Tybalt's death,   ° rear-guard
'Romeo is banishèd'; to speak that word,
Is father, mother, Tybalt, Romeo, Juliet,
All slain, all dead. 'Romeo is banishèd!'
There is no end, no limit, measure, bound,
In that word's death, no words can that woe sound°.   ° express and fathom
Where is my father and my mother, Nurse?
NURSE: Weeping and wailing over Tybalt's corse.
    Will you go to them? I will bring you thither.
JULIET: Wash they his wounds with tears? mine shall be spent,
    When theirs are dry, for Romeo's banishment.
    Take up those cords. Poor ropes, you are beguiled°,   ° tricked, cheated
    Both you and I, for Romeo is exiled.
    He made you for a highway to my bed,
    But I, a maid, die maiden-widowèd.
    Come, cords, come, Nurse, I'll to my wedding bed,
    And death, not Romeo, take my maidenhead!
NURSE: Hie to your chamber. I'll find Romeo
    To comfort you, I wot° well where he is.   ° know
    Hark ye, your Romeo will be here at night.
    I'll to him, he is hid at Lawrence' cell.
JULIET: O find him! Give this ring to my true knight,
    And bid him come to take his last farewell.

(*Exeunt*)

Act Three, Scene Three. Verona: Friar Lawrence's cell.

(*Enter* FRIAR LAWRENCE)

FRIAR LAWRENCE: Romeo, come forth, come forth, thou fearful man:
    Affliction is enamoured of thy parts°,   ° endowments
    And thou art wedded to calamity.

(*Enter* ROMEO)

ROMEO: Father, what news? What is the Prince's doom°?   ° sentence
    What sorrow craves acquaintance at my hand,
    That I yet know not?

FRIAR LAWRENCE: Too familiar
     Is my dear son with such sour company!
     I bring thee tidings of the Prince's doom.
ROMEO: What less than doomsday° is the Prince's doom?   ° death
FRIAR LAWRENCE: A gentler judgement vanished° from his lips: ° issued without chance of recall
     Not body's death, but body's banishment.
ROMEO: Ha, banishment? be merciful, say 'death':
     For exile hath more terror in his look,
     Much more than death. Do not say 'banishment'!
FRIAR LAWRENCE: Here from Verona art thou banishèd.
     Be patient, for the world is broad and wide.
ROMEO: There is no world without° Verona walls,   ° outside
     But purgatory, torture, hell itself:
     Hence 'banishèd' is banished from the world,
     And world's exile° is death; then 'banishèd'   ° his exile from the world
     Is death mistermed°. Calling death 'banishèd',   ° called by the wrong name
     Thou cut'st my head off with a golden axe,
     And smilest upon the stroke that murders me.
FRIAR LAWRENCE: O deadly sin! O rude unthankfulness!
     Thy fault our law calls death, but the kind Prince,
     Taking thy part, hath rushed aside the law,
     And turned that black word 'death' to 'banishment'.
     This is dear° mercy, and thou seest it not.   ° precious
ROMEO: 'Tis torture, and not mercy. Heaven is here
     Where Juliet lives, and every cat and dog
     And little mouse, every unworthy thing,
     Live here in heaven, and may look on her,
     But Romeo may not. More validity°,   ° true worth
     More honourable state, more courtship lives°   ° courtly state
     In carrion flies than Romeo; they may seize
     On the white wonder of dear Juliet's hand,
     And steal immortal blessing from her lips,
     Who even in pure and vestal° modesty   ° virginal
     Still blush, as thinking their own kisses sin;
     But Romeo may not, he is banishèd.
     Flies may do this, but I from this must fly;
     They are free men, but I am banishèd:
     And sayest thou yet that exile is not death?
     Hadst thou no poison mixed, no sharp-ground knife,
     No sudden mean of death, though ne'er so mean,
     But 'banishèd' to kill me? 'Banishèd'?
     O Friar, the damnèd use that word in hell;
     Howling attends it. How hast thou the heart,
     Being a divine, a ghostly° confessor,   ° spiritual
     A sin-absolver, and my friend professed,
     To mangle me with that word 'banishèd'?
FRIAR LAWRENCE: Thou fond° mad man, hear me a little speak.   ° foolish
ROMEO: O thou wilt speak again of banishment.
FRIAR LAWRENCE: I'll give thee armour to keep off that word:
     Adversity's sweet milk, philosophy,
     To comfort thee though thou art banishèd.

ROMEO: Yet 'banishèd'? Hang up philosophy°?   ° Let philosophy hang itself!
    Unless philosophy can make a Juliet,
    Displant° a town, reverse a prince's doom°,   ° uproot ° sentence
    It helps not, it prevails not; talk no more.
FRIAR LAWRENCE: O then I see that mad men have no ears.
ROMEO: How should they when that wise men have no eyes?
FRIAR LAWRENCE: Let me dispute with thee of thy estate°.   ° discuss your situation
ROMEO: Thou canst not speak of that thou dost not feel.
    Wert thou as young as I, Juliet thy love,
    An hour but married, Tybalt murderèd,
    Doting like me, and like me banishèd,
    Then mightst thou speak, then mightst thou tear thy hair,
    And fall upon the ground as I do now,
    Taking the measure of an unmade grave.

(*Enter* NURSE *[within] and knocks*)

FRIAR LAWRENCE: Arise, one knocks. Good Romeo, hide thyself.
ROMEO: Not I, unless the breath of heart-sick groans
    Mist-like infold me from the search of eyes.
    (*knock*)
FRIAR LAWRENCE: Hark how they knock!—Who's there?—Romeo, arise,
    Thou wilt be taken.—Stay a while!—Stand up;
    (*loud knock*)
    Run to my study.—By and by°!—God's will,   ° in a moment
    What simpleness° is this?—I come, I come!   ° foolishness
    (*knock*)
    Who knocks so hard? whence come you? what's your will?
NURSE (*within*): Let me come in, and you shall know my errand:
    I come from Lady Juliet.
FRIAR LAWRENCE: Welcome then. (*unlocks the door*)

(*Enter* NURSE)

NURSE: O holy Friar, O tell me, holy Friar,
    Where's my lady's lord? where's Romeo?
FRIAR LAWRENCE: There on the ground, with his own tears made drunk.
NURSE: O he is even in my mistress' case,
    Just in her case. O woeful sympathy°!   ° similarity of suffering
    Piteous predicament! even so lies she,
    Blubb'ring and weeping, weeping and blubb'ring.
    Stand up, stand up, stand, and you be a man;
    For Juliet's sake, for her sake, rise and stand;
    Why should you fall into so deep an O°?   ° fit of groaning
ROMEO: Nurse! (*He rises.*)
NURSE: Ah, sir, ah, sir, death's the end of all.
ROMEO: Spakest thou of Juliet? how is it with her?
    Doth not she think me an old° murderer,   ° practiced
    Now I have stained the childhood of our joy
    With blood removed but little from her own?
    Where is she? and how doth she? and what says
    My concealed lady° to our cancelled love?   ° secret wife

NURSE: O she says nothing, sir, but weeps and weeps,
　　　And now falls on her bed, and then starts up,
　　　And Tybalt calls, and then on Romeo cries°,　　　　　　° exclaims against
　　　And then down falls again.
ROMEO:　　　　　　　　　　　As if that name,
　　　Shot from the deadly level° of a gun,　　　　　　　　° aim
　　　Did murder her, as that name's cursèd hand
　　　Murdered her kinsman. O tell me, Friar, tell me,
　　　In what vile part of this anatomy
　　　Doth my name lodge? Tell me, that I may sack
　　　The hateful mansion.

(He offers to stab himself, and NURSE *snatches the dagger away.)*

FRIAR LAWRENCE:　　　　　　　Hold thy desperate hand!
　　　Art thou a man? thy form cries out thou art;
　　　Thy tears are womanish, thy wild acts denote
　　　The unreasonable° fury of a beast.　　　　　　　　° irrational
　　　Unseemly woman in a seeming man,
　　　And ill-beseeming beast in seeming both,
　　　Thou hast amazed° me. By my holy order,　　　　　° astonished
　　　I thought thy disposition better tempered°.　　　　° balanced
　　　Hast thou slain Tybalt? wilt thou slay thyself,
　　　And slay thy lady that in thy life lives,
　　　By doing damnèd hate upon thyself?
　　　Why rail'st thou on thy birth? the heaven and earth°?　　° soul and body
　　　Since birth, and heaven, and earth, all three do meet
　　　In thee at once, which thou at once wouldst lose°.　　° through suicide
　　　Fie, fie, thou sham'st thy shape, thy love, thy wit°,　　° intellect
　　　Which° like a usurer abound'st in all,　　　　　　　° Who
　　　And usest none in that true use indeed
　　　Which should bedeck thy shape, thy love, thy wit:
　　　Thy noble shape is but a form of wax°,　　　　　　° waxwork figure
　　　Digressing from the valour of a man;
　　　Thy dear love sworn but hollow perjury,
　　　Killing that love which thou hast vowed to cherish;
　　　Thy wit, that ornament to shape and love,
　　　Misshapen° in the conduct° of them both,　　　　° Wrongly directed　° guidance
　　　Like powder in a skilless soldier's flask°,　　　　° powder horn
　　　Is set afire by thine own ignorance,
　　　And thou dismembered with thine own defence.
　　　What, rouse thee, man! thy Juliet is alive,
　　　For whose dear sake thou wast but lately dead:
　　　There art thou happy°. Tybalt would° kill thee,　　° fortunate　° wished to
　　　But thou slewest Tybalt: there art thou happy.
　　　The law that threatened death becomes thy friend,
　　　And turns it to exile: there art thou happy.
　　　A pack of blessings light upon thy back,
　　　Happiness courts thee in her best array,
　　　But like a mishavèd° and sullen wench,　　　　　° misbehaved
　　　Thou pouts upon thy fortune and thy love:

Take heed, take heed, for such die miserable.
Go get thee to thy love as was decreed°,   ° determined
Ascend her chamber, hence and comfort her;
But look thou stay not till the Watch be set,
For then thou canst not pass to Mantua,[1]
Where thou shalt live till we can find a time
To blaze° your marriage, reconcile your friends°,   ° proclaim ° relatives
Beg pardon of the Prince, and call thee back
With twenty hundred thousand times more joy
Than thou went'st forth in lamentation.
Go before, Nurse, commend me to thy lady,
And bid her hasten all the house to bed,
Which heavy sorrow makes them apt unto.
Romeo is coming.
NURSE: O Lord, I could have stayed here all the night
To hear good counsel. O, what learning is!
My lord, I'll tell my lady you will come.
ROMEO: Do so, and bid my sweet prepare to chide°.   ° reprimand him for Tybalt's death
NURSE: Here, sir, a ring she bid me give you, sir.
Hie you, make haste, for it grows very late.
ROMEO: How well my comfort is revived by this.

(*Exit* NURSE)

FRIAR LAWRENCE: Go hence, good night, and here stands all your state:
Either be gone before the Watch be set,
Or by the break of day disguised from hence.
Sojourn in Mantua; I'll find out your man,
And he shall signify from time to time
Every good hap to you that chances here.
Give me thy hand, 'tis late. Farewell, good night.
ROMEO: But that a joy past joy calls out on me,
It were a grief, so brief° to part with thee: ° hastily
Farewell.

(*Exeunt*)

Act Three, Scene Four. Verona: Capulet's
house.

(*Enter old* CAPULET, *his* WIFE, *and* PARIS)

CAPULET: Things have fall'n out°, sir, so unluckily   ° happened
That we have had no time to move° our daughter.   ° persuade
Look you, she loved her kinsman Tybalt dearly,
And so did I. Well, we were born to die.
'Tis very late, she'll not come down tonight.
I promise° you, but for your company,   ° assure
I would have been abed an hour ago.

---

1. The city gates would be closed at the same time the Watch was set.

PARIS: These times of woe afford no times to woo.
     Madam, good night, commend me to your daughter.
LADY CAPULET: I will, and know her mind early tomorrow;
     Tonight she's mewed up° to her heaviness.

(PARIS offers to go in, and CAPULET calls him again.)

CAPULET: Sir Paris, I will make a desperate tender°
     Of my child's love: I think she will be ruled
     In all respects by me; nay more, I doubt it not.
     Wife, go you to her ere you go to bed,
     Acquaint her here of my son° Paris' love,
     And bid her—mark you me°?—on Wednesday next—
     But soft, what day is this?
PARIS: Monday, my lord.
CAPULET: Monday, ha, ha[2]! Well, Wednesday is too soon,
     A'Thursday let it be—a'Thursday, tell her,
     She shall be married to this noble earl.
     Will you be ready? do you like this haste?
     Well, keep no great ado—a friend or two,
     For hark you, Tybalt being slain so late,
     It may be thought we held him carelessly,
     Being our kinsman, if we revel much:
     Therefore we'll have some half a dozen friends,
     And there an end. But what say you to Thursday?
PARIS: My lord, I would that Thursday were tomorrow.
CAPULET: Well, get you gone, a'Thursday° be it then.—
     Go you to Juliet ere you go to bed,
     Prepare her, wife, against° this wedding day.
     Farewell, my lord. Light to my chamber, ho!
     Afore me°, it is so very late that we
     May call it early by and by. Good night.

(Exeunt)

° shut up with her grief

° bold offer

° son-in-law to be
° are you paying attention?

° on

° in anticipation of

° mild oath

Act Three, Scene Five. Verona: Capulet's orchard.

(Enter ROMEO and JULIET aloft, as at the window)

JULIET: Wilt thou be gone? It is not yet near day:
     It was the nightingale, and not the lark,
     That pierced the fearful hollow of thine ear;
     Nightly she sings on yond pomegranate tree.
     Believe me, love, it was the nightingale.

---

2. "Ha, ha" indicates thoughtful reflection rather than mirth.

ROMEO: It was the lark, the herald of the morn,
No nightingale. Look, love, what envious° streaks   ° malicious
Do lace the severing clouds in yonder east:
Night's candles are burnt out, and jocund° day   ° cheerful
Stands tiptoe on the misty mountain tops.
I must be gone and live, or stay and die.
JULIET: Yond light is not daylight, I know it, I:
It is some meteor that the sun exhaled
To be to thee this night a torch-bearer,
And light thee on thy way to Mantua.
Therefore stay yet, thou need'st not to be gone.
ROMEO: Let me be tane°, let me be put to death,   ° taken
I am content, so thou wilt have it so.
I'll say yon grey is not the morning's eye,
'Tis but the pale reflex° of Cynthia's° brow;   ° reflection   ° moon's
Nor that is not the lark whose notes do beat
The vaulty heaven so high above our heads.
I have more care° to stay than will to go: ° concern
Come, death, and welcome! Juliet wills it so.
How is't, my soul? Let's talk, it is not day.
JULIET: It is, it is, hie hence, be gone, away!
It is the lark that sings so out of tune,
Straining harsh discords and unpleasing sharps.
Some say the lark makes sweet division:
This doth not so, for she divideth us.
Some say the lark and loathèd toad changed eyes;
O now I would they had changed voices too,
Since arm from arm that voice doth us affray°,   ° startle
Hunting thee hence with hunt's-up to the day.
O now be gone, more light and light it grows.
ROMEO: More light and light, more dark and dark our woes!

(*Enter* NURSE *hastily*)

NURSE: Madam!
JULIET: Nurse?
NURSE: Your lady mother is coming to your chamber.
The day is broke, be wary, look about.

(*Exit*)

JULIET: Then, window, let day in, and let life out.
ROMEO: Farewell, farewell! one kiss, and I'll descend.

(*He goes down.*)

JULIET: Art thou gone so, love, lord, ay husband, friend°?   ° lover
I must hear from thee every day in the hour,
For in a minute there are many days.
O, by this count I shall be much° in years   ° old
Ere I again behold my Romeo!
ROMEO (*from below*): Farewell!
I will omit no opportunity
That may convey my greetings, love, to thee.

JULIET: O think'st thou we shall ever meet again?
ROMEO: I doubt it not, and all these woes shall serve
    For sweet discourses in our times to come.
JULIET: O God, I have an ill-divining soul!
    Methinks I see thee now, thou art so low,
    As one dead in the bottom of a tomb.
    Either my eyesight fails, or thou look'st pale.
ROMEO: And trust me, love, in my eye so do you:
    Dry° sorrow drinks our blood. Adieu, adieu!   ° Thirsty
JULIET: O Fortune, Fortune, all men call thee fickle;
    If thou art fickle, what dost thou with him°   ° why are you concerned with him
    That is renowned for faith°? Be fickle, Fortune: ° steadfastness
    For then I hope thou wilt not keep him long,
    But send him back.

(*Enter* LADY CAPULET *below*)

LADY CAPULET: Ho, daughter, are you up?
JULIET: Who is't that calls? It is my lady mother.
    Is she not down so late, or up so early?
    What unaccustomed cause procures her hither?

(*She goes down from the window and enters below.*)

LADY CAPULET: Why how now, Juliet?
JULIET: Madam, I am not well.
LADY CAPULET: Evermore weeping for your cousin's death?
    What, wilt thou wash him from his grave with tears?
    And if thou couldst, thou couldst not make him live;
    Therefore have done. Some grief shows much of love,
    But much of grief shows still some want° of wit.   ° lack
JULIET: Yet let me weep for such a feeling° loss.   ° affecting
LADY CAPULET: So shall you feel the loss, but not the friend
    Which you weep for.
JULIET: Feeling so the loss,
    I cannot choose but ever weep the friend.
LADY CAPULET: Well, girl, thou weep'st not so much for his death
    As that the villain lives which slaughtered him.
JULIET: What villain, madam?
LADY CAPULET: That same villain Romeo.
JULIET (*aside*): Villain and he be many miles asunder.
    God pardon him, I do with all my heart:
    And yet no man like he doth grieve my heart.
LADY CAPULET: That is because the traitor murderer lives.
JULIET: Ay, madam, from the reach of these my hands.
    Would none but I might venge my cousin's death!
LADY CAPULET: We will have vengeance for it, fear thou not:
    Then weep no more. I'll send to one in Mantua,
    Where that same banished runagate° doth live,   ° fugitive
    Shall give him such an unaccustomed dram°   ° unusual draught
    That he shall soon keep Tybalt company;
    And then I hope thou wilt be satisfied.

JULIET: Indeed I never shall be satisfied
　　　With Romeo, till I behold him—dead—
　　　Is my poor heart, so for a kinsman vexed.
　　　Madam, if you could find out but a man
　　　To bear a poison, I would temper° it,　　　　　　　　　　　° compound; moderate
　　　That Romeo should upon receipt thereof
　　　Soon sleep in quiet. O how my heart abhors
　　　To hear him named and cannot come to him,
　　　To wreak the love I bore my cousin
　　　Upon his body that hath slaughtered him!
LADY CAPULET: Find thou the means, and I'll find such a man.
　　　But now I'll tell thee joyful tidings, girl.
JULIET: And joy comes well in such a needy time°.　　　　　　° time in need of joy
　　　What are they, beseech your ladyship?
LADY CAPULET: Well, well, thou hast a careful° father, child,　　° concerned
　　　One who, to put thee from thy heaviness,
　　　Hath sorted out° a sudden day of joy,　　　　　　　　　° selected
　　　That thou expects not, nor I looked not for.
JULIET: Madam, in happy time, what day is that?
LADY CAPULET: Marry, my child, early next Thursday morn,
　　　The gallant, young, and noble gentleman,
　　　The County Paris, at Saint Peter's Church,
　　　Shall happily make thee there a joyful bride.
JULIET: Now by Saint Peter's Church and Peter too,
　　　He shall not make me there a joyful bride.
　　　I wonder at this haste, that I must wed
　　　Ere he that should be husband comes to woo.
　　　I pray you tell my lord and father, madam,
　　　I will not marry yet, and when I do, I swear
　　　It shall be Romeo, whom you know I hate,
　　　Rather than Paris. These are news indeed!
LADY CAPULET: Here comes your father, tell him so yourself;
　　　And see how he will take it at your hands.

(*Enter* CAPULET *and* NURSE)

CAPULET: When the sun sets, the earth doth drizzle dew,
　　　But for the sunset of my brother's son
　　　It rains downright.
　　　How now, a conduit°, girl? What, still in tears?　　　　　° fountain
　　　Evermore show'ring? In one little body
　　　Thou counterfeits° a bark, a sea, a wind:　　　　　　　° imitates
　　　For still thy eyes, which I may call the sea,
　　　Do ebb and flow with tears; the bark thy body is,
　　　Sailing in this salt flood; the winds, thy sighs,
　　　Who, raging with thy tears and they with them,
　　　Without a sudden calm, will overset°　　　　　　　　　° overturn
　　　Thy tempest-tossèd body. How now, wife,
　　　Have you delivered to her our decree?
LADY CAPULET: Ay, sir, but she will none, she gives you thanks.
　　　I would the fool were married to her grave.

CAPULET: Soft, take me with you, take me with you°, wife.   ° let me understand you
How, will she none? doth she not give us thanks?
Is she not proud°? doth she not count her blest,   ° pleased
Unworthy as she is, that we have wrought°   ° persuaded
So worthy a gentleman to be her bride°?   ° bridegroom
JULIET: Not proud you have, but thankful that you have:
Proud can I never be of what I hate,
But thankful even for hate that is meant love.
CAPULET: How how, how how, chopt-logic? What is this?
'Proud', and 'I thank you', and 'I thank you not',
And yet 'not proud', mistress minion you°?   ° madam spoiled child
Thank me no thankings, nor proud me no prouds,
But fettle° your fine joints 'gainst Thursday next,   ° make ready
To go with Paris to Saint Peter's Church,
Or I will drag thee on a hurdle thither.
Out, you green-sickness carrion! out, you baggage°!   ° good-for-nothing
You tallow-face!
LADY CAPULET: Fie, fie, what, are you mad?
JULIET: Good father, I beseech you on my knees,
Hear me with patience but to speak a word.
CAPULET: Hang thee, young baggage°, disobedient wretch!   ° hussy
I tell thee what: get thee to church a 'Thursday,
Or never after look me in the face.
Speak not, reply not, do not answer me!
My fingers itch. Wife, we scarce thought us blest
That God had lent us but this only child,
But now I see this one is one too much,
And that we have a curse in having her.
Out on her°, hilding!   ° indicates indignant reproach
NURSE: God in heaven bless her!
You are to blame, my lord, to rate° her so.   ° berate
CAPULET: And why, my Lady Wisdom? Hold your tongue,
Good Prudence, smatter° with your gossips, go.   ° chatter
NURSE: I speak no treason.
CAPULET: O God-i-goden°!   ° exclamation of annoyance
NURSE: May not one speak?
CAPULET: Peace, you mumbling fool!
Utter your gravity° o'er a gossip's bowl,   ° wise advice
For here we need it not.
LADY CAPULET: You are too hot.
CAPULET: God's bread, it makes me mad! Day, night, work, play,
Alone, in company, still my care hath been
To have her matched; and having now provided
A gentleman of noble parentage,
Of fair demesnes°, youthful and nobly ligned°,   ° estates   ° noble lineage
Stuffed°, as they say, with honourable parts,   ° Crammed full
Proportioned as one's thought would wish a man,
And then to have a wretched puling fool,
A whining mammet°, in her fortune's tender,   ° doll
To answer 'I'll not wed, I cannot love;
I am too young, I pray you pardon me.'

126   WILLIAM SHAKESPEARE

But and you will not wed, I'll pardon you:
Graze where you will, you shall not house with me.
Look to't, think on't, I do not use° to jest.   ° am not accustomed
Thursday is near, lay hand on heart, advise:
And you be mine, I'll give you to my friend;
And you be not, hang, beg, starve, die in the streets,
For by my soul, I'll ne'er acknowledge thee,
Nor what is mine shall never do thee good.
Trust to't, bethink you, I'll not be forsworn.

(Exit)

JULIET: Is there no pity sitting in the clouds
That sees into the bottom of my grief?
O sweet my mother, cast me not away!
Delay this marriage for a month, a week,
Or if you do not, make the bridal bed
In that dim monument where Tybalt lies.
LADY CAPULET: Talk not to me, for I'll not speak a word.
Do as thou wilt, for I have done with thee.

(Exit)

JULIET: O God!—O Nurse, how shall this be prevented?
My husband is on earth, my faith in heaven;
How shall that faith return again to earth,
Unless that husband send it me from heaven
By leaving earth[3]? Comfort me, counsel me.
Alack, alack, that heaven should practise° stratagems   ° devise
Upon so soft° a subject as myself!   ° gentle
What say'st thou? hast thou not a word of joy?
Some comfort, Nurse.
NURSE: Faith, here it is:
Romeo is banished, and all the world to nothing
That he dares ne'er come back to challenge you;
Or if he do, it needs must be by stealth.
Then since the case so stands as now it doth,
I think it best you married with the County°.   ° Count
O, he's a lovely gentleman!
Romeo's a dishclout° to him. An eagle, madam,   ° dishrag
Hath not so green, so quick, so fair an eye
As Paris hath. Beshrew° my very heart,   ° Curse
I think you are happy in this second match,
For it excels your first, or if it did not,
Your first is dead, or 'twere as good he were
As living here and you no use of him.
JULIET: Speak'st thou from thy heart?
NURSE: And from my soul too, else beshrew° them both.   ° curse
JULIET: Amen.
NURSE: What?

---

3. Because Juliet's vow was sworn before God, she cannot marry again unless
Romeo dies.

JULIET: Well, thou hast comforted me marvellous much.
    Go in, and tell my lady I am gone,
    Having displeased my father, to Lawrence' cell,
    To make confession and to be absolved.
NURSE: Marry, I will, and this is wisely done.

(*Exit*)

JULIET (*she looks after* NURSE): Ancient damnation°! O most wicked   ° Cursed old woman
    fiend!
    Is it more sin to wish me thus forsworn,
    Or to dispraise my lord with that same tongue
    Which she hath praised him with above compare
    So many thousand times? Go, counsellor,
    Thou and my bosom° henceforth shall be twain.   ° secret thoughts
    I'll to the Friar to know his remedy;
    If all else fail, myself have power to die.

(*Exit*)

ACT FOUR

Act Four, Scene One. Verona: Friar Lawrence's cell.

(*Enter* FRIAR LAWRENCE *and* COUNTY PARIS)

FRIAR LAWRENCE: On Thursday, sir? the time is very short.
PARIS: My father Capulet will have it so,
    And I am nothing slow° to slack his haste.   ° have no reluctance
FRIAR LAWRENCE: You say you do not know the lady's mind?
    Uneven° is the course, I like it not.   ° Irregular
PARIS: Immoderately she weeps for Tybalt's death,
    And therefore have I little talked of love
    For Venus smiles not in a house of tears.
    Now, sir, her father counts it dangerous
    That she do give her sorrow so much sway;
    And in his wisdom hastes our marriage
    To stop the inundation of her tears,
    Which too much minded by herself alone°   ° too mind-consuming in solitude
    May be put from her by society°.   ° companionship
    Now do you know the reason of this haste.
FRIAR LAWRENCE (*aside*): I would I knew not why it should be slowed.—
    Look, sir, here comes the lady toward my cell.

(*Enter* JULIET)

PARIS: Happily met, my lady and my wife!
JULIET: That may be, sir, when I may be a wife.
PARIS: That 'may be' must be, love, on Thursday next.
JULIET: What must be shall be.
FRIAR LAWRENCE: That's a certain text.
PARIS: Come you to make confession to this father?
CAPULET: To answer that, I should confess to you.

PARIS: Do not deny to him that you love me.

JULIET: I will confess to you that I love him.

PARIS: So will ye, I am sure, that you love me.

JULIET: If I do so, it will be of more price°,   ° greater worth
    Being spoke behind your back, than to your face.

PARIS: Poor soul, thy face is much abused with tears.

JULIET: The tears have got small victory by that,
    For it was bad enough before their spite.

PARIS: Thou wrong's it more than tears with that report.

JULIET: That is no slander, sir, which is a truth,
    And what I spake, I spake it to my face.

PARIS: Thy face is mine, and thou hast slandered it.

JULIET: It may be so, for it is not mine own.
    Are you at leisure, holy father, now,
    Or shall I come to you at evening mass?

FRIAR LAWRENCE: My leisure serves me, pensive° daughter, now.   ° sad
    My lord, we must entreat the time alone.   ° forbid

PARIS: God shield I should disturb devotion!
    Juliet, on Thursday early will I rouse ye;
    Till then adieu, and keep this holy kiss.

(Exit)

JULIET: O shut the door, and when thou hast done so,
    Come weep with me, past hope, past cure, past help!

FRIAR LAWRENCE: O Juliet, I already know thy grief,
    It strains me past the compass° of my wits.   ° range
    I hear thou must, and nothing may prorogue° it,   ° delay
    On Thursday next be married to this County.

JULIET: Tell me not, Friar, that thou hearest of this,
    Unless thou tell me how I may prevent it.
    If in thy wisdom thou canst give no help,
    Do thou but call my resolution wise,
    And with this knife I'll help it presently.
    God joined my heart and Romeo's, thou our hands,
    And ere this hand, by thee to Romeo's sealed°,   ° contracted
    Shall be the label to another deed,
    Or my true heart with treacherous revolt
    Turn to another, this shall slay them both:
    Therefore, out of thy long-experienced time,
    Give me some present counsel, or, behold,
    'Twixt my extremes° and me this bloody knife   ° desperate situation
    Shall play the umpire, arbitrating that
    Which the commission of thy years and art
    Could to no issue° of true honour bring.   ° end
    Be not so long to speak, I long to die,
    If what thou speak'st speak not of remedy.

FRIAR LAWRENCE: Hold, daughter, I do spy a kind of hope,
    Which craves as desperate an execution
    As that is desperate which we would prevent.
    If, rather than to marry County Paris,
    Thou hast the strength of will to slay thyself,

Then is it likely thou wilt undertake
A thing like death to chide away this shame,
That cop'st with Death himself to scape from it;
And if thou dar'st, I'll give thee remedy.

JULIET: O bid me leap, rather than marry Paris,
From off the battlements of any tower,
Or walk in thievish ways°, or bid me lurk   ° lanes endangered by thieves
Where serpents are; chain me with roaring bears,
Or hide me nightly in a charnel-house[4],
O'ercovered quite with dead men's rattling bones,
With reeky shanks° and yellow chapless° skulls;   ° reeking shinbones   ° jawless
Or bid me go into a new-made grave,
And hide me with a dead man in his shroud—
Things that to hear them told have made me tremble—
And I will do it without fear or doubt,
To live an unstained wife to my sweet love.

FRIAR LAWRENCE: Hold then, go home, be merry, give consent
To marry Paris. Wednesday is tomorrow;
Tomorrow night look that thou lie alone,
Let not the Nurse lie with thee in thy chamber.
Take thou this vial, being then in bed,
And this distilling° liquor drink thou off,   ° permeating the body
When presently through all thy veins shall run
A cold and drowsy humour°; for no pulse   ° liquid
Shall keep his native progress, but surcease°;   ° cease
No warmth, no breath shall testify thou livest;
The roses in thy lips and cheeks shall fade
To wanny° ashes, thy eyes' windows° fall,   ° pale   ° shutters
Like Death when he shuts up the day of life;
Each part, deprived of supple government°,   ° muscular control
Shall stiff and stark° and cold appear like death,   ° rigid
And in this borrowed likeness of shrunk death
Thou shalt continue two and forty hours,
And then awake as from a pleasant sleep.
Now when the bridegroom in the morning comes
To rouse thee from thy bed, there art thou dead.
Then as the manner of our country is,
In thy best robes, uncovered on the bier,
Thou shall be borne to that same ancient vault
Where all the kindred of the Capulets lie.
In the mean time, against° thou shalt awake,   ° in anticipation of
Shall Romeo by my letters know our drift°,   ° intent
And hither shall he come, and he and I
Will watch thy waking, and that very night
Shall Romeo bear thee hence to Mantua.
And this shall free thee from this present shame,
If no inconstant toy°, nor womanish fear,   ° capricious state of mind
Abate thy valour in the acting it.

---

4. *Charnel house:* a building, room, or vault in which the bones or bodies of the
dead are placed.

JULIET: Give me, give me! O tell not me of fear.

FRIAR LAWRENCE: Hold, get you gone, be strong and prosperous
    In this resolve; I'll send a friar with speed
    To Mantua, with my letters to thy lord.

JULIET: Love give me strength, and strength shall help afford.
    Farewell, dear father.

(*Exeunt*)

Act Four, Scene Two. Verona: Capulet's house.

(*Enter* CAPULET, LADY CAPULET, NURSE, *and* SERVINGMEN, *two or three*)

CAPULET: So many guests invite as here are writ.

(*Exit* SERVINGMAN)

    Sirrah, go hire me twenty cunning° cooks.   ° skilled

SERVINGMAN: You shall have none ill°, sir, for I'll try° if they can lick their   ° no bad ones ° observe
    fingers.

CAPULET: How canst thou try° them so?   ° test

SERVINGMAN: Marry, sir, 'tis an ill cook that cannot lick his own fingers;
    therefore he that cannot lick his fingers goes not with me.

CAPULET: Go, be gone.

(*Exit* SERVINGMAN)

    We shall be much unfurnished° for this time.   ° unprepared
    What, is my daughter gone to Friar Lawrence?

NURSE: Ay forsooth.

CAPULET: Well, he may chance to do some good on her.
    A peevish self-willed harlotry° it is.   ° hussy

(*Enter* JULIET)

NURSE: See where she comes from shrift° with merry look.   ° confession

CAPULET: How now, my headstrong, where have you been gadding?

JULIET: Where I have learnt me to repent the sin
    Of disobedient opposition
    To you and your behests°, and am enjoined   ° commands
    By holy Lawrence to fall prostrate here
    To beg your pardon.
    (*She kneels down*)
                Pardon, I beseech you!
    Henceforward I am ever ruled by you.

CAPULET: Send for the County, go tell him of this.
    I'll have this knot knit up tomorrow morning.

JULIET: I met the youthful lord at Lawrence's cell,
    And gave him what becomèd° love I might,   ° befitting
    Not stepping o'er the bounds of modesty.

CAPULET: Why, I am glad on't, this is well, stand up.
    This is as't should be. Let me see the County;

Ay, marry, go, I say, and fetch him hither.
Now afore God, this reverend holy Friar,
All our whole city is much bound° to him.   ° beholden
JULIET: Nurse, will you go with me into my closet°,   ° private sitting room
To help me sort° such needful ornaments   ° choose
As you think fit to furnish me tomorrow?
LADY CAPULET: No, not till Thursday, there is time enough.
CAPULET: Go, Nurse, go with her, we'll to church tomorrow.

(*Exeunt* JULIET *and* NURSE)

LADY CAPULET: We shall be short in our provision,
'Tis now near night.
CAPULET: Tush, I will stir about,
And all things shall be well, I warrant thee, wife:
Go thou to Juliet, help to deck up her;
I'll not to bed tonight; let me alone°,   ° leave everything to me
I'll play the huswife° for this once. What ho!   ° housewife
They are all forth. Well, I will walk myself
To County Paris, to prepare up him
Against tomorrow. My heart is wondrous light,
Since this same wayward girl is so reclaimed.

(*Exeunt*)

Act Four, Scene Three. Verona: Capulet's house.

(*Enter* JULIET *and* NURSE)

JULIET: Ay, those attires are best, but, gentle Nurse,
I pray thee leave me to myself tonight:
For I have need of many orisons°   ° prayers
To move the heavens to smile upon my state°,   ° condition
Which, well thou knowest, is cross° and full of sin.   ° perverse

(*Enter* LADY CAPULET)

LADY CAPULET: What, are you busy, ho? need you my help?
JULIET: No, madam, we have culled° such necessaries   ° picked out
As are behoveful° for our state° tomorrow.   ° needful   ° public ceremony
So please you, let me now be left alone,
And let the Nurse this night sit up with you,
For I am sure you have your hands full all,
In this so sudden business.
LADY CAPULET: Good night.
Get thee to bed and rest, for thou hast need.

(*Exeunt* LADY CAPULET *and* NURSE)

JULIET: Farewell! God knows when we shall meet again.
I have a faint cold fear thrills° through my veins   ° pierces
That almost freezes up the heat of life:
I'll call them back again to comfort me.

Nurse!—What should she do here?
My dismal° scene I needs must act alone.   ° fatal
Come, vial.
What if this mixture do not work at all?
Shall I be married then tomorrow morning?
No, no, this shall forbid it; lie thou there.
(*laying down her dagger*)
What if it be a poison which the Friar
Subtly hath ministered to have me dead,
Lest in this marriage he should be dishonoured,
Because he married me before to Romeo?
I fear it is, and yet methinks it should not,
For he hath still been tried° a holy man.   ° proved
How if, when I am laid into the tomb,
I wake before the time that Romeo
Come to redeem me? There's a fearful point!
Shall I not then be stifled in the vault,
To whose foul mouth no healthsome air breathes in,
And there die strangled ere my Romeo comes?
Or if I live, it is not very like
The horrible conceit° of death and night,   ° conception
Together with the terror of the place—
As in a vault, an ancient receptacle,
Where for this many hundred years the bones
Of all my buried ancestors are packed,
Where bloody Tybalt, yet but green in earth°,   ° newly buried
Lies fest'ring in his shroud, where, as they say,
At some hours in the night spirits resort—
Alack, alack, is it not like that I,
So early waking—what with loathsome smells,
And shrieks like mandrakes⁵ torn out of the earth,
That living mortals hearing them run mad—
O, if I wake, shall I not be distraught,
Environèd° with all these hideous fears,   ° Surrounded
And madly play with my forefathers' joints,
And pluck the mangled Tybalt from his shroud,
And in this rage, with some great kinsman's bone,
As with a club, dash out my desp'rate brains?
O look! methinks I see my cousin's ghost
Seeking out Romeo that did spit his body
Upon a rapier's point. Stay, Tybalt, stay°!   ° stop
Romeo, Romeo, Romeo! Here's drink—I drink to thee.

(*She falls upon her bed, within the curtains.*)

---

5. The mandrake, with fleshy, forked roots, supposedly resembled a man. The
shriek of the mandrake, when it was pulled from the earth, caused death or madness to those that heard it.

Act Four, Scene Four. Scene continues.

(*Enter* LADY CAPULET *and* NURSE)

LADY CAPULET: Hold, take these keys and fetch more spices, Nurse.
NURSE: They call for dates and quinces in the pastry.

(*Enter old* CAPULET)

CAPULET: Come, stir, stir, stir! the second cock hath crowed,
    The curfew bell hath rung, 'tis three a'clock.
    Look to the baked meats°, good Angelica,   ° meat pies
    Spare not for cost.
NURSE: Go, you cot-quean°, go,   ° man who plays housewife
    Get you to bed. Faith, you'll be sick tomorrow
    For this night's watching°.   ° staying awake
CAPULET: No, not a whit. What, I have watched ere now
    All night for lesser cause, and ne'er been sick.
LADY CAPULET: Ay, you have been a mouse-hunt° in your time,   ° woman chaser
    But I will watch you from such watching now.

(*Exeunt* LADY CAPULET *and* NURSE)

CAPULET: A jealous hood, a jealous hood°!   ° jealous person

(*Enter three or four* SERVINGMEN *with spits and logs and baskets*)

                  Now, fellow,
    What is there?
FIRST SERVINGMAN: Things for the cook, sir, but I know not what.
CAPULET: Make haste, make haste.

(*Exit* FIRST SERVINGMAN)

               Sirrah, fetch drier logs.
    Call Peter, he will show thee where they are.
SECOND SERVINGMAN: I have a head, sir, that will find out logs,
    And never trouble Peter for the matter.
CAPULET: Mass, and well said, a merry whoreson, ha!
    Thou shalt be loggerhead°.   ° leader of loggers; blockhead

(*Exeunt* SECOND SERVINGMAN *and any others*)

                Good faith, 'tis day.
    The County will be here with music straight°,   ° immediately
    For so he said he would.
    (*play music within*)
              I hear him near.
    Nurse! Wife! What ho! What, Nurse, I say!

(*Enter* NURSE)

    Go waken Juliet, go and trim her up,
    I'll go and chat with Paris. Hie, make haste,
    Make haste, the bridegroom he is come already,
    Make haste, I say.

(*Exit*)

Act Four, Scene Five. Scene continues.

NURSE: Mistress, what mistress! Juliet! Fast°, I warrant her, she.   ° Fast asleep
    Why, lamb! why, lady! fie, you slug-a-bed!
    Why, love I say! madam! sweet heart! why, bride!
    What, not a word? You take your pennyworths° now;   ° small quantities
    Sleep for a week, for the next night I warrant
    The County Paris hath set up his rest
    That you shall rest but little. God forgive me!
    Marry and amen! How sound is she asleep!
    I needs must wake her. Madam, madam, madam!
    Ay, let the County take you in your bed,
    He'll fright you up, i'faith. Will it not be?
    (*draws back the curtains*)
    What, dressed, and in your clothes, and down again?
    I must needs wake you. Lady, lady, lady!
    Alas, alas! Help, help! my lady's dead!
    O weraday° that ever I was born!   ° alas
    Some aqua-vitae°, ho! My lord! My lady!   ° strong liquor

(*Enter* LADY CAPULET)

LADY CAPULET: What noise is here?
NURSE: O lamentable day!
LADY CAPULET: What is the matter?
NURSE: Look, look! O heavy day!
LADY CAPULET: O me, O me, my child, my only life!
    Revive, look up, or I will die with thee.
    Help, help! Call help.

(*Enter* CAPULET)

CAPULET: For shame, bring Juliet forth, her lord is come.
NURSE: She's dead, deceased, she's dead, alack the day!
LADY CAPULET: Alack the day, she's dead, she's dead, she's dead!
CAPULET: Hah, let me see her. Out alas, she's cold,
    Her blood is settled, and her joints are stiff:
    Life and these lips have long been separated;
    Death lies on her like an untimely frost
    Upon the sweetest flower of all the field.
NURSE: O lamentable day!
LADY CAPULET: O woeful time!
CAPULET: Death that hath tane° her hence to make me wail   ° taken
    Ties up my tongue and will not let me speak.

(*Enter* FRIAR LAWRENCE *and the* COUNTY PARIS *with the* MUSICIANS)

FRIAR LAWRENCE: Come, is the bride ready to go to church?
CAPULET: Ready to go, but never to return.—
    O son, the night before thy wedding day
    Hath Death lain with thy wife. There she lies,
    Flower as she was, deflowerèd by him.
    Death is my son-in-law, Death is my heir,

My daughter he hath wedded. I will die,
And leave him all; life, living°, all is Death's.
PARIS: Have I thought long° to see this morning's face,
And doth it give me such a sight as this?
LADY CAPULET: Accursed, unhappy, wretched, hateful day!
Most miserable hour that e'er time saw
In lasting° labour of his pilgrimage!
But one, poor one, one poor and loving child,
But one thing to rejoice and solace in,
And cruel Death hath catched° it from my sight!
NURSE: O woe! O woeful, woeful, woeful day!
Most lamentable day, most woeful day
That ever, ever, I did yet behold!
O day, O day, O day, O hateful day!
Never was seen so black a day as this.
O woeful day, O woeful day!
PARIS: Beguiled, divorcèd, wrongèd, spited, slain!
Most detestable Death, by thee beguiled,
By cruel, cruel thee quite overthrown!
O love! O life! not life, but love in death!
CAPULET: Despised, distressèd, hated, martyred, killed!
Uncomfortable° time, why cam'st thou now
To murder, murder our solemnity°?
O child, O child! my soul, and not my child!
Dead art thou. Alack, my child is dead,
And with my child my joys are burièd.
FRIAR LAWRENCE: Peace ho, for shame! Confusion's° cure lives not
In these confusions°. Heaven and yourself
Had part in this fair maid, now heaven hath all,
And all the better is it for the maid:
Your part in her you could not keep from death,
But heaven keeps his part in eternal life.
The most you sought was her promotion°,
For 'twas your heaven she should be advanced°,
And weep ye now, seeing she is advanced
Above the clouds, as high as heaven itself?
O, in this love, you love your child so ill
That you run mad, seeing that she is well.
She's not well married that lives married long,
But she's best married that dies married young.
Dry up your tears, and stick your rosemary°
On this fair corse, and as the custom is,
And in her best array, bear her to church;
For though fond nature bids us all lament,
Yet nature's tears are reason's merriment.
CAPULET: All things that we ordainèd festival,
Turn from their office° to black funeral:
Our instruments to melancholy bells,
Our wedding cheer to a sad burial feast;
Our solemn hymns to sullen dirges change;

° property
° been impatient

° ceaseless

° snatched

° Comfortless
° festivity

° Ruin's
° outbursts

° material advancement
° socially promoted

° herb signifying remembrance

° function

Our bridal flowers serve for a buried corse;
And all things change them to the contrary.
FRIAR LAWRENCE: Sir, go you in, and, madam, go with him,
And go, Sir Paris. Every one prepare
To follow this fair corse unto her grave.
The heavens do low'r upon you for some ill;
Move them no more by crossing their high will.

(*All but the* NURSE *and the* MUSICIANS *go forth, casting rosemary on her, and shutting the curtains.*)

FIRST MUSICIAN: Faith, we may put up° our pipes and be gone. ° pack up
NURSE: Honest good fellows, ah put up, put up,
For well you know this is a pitiful case.

(*Exit*)

FIRST MUSICIAN: Ay, by my troth, the case may be amended.

(*Enter* PETER)

PETER: Musicians, O musicians, 'Heart's ease', 'Heart's ease'°! O, and   ° a ballad tune
you will have me live, play 'Heart's ease'.
FIRST MUSICIAN: Why 'Heart's ease'?
PETER: O musicians, because my heart itself plays 'My heart is full'.°   ° ballad
O play me some merry dump° to comfort me.   ° mournful song
MUSICIANS: Not a dump we, 'tis no time to play now.
PETER: You will not then?
FIRST MUSICIAN: No.
PETER: I will then give it you soundly.
FIRST MUSICIAN: What will you give us?
PETER: No money, on my faith, but the gleek°; I will give° you the   ° gibe   ° nickname
minstrel°.   ° worthless fellow
FIRST MUSICIAN: Then will I give you the serving-creature.°   ° derogatory reply
PETER: Then will I lay the serving-creature's dagger on your pate. I will
carry no crotchets°, I'll re you, I'll fa you⁶. Do you note° me?   ° endure no whims   ° mark
FIRST MUSICIAN: And you re us and fa us, you note us.
SECOND MUSICIAN: Pray you put up your dagger, and put out your wit.
PETER: Then have at you with my wit! I will dry-beat° you with an iron   ° thrash
wit, and put up my iron dagger. Answer me like men:
'When griping griefs the heart doth wound,
And doleful dumps the mind oppress,
Then music with her silver sound—'
Why 'silver sound'? why 'music with her silver sound'? What say
you, Simon Catling?⁷

---

6. The notes on the scale double as insulting verbs: "re" puns on "ray" and "beray"
(befoul), and "fa" on "fay" (cleanse).
7. Presumably Peter derives the musicians' surnames from their instruments. A
"catling" is a cat-gut lute string.

FIRST MUSICIAN: Marry, sir, because silver hath a sweet sound.

PETER: Prates! What say you, Hugh Rebeck?[8]

SECOND MUSICIAN: I say 'silver sound' because musicians sound° for silver.   ° play

PETER: Prates! What say you, Hugh Rebeck?[8]

THIRD MUSICIAN: Faith, I know not what to say.

PETER: O, I cry you mercy°, you are the singer; I will say for you: It is   ° beg your pardon
    'music with her silver sound' because musicians have no gold for
    sounding.
        'Then music with her silver sound
        With speedy help doth lend redress.'

(*Exit*)

FIRST MUSICIAN: What a pestilent knave is this same!

SECOND MUSICIAN: Hang him, Jack! Come, we'll in here, tarry for the   ° wait till dinner is served
    mourners, and stay dinner°.

(*Exeunt*)

ACT FIVE

Act Five, Scene One. Mantua: a street.

(*Enter* ROMEO)

ROMEO: If I may trust the flattering° truth of sleep,   ° gratifying
    My dreams presage some joyful news at hand.
    My bosom's lord° sits lightly in his throne°,   ° love (Cupid)   ° heart
    And all this day an unaccustomed spirit
    Lifts me above the ground with cheerful thoughts.
    I dreamt my lady came and found me dead
    (Strange dream that gives a dead man leave to think!),
    And breathed such life with kisses in my lips
    That I revived and was an emperor.

    When but love's shadows° are so rich in joy!   ° dreams

(*Enter* ROMEO's *man,* BALTHASAR, *booted*)

    News from Verona! How now, Balthasar?
    Dost thou not bring me letters from the Friar?
    How doth my lady? Is my father well?
    How doth my Juliet? That I ask again,
    For nothing can be ill if she be well.

BALTHASAR: Then she is well and nothing can be ill:
    Her body sleeps in Capels' monument,
    And her immortal part with angels lives
    I saw her laid low in her kindred's vault,
    And presently took post° to tell it you.   ° hired post horses

---

8. Hugh Rebeck is named for an early, three-stringed fiddle.
9. A soundpost is part of the internal structural support of an instrument like the
violin.

O pardon me for bringing these ill news,
Since you did leave it for my office°, sir.   ° duty
ROMEO: Is it e'en so? then I defy you, stars!
    Thou knowest my lodging, get me ink and paper,
    And hire post-horses; I will hence tonight.
BALTHASAR: I do beseech you, sir, have patience:
    Your looks are pale and wild, and do import
    Some misadventure.
ROMEO: Tush, thou are deceived.
    Leave me, and do the thing I bid thee do.
    Hast thou no letters to me from the Friar?
BALTHASAR: No, my good lord.
ROMEO: No matter, get thee gone,
    And hire those horses; I'll be with thee straight.

(*Exit* BALTHASAR)

    Well, Juliet, I will lie with thee tonight.
    Let's see for means°. O mischief, thou art swift   ° think how to do it
    To enter in the thoughts of desperate men!
    I do remember an apothecary,
    And hereabouts 'a dwells, which late I noted
    In tattered weeds°, with overwhelming brows,   ° clothes
    Culling of simples°; meagre were his looks,   ° Gathering herbs
    Sharp misery had worn him to the bones;
    And in his needy shop a tortoise hung,
    An alligator stuffed, and other skins
    Of ill-shaped fishes, and about his shelves
    A beggarly account° of empty boxes,   ° poor store
    Green earthen pots, bladders, and musty seeds,
    Remnants of packthread°, and old cakes of roses°   ° twine   ° compressed rose petals
    Were thinly scattered, to make up a show.
    Noting this penury, to myself I said,
    'And if a man did need a poison now,
    Whose sale is present death° in Mantua,   ° punishable by death
    Here lives a caitiff° wretch would sell it him.'   ° miserable
    O this same thought did but forerun my need,
    And this same needy man must sell it me.
    As I remember, this should be the house.
    Being holiday, the beggar's shop is shut.
    What ho, apothecary!

(*Enter* APOTHECARY)

APOTHECARY: Who calls so loud?
ROMEO: Come hither, man. I see that thou art poor.
    Hold, there is forty ducats°; let me have   ° gold coins
    A dram of poison, such soon-speeding gear
    As will disperse itself through all the veins,
    That the life-weary taker may fall dead,
    And that the trunk may be discharged of breath
    As violently as hasty powder fired
    Doth hurry from the fatal cannon's womb.

APOTHECARY: Such mortal drugs I have, but Mantua's law
    Is death to any he that utters° them.   ° sells
ROMEO: Art thou so bare and full of wretchedness,
    And fearest to die? Famine is in thy cheeks,
    Need and oppression° starveth in thy eyes,   ° oppressive need
    Contempt and beggary hangs upon thy back;
    The world is not thy friend, nor the world's law,
    The world affords no law to make thee rich;
    Then be not poor, but break it° and take this.   ° the law
APOTHECARY: My poverty, but not my will, consents.
ROMEO: I pay thy poverty and not thy will.
APOTHECARY: Put this in any liquid thing you will
    And drink it off, and if you had the strength
    Of twenty men, it would dispatch you straight.
ROMEO: There is thy gold, worse poison to men's souls,
    Doing more murder in this loathsome world,
    Than these poor compounds that thou mayst not sell.
    I sell thee poison, thou hast sold me none.
    Farewell, buy food, and get thyself in flesh°.   ° get fat

(*Exit* APOTHECARY)

    Come, cordial° and not poison, go with me   ° heart-invigorating medicine
    To Juliet's grave, for there must I use thee.

(*Exit*)

Act Five, Scene Two. Verona: Friar Lawrence's cell.

(*Enter* FRIAR JOHN)

FRIAR JOHN: Holy Franciscan Friar, brother, ho!

(*Enter* FRIAR LAWRENCE)

FRIAR LAWRENCE: This same should be the voice of Friar John.
    Welcome from Mantua. What says Romeo?
    Or if his mind be writ, give me his letter.
FRIAR JOHN: Going to find a barefoot brother out,
    One of our order, to associate me°,   ° act as a companion
    Here in this city visiting the sick,
    And finding him, the searchers of the town°,   ° health officials
    Suspecting that we both were in a house
    Where the infectious pestilence did reign,
    Sealed up the doors, and would not let us forth,
    So that my speed° to Mantua there was stayed.   ° successful performance
FRIAR LAWRENCE: Who bare my letter then to Romeo?
FRIAR JOHN: I could not send it—here it is again—
    Nor get a messenger to bring it thee,
    So fearful were they of infection.
FRIAR LAWRENCE: Unhappy fortune! By my brotherhood,
    The letter was not nice° but full of charge°,   ° trivial ° serious matters

Of dear import°, and the neglecting it   ° important consequences
May do much danger. Friar John, go hence,
Get me an iron crow° and bring it straight   ° crowbar
Unto my cell.

FRIAR JOHN: Brother, I'll go and bring it thee.

(*Exit*)

FRIAR LAWRENCE: Now must I to the monument alone,
Within this three hours will fair Juliet wake.
She will beshrew° me much that Romeo   ° reprove
Hath had no notice of these accidents°;   ° happenings
But I will write again to Mantua,
And keep her at my cell till Romeo come,
Poor living corse, closed in a dead man's tomb!

(*Exit*)

Act Five, Scene Three. Verona: a churchyard.

(*Enter* PARIS *and his* PAGE *with flowers and sweet water and a torch*)

PARIS: Give me thy torch, boy. Hence, and stand aloof.°   ° at a distance
Yet put it out, for I would not be seen.
Under yond yew trees lay thee all along°,   ° lie flat on the ground
Holding thy ear close to the hollow ground,
So shall no foot upon the churchyard tread,
Being loose, unfirm with digging up of graves,
But thou shalt hear it. Whistle then to me
As signal that thou hear'st something approach.
Give me those flowers. Do as I bid thee, go.

PAGE (*aside*): I am almost afraid to stand° alone   ° stay
Here in the churchyard, yet I will adventure. (*retires*)

(PARIS *strews the tomb with flowers.*)

PARIS: Sweet flower, with flowers thy bridal bed I strew—
O woe, thy canopy is dust and stones!—
Which with sweet water nightly I will dew,
Or wanting that, with tears distilled by moans.
The obsequies° that I for thee will keep   ° rites for the dead
Nightly shall be to strew thy grave and weep.

(*The* PAGE *whistles.*)

The boy gives warning, something doth approach.
What cursèd foot wanders this way tonight,
To cross° my obsequies and true love's rite?   ° thwart
What, with a torch? Muffle me, night, a while. (*retires*)

(*Enter* ROMEO *and* BALTHASAR *with a torch, a mattock, and a crow bar*)

ROMEO: Give me that mattock and the wrenching iron.°   ° pick-axe and crow-bar
   Hold, take this letter; early in the morning
   See thou deliver it to my lord and father.
   Give me the light. Upon thy life I charge thee,
   What e'er thou hear'st or seest, stand all aloof°,   ° at a distance
   And do not interrupt me in my course.
   Why I descend into this bed of death
   Is partly to behold my lady's face,
   But chiefly to take thence from her dead finger
   A precious ring, a ring that I must use
   In dear employment°; therefore hence, be gone.   ° personally important
   But if thou, jealous°, dost return to pry   ° suspicious
   In what I farther shall intend to do,
   By heaven, I will tear thee joint by joint,
   And strew this hungry churchyard with thy limbs.
   The time and my intents are savage-wild,
   More fierce and more inexorable far
   Than empty tigers or the roaring sea.
BALTHASAR: I will be gone, sir, and not trouble ye.
ROMEO: So shalt thou show me friendship. Take thou that,
   Live and be prosperous, and farewell, good fellow.
BALTHASAR (*aside*): For all this same, I'll hide me hereabout,
   His looks I fear, and his intents I doubt. (*retires*)
ROMEO: Thou detestable maw, thou womb° of death,   ° belly
   Gorged with the dearest morsel of the earth°,   ° Juliet
   Thus I enforce thy rotten jaws to open,
   And in despite I'll cram thee with more food°.   ° himself

(ROMEO *begins to open the tomb.*)

PARIS: This is that banished haughty Montague,
   That murdered my love's cousin, with which grief
   It is supposèd the fair creature died,
   And here is come to do some villainous shame
   To the dead bodies. I will apprehend° him. (*steps forth*)   ° arrest
   Stop thy unhallowed toil, vile Montague!
   Can vengeance be pursued further than death?
   Condemnèd villain, I do apprehend thee.
   Obey and go with me, for thou must die.
ROMEO: I must indeed, and therefore came I hither.
   Good gentle youth, tempt not a desp'rate man,
   Fly hence and leave me. Think upon these gone,
   Let them affright thee. I beseech thee, youth,
   Put not another sin upon my head,
   By urging me to fury: O be gone!
   By heaven, I love thee better than myself,
   For I come hither armed against myself.
   Stay not, be gone; live, and hereafter say,
   A madman's mercy bid thee run away.

142   WILLIAM SHAKESPEARE

PARIS: I do defy thy conjuration°,   ° appeal
    And apprehend thee for a felon here.
ROMEO: Wilt thou provoke me? then have at thee, boy!

(*They fight.*)

PAGE: O Lord, they fight! I will go call the Watch.

(*Exit*)

PARIS: O, I am slain! (*falls*) If thou be merciful,
    Open the tomb, lay me with Juliet. (*dies*)
ROMEO: In faith, I will. Let me peruse this face.
    Mercutio's kinsman, noble County Paris!
    What said my man, when my betossèd soul
    Did not attend him as we rode? I think
    He told me Paris should have married Juliet.
    Said he not so? or did I dream it so?
    Or am I mad, hearing him talk of Juliet,
    To think it was so? O give me thy hand,
    One writ with me in sour misfortune's book!
    I'll bury thee in a triumphant grave.
    A grave? O no, a lantern°, slaughtered youth;   ° tower room glassed on all sides
    For here lies Juliet, and her beauty makes
    This vault a feasting presence full of light.
    Death, lie thou there, by a dead man interred.
    (*laying* PARIS *in the tomb*)
    How oft when men are at the point of death
    Have they been merry, which their keepers° call   ° nurses; jailors
    A light'ning before death! O how may I
    Call this a light'ning? O my love, my wife,
    Death, that hath sucked the honey of thy breath,
    Hath had no power yet upon thy beauty:
    Thou art not conquered, beauty's ensign yet
    Is crimson in thy lips and in thy cheeks,
    And Death's pale flag is not advancèd° there.   ° raised
    Tybalt, liest thou there in thy bloody sheet?
    O, what more favour can I do to thee
    Than with that hand that cut thy youth in twain
    To sunder his that was thine enemy?
    Forgive me, cousin. Ah, dear Juliet,
    Why art thou yet so fair? Shall I believe
    That unsubstantial Death is amorous,
    And that the lean abhorrèd monster keeps
    Thee here in dark to be his paramour?
    For fear of that, I still° will stay with thee,   ° forever
    And never from this palace of dim night
    Depart again. Here, here will I remain
    With worms that are thy chambermaids; O here
    Will I set up my everlasting rest,
    And shake the yoke of inauspicious stars
    From this world-wearied flesh. Eyes, look your last!

Arms, take your last embrace! and, lips, O you
The doors of breath, seal with a righteous kiss
A dateless bargain° to engrossing Death!   ° contract with no expiration date
Come, bitter conduct°, come, unsavoury guide!   ° poison
Thou desperate pilot, now at once run on
The dashing rocks thy seasick weary bark!
Here's to my love! (*drinks*) O true apothecary!
Thy drugs are quick°. Thus with a kiss I die. (*dies*)   ° fast-acting

(*Enter* FRIAR LAWRENCE *with lantern, crow, and spade*)

FRIAR LAWRENCE: Saint Francis be my speed°! how oft tonight   ° aid
    Have my old feet stumbled at graves! Who's there?
BALTHASAR: Here's one, a friend, and one that knows you well.
FRIAR LAWRENCE: Bliss be upon you! Tell me, good my friend,
    What torch is yond that vainly lends his light
    To grubs and eyeless skulls? As I discern,
    It burneth in the Capels' monument.
BALTHASAR: It doth so, holy sir, and there's my master,
    One that you love.
FRIAR LAWRENCE: Who is it?
BALTHASAR: Romeo.
FRIAR LAWRENCE: How long hath he been there?
BALTHASAR: Full half an hour.
FRIAR LAWRENCE: Go with me to the vault.
BALTHASAR: I dare not, sir.
    My master knows not but I am gone hence,
    And fearfully did menace me with death
    If I did stay to look on his intents.
FRIAR LAWRENCE: Stay then, I'll go alone. Fear comes upon me.
    O, much I fear some ill unthrifty° thing.   ° unlucky
BALTHASAR: As I did sleep under this yew tree here,
    I dreamt my master and another fought,
    And that my master slew him. (*retires*)
FRIAR LAWRENCE: Romeo!
    (FRIAR *stoops and looks on the blood and weapons.*)
    Alack, alack, what blood is this which stains
    The stony entrance of this sepulchre?
    What mean these masterless and gory swords
    To lie discoloured by this place of peace?
    (*enters the tomb*)
    Romeo! O, pale! Who else? What, Paris too?
    And steeped in blood? Ah, what an unkind° hour   ° unnatural
    Is guilty of this lamentable chance!
    (JULIET *rises.*)
    The lady stirs.
JULIET: O comfortable Friar, where is my lord?
    I do remember well where I should be;
    And there I am. Where is my Romeo?
    (*noise within*)

FRIAR LAWRENCE: I hear some noise, lady. Come from that nest
    Of death, contagion, and unnatural sleep.
    A greater power than we can contradict
    Hath thwarted our intents. Come, come away.
    Thy husband in thy bosom there lies dead;
    And Paris too. Come, I'll dispose of thee
    Among a sisterhood of holy nuns.
    Stay not to question for the Watch is coming.
    Come go, good Juliet, I dare no longer stay.

(*Exit*)

JULIET: Go get thee hence, for I will not away.
    What's here? a cup closed in my true love's hand?
    Poison I see hath been his timeless° end.   ° untimely
    O churl°, drunk all, and left no friendly drop   ° unmannerly rustic
    To help me after°? I will kiss thy lips,   ° follow
    Haply some poison yet doth hang on them,
    To make me die with a restorative.
    Thy lips are warm.
CAPTAIN OF THE WATCH (*within*): Lead, boy, which way?
JULIET: Yea, noise? Then I'll be brief. O happy° dagger,   ° opportune
    (*taking* ROMEO'S *dagger*)
    This is thy sheath;
    (*stabs herself*)
                   there rust, and let me die.
    (*falls on* ROMEO'S *body and dies*)

(*Enter* PARIS'S BOY *and* WATCH)

PAGE: This is the place, there where the torch doth burn.
CAPTAIN OF THE WATCH: The ground is bloody, search about the church-
    yard.
    Go, some of you, whoe'er you find attach.

(*Exeunt some of the* WATCH)

(*The* CAPTAIN *enters the tomb and returns.*)

    Pitiful sight! here lies the County slain,
    And Juliet bleeding, warm, and newly dead,
    Who here hath lain this two days burièd.
    Go tell the Prince, run to the Capulets,
    Raise up the Montagues; some others search.

(*Exeunt others of the* WATCH)

    We see the ground whereon these woes° do lie,   ° woeful creatures
    But the true ground of all these piteous woes°   ° woeful events
    We cannot without circumstance° descry.   ° details

(*Enter one of the* WATCH *with* ROMEO'S *man,* BALTHASAR)

SECOND WATCHMAN: Here's Romeo's man, we found him in the church-
    yard.
CAPTAIN OF THE WATCH: Hold him in safety° till the Prince come hither.   ° under guard

(*Enter* FRIAR LAWRENCE *and another* WATCHMAN)

THIRD WATCHMAN: Here is a friar that trembles, sighs, and weeps.
    We took this mattock and this spade from him,
    As he was coming from this churchyard's side.
CAPTAIN OF THE WATCH: A great suspicion. Stay the friar too.

(*Enter the* PRINCE *with others*)

PRINCE: What misadventure is so early up,
    That calls our person from our morning rest?

(*Enter* CAPULET, LADY CAPULET)

CAPULET: What should it be that is so shrieked abroad?
LADY CAPULET: O, the people in the street cry 'Romeo',
    Some 'Juliet', and some 'Paris', and all run
    With open outcry toward our monument.
PRINCE: What fear is this which startles° in your ears?   ° springs up
CAPTAIN OF THE WATCH: Sovereign, here lies the County Paris slain,
    And Romeo dead, and Juliet, dead before,
    Warm and new killed.
PRINCE: Search, seek, and know how this foul murder comes.
CAPTAIN OF THE WATCH: Here is a friar, and slaughtered Romeo's man,
    With instruments upon them, fit to open
    These dead men's tombs.

(CAPULET *and* LADY CAPULET *enter the tomb*)

CAPULET: O heavens! O wife, look how our daughter bleeds!
    This dagger hath mistane, for lo his house
    Is empty on the back of Montague,
    And it mis-sheathèd in my daughter's bosom!
LADY CAPULET: O me, this sight of death is as a bell
    That warns my old age to a sepulchre.

(*They return from the tomb*)

(*Enter* MONTAGUE)

PRINCE: Come, Montague, for thou art early up
    To see thy son and heir now early down.
MONTAGUE: Alas, my liege°, my wife is dead tonight;   ° sovereign
    Grief of my son's exile hath stopped her breath.
    What further woe conspires against mine age?
PRINCE: Look and thou shalt see.

(MONTAGUE *enters the tomb and returns*)

MONTAGUE: O thou untaught! what manners is in this,
    To press before thy father to a grave?
PRINCE: Seal up the mouth of outrage° for a while,   ° passionate lament
    Till we can clear these ambiguities,
    And know their spring, their head°, their true descent,   ° leader
    And then will I be general of your woes,
    And lead you even to death. Mean time forbear,
    And let mischance be slave° to patience.   ° be subservient
    Bring forth the parties of suspicion.

FRIAR LAWRENCE: I am the greatest, able to do least,
    Yet most suspected, as the time and place
    Doth make against me, of this direful murder;
    And here I stand both to impeach and purge
    Myself condemnèd and myself excused.
PRINCE: Then say at once what thou dost know in this.
FRIAR LAWRENCE: I will be brief, for my short date of breath
    Is not so long as is a tedious tale.
    Romeo, there dead, was husband to that Juliet,
    And she, there dead, that Romeo's faithful wife:
    I married them, and their stol'n marriage day
    Was Tybalt's doomsday, whose untimely death
    Banished the new-made bridegroom from this city,
    For whom, and not for Tybalt, Juliet pined.
    You, to remove that siege° of grief from her,   ° assault
    Betrothed and would have married her perforce°   ° by compulsion
    To County Paris. Then comes she to me,
    And with wild looks bid me devise some mean
    To rid her from this second marriage,
    Or in my cell there would she kill herself.
    Then gave I her (so tutored by my art)
    A sleeping potion, which so took effect
    As I intended, for it wrought on her
    The form of death. Mean time I writ to Romeo
    That he should hither come as this dire night
    To help to take her from her borrowed grave,
    Being the time the potion's force should cease.
    But he which bore my letter, Friar John,
    Was stayed by accident, and yesternight
    Returned my letter back. Then all alone,
    At the prefixèd hour of her waking,
    Came I to take her from her kindred's vault,
    Meaning to keep her closely at my cell,
    Till I conveniently could send to Romeo.
    But when I came, some minute ere the time
    Of her awakening, here untimely lay
    The noble Paris and true° Romeo dead.   ° faithful
    She wakes, and I entreated her come forth
    And bear this work of heaven with patience.
    But then a noise did scare me from the tomb,
    And she too desperate would not go with me,
    But as it seems, did violence on herself.
    All this I know, and to the marriage
    Her nurse is privy; and if ought in this
    Miscarried by my fault, let my old life
    Be sacrificed, some hour before his time,
    Unto the rigour of severest law.
PRINCE: We still have known thee for a holy man.
    Where's Romeo's man? what can he say to this?
BALTHASAR: I brought my master news of Juliet's death,
    And then in post he came from Mantua

To this same place, to this same monument.
This letter he early bid me give his father,
And threatened me with death, going in the vault,
If I departed not and left him there.

PRINCE: Give me the letter, I will look on it.
Where is the County's page that raised the Watch?
Sirrah, what made your master in this place?

PAGE: He came with flowers to strew his lady's grave,
And bid me stand aloof, and so I did.
Anon comes one with light to ope the tomb,
And by and by my master drew on him,
And then I ran away to call the Watch.

PRINCE: This letter doth make good the Friar's words,
Their course of love, the tidings of her death;
And here he writes that he did buy a poison
Of a poor pothecary, and therewithal
Came to this vault to die, and lie with Juliet.
Where be these enemies? Capulet, Montague?
See what a scourge is laid upon your hate,
That heaven finds means to kill your joys with love!
And I for winking° at your discords too   ° shutting his eyes
Have lost a brace° of kinsmen. All are punished. ° pair

CAPULET: O brother Montague, give me thy hand.
This is my daughter's jointure°, for no more   ° marriage settlement
Can I demand.

MONTAGUE: But I can give thee more,
For I will raise her statue in pure gold,
That whiles Verona by that name is known,
There shall no figure at such rate° be set   ° value
As that of true and faithful Juliet.

CAPULET: As rich shall Romeo's by his lady's lie,
Poor sacrifices of our enmity!

PRINCE: A glooming° peace this morning with it brings, ° cloudy
The sun for sorrow will not show his head.
Go hence to have more talk of these sad things;
Some shall be pardoned, and some punishèd:
For never was a story of more woe
Than this of Juliet and her Romeo.

(*Exeunt omnes*)

CURTAIN

4 THE BOURGEOIS GENTLEMAN

Molière (Jean-Baptiste Poquelin)
1670

The Bourgeois Gentleman is the best known of Molière's Court Plays, which were dramatic entertainments with music and dancing written to be performed before King Louis XIV at his various palaces. This play was written in greater haste than was usual for Molière. King Louis had just received a state visit from the Turkish ambassador, and was dismayed to find that the Turk's finery exceeded his own; he ordered Molière to create a satire on an oriental theme, and on short notice Molière created *The Bourgeois Gentleman*, to be performed before King Louis and his court at the royal hunting lodge of Chambord.

Molière kept to the King's timetable by putting together two plays he was already working on. The result, *The Bourgeois Gentleman*, clearly shows its cut-and-paste construction: it has virtually no plot, no character development, and the principal characters, save the Gentleman himself, are not even introduced until the third act—following two songs and three ballets. The play also contains a rambunctious mixture of Molière's dramatic modes: Roman-style farce, *commedia dell'arte* gags, romantic high comedy, two mini-operas, and great quantities of topical satire. It was, in short, the sort of grab-bag spectacle

one might expect at a country hunting lodge, and it is probable that neither Molière nor his company expected the play to serve any purpose other than as an evening's diversion for the king and his friends.

However, the endurance of this hastily conceived comedy-ballet was astonishing; the King adored it, the public applauded wildly in the subsequent public presentations in Paris, and within a year it was a London hit under the title of *The Citizen Turned Gentleman*. It has been regularly staged in Paris ever since by the legendary Comédie Française, and it is now a repertory staple in theatres all over the world. No rules of dramatic construction—as Molière himself noted many times—can by themselves determine a play's success, and the success of *The Bourgeois Gentleman* is based on the simple fact that it is one of the funniest plays ever written. Also, its theme—social pretension—is one that has no temporal or geographical boundaries. Comic genius allied with universal concerns can always find a lasting home in the theatre.

The play's success may also be due to the fact that its author was poking fun at his own social class. Not a soul in the original audience was unaware that Molière was himself a bourgeois (i.e.

middle-class) gentleman: he was the son of an up-holsterer and had become the favorite of the King's Court. But there are other targets for Molière's deft satirical jabs; the "paytrones of the ahts" that the music Master derides must have made that audience think of, among others, King Louis himself. Like Monsieur Jourdain, King Louis organized plays and ballets for the entertainment of his friends, kept a retinue of singers and dancers at his beck and call, and even performed in some of Molière's musical works. Molière's play is universal, but it is not abstract; the people he satirizes include his royal patron and himself, and both he and his audience knew whom and what he was talking about. This lends the play a special piquancy today.

Molière (1622–1673) is perhaps better known for his more serious comedies: *Tartuffe*, *The Miser*, *Don Juan*, *The Misanthrope*, and *The School for Wives*. He was also the author of two superb pieces of dramatic criticism, which took the form of plays about the theatre (*The Versailles Rehearsal*, *The "School for Wives" Critique*), and he served his company as director, producer, and principal actor. He died hours after collapsing onstage while playing the title role in his *The Imaginary Invalid*. For a man whose life had been the theatre, his death was particularly, if sadly, fitting.

A NOTE ON THE TEXT

This translation, by Robert Cohen, was prepared for a stage production of the play in 1982. Stage directions in the current text are from the 1982 production; there are no stage directions in Molière's original, but the directions here employed are presumably similar to those originally used by the author.

This translation takes many other liberties, for the most crucial goal in a translation of comedy is to make the play funny; if *The Bourgeois Gentleman* doesn't read funnily, then it isn't *The Bourgeois Gentleman*. Timing, rhyming, alliteration, and topical references, while not precisely "updated," are given a modern idiom. The translation also makes use of some literary borrowings (from the Book of Ecclesiastes, Shakespeare, Milton, Keats, Proust, and Beckett), which are not simply inserted as gags but serve to fit the text into a cultural and satirical context—a textual consanguinity that the original possessed and no contemporary version should ignore. Some French words appear in the English translation, but these are not from the original; the only French used herein is of the "fractured French" variety that an American "culture climber" would understand, and that Monsieur Jourdain would (mis) use to impress his friends.

THE BOURGEOIS GENTLEMAN

CAST OF CHARACTERS

A MUSIC MASTER
A DANCING MASTER
MONSIEUR JOURDAIN
A FENCING MASTER
A PHILOSOPHY TEACHER
A TAILOR
NICOLE
MADAME JOURDAIN
DORANTE

CLEONTE
COVIELLE
LUCILE
DORANTE
DORIMENE
THE MUFTI

STUDENTS, LACKEYS, DERVISHES, TURKISH DANCERS, SINGERS, *and* INSTRUMENTALISTS.

ACT ONE

(*Overture. In the middle of the stage we see one of the Music Master's students seated at a table, composing a serenade. The* MUSIC MASTER *and the* DANCING MASTER, *each with several students, enter from either side.*)

MUSIC MASTER (*to his singers*): Come on, get in here. Now stay there until he comes!

DANCING MASTER (*to his dancers*): You too. Over there!

MUSIC MASTER (*to his student*): Finished?

STUDENT: Yes. (*gives him the song*)

MUSIC MASTER: Let me see . . . ah yes, very good.

DANCING MASTER: A new piece?

MUSIC MASTER: Yes, it's a new "wake-up serenade." I've had it prepared for you know who.

DANCING MASTER: Ah, let's hear it!

MUSIC MASTER: No, no, you'll hear it, words and all, when he gets here. It won't be long, I assure you!

DANCING MASTER: We also serve, who only stand and wait.

MUSIC MASTER: Ah yes! And we have here just the man to wait upon: our "ticket to ride man," this Monsieur Jourdain, with his visions of gallantry and *noblesse oblige* flitting about in his head. A true "paytrone of the ahts," this "monsewer," I only wish there were more where he came from.

DANCING MASTER: Well, I suppose, but I certainly wish he knew something about the "ahts" he so adores!

MUSIC MASTER: He knows nothing, doesn't he? (*they both laugh*) But he pays through the nose and that's what counts. That's what the arts need these days, my dancing friend, MONEY!

DANCING MASTER: But to produce art for these imbeciles, it's abominable! I must admit to you, my *maestro profondo*, that I yearn for the glory of *noble* approval; of the applause of the discriminating critic and the bravos echoing down gilded salons of the court. It pleases me—as it pleases you, don't argue—to fashion our creations for the tastes of those whose sensitivities are refined, and whose approbation is both cultured and cordial. Their approval *means* something; it caresses the soul as it honors the achievement; and that reward, believe me, is far greater than any paycheck!

MUSIC MASTER: Yes, yes, yes, but it doesn't pay the rent! Clever praise and cultured applause are wonderful, I agree, but one must live, one must be comfortable, one must eat! When people give me a hand (*he claps his hands*) there should be something in it! (*he makes a money gesture*). Now our Monsieur Jourdain, it's true, is a bit unenlightened—he speaks backwards and forwards at the same time—he applauds only when he's not supposed to—but his money makes up for much misery; he has great wisdom in his purse, and his praise is coined in legal tender. Indeed, this ignorant bourgeois is worth far more to us than the *grand seigneur* who brought us here in the first place.

DANCING MASTER: Well, there's some truth to all this, I suppose, but I don't like it. You're just too moneymad; it's unseemly.

MUSIC MASTER: You take it when he gives it to you.

DANCING MASTER: Yes, but it breaks my heart. If I had my wish . . .

MUSIC MASTER (*completing his thought*): And if I had mine . . . But that's life now, isn't it? In any event, M. Jourdain is giving us the chance to make names for ourselves at the Court—and if you take my advice, you'll let him pay us what the court won't, and let the court praise us as this jackass can't!

DANCING MASTER: Shh. Here he comes.

M. JOURDAIN (*entering and nodding grandly*): Well, gentlemen? And what do we have here? You have made for me, I presume, some little drollery for the afternoon?

DANCING MASTER (*confused*): Drollery?

M. JOURDAIN (*delighted*): Ah, yes! (*then, fearful he has said something wrong*) Ah, no! (*desperate*) But how do you call it? (*to each of them, in turn*) Your prologue? Your, um, dialogue? Your singing and dancing?

DANCING MASTER: Ah, yes!

MUSIC MASTER: At your service!

M. JOURDAIN: I know I've made you wait a bit, but it is only because I have decided today to dress in the fashion of quality folk, and my tailor has sent me (*he raises the hem of his gown*) these stockings—silk, of course—which take forever to get on!

MUSIC MASTER: We are here to attend your convenience.

M. JOURDAIN: Well, then, you mustn't go—they are bringing my new suit, and you must see me in it!

DANCING MASTER: Whatever pleases you.

M. JOURDAIN: Then you will see me in the height of fashion—from toe to head!

MUSIC MASTER (*trying not to laugh*): We don't doubt it.

M. JOURDAIN (*turning about*): My dressing gown *à l'indienne*—do you like it?

DANCING MASTER: *Très, très chic!*

M. JOURDAIN: My tailor tells me it's the morning fashion of quality folk!

MUSIC MASTER: Suits you perfectly!

M. JOURDAIN (*suddenly and imperiously*): Lackeys! I say LACKEYS!

THE LACKEYS (*springing forward in terror*): Yes, Monsieur?

M. JOURDAIN: Oh, nothing, nothing. Just checking! (*the lackeys return to their position*) How do you like their liveries?

DANCING MASTER: Magnificent.

M. JOURDAIN (*as one bestowing a precious gift, opens his gown, revealing red velvet tights and a hideous green velvet jacket*): My little underdress outfit for the morning exercises!

MUSIC MASTER (*grinning through his revulsion*): Oh, *très gallant, très gallant* indeed.

M. JOURDAIN: Lackey!

FIRST LACKEY (*coming forward*): Monsieur!

M. JOURDAIN: No, no, the other one!

SECOND LACKEY: Monsieur!

M. JOURDAIN: Hold my gown. (*to the masters*) How do you find me?

DANCING MASTER: Wonderful. Couldn't be better.

M. JOURDAIN: Let's see your dance!

MUSIC MASTER: Ah, but first, your "wake up serenade," remember—composed just for you this morning . . .

M. JOURDAIN: Ah!

MUSIC MASTER: By my student here.

M. JOURDAIN: By your student! And are you too good for that sort of thing?

MUSIC MASTER: Oh no, I mean yes, I mean . . . don't abuse the name of student, Monsieur. *Studenten, studere,* studiosity . . . why, my scholars are wiser than their masters, and this song is as beautiful as any ever written. Just *écoutez, Monsieur, écoutez!*

M. JOURDAIN: Give me back my gown; I hear better with it on. On second thought, forget it. No! Give it here. That's better.

MUSIC STUDENT (*sings*):

I languish night and day, I suffer deep.
Your lovely eyes have stolen all my sleep.
Oh, Iris, dear, if thus your lovers treat
What ills befall the enemies you meet?

M. JOURDAIN: A bit lugubrious, don't you think? A bit too sad and boring. Liven it up, can't you a little?

MUSIC MASTER: But the words have to go with the music, Monsieur.

M. JOURDAIN: Hey, I learned a cute little number a few days ago, listen . . . la la la . . . now how does it go?

DANCING MASTER: I'm afraid I . . .

M. JOURDAIN: It's got a sheep in it.

DANCING MASTER: A sheep?

MUSIC MASTER: A sheep?

M. JOURDAIN: A sheep! I got it! (sings)

> Aye Jenny! Dear Jenny! Oh Jenny my love!
> As sweet as a lambkin with sheep's eyes above.
> Alas and alas
> She's a snake in the grass,
> And a wildcat whenever I tickle her ass!

Isn't that sweet?

MUSIC MASTER: The sweetest I ever heard.

DANCING MASTER: And you sing it so well.

M. JOURDAIN: Without even learning to read music!

MUSIC MASTER: You must learn music, Monsieur, as well as the dance. These are the two arts which always lie together, intertwined, you might say.

DANCING MASTER: And which open a man's soul to beauty, passion, rapture!

M. JOURDAIN: Quality folk learn music?

MUSIC MASTER: Yes, Monsieur.

M. JOURDAIN: Then I shall too! But I don't know where I'll find the time, because besides the two of you and my fencing lessons, I've just hired a philosophy teacher, who's starting me up this morning.

MUSIC MASTER: Philosophy is something, I suppose, but music, Monsieur, MUSIC . . .

DANCING MASTER: Music and dance, dance and music, that's all ye know and all ye need to know.

MUSIC MASTER: Nothing is more important than music.

DANCING MASTER: Nothing so necessary as dance.

MUSIC MASTER: Without music, our government would fall.

DANCING MASTER: Without dance, man would become helpless.

MUSIC MASTER: All the world's problems, poverty, prejudice, and war, come about solely because people refuse to study music.

DANCING MASTER: All human misery, all historical disasters, all political catastrophes and all military fiascos, *all* comes from not knowing how to dance!

M. JOURDAIN: Are you sure?

MUSIC MASTER: Doesn't war come from a lack of harmony among men?

M. JOURDAIN: Well, yes . . .

MUSIC MASTER: And if men learned music, wouldn't they learn to harmonize?

M. JOURDAIN: I suppose so.

DANCING MASTER: When a man makes a big mistake in ordering about his wife, or his troops, or the government of his country, don't we say: "he made a false step?"

M. JOURDAIN: Yes, yes we do!

DANCING MASTER: Well how would you ever take a false step, if you knew how to dance?

M. JOURDAIN: That's right—you're both right!

DANCING MASTER: We only want you to understand the usefulness of dance and music.

M. JOURDAIN: I'm beginning to.

MUSIC MASTER: Would you like to witness our creations?

M. JOURDAIN: Yes.

MUSIC MASTER: Well, this song, as I've already explained, is a *petit* attempt to express, through music, earthly passion.

M. JOURDAIN: Very good.

MUSIC MASTER (*to musicians*): Come on, come on in. (*to* M. JOURDAIN) You must imagine them dressed as shepherds.

M. JOURDAIN: Why shepherds? They're always shepherds.

MUSIC MASTER: Who else would *sing* of earthly passions? Princes don't, neither do the bourgeoisie. Shepherds do. Realism, Monsieur, Realism.

M. JOURDAIN: Okay, okay. Let's see it.

SONG (*mock heroic*)

SHEPHERDESS: Love is a tyrant
A tormenting giant
Collection of headaches and pains.
Love is a cancer.
Freedom's the answer,
The freedom a lover disdains.

1ST SHEPHERD: Love is a treasure
Love is life's pleasure
Two hearts beating warmly as one.
Love is no trap. E—
Gregariously happy's
The person whom love has undone.

2ND SHEPHERD: Love is a nuisance.
And filled with abuse. Since
I quit love my troubles are few.
All women are liars.

They stoke our male fires
They turn on us: bid love adieu!

1ST SHEPHERD: I am impassioned!

SHEPHERDESS: Freedom is best.

2ND SHEPHERD: Honesty's rationed!

1ST SHEPHERD: Lovers are blessed!

SHEPHERDESS (*to* 2ND SHEPHERD): You make my heart shiver.

2ND SHEPHERD (*to* HER): Why don't you grow up?

1ST SHEPHERD (*to* HER): You make my thighs quiver.

2ND SHEPHERD (*to* 1ST SHEPHERD): You make me throw up.

1ST SHEPHERD: Let's stop this disputing.

SHEPHERDESS (*to* 1ST SHEPHERD): I love *him* you see.

2ND SHEPHERD (*to* HER): You're husband-recruiting!

SHEPHERDESS (*to* 2ND SHEPHERD): Hear, my shepherdess' plea: I will be faithful!

2ND SHEPHERD: And honest and true?

GIRL: And never a wraith. All
My love goes to you.

2ND SHEPHERD: Well, there goes my chance
To abandon romance,
But fail me my dear,
And I'll CHOP OFF YOUR EAR!

ALL: Love is a treasure
Love is life's pleasure
Two hearts beating warmly as one.
Love is no trap. E—

Gregariously happy's
The couple whom love's bounty won.

M. JOURDAIN: Is that it?
MUSIC MASTER: Yes.
M. JOURDAIN: Very nice, with some very nice sayings. Catchy.
DANCING MASTER: And here, Monsieur, is my little essay in choreography, the most beautiful movements, and the loveliest positions, of which man is capable.
M. JOURDAIN: More shepherds?
DANCING MASTER: They are, Monsieur, as you may imagine them. (*to the dancers*) Allons!

(*Four dancers dance.*)

ACT II

M. JOURDAIN: Not at all bad, they know how to shake a leg, don't they?
MUSIC MASTER: And with words, it's even better; you'll see in the ballet we've prepared for you.
M. JOURDAIN: Soon, soon! The lady I commissioned it for will be dining here this evening. This evening!
DANCING MASTER: It's ready, it's ready!
MUSIC MASTER: But, Monsieur, truly, just one ballet . . . I must say a person as yourself, a splendid person as yourself, one with a bent for the arts as we say, such a person should have a musical concert in one's home every Wednesday . . .
M. JOURDAIN: Every Wednesday?
MUSIC MASTER: Or Thursday . . .
M. JOURDAIN: Do quality folk do that?
MUSIC MASTER: But of course.
M. JOURDAIN: And I will too! Beautiful concerts!
MUSIC MASTER: To be sure. You'll need three voices, a tenor, a soprano, and a basso profundo; and let me see, a bass viol, a lute, and a harpsichord for the *continuos*; then two violins for the refrains . . .
M. JOURDAIN: And a fog horn! I love the sound of a fog horn!
MUSIC MASTER: Let us arrange things.
M. JOURDAIN: And don't forget the dinner music! I adore the *chansons* with the *soufflé!*
MUSIC MASTER: You'll have everything you need.
M. JOURDAIN: As long as the ballet is beautiful . . .
MUSIC MASTER: You will be happy. The ballet is beautiful, and the minuets sublime!

M. JOURDAIN: Ah! Minuets! That's my dance! You must see me minuet! Come, my dancing master, my *maître de danser!*

DANCING MASTER (*to a servant*): Un chapeau, Monsieur, s'il vous plaît.

(M. JOURDAIN *dons a hat; the music master teaches him a dance*)

> La, la, la; la, la, la, la, la; la, la, la, again; la, la, la; la, l—In time now, please, la, la, la, la. Your right leg. La, la, la. Don't wiggle your shoulders so much. La, la, la, la, la; la, la, la, la, la. Your arms are drooping, Monsieur, la, la, la, la, la. Raise your head. Turn your toes out. La, la, la. Straighten up!

M. JOURDAIN: Eh?

MUSIC MASTER: Marvellous!

M. JOURDAIN: Glad you think so. Now, teach me how to bow, as to greet a marquise, which I must do shortly.

DANCING MASTER: A bow to a marquise?

M. JOURDAIN: Yes, a marquise called Dorimene.

DANCING MASTER: Give me your hand.

M. JOURDAIN: No! You do it, I'll remember how.

DANCING MASTER: Well, for your respectful bow . . .

M. JOURDAIN: Oh, yes . . .

DANCING MASTER: You must first bow to the rear, and then walk towards her in three salutations, lower and lower until you complete your reverences nose to her knees.

M. JOURDAIN: You do it. (THE DANCING MASTER *demonstrates*) Good.

FIRST LACKEY: Monsieur, your fencing master has arrived.

M. JOURDAIN: Ah, my lesson! Tell him to *entrez tout de suite.* (*to the masters*) I want you to watch!

FENCING MASTER (*entering and giving* JOURDAIN *a sword*): Come, sir, your bow! (JOURDAIN *bows deeply and stiffens: his back has gone out*) Up! (FENCING MASTER *playfully points his sword at* JOURDAIN's *belly:* JOURDAIN *quickly straightens up*) Body erect! More to your left! Not so far apart, those legs! Square your feet! Your wrist opposite your hip! (JOURDAIN *grows confused as the* FENCING MASTER *barks his orders faster and faster*) The tip of your sword across from your shoulder. Relax your arm! Your left hand at eye level! Your left shoulder—square it! Head up! (JOURDAIN *is now twisted like a pretzel*) Look fierce! (JOURDAIN *makes a ludicrous attempt to look warlike*) Ad-

vance! (JOURDAIN *advances and stumbles*) Body firm! (JOURDAIN *sighs;* FENCING MASTER *slashes at* JOURDAIN's *sword;* JOURDAIN *screams as his sword vibrates out of control*) Touché! One, two, retreat! (JOURDAIN *retreats, still trying to gain control of his vibrating sword*) Again: stand firm! (JOURDAIN *tries to resume his warlike mien*) Jump back! (JOURDAIN *does so*) The sword forward and the body back. One! Two! (FENCING MASTER *hits* JOURDAIN's *sword again,* JOURDAIN *yelps*) Touché! Keep coming! Advance! (JOURDAIN *begins to whimper*) Body firm! Advance! (JOURDAIN *is crying*) From there! One! Two! Retreat! (JOURDAIN *starts to run away;* FENCING MASTER *"spanks" him with his sword*) Again! Jump Back! En garde, sir, *en garde!*

M. JOUDAIN: Owwwwwww!

MUSIC MASTER: You're doing fine!

M. JOURDAIN: Oh, no I'm not!

FENCING MASTER (*didactically, illustrating each point with a flourish of his foil*): It is as I said before, the whole secret of fencing lies simply in hitting (*swats* JOURDAIN) and not being hit. Do you understand? It is more blessed to give blows (*swats again*) than to receive them—did I not explain that sufficiently the other day? All you need concentrate on is that little outward movement of the wrist—(*stops for a moment, afraid of having contradicted himself*) or is it a little inward movement . . .

M. JOURDAIN: You mean if I could learn that, I could be certain of killing my opponent—without myself being killed?

FENCING MASTER: Of course! Isn't that what I just showed you?

M. JOURDAIN: Oh! Yes, of course.

FENCING MASTER: And that's why we must be elevated above the other arts and sciences, particularly the useless ones such as music and dance.

DANCING MASTER: Ah, ah, ah, Monsieur fencer, don't speak of dance, you know nothing about it.

MUSIC MASTER: Nor music, beautiful music!

FENCING MASTER: Don't jest, gentlemen! You certainly wouldn't compare your sciences with mine!

MUSIC MASTER: Well, look at the Big Shot.

DANCING MASTER: Scaramouche in chain mail.

FENCING MASTER: My little twinkletoes, I'll make you dance, all right. And you my little songbird, prepare to lose your lower register!

DANCING MASTER: You iron monger, I'll teach you a few tricks.

M. JOURDAIN (*in the middle of all this, to* THE DANCING MASTER): Don't argue with him, are you crazy? He'll attack you in the third position! In the fourth position! He'll run you through with pure reason if he has to!

DANCING MASTER: His reason is ridiculous, and his positions even more so.

M. JOURDAIN: Now, now, please . . .

FENCING MASTER: What? You nasty little . . .

M. JOURDAIN: Now, my dear fencing master . . .

DANCING MASTER: You carthorse! Dromedary!

M. JOURDAIN: My good dancing master . . .

FENCING MASTER: Oh, let me at him!

M. JOURDAIN: Easy, easy . . .

DANCING MASTER: If I get my hands on him!

M. JOURDAIN: Okay. Okay.

FENCING MASTER: I'll comb your locks!

M. JOURDAIN: Please!

DANCING MASTER: I'll smash your flanks!

M. JOURDAIN: I beg you!

MUSIC MASTER: We'll show him how to talk!

M. JOURDAIN: Good God, stop, please, stop . . .

FENCING MASTER (*roars*): Arrghhh!!

M. PHILOSOPHER (*entering*): Ah . . .

M. JOURDAIN: Oh good lord, Monsieur Philosopher, you've come just in time. Philosophize, philosophize!

M. PHILOSOPHER: What's the matter, sirs?

M. JOURDAIN: They're angry. Professional quarrels. Body blows!

M. PHILOSOPHER: What what? Gentlemen, must you? Have you not read Seneca on anger? Is there anything worse? More shameful? It is anger that makes man a beast of the jungle—it is reason which calms the savage beast.

DANCING MASTER: But sir, he insulted the Dance!

MUSIC MASTER: And Music!

M. PHILOSOPHER: The wise man is above insults; the wise response is patience and moderation.

FENCING MASTER: They have a nerve, comparing their profession to mine!

M. PHILOSOPHER: Vanity, vanity. We are all one humankind; only wisdom and virtue proclaim one as superior.

DANCING MASTER: Dance is superior. It is art!

MUSIC MASTER: Music! For centuries, the finest of arts!

FENCING MASTER: Fencing! Fighting! The science of War!

M. JOURDAIN: Oh, my God!

M. PHILOSOPHER: And philosophy? You are all impertinent, arrogant, and impudent. Art? Science?

Presumptuous pigs, you are tradesmen: the gladiator, the minstrel, and the mountebank!

FENCING MASTER: *En garde*, sagacious dog!

MUSIC MASTER: Fists up, pedantic prune!

DANCING MASTER: Take that, you peasant pedagogue!

M. PHILOSOPHER: Villains!

(*They all fight.*)

M. JOURDAIN: Monsieur Philosopher!

M. PHILOSOPHER: Scoundrels! Jerks! Rascals!

M. JOURDAIN: Monsieur Philosopher!

FENCING MASTER: A plague on all your houses!

M. JOURDAIN: Gentlemen!

M. PHILOSOPHER: Upstarts!

DANCING MASTER: Stupid ass!

M. JOURDAIN: Gentlemen!

M. PHILOSOPHER: Knaves!

M. JOURDAIN: Monsieur Philosopher!

MUSIC MASTER: To hell with him!

M. JOURDAIN: Gentlemen!

M. PHILOSOPHER: Dolts! Serfs! Traitors! Imposters!

(*They leave.*)

M. JOURDAIN: Monsieur Philosopher, Monsieur Philosopher, Gentlemen, Monsieur Philosopher! Oh well, go on and fight, then, I don't know what to do. And watch out for my gown! (*aside*) I'm crazy to try and stop them, I could get hurt!

M. PHILOSOPHER (*re-enters*): Well, let's to our lesson, shall we?

M. JOURDAIN: Ah, my dear Philosopher, they struck you, I'm so embarrassed, and in my house too!

M. PHILOSOPHER: Nothing, it is nothing. A philosopher, my good man, transcends his environment. I shall compose a satire against them, after Juvenal, which shall RIP THEM TO SHREDS!! But let that pass. What would you like me to teach you?

M. JOURDAIN: Everything! I adore learning! I am furious at my parents—they never made me study when I was young.

M. PHILOSOPHER: Yes, I see. *Nam sine doctrina vita est quasi mortis imago.* Of course you know Latin . . .

M. JOURDAIN: Of course, but pretend that I don't— explain it to me!

M. PHILOSOPHER: Without knowledge, life is virtually the reflection of death.

M. JOURDAIN: Latin is always right.

M. PHILOSOPHER: You know, I suppose, the foundations of knowledge?

M. JOURDAIN: Well, yes, I know how to read and write.

M. PHILOSOPHER: Then where shall we begin? With logic?

M. JOURDAIN: What's that?

M. PHILOSOPHER: It's what organizes the mind into its three functions.

M. JOURDAIN: Three functions? What are they?

M. PHILOSOPHER: The first, the second, and the third.

M. JOURDAIN: Oh!

M. PHILOSOPHER: The first is to conceptualize, through universal understandings, the second is to evaluate, through categorical reasoning, and the third is to draw conclusions, through identifications and syllogisms.

M. JOURDAIN: Uh huh. Too hard. I'm afraid logic doesn't suit me very well, do you have anything jollier?

M. PHILOSOPHER: How about morality?

M. JOURDAIN: Morality?

M. PHILOSOPHER: Yes.

M. JOURDAIN: What's that?

M. PHILOSOPHER: Happiness, moderation . . .

M. JOURDAIN: No, no, no, none of that. I rage like the devil, no morality can hold me back. No morality today!

M. PHILOSOPHER: Physics then?

M. JOURDAIN: Can you sing it?

M. PHILOSOPHER: Physics is the science of natural order, of the properties of matter: the elements, the metals, the minerals, the stones, the plants and animals; the causes of meteors, the rainbow, the northern lights, the comets, lightning, thunder, thunderclaps, rain, snow, hail, winds, tornados . . .

M. JOURDAIN: A lot of hullabaloo if you ask me.

M. PHILOSOPHER: What then?

M. JOURDAIN: How about spelling?

M. PHILOSOPHER: Marvellous.

M. JOURDAIN: And then the almanack, so I can tell when there's a moon out, and when there's not.

M. PHILOSOPHER: Very good. To accomplish this philosophically, we must begin at the beginning, by an understanding of the nature of letters and their various pronunciations. Now first, there are the vowels, so named because they *avow* the voice; and then there are the consonants, so called because they consonate the vowels, and mark the many measures of vowelization. There are five vowels: ah, eh, ee, oh, yu.[1]

M. JOURDAIN: Yes, I know.

M. PHILOSOPHER: The sound "ah" is formed by opening the mouth wide (*he does so, saying*) "ah."

M. JOURDAIN (*imitating*): "Ah" . . . "ah" Yes!

M. PHILOSOPHER: The sound "eh" is made by closing the jaws (*opening his mouth*) "ah" (*closing it*) "eh."

M. JOUDAIN (*opens and closes his mouth mechanically*): "Ah"—"eh," "Ah"—"eh" My God! You're right! How wonderful learning is!

M. PHILOSOPHER: And to make an "ee" you close your jaws even further, and spread your cheeks to your ears: "Ah"—"eh"—"ee."

M. JOURDAIN (*with exaggerated movement*): "Ah"—"eh"—"ee." "Ee." (*spreads his cheeks as wide as he can with his fingers*) "Ee!" "ee!" It's true! Magnificent! Long live science!

M. PHILOSOPHER: To make an "oh" you must open your jaw and bring together the corners of your lips: "Oh."

M. JOURDAIN: "Oh." "Oh." Nothing could be more wonderful than this! (*moving his face in absurdly exaggerated configurations*) "Ah"—"eh"—"ee"—"Oh." "Ee"—"oh!" Splendid! "Ee"—"oh!" "ee"—"oh!"

M. PHILOSOPHER (*making a circle with his finger*): The shape of your mouth, you see, is a little round "o."

M. JOURDAIN (*astounded, making the same circle with his finger and then tracing his lips in an "o"*): "O"—"O"—"O"—you're soooooooo right. Ooooooooo. Ah, what a beautiful thing to knooooooow something.

M. PHILOSOPHER: The sound "yu" is made by bringing the teeth together, by spreading the lips, and then making them come together without quite touching: "Yu."

M. JOURDAIN: "Yu." "Yu"—nothing could be truer: "Yu"!

M. PHILOSOPHER (*suddenly making a grotesque face at* JOURDAIN, *who recoils in shocked surprise*): It's like making a face at someone: if you want to make fun of somebody, just say "yu" at them.

(*He coaches* JOURDAIN, *who finally "gets" it.*)

M. JOURDAIN: "Yu"—"yu"! Oh, it's truuuuuuuue! Oh, why didn't I take up education earlier, I would have known all this!

---

1. The vowels are pronounced in the French manner.

M. PHILOSOPHER: Tomorrow we'll take a look at the consonants.

M. JOURDAIN: Are they as wonderful as the vowels?

M. PHILOSOPHER: Of course. The consonant "d" for example, is pronounced with the tip of the tongue at the tip of the teeth: "da."

M. JOURDAIN: "da," "da." Yes! Magnificent! Magnificent!

M. PHILOSOPHER: The "f" is made by digging the upper teeth into the lower lip: "fa."

M. JOURDAIN: "fa," "fa." It's true! Oh how I despise my parents. "fa!"

M. PHILOSOPHER: And the "r" is made by the tip of the tongue and the roof of the mouth so close as to shake up the air, to make it tremble: "rra!"

M. JOURDAIN: "rra," "rra," "r," "r." "rra!" True! What a brilliant man! And how much time I've lost, how much *temps* has been *perdu*! "RrrrrrrA!" "Fa!" "Da!" "Da!" "yu!"

M. PHILOSOPHER: All this shall I explain to you.

M. JOURDAIN: Oh, please, please. And now I must share with you a great confidence. I am in love with a grand lady of quality, and I want you to help me write a little love note (*he giggles*) that I can drop at her feet (*giggles again*).

M. PHILOSOPHER: Very well.

M. JOURDAIN: Something *très gallant*, okay?

M. PHILOSOPHER: Of course. Some verses?

M. JOURDAIN: No, no. No verses.

M. PHILOSOPHER: Ahah! Entirely in prose, then.

M. JOURDAIN: No, no, no—no prose either.

M. PHILOSOPHER: Well, it must be one or the other.

M. JOURDAIN: Why?

M. PHILOSOPHER: Because, Monsieur, there are only the two: prose—and verse.

M. JOURDAIN: There is only prose—and verse?

M. PHILOSOPHER: Only. Whatever is not prose—is verse; and whatever is not verse—is prose.

M. JOURDAIN (*beginning to understand*): And talking, what is that?

M. PHILOSOPHER: That is prose.

M. JOURDAIN (*on the verge of a great discovery, his eyes widening all the time*): When I say, "Nicole, bring me my slippers and my nightcap." that's—(*almost unwilling to believe it*) prose?!

M. PHILOSOPHER (*as in benediction*): That's prose.

M. JOURDAIN: My God! (*starts dancing about*) For forty years I've been speaking PROSE without knowing it! Oh, thank you, THANK YOU, thank you, thank you.

(M. PHILOSOPHER *bows graciously*)

M. JOURDAIN: Then, would you write this up for me in a note: "Beautiful Marquise, your beautiful eyes make me die for love"—but gallantly put, elegantly turned . . .

M. PHILOSOPHER: You should say that the fire of her eyes turns your heart to cinders, that night and day you are tortured by . . .

M. JOURDAIN: No, no, no, that's not it! I want "Beautiful Marquise, your beautiful eyes make me die for love."

M. PHILOSOPHER: You must elaborate.

M. JOURDAIN: No. No elaboration. Just gallantly put, elegantly turned. Please, give me some suggestions??

M. PHILOSOPHER: Well, there's "Beautiful Marquise, your beautiful eyes make me die for love."

M. JOURDAIN: Yes!

M. PHILOSOPHER: Or better, perhaps, "Of love to death, beautiful Marquise, your beautiful eyes make me." Or better yet, "Your beautiful eyes, of love, beautiful Marquise, make me die." Or how about "To die of your beautiful eyes, my beautiful Marquise, makes me love." Or "Make me die of your beautiful eyes, beautiful Marquise, of love."

M. JOURDAIN: All those ways! Now which one is best?

M. PHILOSOPHER: Yours, Monsieur. "Beautiful Marquise, your beautiful eyes make me die for love."

M. JOURDAIN: Got it in one! And you know, I've never studied. Well, I thank you from the bottom of my heart, and I beg you to come back tomorrow early on.

M. PHILOSOPHER: Never fear.

(*He leaves.*)

M. JOURDAIN (*to a lackey*): Where's my suit? Hasn't it been delivered yet?

LACKEY: No. Monsieur.

M. JOURDAIN: Curse the tailor, keeping me waiting all day. Doesn't he know I'm a busy man; I'm furious! May malaria mangle him! May the plague pickle him! A detestable tailor, a devilish tailor, a dog of a tailor, a traitorous tailor, a . . .

(*The tailor arrives with his assistant and* JOURDAIN'S *suit.*)

Ah, there you are tailor, I was just about to get angry with you.

TAILOR: I couldn't come earlier, I've had twenty of my boys working night and day on this.

M. JOURDAIN: Those stockings you sent me were too tight; it takes forever to put them on, and I've already broken through the toes!

TAILOR: They stretch.

M. JOURDAIN: Yes, when I burst the stitches! Also your shoes hurt.

TAILOR: Nonsense.

M. JOURDAIN: What do you mean, nonsense?

TAILOR: They don't hurt at all.

M. JOURDAIN: I'm telling you that they hurt; they hurt *me.*

TAILOR: You imagine it.

M. JOURDAIN: I imagine it, because I feel it. What is this?

TAILOR (*presenting the gown*): Voilà, my friend, this is the most beautiful new suit ever fashioned for the Court, serious but colorful, a masterpiece no one in Paris could even touch.

(*With a flourish, he and his assistants hold the gown up for general examination.* JOURDAIN *gasps.*)

M. JOURDAIN: But—my good man—the flowers are upside down!

MASTER TAILOR (*stunned, looks at his mistake, but immediately recovers and takes the offensive*): Well—you never told me you wanted them rightside up!

M. JOURDAIN (*dismayed*): You mean I'm supposed to tell you?

MASTER TAILOR: (*vastly relieved, he boldly continues*): Of course! Persons of quality like them like this!

M. JOURDAIN (*utterly perplexed*): Persons of quality like their flowers upside down?

MASTER TAILOR: Yes, of course.

M. JOURDAIN (*making the best of it*): Oh. Well, it's all right then.

MASTER TAILOR (*pressing advantage*): If you wish, I'll redo them.

M. JOURDAIN (*frightened*): Oh, no, no.

MASTER TAILOR (*wickedly*): Just say the word—

M. JOURDAIN (*urgently*): No, no, I tell you, they're PERFECT . . . Do you think it looks right?

MASTER TAILOR: What a question! I defy any painter with his brush to paint a better one! Why, one of my boys is a virtual genius at breeches; another, who arranged the doublet, is a national hero.

M. JOURDAIN: And my wig feathers?

MASTER TAILOR: Magnificent.

M. JOURDAIN: Ah . . . Hey! What's that you're wearing? That's the fabric of the last suit you made for me! I recognize it!

MASTER TAILOR: Yes, well, I liked it so much, I made one for myself.

M. JOURDAIN: With my fabric? You shouldn't have done that . . .

MASTER TAILOR: Would you care to dress now, Monsieur?

M. JOURDAIN: Oh, yes, give it here.

MASTER TAILOR: Wait, wait. That's just not DONE, Monsieur. I've brought my people to dress you *properly*—(*his eyes lofting heavenward*) in RHYTHM! (*reverentially*) Clothing like this must be put on with ceremony—BOYS!

(*The orchestra strikes up a minuet: four tailoring assistants dance forward and* JOURDAIN *whirls around.*)

Dress our Friend as a Man of Quality.

(*A ballet ensues, with the assistants undressing* JOURDAIN *and redressing him in his new suit, to the light strains of Lully's orchestral rendition.* JOURDAIN *parades around in his new garments as the dancers pretend to admire him.*)

MASTER TAILOR (*as the dance concludes, to* JOURDAIN): My dear gentleman, you may now give my boys their gratuity.

M. JOURDAIN: What did you call me?

MASTER TAILOR (*a little frightened*): My dear gentleman?

M. JOURDAIN (*overjoyed*): Gentleman! That's what happens when you dress in quality, they call you gentleman! No one calls you that if you dress like a petty bourgeois! Here (*giving money to the tailor*)—this is from your "dear gentleman"!

MASTER TAILOR: My lord, we are all obliged to you.

M. JOURDAIN: My lord! Oh! Oh! My lord! Wait, HEY! wait my friend, "My Lord" means something more. "My Lord," why that's not inconsiderable; here, here's what "My Lord" will give you.

(*He gives money to the* TAILOR.)

MASTER TAILOR: Well, well, we drink the health of Your Excellency, don't we, boys?

M. JOURDAIN: Your Excellency? Oh, oh oh! Wait, wait! Me, Your Excellency! (*turns away from them, to the audience*) My God, if he goes up to "Your Highness, my purse is his. (*turns back to the*

TAILOR) Here, here's from "Your Excellency."
(*gives yet more money*)

MASTER TAILOR (*now would rather leave than milk* JOURDAIN *further*): My lord, we thank you humbly.

(*He bows and turns away.*)

M. JOURDAIN (*turning again to the audience, confidentially*): Thank God. I was just about to give him all I had!

(*The Second Interlude, a Ballet performed by the Tailor's Assistants, takes place.*)

ACT III

M. JOURDAIN (*to his lackeys*): Follow me, boys, I'm going to show off my gown in the town; you walk right behind me, now; I want everybody to know you're mine.

LACKEYS: Yes sir!

M. JOURDAIN: Call Nicole, I want to give her some orders. No, wait! Here she comes. (NICOLE *enters*) Nicole!

NICOLE: Yes?

M. JOURDAIN: Listen to me.

NICOLE (*seeing the flowers, and bursting into giggles*): Hee hee hee hee hee hee hee hee hee hee!

M. JOURDAIN: What are you laughing at?

NICOLE: Hee hee hee hee hee hee hee hee hee hee!

M. JOURDAIN: What's that supposed to mean?

NICOLE: Hee hee hee. The way you're dressed! Hee hee hee.

M. JOURDAIN: Dressed? How am I dressed?

NICOLE: Ahhh, well, (*pointing*) My God! The flowers are. . . . Hee hee hee hee hee hee!

M. JOURDAIN: Detested minx! Are you making fun of me?

NICOLE: Not at all, sir, not at all. Hee hee hee hee hee hee hee!

M. JOURDAIN: I'll smack you on the nose! Just one more laugh . . . !

NICOLE (*wailing*): I can't help it! Hee hee hee hee hee hee!

M. JOURDAIN: You won't stop?!

NICOLE: Sir, sir, I'm sorry, I'm sorry, but you look so funny, I don't know *how* to stop. Hee hee hee hee.

M. JOURDAIN: Insolent hussy!

NICOLE: You look so *ridiculous!* Hee hee hee hee hee hee!

M. JOURDAIN: Now, that's enough!

NICOLE: Please, please, I beg you to excuse meeee— hee hee hee hee!

M. JOURDAIN: Enough! If you even so much as *smile* at me, I'm going to give you such a smacking your cheeks will burn!

NICOLE (*holding back her laughter*): It's over. I'm finished. No more laughing.

M. JOURDAIN: Good. I want you to start cleaning up the . . .

NICOLE: Hee hee . . .

M. JOURDAIN: Yes, now I want you to start cleaning up the . . .

NICOLE: Hee hee . . .

M. JOURDAIN: I say, I WANT YOU TO START CLEANING UP THE . . .

NICOLE: Hee hee!

M. JOURDAIN: Again!!

NICOLE: Go ahead, sir, beat me! Beat me, but let me laugh! I have to laugh! Hee hee hee hee hee hee hee hee hee!!

M. JOURDAIN: I am FURIOUS!

NICOLE: Please, sir, let me laugh, I beg you! Hee hee hee hee!

M. JOURDAIN: I'm going to take you between my . . .

NICOLE: Sirrrrr, I'm going to burrrrrrrrrrst, if I can't laffffffffffffffffffff! Hee hee hee hee hee hee hee!

M. JOURDAIN (*to the lackeys*): Have you ever seen anything like this? Insolent wench! Laughing in my face! Refuses to take her orders!

NICOLE (*controlling herself*): What do you want, Monsieur?

MONSIEUR JOURDAIN: I want, my little trollop, for you to start cleaning up the room, for company that's coming IN JUST A FEW MINUTES!

NICOLE: Well why didn't you say so? Your "company" would stop anybody from laughing—they're as miserable as they are unruly.

M. JOURDAIN: Are you telling me I'm to close *my* door on people *you* don't like?

NICOLE: Some of them, yes!

MADAME J. (*entering*): Ahah! So, what's the story this time? A new little outfit, my darling husband? Your equipage for the day? That's the most idiotic get up I've ever seen. Have you gone mad? Out of your mind? You're the laughingstock of all Paris.

M. JOURDAIN: Only fools will laugh, my dear wife.

MADAME J.: Everyone will laugh; everyone's already laughing—in fact, everyone's been laughing at you for a long time now.

M. JOURDAIN: And who is this "everyone," if you please?

MADAME J.: Everyone who's smart, everyone who's intelligent—it's a scandal! This isn't a house anymore, it's a stinking carnival, with fiddlers and fencers and warblers; we're the joke of the neighborhood!

NICOLE: Madame's right. I can't even keep house with this crowd you bring in here every day, tracking in mud from every quarter of Paris; poor Françoise is down on her knees all day scrubbing after them.

M. JOURDAIN: Nicole, you jabber pretty well for a country peasant.

MADAME J.: Nicole's right, and she has better sense than you do. What are you doing with a dancing master at your age, anyway.

NICOLE: And a foot-clomping swordsman who's going to tear the house apart with his "lessons?"

M. JOURDAIN: Shut up, both of you!

MADAME J.: You want to dance 'til you can't walk?

NICOLE: You want to murder somebody?

M. JOURDAIN: Be quiet I tell you! You know nothing of the prerogatives of privilege!

MADAME J.: Privilege! You'd be better off trying to get your daughter married; she's rather getting on, you know.

M. JOURDAIN: I will take care of that when the right man comes along, but I shall also study the arts!

NICOLE (*to* MADAME J.): He also took on a philosophy teacher, another mussel in his marinière, I suppose.

M. JOURDAIN: I want to be able to make spirited conversation with intelligent people, what's wrong with that?

MADAME J.: Why don't you go to college? They'd whip it into you.

M. JOURDAIN: Well maybe I shall! It would be worth a dozen whippings to learn what you can learn in college!

NICOLE: They'd teach you to bow down, anyway.

M. JOURDAIN: Absolutely!

MADAME J.: And how is all this education going to help you run the household, may I ask?

M. JOURDAIN: Don't be such an ignoramus; I am ashamed of both of you. Listen: do either of you know, for just one example, what it is you are *talking* right now?

MADAME J.: Talking? I'm talking good common sense, and you better think about getting some of that yourself.

M. JOURDAIN: That's not what I'm asking you; I'm asking what are the WORDS you're speaking?

MADAME J.: Sensible ones, as opposed to yours!

M. JOURDAIN: No, that's not what I'm saying! I'm asking you—what we're saying, what we have been speaking, what is it?

MADAME J.: Drivel?

M. JOURDAIN: No, no, I don't mean that! Idiot! What are we saying, the language we're speaking, right now, what is it?

MADAME J.: What the hell are you talking about??

M. JOURDAIN: WHAT IS IT CALLED!!??

MADAME J.: WHATEVER YOU WANT! FRENCH! ENGLISH! SANSKRIT!

M. JOURDAIN: NO! (*triumphant*) It's prose, you imbecile!

MADAME J. (*pause*): Prose?

M. JOURDAIN (*as if announcing a new religion*): Yes, prose! Everything that is not verse is prose. And everything that is not prose is verse! There's education for you! And now you, Nicole, do you know how you're supposed to say "yu"?

NICOLE: Huh?

M. JOURDAIN: "Yu"—What do you do to say "yu"?

NICOLE: What do you mean?

M. JOURDAIN: Say a little "yu"—you'll see.

NICOLE: Okay. "Yu."

M. JOURDAIN: Now what did you do?

NICOLE: I said "yu."

M. JOURDAIN: Yes, when you said "yu"—what did you do?

NICOLE: What you told me to do.

M. JOURDAIN: Oh God, to have to deal with these morons? (*patiently*) You pout your lips outwards, and bring your jaw inwards—"yu"—do you see now? "Yu" I'm making a face, see? "Yu"!

NICOLE: Beauuuuuuuuuutiful.

MADAME J. (*sarcastically*): How extraordinary!

M. JOURDAIN: I'm glad you appreciate it. The "oh," the "da da" and the "fa fa" are far more complicated.

MADAME J.: You're off your rocker.

NICOLE: He's the most ridiculous thing I've ever seen.

M. JOURDAIN: You two are infuriating! Ignorant WOMEN!

MADAME J.: Get rid of these master idiots; send them packing!

NICOLE: And that filthy fencing master with his muddy boots!

M. JOURDAIN: Aha, my fencing master really gets to you, doesn't he? Let me show you your impertinence, Nicole; take this! (*gives a foil to* NICOLE) The body's line is the mind's reason; when one thrusts in the fourth position, one thinks in fours, when one thrusts in the third, one responds in threes. That's how to prevent being killed—isn't that important? Here, thrust at me.

NICOLE: Okay.

(*She thrusts several times.*)

M. JOURDAIN: Hey! HEY! Easy now. Hey! WATCH IT! She-devil!

NICOLE: You told me to thrust.

M. JOURDAIN: Yes, but you thrusted in the third position when I was in the fourth position; you're supposed to wait until I parry!

MADAME J.: Husband, you have gone crazy, you are living in some kind of fantasy! Ever since you decided to mix with your marquises and marquesses and to haunt the antechambers of the court. . . .

M. JOURDAIN: If I haunt the court, my dear wife, I show much better judgment than to haunt your beloved bourgeoisie.

MADAME J.: Oh for God sakes! You are beguiled by titles, by positions, and most of all by that oh-so-splendid Count Dorante that you're in love with.

M. JOURDAIN: PEACE! Watch what you say! Understand, my dear wife, THAT YOU HAVE NO IDEA WHAT YOU'RE TALKING ABOUT when you talk about him. He is an important person, more than you could ever know, a *seigneur*, respected at court; why he talks to the King as easily as I talk to you. He honors us with his presence—this a man of such importance who treats me as if I were an equal. His kindnesses to me, his open affection towards me before the whole world, his public caresses leave me in a state of bewilderment and joy.

MADAME J.: Sure, he gives you caresses, and he borrows your money.

M. JOURDAIN: Very well then! It is, I tell you, an honor to loan funds to a man of his importance! Could I do less for a *seigneur* who calls me his dear friend?

MADAME J.: What does he actually *do* for you?

M. JOURDAIN: Astonishing things!

MADAME J.: Yes?

M. JOURDAIN: Yes! You wouldn't understand, so I won't bother to explain. Just know that he has borrowed some money, and he will be paying it back.

MADAME J.: When?

M. JOURDAIN: Uh . . . before long.

MADAME J.: Sure. We'll wait for it!

M. JOURDAIN: Of course we will. He said he would and he will.

MADAME J.: Without fail.

M. JOURDAIN: On his honor as a gentleman.

MADAME J.: Bulldirt!

M. JOURDAIN: Yiiiiii! God, you're obstinate. Wife, I tell you, he gave his word, and he'll keep his word, I know he will, I'm sure he will!

MADAME J.: And I'm sure he won't, not as long as caresses are cheaper than good French Francs.

M. JOURDAIN: QUIET, wench, here he is.

MADAME J.: Oh boy! To borrow more money, I'll bet. The very sight of him makes me want to throw up.

M. JOURDAIN: QUIET, I tell you!!

DORANTE: My dear, dear friend, Monsieur Jourdain, how are you?

M. JOURDAIN: Very, very well, Monsieur. Monsieur, your servant ever.

DORANTE: And Madame Jourdain, over there in the corner, how is she?

M. JOURDAIN: As well as possible, Monsieur.

DORANTE (*pretending to admire* JOURDAIN's *costume*): Why, Monsieur Jourdain, how magnificent you look!

M. JOURDAIN: Ah, you like it?

DORANTE: The suit is—well it's—(*he searches for the right description*) it gives you a splendid appearance—(*and, finding the perfect ambiguous compliment*) none of the young men at court could possibly come up with anything like it!

M. JOURDAIN (*ecstatic*): Ay yi! Ay yi!

MADAME J. (*to the audience*): It's you scratch my back, and I'll . . .

DORANTE: Turn around . . . (JOURDAIN *does so*) Ah, how gallant, how . . .

MADAME J. (*still to the audience*): It's as stupid in the be-hind as in the front . . .

DORANTE (*hurrying to interrupt*): In faith, Monsieur Jourdain, I could hardly wait to get here this morning, for I esteem you far above all other men. Why this very morning, I found myself speaking of you, once again, right in the King's Chamber!

M. JOURDAIN (*stunned, suddenly doffs his hat and bows clumsily, obsequiously to* DORANTE; *with true humility*): You do me too much honor, Monsieur! (*to his wife*) Did you hear that? In the King's Chamber!

DORANTE: Ah, Monsieur, please, put on your . . .

M. JOURDAIN: I am overcome with respect, Monsieur.

DORANTE (*with ingratiating sincerity*): My God, please, put on your hat, I beg you, there must be no artificial ceremony between us.

M. JOURDAIN (*utterly overawed at* DORANTE's *kindness*): Monsieur!

DORANTE (*with oily charm, taking off his own hat*): Put it back on, I tell you, you are my FRIEND.

M. JOURDAIN (*almost falling to his knees, his legs trembling*): Monsieur, I am your servant.

DORANTE (*with sudden mock anger*): I will not put on my hat unless you do!

M. JOURDAIN (*quickly, with mustered dignity, puts on his hat*): If you insist.

(*His hand trembles with anxiety as he lets go of the brim;* DORANTE *puts his hat back on also.*)

DORANTE (*coming to his true subject, now that* JOURDAIN *has been primed*): I am your debtor, as you know.

MADAME J.: Oh yes, we know all right!

DORANTE: You have generously loaned me money on several occasions, with the greatest graciousness the world could ever know.

M. JOURDAIN: You embarrass me, sir.

DORANTE: But I understand that debts must be repaid, and that gratitude must be accounted for.

M. JOURDAIN: I doubt it not, Monsieur.

DORANTE: So I have come to clear our ledgers.

M. JOURDAIN (*to his wife*): There, you see how impertinent you've been!

DORANTE: I'm a man who likes to settle his affairs as soon as possible.

M. JOURDAIN (*to* MADAME J.): I told you so, dummy!

DORANTE: Let's see how much I owe you.

M. JOURDAIN (*to* MADAME J.): . . . and as for your ridiculous suspicions . . .

DORANTE: Perhaps you recall the amounts I've borrowed?

M. JOURDAIN: I think so, yes; I've made a little note of it; here it is. First a loan of two hundred gold *louis*.

DORANTE: That's right.

M. JOURDAIN: Then one of a hundred and twenty.

DORANTE: Right.

M. JOURDAIN: Another of a hundred and forty.

DORANTE: Right again.

M. JOURDAIN: That's four hundred and sixty gold *louis*, or five thousand and sixty *livres*.

DORANTE: Good counting. Five thousand and sixty.

M. JOURDAIN: A bill of one thousand eight hundred and thirty-two *livres* paid to the man that makes your hat plumes.

DORANTE: Good.

M. JOURDAIN: One of two thousand seven hundred and eighty to your tailor.

DORANTE: Fine.

M. JOURDAIN: One of four thousand three hundred and seventy-nine *livres*, twelve *sols*, eight *deniers* to your provisioner.

DORANTE: Quite right. Twelve *sols*, eight *deniers*, exactly; what records!

M. JOURDAIN: And one thousand seven hundred and forty-eight *livres*, seven *sols*, four *deniers* to your saddler.

DORANTE: Everything is correct. Now what does it make?

M. JOURDAIN: The total is fifteen thousand eight hundred *livres*.

DORANTE: Very good: fifteen thousand eight hundred. Now add to that two hundred *pistoles* that you're going to give me today and that makes it exactly eighteen thousand francs, which I will pay you just as soon as I can.

MADAME J.: Well, did I guess it or did I guess it?

M. JOURDAIN: Peace!

DORANTE: This won't put you out any, will it?

M. JOURDAIN: Oh, no!

MADAME J.: He milks you like a cow!

M. JOURDAIN: Shut up!

DORANTE: If this is inconvenient, I can go elsewhere . . .

M. JOURDAIN: No, Monsieur!

MADAME J.: He won't be happy until you're ruined.

M. JOURDAIN: I said shut up!

DORANTE: You only have to say the word if this would put you in, shall I say, a ticklish position.

M. JOURDAIN: Not at all, sir, not at all!

MADAME J.: What a charmer.

M. JOURDAIN: If you don't shut up . . .

MADAME J.: He'll suck you to your last *sou!*

M. JOURDAIN: Will you be quiet!

DORANTE: Of course, there are lots of people who would love to loan me the money, but since you are my best friend, I thought you might be offended if I went to anyone else.

M. JOURDAIN: Oh, I would be indeed! You do me too much honor, Monsieur. I will arrange everything.

MADAME J.: What?! You're not going to give him more?

M. JOURDAIN: And what am I supposed to do? Do you want me to refuse to help a man like that, a *seigneur* who spoke of me this morning in the King's chamber?

MADAME J. (*as he goes off*): Husband, you are a total fool!

DORANTE: You seem unhappy, Madame, is there anything wrong?

MADAME J.: My head's not as swollen as my husband's, but it's still bigger than my fist.

DORANTE: Mademoiselle your daughter, now where is she? I don't see her around?

MADAME J.: Lucky for her.

DORANTE: And how goes the dear girl?

MADAME J.: On foot, thank you very much!

DORANTE: Won't you bring her to court some day, to catch a play or ballet?

MADAME J.: Oh, of course, that would be good for a laugh, wouldn't it?

DORANTE (*laughs*): Oh, Madame Jourdain, you must have had many lovers in your youth, with your beauty and such wit . . .

MADAME J.: Are you suggesting, Monsieur, that I am now old and decrepit? Palsied maybe?

DORANTE: Ah, *ma foi!* I beg your pardon, Madame, I don't know what I was thinking of, of course you are still a young, *young* woman, excuse me, please, for such impertinence!

M. JOURDAIN (*returning*): Here's the two hundred gold *louis*, Monsieur.

DORANTE: Ah, Monsieur Jourdain, your servant ever I assure you. I simply burn to support you at court!

M. JOURDAIN: Too obliged, too obliged.

DORANTE: If Madame Jourdain wishes to see the royal entertainment, I will get her the best seats in the house.

MADAME J.: Madame Jourdain kisses both your hands, knuckle by knuckle by knuckle.

DORANTE (*aside, to* JOURDAIN): Listen, our lovely marquise is coming tonight for dinner and a dance, as you asked me to invite her, and I have also persuaded her to accept your little gift!

M. JOURDAIN (*pulling him aside*): Over here, over here!

DORANTE: She put up a fight—but she agreed this morning to take your diamond! You must imagine how difficult it was—it took me eight days to overcome her scruples—that's why I haven't been able to come here all week!

M. JOURDAIN: How did she like it?

DORANTE: Marvellously! It's put her in a wonderful mood!

M. JOURDAIN: Thank the Lord!

DORANTE: I explained to her that the value of the diamond was only equal to the magnitude of your love.

M. JOURDAIN: Your kindness overwhelms me—why a person of your rank even bothers with someone like me is beyond my . . .

DORANTE: Don't be silly! What are friends for? To worry about trifles like rank and social standing? You'd do the same for me, wouldn't you?

M. JOURDAIN: Ah, my God, but of course! Of course! With all my heart!

MADAME J. (*to* NICOLE): Ohhhhh he weighs me down!

DORANTE: Well, listen, as far as I'm concerned, nothing stops me from helping my friends, nothing! From the moment you confided in me of your love for this delightful marquise, I have been happy to act as your amorous go-between.

M. JOURDAIN: Such kindness, such overwhelming loyalty . . .

MADAME J.: Is he never going to leave?

NICOLE (*to* MADAME): Well, they do make a charming couple!

DORANTE: Monsieur, your approach has been perfect; women love to be fussed over, and to know we're lavishing lots of money on them. Your serenades, your bouquets of flowers, the fireworks display you arranged over the pond beneath her window, the diamond you've sent her, tonight's planned entertainment: all this signifies your love far more than any possible words that could come from your own mouth.

M. JOURDAIN: There is nothing I wouldn't spend to reach her heart; a woman of her quality, of her station, of her ravishing charms: her love would be an honor at any price!

MADAME J.: What can they still be talking about? Nicole, go listen, won't you?

(NICOLE *moves nearer*)

DORANTE: It won't be long—soon, soon, you will rejoice in seeing her, you will stare at her leisurely, longingly, your eyes will drink her in, lovingly . . .

M. JOURDAIN: Ah, yes . . . I'm sending my wife to her

sister's so we can be alone, so we can be free, free, free!

DORANTE: Wise, wise, how wise! Your wife would only prove an embarrassment! I have already ordered the dinner from the caterers, and I've arranged everything for the ballet, which I have composed myself. If the execution matches the idea, I know that you'll love it!

M. JOURDAIN (*sees* NICOLE *eavesdropping and slaps her*): Ahah! Nosy wench! (*to* DORANTE) Come on, let's get out of here!

(*They leave.*)

NICOLE (*rubbing her slapped cheek*): Well, Madame, curiosity may kill Nicole, but I think we've found a snake in the grass here. They're keeping something secret, that's for sure.

MADAME J.: It's not the first time, Nicole. I'm afraid that love is in the air, and I'm going to hunt it down! But first we must take care of my daughter. Lucile is in love with Cleonte. Cleonte is in love with Lucile. I like him, I'd like to give her to him.

NICOLE: Good heavens, Madame, that's the most wonderful thing I've ever heard! For if you like Cleonte, I love his valet, Covielle; we were hoping we could get married—in their shadow as it were.

MADAME J.: Go tell Cleonte what I said, and tell him to come here so we can go ask my husband's approval.

NICCLE: At once, Madame, Oh Madame, you couldn't ask me to do anything I'd rather do! Oh, we're all going to be so very happy!

(MADAME J. *exits.* CLEONTE *and* COVIELLE *enter, meeting* NICOLE.)

Ah, there you are! Just the man I want! Listen, I have great news, I want . . .

CLEONTE: Witch, get out of here! I am no longer amused by your treachery!

NICOLE: What? I'm trying to tell you . . .

CLEONTE: Out, I say, get out of here and tell your faithless mistress I'm not such a fool as she thinks I am! Out!

NICOLE: Are you dizzy? Dear Covielle, tell me what's going on.

COVIELLE: Your dear Covielle is it? Traitoress! Out of my sight and fast, you harridan, leave me in peace!

NICOLE: What??? You too?

COVIELLE: Out of my sight, I tell you, and never speak to me again.

NICOLE: Okay! Okay! You've both been bitten by the same bug I see; and what a story this will make!

(*Exits*)

CLEONTE: How could she do it? To treat a lover like this—the most faithful and passionate of lovers!

COVIELLE: To both of us! It's an atrocity!

CLEONTE: I give her the greatest ardor, the greatest tenderness that can be imagined, I love no one in the world but her, I think of no one in the world but her; she inhabits all my cares, all my desires, all my joy; I speak nothing but her, I think of nothing but her, I dream of nothing but her; when I breathe, I breathe Lucile, when my heart beats, it beats "Lucile, Lucile!" And see what I get for it! Two days without seeing her—days that seem like centuries to me—I meet her by chance, my heart leaps into my throat, joy sets my cheek aflame, I fly passionately to her arms—and the infidel stares straight ahead and passes by like she never saw me!

COVIELLE: Exactly the same with me.

CLEONTE: Has anyone ever seen anything like this? Perfidious women! Ingratitude, thou marble-hearted fiend!

COVIELLE: Ditto Nicole!

CLEONTE: After the sacrifices, the sighs, the vows to her charms!

COVIELLE: After all my kind words and care, helping her with the dishes and cleaning the kitchen!

CLEONTE: The tears I've shed at her knees!

COVIELLE: The times I've gone to the well for her.

CLEONTE: The heat of passion I've spent cherishing her!

COVIELLE: The heat of the oven I've suffered helping her cook!

CLEONTE: She has fled from me with contempt!

COVIELLE: She's turned her back on me with abandon!

CLEONTE: To the dungeon with her!

COVIELLE: To the whipping post!

CLEONTE: Covielle, never mention her name in my presence!

COVIELLE: Me? Never!

CLEONTE: Never forget. Never forgive.

COVIELLE: Fear me not!

CLEONTE: No! I mean it! Don't defend her!

COVIELLE: Who could dream of such a thing?

CLEONTE: I want to remember her in hatred, not in love.

COVIELLE: Absolutely!

CLEONTE: This Monsieur the Count—this Dorante who comes to her house, perhaps she sees him, perhaps her head is turned by his title. But I can't let it be known that she jilted me for him; my honor is at stake, Covielle! I'm leaving her first!

COVIELLE: Rightly said. My sentiments exactly.

CLEONTE: Give me a hand, Covielle; support my resolution against the urgings of my heart. Tell me, I beg you, how bad she is; make her ugly and evil in my eyes; tell me her faults—come on, disgust me!

COVIELLE: Ah, Monsieur, Lucile . . . she is a cute little minx, nothing else, stuck-up, conceited, a waste of your time. I've never seen anyone more mediocre; there are hundreds better all around you.

CLEONTE: Her faults, her faults!

COVIELLE: Well, right off, she's got these tiny eyes . . .

CLEONTE: Tiny! But with such fire, such luminosity; such piercing, touching eyes . . .

COVIELLE: A big mouth.

CLEONTE: Huge! But graceful, not like other mouths. A mouth filled with desire, a beautiful mouth, an amourous mouth . . .

COVIELLE: Small . . .

CLEONTE: But shapely . . .

COVIELLE: Careless . . .

CLEONTE: But charming and engaging; a certain *je ne sais quoi* that goes right to the heart . . .

COVIELLE: As for her wit . . .

CLEONTE: Oh no, Covielle, her wit is the finest, the most delicate, the most subtle . . .

COVIELLE: Conversationally . . .

CLEONTE: Brilliant!

COVIELLE: Too serious!

CLEONTE: Would you have her frivolous? Empty-headed? Laughing giddily all over the place? How banal!

COVIELLE: But she's capricious! Fickle!

CLEONTE: And I love it! I love it! Damn beautiful women, they can get away with anything!!!

COVIELLE: The way things are going, I think I'd better quit. You'll love her forever.

CLEONTE: I'd love to see her dead; I'll hate her as soon as I can stop myself from loving her.

COVIELLE: How will you do that, if you think she's so perfect?

CLEONTE: All the better; I'll hate her perfectly, with all the passion of this passionate heart. The more beautiful she is, the more adorable, the more I'll hate her! Here she is!

(NICOLE *and* LUCILE *enter.*)

NICOLE: Let me tell you, I was stunned.

LUCILE: I'm sure it's what I told you, Nicole. But there they are.

CLEONTE: I have no intention of speaking to her.

COVIELLE: Me neither.

LUCILE: What is it, Cleonte? What's the matter with you?

NICOLE: You too, Covielle?

LUCILE: Did I say something wrong?

NICOLE: You're out of sorts?

LUCILE: Can't you speak, Cleonte?

NICOLE: Tongue-tied, Covielle?

CLEONTE: Faithless!

COVIELLE: Judas!

LUCILE: I have a feeling that our little meeting a while back has upset your spirits.

CLEONTE: Ah! Ah! Now we're getting somewhere.

NICOLE: Our little greeting this morning got your goat, did it?

COVIELLE: Good guess.

LUCILE: Is this what's bothering you, Cleonte?

CLEONTE: Yes, you mistress of perfidy, since you mention it, and I'm here to tell you that you won't triumph over me! You can't break up with me because I hereby break up with you! I will suffer, no doubt, but I will overcome my grief, I will overcome my love, and I shall emerge victorious! Far better to fall upon my sword than to crawl upon my knees!

COVIELLE: Me too! I also!

LUCILE: Much ado about nothing! Let me explain what happened this morning.

CLEONTE: I don't want to hear about it.

NICOLE: I'll tell you why we passed you by.

COVIELLE: I'm not listening.

LUCILE: This morning . . .

CLEONTE: No, I tell you.

NICOLE: We were . . .

COVIELLE: No, traitoress!

LUCILE: Listen!

CLEONTE: Forget it!

NICOLE: Let me speak.

COVIELLE: I'm deaf.

LUCILE: Cleonte!

CLEONTE: No.

NICOLE: Covielle!

COVIELLE: Sorry!

LUCILE: Come back here!

CLEONTE: Stuff!

NICOLE: Hear us!

COVIELLE: Nonsense!

LUCILE: Just a moment!

CLEONTE: Never!

NICOLE: Wait!

COVIELLE: Fiddlesticks!

LUCILE: Two words!

CLEONTE: No, I've heard enough!

NICOLE: One word!

COVIELLE: That's it!

LUCILE: Okay! Okay! Since you won't listen, do what you please and think what you will!

NICOLE: If that's the way you're going to be, just take it as you like it!

CLEONTE: Well, then explain.

LUCILE: No, I've said enough.

COVIELLE: Tell me . . .

NICOLE: No, I have nothing to tell.

CLEONTE: Please.

LUCILE: No, I tell you.

COVIELLE: Have a heart.

NICOLE: No.

CLEONTE: I beg you.

LUCILE: Leave me alone.

COVIELLE: I implore you.

NICOLE: Go away from me.

CLEONTE: Lucile!

LUCILE: No.

COVIELLE: Nicole!

NICOLE: No! No!

CLEONTE: In the name of God!

LUCILE: I don't want to.

COVIELLE: Speak to me!

NICOLE: Absolutely not.

CLEONTE: Enlighten my suspicions.

LUCILE: I can't be bothered.

COVIELLE: Ameliorate my anxiety!

NICOLE: I have no wish to do so.

CLEONTE: All right! Since you care so little about relieving my agony, and about explaining the vile manner in which you have abused my passion, let us part forever. Ingrateful wretch, you see me for the last time. I shall go far away and die of grief and vanquished love!

COVIELLE: I'll follow you!

LUCILE: Cleonte!

NICOLE: Covielle!

CLEONTE: Eh?

COVIELLE: What was that?

LUCILE: Where are you going?

CLEONTE: Where I told you.

COVIELLE: To die.

LUCILE: You're going to die, Cleonte?

CLEONTE: Yes, you cruel angel, as you wish me to.

LUCILE: I? I wish you to die?

CLEONTE: Yes, you have demanded it!

LUCILE: Who said?

CLEONTE: You did, when you refused to allay my suspicions!

LUCILE: Is it my fault? If you had only listened, I would have explained to you that the unfortunate event of earlier this morning was caused quite simply by the presence of my old auntie, who thinks that all men are devils in disguise, and who lectures me daily that for a man to approach an unmarried woman on the street eternally dishonors her, and for that reason must be pointedly ignored!

NICOLE: And that's what happened.

CLEONTE: Are you sure?

COVIELLE: Is that the whole truth?

LUCILE: And nothing but the truth!

NICOLE: So help us God!

COVIELLE: Are we going to buy this?

CLEONTE (*pause*): Yup! Ah, Lucile! How one word from your mouth can put my heart's agonies to rest! And how easily we can be convinced by the woman we love!

COVIELLE: How easily bamboozled by she-devils!

MADAME J. (*enters*): Cleonte! I am delighted to find you, and just in time, too. My husband is coming, this is the time to ask him for Lucile's hand in marriage.

CLEONTE: Madame! What lovely words, so in tune with my desire! Could I ever be given a more charming task? A more delicious assignment?

(MONSIEUR JOURDAIN *enters.*)

CLEONTE: Monsieur Jourdain!

M. JOURDAIN: Yes?

CLEONTE: Monsieur, I wish to deliver in person a request I have long considered; in person because it is a request that comes from the bottom of my heart. Monsieur, without further ado, I wish to declare that the honor of being your son-in-law is the most glorious favor which I could ever so humbly beseech of you.

M. JOURDAIN: Ah, well, let me see, now before I answer you, young man, I must inquire if you are of the bourgeois or the gentle class? Are you a gentleman?

CLEONTE: Monsieur, most people would answer that question right away—a snappy reply, and, most likely, an unscrupulous one as well. People steal titles these days, and nobody seems to care. I, however, am a delicate man, Monsieur. I believe that presumption is unworthy of an honest man, and to pretend to a gentility above the one that God delivered us in would be an act of the greatest cowardice. My parents were fine people. I served six years in the army with great honor, and I earn my own living quite comfortably. But I cannot give myself that which others in my place often pretend to: I tell you frankly that I am not of the gentle class: I am not a gentleman.

M. JOURDAIN: Good. Let's shake on that! My answer is No.

CLEONTE: No!

M. JOURDAIN: No. You are not a gentleman, you can't have my daughter.

MADAME J.: What is this "gentleman" nonsense? Who do you think we are anyway, descendants of the Pope?

M. JOURDAIN: Quiet woman, I'll hear no more about it!

MADAME J.: We are both bourgeois, both good middle-class citizens!

M. JOURDAIN: Keep your insults to yourself.

MADAME J.: Our fathers were tradesmen!

M. JOURDAIN: A plague on you! You can't forget that, can you! If your father was a tradesman, too bad for him, but my father—well, only scoundrels would bring him into this. But it doesn't matter anyway—I'm going to have a gentleman for a son-in-law—or else!

MADAME J.: Your daughter will have a husband—or else; a good, honest man, self-sufficient and handsome—not some pigeon-livered, inbred, mincing aristocrat!

NICOLE: She's right. We had a gentleman's son in our village; he was a deformed nincompoop!

M. JOURDAIN: Quiet, you. Stop interrupting all the time. I can support my daughter well enough financially. I want a son-in-law who can give her a title!

MADAME J.: A title?

M. JOURDAIN: Yes—I want her to be a marquise.

MADAME J.: Oh my God!

M. JOURDAIN: My mind is made up!

MADAME J.: I will never agree! Never! Mixed marriages don't ever work. Do you want a son-in-law who will reproach our daughter with our birth, or who will make our grandchildren ashamed of us? Ashamed to call me "grandma"? Do you want Lucile to come home in a fine carriage, like some sort of Princess? If she were to ignore anybody in the neighborhood, we'd be hearing them all right: "Look at her, Madame Marquise, Madame stuck-on-herself! It's the daughter of Monsieur Jourdain, remember when she was a happy little girl only playing at dress-up? She may be high and mighty now, but her grandparents were dry goods dealers by the city gate. They got rich, yes, but they're paying for it now in the other world, for you can't get rich honestly these days." Is that what you want to hear about your Marquise? No. I want Lucile to have a man of her own rank, whom she need not feel inferior to: a man to whom I can always say, "Come on over, son, let's have dinner."

M. JOURDAIN: It's very narrow-minded of you, my dear, to want to remain forever at your low station in life. No more of this! My daughter will be a marquise despite you and you and everybody else: and if you persist in making me angry—I will make her a duchess!

(*He leaves.*)

MADAME J.: Courage, Cleonte, courage. Come, Lucile, tell your father that if you can't marry the man you want, you won't marry anyone at all!

(*They leave;* CLEONTE *and* COVIELLE *remain.*)

COVIELLE: Good going with the noble sentiments.

CLEONTE: How could I know? I feel these things very strongly.

COVIELLE: Don't you see he's nuts? You speak seriously with a man like that? Couldn't you just play along with him a little?

CLEONTE: You're right. But I didn't think I was going to have to give him a birth certificate. (COVIELLE *laughs*) What are you laughing about?

COVIELLE: I have an idea.

CLEONTE: What?

COVIELLE: It's pretty cute.

CLEONTE: Go on.

COVIELLE: I remember a little masquerade which could serve us well right now, a little burlesque which we can play around Monsieur Ridiculous. It will be a comedy in which he'll play his part to perfection! Just leave it to me: I'll get the actors, the costumes, and I'll slip him into his role before he has the foggiest notion of what's happening.

CLEONTE: But tell me more!

COVIELLE: I'll tell you everything. But over here; he's coming.

(*They leave.* MONSIEUR JOURDAIN *and a* LACKEY *enter.*)

M. JOURDAIN: What the hell's the matter with them, anyway. They're continually carping about my hobnobbing with aristocrats; what's wrong with that? Aristocrats are honorable, they are civilized, they are aristocratic! Why to be a count or a marquis I'd gladly give two of my fingers!

LACKEY (*enters, announcing*): Monsieur, Count Dorante and Lady Dorimene!

M. JOURDAIN: Good God. Uh, tell them I'll be right back! I have some orders to give! (*rushes out*)

LACKEY (*as* DORIMENE *and* DORANTE *enter*): Monsieur says that he will return in just a moment.

DORANTE: Very good.

DORIMENE: Well, here I am again, Dorante, in a house where I know no one! I don't know, Dorante . . .

DORANTE: Where else can we go, my sweet, since we obviously can't go to my house, and we obviously can't go to yours! I love you. I love you!

DORIMENE: Stop saying that! Can't you see I'm trying to resist you? But your persistence is wearing me down, Dorante—I'm afraid you'll soon have me doing very sweetly just as you please. Day after day, your visits, your letters of affection, your serenades, your little entertainments and ballets, your presents, your flowers, your fireworks at my window. I'm trying to stop you, but you won't be stopped; little by little you are breaking down all my resistance. Soon, Dorante, I will be unable to put up any fight at all, and I fear that you will end up driving me into marriage; which, I assure you, is an honor that I've dreamt not of.

DORANTE: Faith, Madame, you should be married. Your widowhood is a prison where you can think only of yourself. I know what I am doing, and I love you more than my whole life. You are my happiness: marry me today!

DORIMENE: Lord, Dorante, we must each be happy alone, if we are both to be happy together—and that's not always easy, even for rational people.

DORANTE: You're joking, Madame, your past former marriage is no guide to *our* future.

DORIMENE: But your debts, incurred on my account—they bother me for two reasons: first, because they oblige me to you more than I would wish, and second, because I don't think you can afford them, and that displeases me.

DORANTE: Ah, Madame, they are mere trifles, don't think about them further.

DORIMEME: I know what I am talking about. For example, the diamond you gave me—forced on me—is much more expensive . . .

DORANTE: Ah, Madame, please think nothing of it—it is nothing compared to my love for you, please . . . but here comes the man of the house!

M. JOURDAIN (*enters and starts to bow—but he is too near* DORIMENE *to do the bow he learned*): A little further back, Madame.

DORIMENE: What?

M. JOURDAIN: A step back, please.

DORIMENE: What are you talking about?

M. JOURDAIN: Just a little bit, please, for the third salutation!

DORANTE: Madame, Monsieur Jourdain knows his manners.

(JOURDAIN *completes his bow.*)

M. JOURDAIN: Madame, it is a great honor for me to see myself so blessed as to be able to be so happy as to have the great and good fortune of having your good will to grant me the grace of doing you the honor of honoring me with the favor of your presence—and if I could also have the merit of meriting a merit such as you provide, and that heaven—envious of my great fortune—has granted me—the advantage of making me worthy—of—

DORANTE: That's quite all right, Monsieur Jourdain. She doesn't like compliments, actually, and she knows a man of spirit when she sees one. (*to* DORIMENE) Ridiculous, isn't he?

DORIMENE (*to* DORANTE *sarcastically*): How clever of you to notice.

DORANTE: Madame, my very best friend.

M. JOURDAIN: You do me too much honor.

DORANTE: Gallant, through and through.

DORIMENE (*to* DORANTE): Pay him my esteemed respects.

M. JOURDAIN: I have deserved neither, not yet anyway.

DORANTE: Listen (*taking* M. JOURDAIN *aside*), make sure not to mention the diamond you gave her.

M. JOURDAIN: (*to* DORANTE): Can't I ask her if she liked it?

DORANTE: Good God no! That would be terrible; a gentleman must pretend he's never even *heard* of it. (*to* DORIMENE) Monsieur Jourdain says, Madame, that he is delighted to welcome you to his humble home.

DORIMENE: He honors me greatly.

M. JOURDAIN (*aside to* DORANTE): Thanks for speaking for me!

DORANTE: No trouble. But it was hard to get her to come.

M. JOURDAIN: How can I thank you?

DORANTE (*aloud*): He says, Madame, that you are the most beautiful creature in the entire world.

DORIMENE: Very gracious, indeed.

M. JOURDAIN: It is you who are gracious, my sweet, sweet angel, and let me . . .

DORANTE: Let's eat!

LACKEY: Everything's ready, sir.

DORANTE: Let's to table, shall we? Musicians—play!

(*Six cooks dance, making the third interlude; then they bring out a laden banquet table.*)

ACT IV

DORIMENE: Dorante, this is magnificent! What a feast!

M. JOURDAIN: You jest, Madame, I only wish it were worthier of you!

(*They sit and eat.*)

DORANTE: Monsieur Jourdain is quite correct, however obliged we are at the treatment we receive here, the meal, Madame, is unworthy of you . . . Yes, I ordered it, but I confess I am not as enlightened in the art of cuisine as are some of our more eloquent friends—Count Damis, for example—and so I am afraid that this will not be quite so sophisticated a repast, quite so intellectual a culinary diversion, as greater elegance and erudition would have provided. So you must excuse some of the incongruities of the *charcuterie*, some of the barbaric excesses of *le bon gôut*. If Damis were here, he would wax poetic on the courses, one by one, overwhelm-

ing us with the science of gourmet-ology. Why Damis would speak to us of this glorious Parisian bread, its dense interior wrapped, as is a river by its banks, with a gilded crust, capturing the flowing flavor with a crackling tenderness that titillates the teeth. He would tell us of this wine, its depth, its age, its color, its sagacity, as smooth as fine velvet with just a touch of youth in the aftertaste; he would point out this saddle of lamb, perfectly gormandized with shreds of mint and parsley; this loin of veal *à la rivière*, as long as my arm; white and delicate, melting in your mouth like a pûree of almonds. He would mention the partridges, tenderly simmered in frothy *fumet*, and finally, the main course—*le grand opera* of this occasion—this magnificently plump, magnificently young spring turkey, surrounded by poached pigeons, crowned by endives and white onions, and set into an aspic dotted with pearls. That, of course, is what Damis would say, while I . . . I, of course, admit my ignorance of all of this, and, with Monsieur Jourdain, can only say that I wish the meal were worthier of you, Madame.

DORIMENE: I'm eating it anyway.

M. JOURDAIN: Ah, what beautiful hands you have.

DORIMENE: The hands are so-so, Monsieur, you're probably referring to the diamond.

M. JOURDAIN: Me? Refer to the diamond? God forbid, Madame, no gentleman would dream of such a thing. The diamond is a mere bagatelle, it's a little nothing!

DORIMENE: You are very difficult.

M. JOURDAIN: You are much too kind.

DORANTE: Here, give Monsieur Jourdain some wine, and some to the singers. Come, a drinking song!

DORIMENE: To season meat with music is most marvelous, I am most admirably regaled!

M. JOURDAIN: Madame, let me . . .

(*Singers enter.*)

DORANTE: Monsieur Jourdain, let's listen to the singers; the words of their song will be much better than anything we can say.

SONG

FIRST MAN: Drink, Phyllis, drink, darling, and
Pass it to me.
The wine, you and I make a
Menage of three.
So let's not tarry here at all

But plunge into our bacchanal
'Cause when you are tipsy
You bring out the gypsy
In me!

SECOND MAN: Drink, Phyllis, drink, darling, and
Take a few sips.
You're so alluring with
Wine on your lips.
Now what I'm trying to imply,
Is that I love you high—not dry.
'Cause when you are mellow
You make quite a fellow
Of me!

PHYLLIS: Drink boys, drink.
It' later than you think.
Life's candle could go out,
With wine still in the spout.
So let us have a taste
While there's still time to waste,
And drink, boys, drink,
While you're still in the pink!

Let this academy (*pointing to audience*)
Dispense philosophy,
But let our thoughts incline
Towards our vat of wine.
Money, wisdom, fame,
Is just a foolish game,
For happiness, I think
Is only found in drink!

ALL: So pour, *garcons*, pour! Pour on your sacred stuff!
And damned oh damned be he that first cries 'Hold, Enough!'

DORIMENE: I don't think I've ever heard better singing in my life!
M. JOURDAIN: And yet, Madame, I can imagine something you'd like even better yet!
DORIMENE: Well! Monsieur Jourdain is more of a *galant* than I realized.
DORANTE: Why, Madame, what did you take him for?
M. JOURDAIN: I'll tell you what she can take me for! She can take me . . .
DORIMENE: Take you?
DORANTE: You don't yet know him, Madame.
M. JOURDAIN: She may know me whenever she likes!
DORIMENE: I think it's time to go . . .

DORANTE: Isn't he clever? Such repartee! And notice, Madame, how he eats off your plate!
DORIMENE: Delightful!
M. JOURDAIN: To be delightful in your eyes, to ravish your heart, why I would . . .
MADAME J. (*entering*): Ahah! Company for dinner? And I'm not invited, am I; that's why you've sent me to my sister's, isn't it? It's a stinking *theatre* in here; singing and dancing, and what's this? A wedding banquet? How much did all this cost? How much to feast your ladies and put on your little theatricals?
DORANTE: What are you talking about, Madame Jourdain? Your head's full of fantasies; this is *my* party, I've borrowed your husband's house for the evening. Please understand.
M. JOURDAIN: Yes, you fool, Monsieur the Count is giving all this in honor of Madame, the Marquise, a lady of high quality. He has honored me by using my house, and by asking me to join them.
MADAME J.: Bulldirt! I know what I know.
DORANTE: Please, Madame Jourdain, please put on your glasses.
MADAME J.: I do not wear glasses, Monsieur, and I see plenty clearly. I'm not stupid, and I've known what's going on for long time. It's despicable of you—a so-called *noble*man—to lead my idiot husband around by the nose like this. And you, Madame—a great lady if you are—it is neither fair nor becoming of you to disrupt my home like this, and let my husband make love to you.
DORIMENE: Love! What's all this about? Dorante, how dare you let this old hag talk to me like this?

(*She leaves*, DORANTE *following*.)

DORANTE: Dorimene! Where are you going? Wait!
M. JOURDAIN: Madame! Oh God. Monsieur Count, get her, bring her back, make some excuses! (*to* MADAME JOURDAIN) Impertinent woman! Look what you've done! Insulting me in public! Chasing out people of quality!
MADAME J.: You know what you can do with their quality!
M. JOURDAIN: I don't know what's keeping me from picking up this banquet table, and smashing you on the head with it!
MADAME J.: You know what you can do with your banquet table! I'm defending my rights! I'm defending women's rights! All women are on my side!

(*She leaves.*)

M. JOURDAIN (*yelling after her*): And stay out! God! What a time for her to come in here. I was just about to say the cleverest things; I've never been wittier in my life! What's this? Who the hell are you?

COVIELLE (*entering, disguised*): Monsieur, I do not know if I have the honor of being recognized by you.

M. JOURDAIN: No, Monsieur. Excuse me.

(*He starts to leave.*)

COVIELLE: I knew you when you were a little boy.

M. JOURDAIN: Me?

COVIELLE: Yes, you were the prettiest child in the world, and all the ladies took you in their arms to kiss you.

M. JOURDAIN: To kiss me!

COVIELLE: Yes. I was a great friend of your late father.

M. JOURDAIN: Of my late father!

COVIELLE: Yes, a great gentleman.

M. JOURDAIN: What did you say?

COVIELLE: I said "a great gentleman."

M. JOURDAIN: My father?

COVIELLE: Yes.

M. JOURDAIN: You knew him well?

COVIELLE: I certainly did.

M. JOURDAIN: And you knew him as a gentleman?

COVIELLE: Certainly.

M. JOURDAIN: Then I don't understand what people have been saying.

COVIELLE: What do you mean?

M. JOURDAIN: Oh, stupid idiots, who've made me believe he was a dry goods merchant.

COVIELLE: Dry goods? Lies, all lies, never! All he ever did, well, he was a very gracious man, and he happened to be an expert in imported fabrics, which he selected from all over the world and brought home with him; often he would give them to his friends—for a little money and that's all there was to it.

M. JOURDAIN: I am overwhelmed! I am delighted to know you—you can testify, then, that my father was a gentleman?

COVIELLE: I will announce it to the world.

M. JOURDAIN: I am your servant ever. But what brings you here?

COVIELLE: Since I knew your late father, worthy gentleman that he was, as I have said, I have travelled all over the world.

M. JOURDAIN: All over the world!

COVIELLE: Yes.

M. JOURDAIN: That's a long way away!

COVIELLE: It certainly is. I just got back four days ago, and as I loved your father dearly, I thought I'd come right over here with the news.

M. JOURDAIN: What?

COVIELLE: You know that the son of the Grand Turk is in town?

M. JOURDAIN: Me? No.

COVIELLE: Really? He has a most magnificent retinue—the whole town has come to see him; he's being received as a *grand seigneur.*

M. JOURDAIN: My word. I had no idea.

COVIELLE: And what's more, he's in love with your daughter.

M. JOURDAIN: The son of the Grand Turk?

COVIELLE: Yes indeed, he wants to be your son.

M. JOURDAIN: My Son? The son of the Grand Turk?

COVIELLE (*grandly*): The son of the Grand Turk! Your son-in-law! Indeed, he was just telling me that. We had hardly begun our conversation when he said to me (*in heroic mock-Turkish*) "*Acciam croc coler ouch alla moustaph gidelum amanahem varahini oussere carbulath.*" That is, "Do you know the pretty young girl who's the daughter of Monsieur Jourdain, the Parisian gentleman?"

M. JOURDAIN: The son of the Grand Turk said that of me? A Parisian gentleman?

COVIELLE (*pouring it on*): Yes, he did. And I told him I knew you well, and that I knew Lucile. "Ah," he said to me, "*Marababa sahem.*" "How I love her."

M. JOURDAIN (*figuring it out*): *Marababa sahem* means "how I love her?"

COVIELLE: Yes.

M. JOURDAIN: Lordy, thanks for telling me. I never would have thought *marababa sahem* meant "how I love her." What a magnificent language. Turkish!

COVIELLE: More magnificent yet! Do you know what *cacaracamouchen* means?

M. JOURDAIN: *Cacaracamouchen?* No.

COVIELLE: It means "my darling."

M. JOURDAIN: *Cacaracamouchen* means "my darling"?

COVIELLE: Yes.

M. JOURDAIN: How wonderful. *Cacaracamouchen:* "my darling." Has there ever been anything so wonderful? I'm amazed!

COVIELLE: Exactly; now to come to the point, he wants to ask you for your daughter's hand in marriage, and, in order that he have a father-in-law worthy of his station, he wishes to make you a *Mamamouchi*, which is a grand Lord of his country.

M. JOURDAIN: *Mamamouchi?*

COVIELLE: Yes, *Mamamouchi*. That is, in our language, a knight. You know, a knight, one of the ancient . . . well, a knight, anyway. There is nothing nobler than that, anywhere. You will be a member of the greatest nobility on earth.

M. JOURDAIN: The son of the Grand Turk honors me more than I can say, and I beg you to bring me to him so that I may render my thanks unto him.

COVIELLE: You don't have to, he's coming here.

M. JOURDAIN: He's coming here!

COVIELLE: Yes, and he's bringing with him everything for the ceremony of your investiture!

M. JOURDAIN: That's quick!

COVIELLE: His love brooks no delay.

M. JOURDAIN: But there's one problem, my daughter is very stubborn, she has got it in her head that she will only marry one Cleonte; she swears she'll marry no one else!

COVIELLE: She'll change her mind when she sees the son of the Grand Turk, I assure you; as a matter of fact, by an extraordinary coincidence, I ran into this one Cleonte on my way here, and I can tell you he resembles the son of the Grand Turk amazingly; the love she has for the one can just be passed over to the other! Ah! I hear him coming—here he is!

CLEONTE (*entering grandly*): *Ambousahim oqui boraf, lordina salamalequi.*

COVIELLE (*translating*): That means: "Monsieur Jourdain, may your heart flourish like a year-round rose." (*whispers*) They go in big for compliments in Turkey.

M. JOURDAIN (*responding through* COVIELLE, *with a bow*): I am the very humble servant of his "Turkish Highness."

COVIELLE: *Carigar comboto outsin moraf.*

CLEONTE: *Outsin voc catamelequi basum base alla moran.*

COVIELLE: He says, "Let heaven grant you the strength of the lion and the wisdom of the serpent."

M. JOURDAIN: His Turkish Highness honors me too much, and I wish him all sorts of prosperity.

COVIELLE: *Ossa binamen sadoc babally oracaf ouram.*

CLEONTE: *Bel men.*

COVIELLE (*excitedly*): He says you must go right away

with him and prepare yourself for the ceremony, and bring your daughter so that he and she can get married.

M. JOURDAIN (*puzzled*): All that in two words?

COVIELLE (*reassuring*): O yes, Turkish is like that: few words suffice. Go quickly!

(CLEONTE *and* JOURDAIN *exit.*)

COVIELLE: Ha ha ha! Oh this is funny! What a dupe! He couldn't play his part better if he had memorized and rehearsed it! (DORANTE *enters*) Ah, Monsieur, I beg you give us a hand here.

DORANTE: Ah, Covielle, my boy, I didn't recognize you! What's this get up?

COVIELLE: Ha ha ha ha ha. You'll see. Ha ha ha . . .

DORANTE: What's so funny?

COVIELLE: Funny? It's hilarious!

DORANTE: What?

COVIELLE: Three guesses as to who we're duping!

DORANTE: Jourdain?

COVIELLE: We're putting him in mind to marry his daughter to my master!

DORANTE: On him, anything would work.

COVIELLE: Then you know him very well. Ha ha ha ha.

DORANTE: Tell me what's going on.

COVIELLE: Step aside, first; you'll see. Here, watch this; I'll fill in the rest.

(*The* turkish *ceremony proceeds, forming the fourth interlude. The* MUFTI, *four Dervishes, six Turkish dancers, six Turkish singers, together with other Turkish instrumentalists, are the participants. The* MUFTI, *the twelve Turks, and the four Dervishes invoke Mohammed, after which they lead* JOURDAIN, *clothed as a Turk but without turban or sword, into the center of the room, dancing and singing around him.*)

MUFTI: Se ti sabir
    Ti respondir
    Se no sabir,
    Tazir, tazir.
    Mi star Mufti
    Ti qui star ti?
    Non intendir:
    Tazir, tazir.

(*The* MUFTI, *in the same language, asks the Turkish assistants what* JOURDAIN's *religion is, and they assure him that he is a Mohammedan. The* MUFTI *invokes Mohammed in pidgin-French, singing:*)

MUFTI: Mahametta per Giordina
    Mi pregar sera e mattina
    Voler far un Paladina
    De Giordina, de Giordina,
    Dar turbanta e dar scarcina,
    Con galera e brigantina
    Per deffender Palestina
    Mahametta (etc.)

(*The* MUFTI *asks the Turks if* JOURDAIN *will become a Mohammedan, and they sing:*)

MUFTI: Star bon Turca Giordina?
THE TURKS: Hi valla
MUFTI (*singing and dancing*): Hu la ba ba la chou ba la ba ba la da.

(*The Turks reply in the same word. The* MUFTI *proceeds to give* JOURDAIN *the turban, and to sing:*)

MUFTI: Ti no star furba?
THE TURKS: No, no, no.
MUFTI: Non star furfanta?
THE TURKS: No, no, no.
MUFTI: Donar turbanta, donar turbanta.

(*The Turks repeat all this as the* MUFTI *gives* JOURDAIN *the turban. The* MUFTI *and the Dervishes then put on their turbans with great ceremony, and the* MUFTI, *Koran in hand, gives* JOURDAIN *a sword, while singing:*)

MUFTI: Ti star nobile, e non star babbola Pigliar schiabbola.

(*The Turks repeat all this, sabres in hand, and six dance around* JOURDAIN, *feinting blows toward him. The* MUFTI *directs the Turks to slap* JOURDAIN *with their swords, which they do as he sings:*)

MUFTI: Dara, dara,
    Bastonnara, bastonnara.

(*The Turks repeat all this, slapping him in cadence with the song. The* MUFTI *then sings:*)

MUFTI: Non tener honta:
    Questa star ultima affronta.

(*The Turks repeat all this, and after more dancing and singing, the Turks all leave the stage.*)

ACT V

MADAME J. (*entering*): Oh my God, What a sight! Is this a masquerade? Are you going Christmas carolling? One of the three wise men? Speak up. Who's wrapped you in that—that—*thing*?

M. JOURDAIN: Listen to her, Madame impertinence herself, speaking in such a way to a *Mamamouchi!*

MADAME J.: A what?

M. JOURDAIN: Yes, my dear, you must show me some respect now, as I have just been made a *Mamamouchi!*

MADAME J.: What the hell is a *mamamouchi?*

M. JOURDAIN: *Mamamouchi, mamamouchi*—that is to say, in our language, a knight.

MADAME J.: A knight? Good night to you!

M. JOURDAIN: Knight! K-night! Ignoramus! I said K-night, which is a title with which I have just been ceremoniously invested.

MADAME J.: What ceremony?

M. JOURDAIN: *Hamemetta por Iordina.*

MADAME J.: What does that mean?

M. JOURDAIN: *Iordina,* that is to say, Jourdain, Mohammed to Knight Jourdain!

MADAME J.: You?

M. JOURDAIN: *Voler far un Paladina de Iordina.*

MADAME J.: What?

M. JOURDAIN: *Dar turbanta con galeria.*

MADAME J.: What's that mean?

M. JOURDAIN: *Per deffender Palestina.*

MADAME J.: You're going to defend Palestine?

M. JOURDAIN: *Dara dara bastonara.*

MADAME J.: How does your garden grow! It's gibberish you fool.

M. JOURDAIN: *Non tener honta; questa star l'ultima affronta!*

MADAME J.: I'll say I'm affronted.

M. JOURDAIN (*dancing and singing*): Hou la ba, ba la chou, ba la ba, ba la da.

MADAME J.: He's lost his mind.

M. JOURDAIN (*leaving*): Peace, Madame Insolence, show some respect for your husband the *Mamamouchi.*

MADAME J.: He's as mad as a mongoose; I'd better stop him—(*sees* DORANTE) Oh God, as if we didn't have enough problems. Misery all around us!

(*She leaves.*)

DORANTE (*entering with* DORIMENE): Yes, Madame, you will see him in a moment; I've never seen anything so comical in my life, nor no one so ridiculous. But play along with him, please, it will only help serve Cleonte's suit to Lucile, and Cleonte is a very gallant young man.

DORIMENE: He's cute; he deserves well.

DORANTE: Besides, there's about to be a ballet which we can't miss: it was my idea, and I want to see if it works.

DORIMENE: Yes, I have seen all the extravagant preparations: Dorante, I can no longer put up with this. Yes, that's right—I'm putting a stop to your prodigal expenditures; you may spend no more money on me: I won't tolerate it. Don't protest! I have decided to marry you immediately—therefore you can stop wasting all this money courting me; these things come to an end at the altar, after all, and that, my dear Dorante, is the most unassailable truth in the world.

DORANTE: Ah! Madame, is it possible that you have been able to reach such a delightful decision?

DORIMENE: Only to keep you from the poor house. If I weren't to marry you, you'd be utterly ruined.

DORANTE: You are, Madame, ever my adored accountant; I give you my estate along with my heart, you must use both in whatever way you please.

DORIMENE: I will use both well. But here is your friend, he looks a sight.

(JOURDAIN *enters.*)

DORANTE: Monsieur, we have come to pay you our respects, O mighty Mamamouchi, and we rejoice with you in the fortuitous marriage of your daughter and the son of the Grand Turk!

M. JOURDAIN (*with a Turkish bow*): Monsieur, I am happy to wish for you the strength of the serpent and the wisdom of the lion!

DORIMENE: May I be the first, Monsieur, to congratulate you on the glorious position to which you have ascended.

M. JOURDAIN (*with another bow*): Madame, I wish your rosebushes to flower perpetually: I am forever obliged to you for honoring my honors today, and for coming to receive my humble apologies for my wife's unforgivable gaucheries.

DORIMENE: It's nothing, believe me; I understand only too well how she esteems you, and how alarmed she must have been to think of losing you.

M. JOURDAIN: Let her lose me! Let her lose me!

DORANTE: You see, Madame, that Monsieur Jourdain is the kind of man who remembers his friends, even after greatness has been thrust upon him.

DORIMENE: It's the mark of true nobility.

DORANTE: Where is his Royal Turkish Highness? We must pay him homage!

M. JOURDAIN: He's coming; I have sent for Lucile to give him her hand.

(CLEONTE *enters.*)

DORANTE: Monsieur, we have come to pay our reverence to his Royal Highness, as friends of your future father-in-law, and to assure you of our very humble and respectful services forever.

M. JOURDAIN: Now where's the interpreter? He'll introduce you and let you know what he's talking about. You'll see—he talks great Turkish—where the hell is he? (*to* CLEONTE) *Strouf, strif, strof, straf,* Monsieur is a Grand Segnore, grand Segnore, grande Segnore; and Madame, she's a granda Dama, granda Dama . . . Ahi, he, Monsieur, he French *Mamamouchi,* and Madame, she's a French *Mamamouchesse,* I can't say it any better than that, da-mit. (COVIELLE *reappears*) Ah good, here's my interpreter. Where the heck did you go to? We haven't been able to say anything. Just tell him that Monsieur and Madame are persons of high rank, and, as my friends, they have come to pay their respects and proffer their services. (*to* DORIMENE *and* DORANTE) Now watch them talk Turkish!

COVIELLE: *Alabala crociam acci boram alabamen.*

CLEONTE: *Catelequi tubal ourin soter amalouchan.*

M. JOURDAIN: You see.

COVIELLE: He prays that the rain of prosperity shall ever water the garden of your family.

M. JOURDAIN: Now that's Turkish!

DORANTE: Wonderful.

(LUCILE *enters.*)

M. JOURDAIN: Daughter, come here—approach, will you! And give your hand to this gentleman who has done us the honor of demanding it in marriage.

LUCILE: Why on earth are you dressed up like that? Is this some kind of costume play? A comedy! How marvellous!

M. JOURDAIN: No, no, it's no comedy, it's serious! Here is your new husband!

LUCILE: My husband? Father . . .

M. JOURDAIN: Yes yours, yours, come on, give him your hand!

LUCILE: I do not want to get married.

M. JOURDAIN: I want you to, and I'm your father.

LUCILE: I won't do it!

M. JOURDAIN: Stuff and nonsense, girl! Go on, I tell you, here, give him your hand!

LUCILE: I won't!

M. JOURDAIN: You will!

LUCILE: No, I tell you, no power on earth will make me marry anyone but Cleonte! Go ahead and torture me! I am resolved; I am resolute! I am . . . (*recognizes* CLEONTE) . . . on the other hand, Dad, it *is* true that I owe you my complete devotion and obedience, and, well, of course, if you wish it, I must above all else bend my desire to your sacred will.

M. JOURDAIN: Ahah! Ahah! Well, I am delighted to see you come so quickly to your duty as a daughter. How sweeter than a lapdog's kiss it is, to have a thankful child!

MADAME J. (*entering*): What, what, what's going on here? I understand you're marrying our daughter to a sabre dancer!

M. JOURDAIN: Will you hold off, weasel? Can't you be a little reasonable?

MADAME J.: I? Be reasonable? When you're going from one insanity to another? What are all these people doing here?

M. JOURDAIN: I'm marrying Lucile to this Son of a Turk!

MADAME J.: A son of a Turk?

M. JOURDAIN: Yes, the son of a Grand Turk! Now pay him your respects—there's his translator.

MADAME J.: I don't need no translator—I'll tell him myself, face to face and nose to nose; HE'S NOT GETTING MY DAUGHTER!

M. JOURDAIN: Won't you be quiet, won't you be quiet, won't you be quiet??

DORANTE: Now what is this, Madame, surely you won't stand in the way of your daughter's great fortune! Wouldn't you like to have his Royal Turkish Highness for a son-in-law?

MADAME J.: Mind your own business, Count.

DORIMENE: But such an honor, surely you won't turn it down!

MADAME J.: I don't see how this concerns you, Madame.

DORANTE: Our friendship bids us speak!

MADAME J.: Thanks anyway. Lucile!

DORANTE: But your daughter has consented!

MADAME J.: What? To marry a Turk?

DORANTE: That's right.

MADAME J.: She could never forget Cleonte.

DORANTE: Ah, what young girls will do to become great ladies!

MADAME J.: I'll strangle her with my bare hands—but she couldn't . . .

M. JOURDAIN: Cackle cackle! I tell you the marriage will take place!

MADAME J.: And I tell you it won't!

M. JOURDAIN: Don't you shout at me!

LUCILE: Mother!

MADAME J.: Go away, slut!

M. JOURDAIN: What's that? You insult her for obeying me!

MADAME J.: Yes, she's my daughter as much as yours, she should obey *me!*

COVIELLE: Madame.

MADAME J.: Yes, what's your story?

COVIELLE: A word with you.

MADAME J.: Who needs it?

M. JOURDAIN: Oh, my God!

COVIELLE (*to* JOURDAIN): Monsieur, if I can take her aside for a minute, I think I can explain everything to her quite satisfactorily.

MADAME J.: Take yourself aside.

COVIELLE: Listen to me, please.

MADAME J.: No.

M. JOURDAIN: Listen to him.

MADAME J.: No! No!

M. JOURDAIN: He'll tell you . . .

MADAME J.: He'll tell me nothing!

COVIELLE: Just listen once, then you can do anything you like!

MADAME J.: Well then?

(*They go off.*)

COVIELLE (*aside to her*): We've been signalling to you for the past hour, Madame; can't you see we're only doing this to fool your husband? That's Cleonte, in disguise; he's the son of the Grand Turk.

MADAME J.: Ahhhh.

COVIELLE: And I'm Covielle, your translator.

MADAME J.: Ahhhhhh. Well, in that case . . .

COVIELLE: Pretend you know nothing.

MADAME J. (*aloud*): Yes, all right, I consent to the marriage!

M. JOURDAIN: Aha, well, good, now everybody's quite reasonable. And you didn't want to listen to him. I knew that he would explain everything to you about the son of the Grand Turk!

MADAME J.: He has explained perfectly; I'm satisfied. Send for the notary! And may they live happily ever after!

DORANTE: Consider it done! And, Madame Jourdain, to set your mind at rest and relieve you of any jealousy you may have felt towards your husband, the Marquise Dorimene and I will use that self-same notary to perform our marriage!

MADAME J.: Okay, I consent to that too.

M. JOURDAIN (*aside to* DORANTE): You're just trying to make her go along with it, right?

DORANTE (*aside to* JOURDAIN): Yes, of course. I'm just pretending.

M. JOURDAIN (*aloud*): Brilliant! Brilliant! A notary, ho! Ho!

(*A* LACKEY *runs out.*)

DORANTE: Until he comes with his contracts, let's see the ballet, and entertain his Royal Turkish Highness!

M. JOURDAIN: Good idea, everyone sit down!

MADAME J.: And Nicole?

M. JOURDAIN: I give her to the translator! And my wife—I give her to whoever wants her!

COVIELLE: Monsieur, we thank you. (*to the audience*) And if there is a greater fool on this earth, let's report him to the Pope!

(*The play concludes with a little ballet prepared for the occasion.*)

CURTAIN

5 MISS JULIE
A TRAGEDY IN ONE ACT

August Strindberg
1888

Translated by Elizabeth Spriggs

Since the play is here reprinted with its author's original preface, it requires little introduction.

August Strindberg (1849–1912) is considered Sweden's greatest author. Many of his plays are deeply concerned with parochial Scandinavian themes; however, his works include both early masterpieces of naturalism, such as *Miss Julie*, and expressionism, such as *The Dream Play* (1901). A deeply pessimistic man, his life was marked by severe marital discord and mental illness; still, his dramatic craftsmanship was superb and his probing into the human condition was relentless—almost to the degree of self-destruction.

Miss Julie is a play of stunning power; few plays have explored such psychological brutality or such a poisonous admixture of love and hate (Strindberg's great preoccupation) between two seemingly civilized persons. In his famous preface, Strindberg develops not only the main attributes of the naturalistic theatre, which was then in its infancy, but delivers a death blow to the excesses of nineteenth-century romanticism and the sentimentalized theatre of his contemporaries.

AUTHOR'S FOREWORD

Theatre has long seemed to me—in common with much other art—a *Biblia Pauperum*, a Bible in pictures for those who cannot read what is written or printed; and I see the playwright as a lay preacher peddling the ideas of his time in popular form, popular enough for the middle-classes, mainstay of theatre audiences, to grasp the gist of the matter without troubling their brains too much. For this reason theatre has always been an elementary school for the young, the semi-educated, and for women who still have a primitive capacity for deceiving themselves and letting themselves be deceived—who, that is to say, are susceptible to illusion and to suggestion from the author. I have therefore thought it not unlikely that in these days, when that rudimentary and immature thought process operating through fantasy appears to be developing into reflection, research and analysis, that theatre, like religion, might be discarded as an outworn form for whose appreciation we lack the necessary conditions. This opinion is confirmed by the major crisis still prevailing in the theatres of Europe, and still more by the fact that in those countries of culture, producing the greatest thinkers of the age, namely England and Germany, drama—like other fine arts—is dead.

Some countries, it is true, have attempted to create a new drama by using the old forms with up-to-date contents, but not only has there been insufficient time for these new ideas to be popularized, so that the audience can grasp them, but also people have been so wrought up by the taking of sides that pure, disinterested appreciation has become impossible. One's deepest impressions are upset when an applauding or a hissing majority dominates as forcefully and openly as it can in the theatre. Moreover, as no new form has been devised for these new contents, the new wine has burst the old bottles.

In this play I have not tried to do anything new, for this cannot be done, but only to modernize the form to meet the demands which may, I think, be made on this art today. To this end I chose—or surrendered myself to—a theme which claims to be outside the controversial issues of today, since questions of social climbing or falling, of higher or lower, better or worse, of man and woman, are, have been and will be of lasting interest. When I took this theme from a true story told me some years ago, which made a deep impression, I saw it as a subject for tragedy, for as yet it is tragic to see one favored by fortune go under, and still more to see a family heritage die out, although a time may come when we have grown so developed and enlightened that we shall view with indifference life's spectacle, now seeming so brutal, cynical, and heartless. Then we shall have dispensed with those inferior, unreliable instruments of thought called feelings, which become harmful and superfluous as reasoning develops.

The fact that my heroine rouses pity is solely due to weakness; we cannot resist fear of the same fate overtaking us. The hyper-sensitive spectator may, it is true, go beyond this kind of pity, while the man with belief in the future may actually demand some suggestion for remedying the evil—in other words some kind of policy. But, to begin with, there is no such thing as absolute evil; the downfall of one family is the good fortune of another, which thereby gets a chance to rise, and, fortune being only comparative, the alternation of rising and falling is one of life's principal charms. Also, to the man of policy, who wants to remedy the painful fact that the bird of prey devours the dove, and lice the bird of prey, I should like to put the question: why should it be remedied? Life is not so mathematically idiotic as only to permit the big to eat the small; it happens just as often that the bee kills the lion or at least drives it mad.

That my tragedy depresses many people is their own fault. When we have grown strong as the pioneers of the French revolution, we shall be happy and relieved to see the national parks cleared of ancient rotting trees which have stood too long in the way of others equally entitled to a period of growth—as relieved as we are when an incurable invalid dies.

My tragedy "The Father" was recently criticised for being too sad—as if one wants cheerful tragedies! Everybody is clamouring for this supposed "joy of life," and theatre managers demand farces, as if the joy of life consisted in being ridiculous and portraying all human beings as suffering from St. Vitus's dance or total idiocy. I myself find the joy of life in its strong and cruel struggles, and my pleasure in learning, in adding to my knowledge. For this reason I have chosen for this play an unusual situation, but an instructive one—an exception, that is to say, but a great exception, one proving the rule, which will no doubt annoy all lovers of the commonplace. What will offend simple minds is that my plot is not simple, nor its point of view single. In real life an action—this, by the way, is a somewhat new discovery—is generally caused by a whole series of motives, more or less fundamental, but as a rule the spectator chooses just one of these—the one that his mind can most easily grasp or that does most credit to his intelligence. A suicide is committed. Business troubles, says the man of affairs. Unrequited love, say the women. Sickness, says the invalid. Despair, says the down-and-out. But it is possible that the motive lay in all or none of these directions, or that the dead man concealed his actual motive by revealing quite another, likely to reflect more to his glory.

I see Miss Julie's tragic fate to be the result of many circumstances: the mother's character, the father's mistaken upbringing of the girl, her own nature, and the influence of her fiancé on a weak, degenerate mind. Also, more directly, the festive mood of Midsummer Eve, her father's absence, her monthly indisposition, her preoccupation with animals, the excitement of dancing, the magic of dusk, the strongly aphrodisiac influence of flowers, and finally the chance that drives the couple into a room alone—to which must be added the urgency of the excited man.

My treatment of the theme, moreover, is neither exclusively physiological nor psychological. I have not put the blame wholly on the inheritance from her mother, nor on her physical condition at the time, nor on immorality. I have not even preached a moral sermon; in the absence of a priest I leave this to the cook.

I congratulate myself on this multiplicity of motives as being up-to-date, and if others have done the same thing before me, than I congratulate myself on not being alone in my "paradoxes," as all innovations are called.

In regard to the drawing of the characters, I have made my people somewhat "characterless" for the following reasons. In the course of time the word character has assumed manifold meanings. It must have originally signified the dominating trait of the soul-complex, and this was confused with temperament. Later it became the middle-class term for the automaton, one whose nature had become fixed or who had adapted himself to a particular rôle in life. In fact a person who had ceased to grow was called a character, while one continuing to develop—the skilful navigator of life's river, sailing not with sheets set fast, but veering before the wind to luff again—was called characterless, in a derogatory sense, of course, because he was so hard to catch, classify, and keep track of. This middle-class conception of the immobility of the soul was transferred to the stage where the middle-class has always ruled. A character came to signify a man fixed and finished: one who invariably appeared either drunk or jocular or melancholy, and characterization required nothing more than a physicial defect such as a club-foot, a wooden leg, a red nose; or the fellow might be made to repeat some such phrase as "That's capital!" or "Barkis is willin'!" This simple way of regarding human beings still survives in the great Molière. Harpagon is nothing but a miser, although Harpagon might have been not only a miser, but also a first-rate financier, an excellent father and a good citizen. Worse still, his "failing" is a distinct advantage to his son-in-law and his daughter, who are his heirs, and who therefore cannot criticize him, even if they have to wait a while to get to bed. I do not believe, therefore, in simple stage characters; and the summary judgments of authors—this man is stupid, that one brutal, this jealous, that stingy, and so forth—should be challenged by the Naturalists who know the richness of the soul-complex and realize that vice has a reverse side very much like virtue.

Because they are modern characters, living in a period of transition more feverishly hysterical than its predecessor at least, I have drawn my figures vacillating, disintegrated, a blend of old and new. Nor does it seem to me unlikely that, through newspapers and conversations, modern ideas may have filtered down to the level of the domestic servant.

My souls (characters) are conglomerations of past and present stages of civilization, bits from books and newspapers, scraps of humanity, rags and tatters of fine clothing, patched together as is the human soul. And I have added a little evolutionary history by making the weaker steal and repeat the words of the stronger, and by making the characters borrow ideas or "suggestions" from one another.

Miss Julie is a modern character, not that the half-woman, the man-hater, has not existed always, but because now that she has been discovered she has stepped to the front and begun to make a noise. The half-woman is a type who thrusts herself forward, selling herself nowadays for power, decorations, distinctions, diplomas, as formerly for money. The type implies degeneration; it is not a good type and it does not endure; but it can unfortunately transmit its misery, and degenerate men seem instinctively to choose their mates from among such women, and so they breed, producing offspring of indeterminate sex to whom life is torture. But fortunately they perish, either because they cannot come to terms with reality, or because their repressed instincts break out uncontrollably, or again because their hopes of catching up with men are shattered. The type is tragic, revealing a desperate fight against nature, tragic too in its Romantic inheritance now dissipated by Naturalism, which wants nothing but happiness—and for happiness strong and sound species are required.

But Miss Julie is also a relic of the old warrior nobility now giving way to the new nobility of nerve and brain. She is a victim of the discord that a mother's "crime" has produced in a family, a victim too of the day's complaisance, of circumstances, of her own defective constitution, all of which are equivalent to the Fate or Universal Law of former days. The Naturalist has abolished guilt with God, but the consequences of the action—punishment, imprisonment or the fear of it—he cannot abolish, for the simple reason that they remain whether he is acquitted or not. An injured fellow-being is not so complacent as outsiders, who have not been injured, can afford to be. Even if the father had felt impelled to take no vengeance, the daughter would have taken vengeance on herself, as she does here, from that innate or acquired sense of honor which the upper-classes inherit—whether from Barbarism or Aryan forebears, or from the chivalry of the Middle Ages, who knows? It is a very beautiful thing, but it has become a danger nowadays to the preservation of the race. It is the nobleman's *hara-kiri*, the Japanese law of inner conscience which compels him to cut his own stomach open at the insult of another, and which survives in modified form in the duel, a privilege of the nobility. And so the valet Jean lives on, but Miss Julie cannot live without honor. This is the thrall's advantage over the nobleman, that he lacks this fatal preoccupation with honor. And in all of us Aryans there is something of the nobleman, or the Don Quixote, which makes us sympathize with the man who commits suicide because he has done something ignoble and lost his honor. And we are noblemen enough to suffer at the sight of fallen greatness littering the earth like a corpse—yes, even if the fallen rise again and make restitution by honorable deeds. Jean, the valet, is a race-builder, a man of marked characteristics. He was a laborer's son who has educated himself towards becoming a gentleman. He has learnt easily, through his well-developed senses (smell, taste, vision)—and he also has a sense of beauty. He has already bettered himself, and is thick-skinned enough to have no scruples about using other people's services. He is already foreign to his associates, despising them as part of the life he has turned his back on, yet also fearing and fleeing from them because they know his secrets, pry into his plans, watch his rise with envy, and look forward with pleasure to his fall. Hence his dual, indeterminate character, vacillating between love of the heights and hatred of those who have already achieved them. He is, he says himself, an aristocrat; he has learned the secrets of good society. He is polished, but vulgar within; he already wears his tails with taste, but there is no guarantee of his personal cleanliness.

He has some respect for his young lady, but he is frightened of Kristin, who knows his dangerous secrets, and he is sufficiently callous not to allow the night's events to wreck his plans for the future. Having both the slave's brutality and the master's lack of squeamishness, he can see blood without fainting and take disaster by the horns. Consequently he emerges from the battle unscathed, and probably ends his days as a hotel-keeper. And even if *he* does not become a Romanian Count, his son will doubtless go to the university and perhaps become a county attorney.

The light that Jean sheds on a lower-class conception of life, life seen from below, is on the whole illuminating—when he speaks the truth, which is not often, for he says what is favorable to himself rather than what is true. When Miss Julie suggests that the lower classes must be oppressed by the attitude of their superiors, Jean naturally agrees, as his object is to gain her sympathy; but when he perceives the advantage of separating himself from the common herd, he at once takes back his words.

It is not because Jean is now rising that he has the upper hand of Miss Julie, but because he is a man. Sexually he is the aristocrat because of his virility, his keener senses and his capacity for taking the initiative. His inferiority is mainly due to the social environment in which he lives, and he can probably shed it with his valet's livery.

The slave mentality expresses itself in his worship of the Count (the boots), and his religious superstition; but he worships the Count chiefly because he holds that higher position for which Jean himself is striving. And this worship remains even when he has won the daughter of the house and seen how empty is that lovely shell.

I do not believe that a love relationship in the "higher" sense could exist between two individuals of such different quality, but I have made Miss Julie imagine that she is in love, so as to lessen her sense of guilt, and I let Jean suppose that if his social position were altered he would truly love her. I think love is like the hyacinth that has to strike roots in darkness *before* it can produce a vigorous flower. In this case it shoots up quickly, blossoms and goes to seed all at the same time, which is why the plant dies so soon.

As for Kristin, she is a female slave, full of servility and sluggishness acquired in front of the kitchen fire, and stuffed full of morality and religion, which are her cloak and scape-goat. She goes to church as a quick and easy way of unloading her household thefts on to Jesus and taking on a fresh cargo of guiltlessness. For the rest she is a minor character, and I have therefore sketched her in the same manner as the Pastor and the Doctor in "The Father," where I wanted ordinary human beings, as are most country pastors and provincial doctors. If these minor characters seem abstract to some people, this is due to the fact that ordinary people are to a certain extent abstract in pursuit of their work; that is to say, they are without individuality, showing, while working, only one side of themselves. And as long as the spectator does not feel a need to see them from other sides, there is nothing wrong with my abstract presentation.

In regard to the dialogue, I have departed somewhat from tradition by not making my characters catechists who ask stupid questions in order to elicit a smart reply. I have avoided the symmetrical, mathematical construction of French dialogue, and let people's minds work irregularly, as they do in real life where, during a conversation, no topic is drained to the dregs, and one mind finds in another a chance cog to engage in. So too the dialogue wanders, gathering in the opening scenes material which is later picked up, worked over, repeated, expounded and developed like the theme in a musical composition.

The plot speaks for itself, and as it really only concerns two people, I have concentrated on these, introducing only one minor character, the cook, and keeping the unhappy spirit of the father above and behind the action. I have done this because it seems to me that the psychological process is what interests people most today. Our inquisitive souls are no longer satisfied with seeing a thing happen; we must also know how it happens. We want to see the wires themselves, to watch the machinery, to examine the box with the false bottom, to take hold of the magic ring in order to find the join, and look at the cards to see how they are marked.

In this connection I have had in view the documentary novels of the brothers de Goncourt, which appeal to me more than any other modern literature.

As far as the technical side of the work is concerned I have made the experiment of abolishing the division into acts. This is because I have come to the conclusion that our capacity for illusion is disturbed by the intervals, during which the audience has time to reflect and escape from the suggestive influence of the author-hypnotist. My play will probably take an hour and a half, and as one can listen to a lecture, a sermon or a parliamentary debate for as long as that or longer, I do not think a theatrical performance will be fatiguing in the same length of time. As early as 1872, in one of my first dramatic attempts, "The Outlaw," I tried this concentrated form, although with scant success. The play was written in five acts, and only when finished did I become aware of the restless, disjointed effect that it produced. The script was burnt and from the ashes rose a single well-knit act—fifty pages of print, playable in one hour. The form of the present play is, therefore, not new, but it appears to be my own, and changing tastes may make it timely. My hope is one day to have an audi-ence educated enough to sit through a whole evening's entertainment in one act, but one would have to try this out to see. Meanwhile, in order to provide respite for the audience and the players, without allowing the audience to escape from the illusion, I have introduced three art forms: monologue, mime, and ballet. These are all part of drama, having their origins in classic tragedy, monody having become monologue and the chorus, ballet.

Monologue is now condemned by our realists as unnatural, but if one provides motives for it one makes it natural, and then can use it to advantage. It is, surely, natural for a public speaker to walk up and down the room practicing his speech, natural for an actor to read his part aloud, for a servant girl to talk to her cat, a mother to prattle to her child, an old maid to chatter to her parrot, and a sleeper to talk in his sleep. And in order that the actor may have a chance, for once, of working independently, free from the author's direction, it is better that the monologue should not be written, but only indicated. For since it is of small importance what is said in one's sleep or to the parrot or to the cat—none of it influences the action—a talented actor, identifying himself with the atmosphere and the situation, may improvise better than the author, who cannot calculate ahead how much may be said or how long taken without waking the audience from the illusion.

Some Italian theatres have, as we know, returned to improvisation, thereby producing actors who are creative, although within the bounds set by the author. This may well be a step forward, or even the beginning of a new art-form worthy to be called *productive*.

In places where monologue would be unnatural I have used mime, leaving here an even wider scope for the actor's imagination, and more chance for him to win independent laurels. But so as not to try the audience beyond endurance, I have introduced music—fully justified by the Midsummer Eve dance—to exercise its powers of persuasion during the dumb show. But I beg the musical director to consider carefully his choice of compositions, so that conflicting moods are not induced by selections from the current operetta or dance show, or by folk-tunes of too local a character.

The ballet I have introduced cannot be replaced by the usual kind of "crowd-scene," for such scenes are too badly played—a lot of grinning idiots seizing the opportunity to show off and thus destroying the illusion. And as peasants cannot improvise their taunts, but use ready-made phrases with a double meaning, I have not composed their lampoon, but taken a little-known song and dance which I myself noted down in the Stockholm district. The words are not quite to the point, but this too is intentional, for the cunning, i.e. weakness, of the slave prevents him from direct attack. Nor can there be clowning in a serious action, or coarse joking in a situation that nails the lid on a family coffin.

As regards the scenery, I have borrowed from impressionist painting its asymmetry and its economy; thus, I think, strengthening the illusion. For the fact that one does not see the whole room and all the furniture leaves scope for conjecture—that is to say imagination is roused and complements what is seen. I have succeeded too in getting rid of those tiresome exits through doors, since scenery doors are made of canvas, and rock at the slightest touch. They cannot even express the wrath of an irate head of the family who, after a bad dinner, goes out slamming the door behind him, "so that the whole house shakes." On the stage it rocks. I have also kept to a single set, both in order to let the characters develop in their métier and to break away from over-decoration. When one has only one set, one may expect it to be realistic; but as a matter of fact nothing is harder than to get a stage room that looks something like a room, however easily the scene painter can produce flaming volcanoes and waterfalls. Presumably the walls must be of canvas; but it seems about time to dispense with painted shelves and cooking utensils. We are asked to accept so many stage conventions that we might at least be spared the pain of painted pots and pans.

I have set the back wall and the table diagonally so that the actors may play full-face and in half-profile when they are sitting opposite one another at the table. In the opera *Aïda* I saw a diagonal background, which led the eye to unfamiliar perspectives and did not look like mere reaction against boring, straight lines.

Another much needed innovation is the abolition of foot-lights. This lighting from below is said to have the purpose of making the actors' faces fatter. But why, I ask, should all actors have fat faces? Does not this underlighting flatten out all the subtlety of the lower part of the face, specially the jaw, falsify the shape of the nose and throw shadows up over the eyes? Even if this were not so, one thing is certain: that the lights hurt the performers' eyes, so that the full play of their expression is lost. The foot-lights strike part of the retina usually protected—except in sailors who have to watch sunlight on water—and therefore one seldom sees anything other than a crude rolling of the eyes, either sideways or up towards the gallery, showing their whites. Perhaps this too causes that tiresome blinking of the eyelashes, especially by actresses. And when anyone on the stage wants to speak with his eyes, the only thing he can do is to look straight at the audience, with whom he or she then gets into direct communication, outside the framework of the set—a habit called, rightly or wrongly, "greeting one's friends."

Would not sufficiently strong side-lighting, with some kind of reflectors, add to the actor's powers of expression by allowing him to use the face's greatest asset—the play of the eyes?

I have few illusions about getting the actors to play *to* the audience instead of *with* it, although this is what I want. That I shall see an actor's back throughout a critical scene is beyond my dreams, but I do wish crucial scenes could be played, not in front of the prompter's box, like duets expecting applause, but in the place required by the action. So, no revolutions, but just some small modifications, for to make the stage into a real room with the fourth wall missing would be too upsetting altogether.

I dare not hope that the actresses will listen to what I have to say about make-up, for they would rather be beautiful than life-like, but the actor might consider whether it is to his advantage to create an abstract character with grease-paints, and cover his face with it like a mask. Take the case of a man who draws a choleric charcoal line between his eyes and then, in this fixed state of wrath, has to smile at some repartee. What a frightful grimace the result is! And equally, how is that false forehead, smooth as a billiard ball, to wrinkle when the old man loses his temper?

In a modern psychological drama, where the subtlest reactions of a character need to be mirrored in the face rather than expressed by sound and gesture, it would be worth while experimenting with powerful side-lighting on a small stage and a cast without make-up, or at least with the minimum.

If, in addition, we could abolish the visible orchestra, with its distracting lamps and its faces turned toward the audience; if we could have the stalls raised so that the spectators' eyes were higher than the players' knees; if we could get rid of the boxes (the center of my target), with their tittering diners and supperparties, and have total darkness in the auditorium during the performance; and if, first and foremost, we could have a *small* stage and a *small* house, then perhaps a new dramatic art might arise, and theatre once more become a place of entertainment for educated people. While waiting for such a theatre it is as well for us to go on writing so as to stock that repertory of the future.

I have made an attempt. If it has failed, there is time enough to try again.

MISS JULIE:
A TRAGEDY IN ONE ACT

CAST OF CHARACTERS

MISS JULIE, *aged 25*
JEAN, *the valet, aged 30*
KRISTIN, *the cook, aged 35*

Scene: The large kitchen of a Swedish manor house in a country district in the eighties.

Midsummer Eve.
The kitchen has three doors, two small ones into JEAN's *and* KRISTIN's *bedrooms, and a large, glass-fronted double one, opening on to a courtyard. This is the only way to the rest of the house.*
Through these glass doors can be seen part of a fountain with a cupid, lilac bushes in flower, and the tops of some Lombardy poplars. On one wall are shelves edged with scalloped paper on which are kitchen utensils of copper, iron, and tin.
To the left is the corner of a large tiled range and part of its chimney-hood, to the right the end of the servants' dinner table with chairs beside it.
The stove is decorated with birch boughs, the floor strewn with twigs of juniper. On the end of the table is a large Japanese spice jar full of lilac.
There are also an ice-box, a scullery table, and a sink. Above the double door hangs a big, old-fashioned bell; near it is a speaking-tube.
A fiddle can be heard from the dance in the barn nearby. KRISTIN *is standing at the stove, frying something in a pan. She wears a light-coloured cotton dress and a big apron.*
JEAN *enters, wearing livery and carrying a pair of large*

riding-boots with spurs, which he puts in a conspicuous place.

JEAN: Miss Julie's crazy again tonight, absolutely crazy.

KRISTIN: Oh, so you're back, are you?

JEAN: When I'd taken the Count to the station, I came back and dropped in at the Barn for a dance. And who did I see there but our young lady leading off with the game-keeper. But the moment she sets eyes on me, up she rushes and invites me to waltz with her. And how she waltzed—I've never seen anything like it! She's crazy.

KRISTIN: Always has been, but never so bad as this last fortnight since the engagement was broken off.

JEAN: Yes, that was a pretty business, to be sure. He's a decent enough chap, too, even if he isn't rich. Oh, but they're choosy! (*sits down at the end of the table*) In any case, it's a bit odd that our young—er—lady would rather stay at home with the yokels than go with her father to visit her relations.

KRISTIN: Perhaps she feels a bit awkward, after that bust-up with her fiancé.

JEAN: Maybe. That chap had some guts, though. Do

you know the sort of thing that was going on, Kristin? I saw it with my own eyes, though I didn't let on I had.

KRISTIN: You saw them . . . ?

JEAN: Didn't I just! Came across the pair of them one evening in the stable-yard. Miss Julie was doing what she called "training" him. Know what that was? Making him jump over her riding-whip—the way you teach a dog. He did it twice and got a cut each time for his pains, but when it came to the third go, he snatched the whip out of her hand and broke it into smithereens. And then he cleared off.

KRISTIN: What goings on! I never did!

JEAN: Well, that's how it was with that little affair . . . Now, what have you got for me, Kristin? Something tasty?

KRISTIN (*serving from the pan to his plate*): Well, it's just a little bit of kidney I cut off their joint.

JEAN (*smelling it*): Fine! That's my special *delice*. (*feels the plate*) But you might have warmed the plate.

KRISTIN: When you choose to be finicky you're worse than the Count himself. (*pulls his hair affectionately*)

JEAN (*crossly*): Stop pulling my hair. You know how sensitive I am.

KRISTIN: There, there! It's only love, you know.

(JEAN *eats.* KRISTIN *brings a bottle of beer.*)

JEAN: Beer on Midsummer Eve? No thanks! I've got something better than that. (*from a drawer in the table brings out a bottle of red wine with a yellow seal*) Yellow seal, see! Now get me a glass. You use a glass with a stem of course when you're drinking it straight.

KRISTIN (*giving him a wine-glass*): Lord help the woman who gets you for a husband, you old fusser!

(*She puts the beer in the ice-box and sets a small saucepan on the stove.*)

JEAN: Nonsense! You'll be glad enough to get a fellow as smart as me. And I don't think it's done you any harm people calling me your fiancé. (*tastes the wine*) Good. Very good indeed. But not quite warmed enough. (*warms the glass in his hand*) We bought this in Dijon. Four francs the litre without the bottle, and duty on top of that. What are you cooking now? It stinks.

KRISTIN: Some bloody muck Miss Julie wants for Diana.

JEAN: You should be more refined in your speech, Kristin. But why should you spend a holiday cooking for that bitch? Is she sick or what?

KRISTIN: Yes, she's sick. She sneaked out with the pug at the lodge and got in the usual mess. And that, you know, Miss Julie won't have.

JEAN: Miss Julie's too high-and-mighty in some respects, and not enough in others, just like her mother before her. The Countess was more at home in the kitchen and cowsheds than anywhere else, but would she ever go driving with only one horse? She went round with her cuffs filthy, but she had to have the coronet on the cuff-links. Our young lady—to come back to her—hasn't any proper respect for herself or her position. I mean she isn't refined. In the barn just now she dragged the gamekeeper away from Anna and made him dance with her—no waiting to be asked. We wouldn't do a thing like that. But that's what happens when the gentry try to behave like the common people—they become common . . . Still she's a fine girl. Smashing! What shoulders! And what—er—etcetera!

KRISTIN: Oh come off it! I know what Clara says, and she dresses her.

JEAN: Clara? Pooh, you're all jealous! But I've been out riding with her . . . and as for her dancing!

KRISTIN: Listen, Jean. You will dance with me, won't you, as soon as I'm through.

JEAN: Of course I will.

KRISTIN: Promise?

JEAN: Promise? When I say I'll do a thing I do it. Well, thanks for the supper. It was a real treat. (*corks the bottle*)

(JULIE *appears in the doorway, speaking to someone outside.*)

JULIE: I'll be back in a moment. Don't wait.

(JEAN *slips the bottle into the drawer and rises respectfully.* JULIE *enters and joins* KRISTIN *at the stove.*)

Well, have you made it?

(KRISTIN *signs that* JEAN *is near them*)

JEAN (*gallantly*): Have you ladies got some secret?

JULIE (*flipping his face with her handkerchief*): You're very inquisitive.

JEAN: What a delicious smell! Violets.

JULIE (*coquettishly*): Impertinence! Are you an expert of scent too? I must say you know how to dance. Now don't look. Go away.

(*The music of a schottische begins.*)

JEAN (*with impudent politeness*): Is it some witches' brew you're cooking on Midsummer Eve? Something to tell your stars by, so you can see your future?

JULIE (*sharply*): If you could see that you'd have good eyes. (*to* KRISTIN) Put it in a bottle and cork it tight. Come and dance this schottische with me, Jean.

JEAN (*hesitating*): I don't want to be rude, but I've promised to dance this one with Kristin.

JULIE: Well, she can have another, can't you, Kristin? You'll lend me Jean, won't you?

KRISTIN (*bottling*): It's nothing to do with me. When you're so condescending, Miss, it's not his place to say no. Go on, Jean, and thank Miss Julie for the honor.

JEAN: Frankly speaking, Miss, and no offence meant, I wonder if it's wise for you to dance twice running with the same partner, specially as those people are so ready to jump to conclusions.

JULIE (*flaring up*): What did you say? What sort of conclusions? What do you mean?

JEAN (*meekly*): As you choose not to understand, Miss Julie, I'll have to speak more plainly. It looks bad to show a preference for one of your retainers when they're all hoping for the same unusual favor.

JULIE: Show a preference! The very idea! I'm surprised at you. I'm doing the people an honor by attending their ball when I'm mistress of the house, but if I'm really going to dance, I mean to have a partner who can lead and doesn't make me look ridiculous.

JEAN: If those are your orders, Miss, I'm at your service.

JULIE (*gently*): Don't take it as an order. Tonight we're all just people enjoying a party. There's no question of class. So now give me your arm. Don't worry, Kristin. I shan't steal your sweetheart.

(JEAN *gives* JULIE *his arm and leads her out. Left alone,* KRISTIN *plays her scene in an unhurried, natural way, humming to the tune of the schottische, played on a distant violin. She clears* JEAN's *place, washes up and puts things away, then takes off her apron, brings out a small mirror from a drawer, props it against the jar of lilac, lights a candle, warms a small pair of tongs and curls her fringe. She goes to the door and listens, then turning back to the table finds* MISS JULIE's *forgotten handkerchief. She smells it, then meditatively smooths it out and folds it. Enter* JEAN.)

JEAN: She really *is* crazy. What a way to dance! With people standing grinning at her too from behind the doors. What's got into her, Kristin?

KRISTIN: Oh, it's just her time coming on. She's always queer then. Are you going to dance with me now?

JEAN: Then you're not wild with me for cutting that one.

KRISTIN: You know I'm not—for a little thing like that. Besides, I know my place.

JEAN (*putting his arm round her waist*): You're a sensible girl, Kristin, and you'll make a very good wife . . .

(*Enter* JULIE *unpleasantly surprised.*)

JULIE (*with forced gaiety*): You're a fine beau—running away from your partner.

JEAN: Not away, Miss Julie, but as you see back to the one I deserted.

JULIE (*changing her tone*): You really can dance, you know. But why are you wearing your livery on a holiday. Take it off at once.

JEAN: Then I must ask you to go away for a moment, Miss. My black coat's here. (*indicates it hanging on the door to his room*)

JULIE: Are you so shy of me—just over changing a coat? Go into your room then—or stay here and I'll turn my back.

JEAN: Excuse me then, Miss

(*He goes to his room and is partly visible as he changes his coat.*)

JULIE: Tell me, Kristin, is Jean your fiancé? You seem very intimate.

KRISTIN: My fiancé? Yes, if you like. We call it that.

JULIE: Call it?

KRISTIN: Well, you've had a fiancé yourself, Miss, and . . .

JULIE: But we really were engaged.

KRISTIN: All the same it didn't come to anything.

(JEAN *returns in his black coat.*)

JULIE: *Très gentil, Monsieur Jean. Très gentil.*

JEAN: *Vous voulez plaisanter, Madame.*

JULIE: *Et vous voulez parler français.* Where did you learn it?

JEAN: In Switzerland, when I was sommelier at one of the biggest hotels in Lucerne.

JULIE: You look quite the gentleman in that get-up. Charming. (*sits at the table*)

JEAN: Oh, you're just flattering me!

JULIE (*annoyed*): Flattering you?

JEAN: I'm too modest to believe you would pay real compliments to a man like me, so I must take it you are exaggerating—that this is what's known as flattery.

JULIE: Where on earth did you learn to make speeches like that? Perhaps you've been to the theatre a lot.

JEAN: That's right. And travelled a lot too.

JULIE: But you come from this neighborhood, don't you?

JEAN: Yes, my father was a laborer on the next estate—the District Attorney's place. I often used to see you, Miss Julie, when you were little, though you never noticed me.

JULIE: Did you really?

JEAN: Yes. One time specially I remember . . . but I can't tell you about that.

JULIE: Oh do! Why not? This is just the time.

JEAN: No, I really can't now. Another time perhaps.

JULIE: Another time means never. What harm in now?

JEAN: No harm, but I'd rather not. (*points to* KRISTIN, *now fast asleep*) Look at her.

JULIE: She'll make a charming wife, won't she? I wonder if she snores.

JEAN: No, she doesn't, but she talks in her sleep.

JULIE (*cynically*): How do you know she talks in her sleep?

JEAN (*brazenly*): I've heard her.

(*Pause. They look at one another.*)

JULIE: Why don't you sit down?

JEAN: I can't take such a liberty in your presence.

JULIE: Supposing I order you to.

JEAN: I'll obey.

JULIE: Then sit down. No, wait a minute. Will you get me a drink first?

JEAN: I don't know what's in the ice-box. Only beer, I expect.

JULIE: There's no only about it. My taste is so simple I prefer it to wine.

(JEAN *takes a bottle from the ice-box, fetches a glass and plate, and serves the beer.*)

JEAN: At your service.

JULIE: Thank you. Won't you have some yourself?

JEAN: I'm not really a beer-drinker, but if it's an order . . .

JULIE: Order? I should have thought it was ordinary manners to keep your partner company.

JEAN: That's a good way of putting it.

(*He opens another bottle and fetches a glass*)

JULIE: Now drink my health. (*he hesitates*) I believe the man really is shy.

(JEAN *kneels and raises his glass with mock ceremony.*)

JEAN: To the health of my lady!

JULIE: Bravo! Now kiss my shoe and everything will be perfect. (*he hesitates, then boldly takes hold of her foot and lightly kisses it*) Splendid. You ought to have been an actor.

JEAN (*rising*): We can't go on like this, Miss Julie. Someone might come in and see us.

JULIE: Why would that matter?

JEAN: For the simple reason that they'd talk. And if you knew the way their tongues were wagging out there just now, you . . .

JULIE: What were they saying? Tell me. Sit down.

JEAN (*sitting*): No offence meant, Miss, but . . . well, their language wasn't nice, and they were hinting . . . oh, you know quite well what. You're not a child, and if a lady's seen drinking alone at night with a man—and a servant at that—then . . .

JULIE: Then what? Besides, we're not alone. Kristin's here.

JEAN: Yes, asleep.

JULIE: I'll wake her up. (*rises*) Kristin, are you asleep? (KRISTIN *mumbles in her sleep*) Kristin! Goodness, how she sleeps!

KRISTIN (*in her sleep*): The Count's boots are cleaned—put the coffee on—yes, yes, at once . . . (*mumbles incoherently*)

JULIE (*tweaking her nose*): Wake up, can't you!

JEAN (*sharply*): Let her sleep.

JULIE: What?

JEAN: When you've been standing at the stove all day you're likely to be tired at night. And sleep should be respected.

JULIE (*changing her tone*): What a nice idea. It does you credit. Thank you for it. (*holds out her hand to him*) Now come out and pick some lilac for me.

(*During the following* KRISTIN *goes sleepily in to her bedroom.*)

JEAN: Out with you, Miss Julie?

JULIE: Yes.

JEAN: It wouldn't do. It really wouldn't.

JULIE: I don't know what you mean. You can't possibly imagine that . . .

JEAN: I don't, but others do.

JULIE: What? That I'm in love with the valet?

JEAN: I'm not a conceited man, but such a thing's been known to happen, and to these rustics nothing's sacred.

JULIE: You, I take it, are an aristocrat.

JEAN: Yes, I am.

JULIE: And I am coming down in the world.

JEAN: Don't come down, Miss Julie. Take my advice. No one will believe you came down of your own accord. They'll all say you fell.

JULIE: I have a higher opinion of our people than you. Come and put it to the test. Come on. (*gazes into his eyes*)

JEAN: You're very strange, you know.

JULIE: Perhaps I am, but so are you. For that matter everything is strange. Life, human beings, everything, just scum drifting about on the water until it sinks—down and down. That reminds me of a dream I sometimes have, in which I'm on top of a pillar and can't see any way of getting down. When I look down I'm dizzy; I have to get down but I haven't the courage to jump. I can't stay there and I long to fall, but I don't fall. There's no respite. There can't be any peace at all for me until I'm down, right down on the ground. And if I did get to the ground I'd want to be under the ground . . . Have you ever felt like that?

JEAN: No. In my dream I'm lying under a great tree in a dark wood. I want to get up, up to the top of it, and look out over the bright landscape where the sun is shining and rob that high nest of its golden eggs. And I climb and climb, but the trunk is so thick and smooth and it's so far to the first branch. But I know if I can once reach that first branch I'll go to the top just as if I'm on a ladder. I haven't reached it yet, but I shall get there, even if only in my dreams.

JULIE: Here I am chattering about dreams with you. Come on. Only into the park.

(*She takes his arm and they go towards the door.*)

JEAN: We must sleep on nine midsummer flowers tonight; then our dreams will come true, Miss Julie.

(*They turn at the door. He has a hand to his eye.*)

JULIE: Have you got something in your eye? Let me see.

JEAN: Oh, it's nothing. Just a speck of dust. It'll be gone in a minute.

JULIE: My sleeve must have rubbed against you. Sit down and let me see to it. (*takes him by the arm and makes him sit down, bends his head back and tries to get the speck out with the corner of her handkerchief*) Keep still now, quite still. (*slaps his hand*) Do as I tell you. Why, I believe you're trembling, big, strong man though you are! (*feels his biceps*) What muscles!

JEAN (*warning*): Miss Julie!

JULIE: Yes, Monsieur Jean?

JEAN: Attention. Je ne suis qu'un homme.

JULIE: Will you stay still! There now. It's out. Kiss my hand and say thank you.

JEAN (*rising*): Miss Julie, listen. Kristin's gone to bed now. Will you listen?

JULIE: Kiss my hand first.

JEAN: Very well, but you'll have only yourself to blame.

JULIE: For what?

JEAN: For what! Are you still a child at twenty-five? Don't you know it's dangerous to play with fire?

JULIE: Not for me. I'm insured.

JEAN (*bluntly*): No, you're not. And even if you are, there's still stuff here to kindle a flame.

JULIE: Meaning yourself?

JEAN: Yes. Not because I'm me, but because I'm a man and young and . . .

JULIE: And good-looking? What incredible conceit! A Don Juan perhaps? Or a Joseph? Good Lord, I do believe you are a Joseph!

JEAN: Do you?

JULIE: I'm rather afraid so.

(JEAN *goes boldly up and tries to put his arms round her and kiss her. She boxes his ears.*)

How dare you!

JEAN: Was that in earnest or a joke?

JULIE: In earnest.

JEAN: Then what went before was in earnest too. You take your games too seriously and that's dangerous. Anyhow I'm tired of playing now and beg leave to return to my work. The Count will want his boots first thing and it's past midnight now.

JULIE: Put those boots down.

JEAN: No. This is my work, which it's my duty to do. But I never undertook to be your playfellow and I never will be. I consider myself too good for that.

JULIE: You're proud.

JEAN: In some ways—not all.

JULIE: Have you even been in love?

JEAN: We don't put it that way, but I've been gone on quite a few girls. And once I went sick because I couldn't have the one I wanted. Sick, I mean, like those princes in the Arabian Nights who couldn't eat or drink for love.

JULIE: Who was she? (*no answer*) Who was she?

JEAN: You can't force me to tell you that.

JULIE: If I ask as an equal, ask as a—friend? Who was she?

JEAN: You.

JULIE (*sitting*): How absurd!

JEAN: Yes, ludicrous if you like. That's the story I wouldn't tell you before, see, but now I will . . . Do you know what the world looks like from below? No, you don't. No more than the hawks and falcons do whose backs one hardly ever sees because they're always soaring up aloft. I lived in a laborer's hovel with seven other children and a pig, out in the grey fields where there isn't a single tree. But from the window I could see the wall round the Count's park with apple-trees above it. That was the Garden of Eden, guarded by many terrible angels with flaming swords. All the same I and the other boys managed to get to the tree of life. Does all this make you despise me?

JULIE: Goodness, all boys steal apples!

JEAN: You say that now, but all the same you do despise me. However, one time I went into the Garden of Eden with my mother to weed the onion beds. Close to the kitchen garden there was a Turkish pavilion hung all over with jasmine and honeysuckle. I hadn't any idea what it was used for, but I'd never seen such a beautiful building. People used to go in and then come out again, and one day the door was left open. I crept up and saw the walls covered with pictures of kings and emperors, and the windows had red curtains with fringes—you know now what the place was, don't you? I . . . (*Breaks off a piece of lilac and holds it for* JULIE *to smell. As he talks, she takes it from him.*) I had never been inside the manor, never seen anything but the church, and this was more beautiful. No matter where my thoughts went, they always came back—to that place. The longing went on growing in me to enjoy it fully, just once. *Enfin,* I sneaked in, gazed and admired. Then I heard someone coming. There was only one way out for the gentry, but for me there was another and I had no choice but to take it. (JULIE *drops the lilac on the table*) Then I took to my heels, plunged through the raspberry canes, dashed across the strawberry beds and found myself on the rose terrace. There I saw a pink dress and a pair of white stockings—it was you. I crawled into a weed pile and lay there right under it among prickly thistles and damp rank earth. I watched you walking among the roses and said to myself: "If it's true that a thief can get to heaven and be with the angels, it's pretty strange that a laborer's child here on God's earth mayn't come in the park and play with the Count's daughter."

JULIE (*sentimentally*): Do you think all poor children feel the way you did?

JEAN (*taken aback, then rallying*): *All* poor children? . . . Yes, of course they do. Of course.

JULIE: It must be terrible to be poor.

JEAN (*with exaggerated distress*): Oh yes, Miss Julie, yes. A dog may lie on the Countess's sofa, a horse may have his nose stroked by a young lady, but a servant . . . (*change of tone*) well, yes, now and then you meet one with guts enough to rise in the world, but how often? Anyhow, do you know what I did? Jumped in the millstream with my clothes on, was pulled out and got a hiding. But the next Sunday, when Father and all the rest went to Granny's, I managed to get left behind. Then I washed with soap and hot water, put my best clothes on and went to church so as to see you. I did see you and went home determined to die. But I wanted to die beautifully and peacefully, without any pain. Then I remembered it was dangerous to sleep under an elder bush. We had a big one in full bloom, so I stripped it and climbed into the oats-bin with the flowers. Have you ever noticed how smooth oats are? Soft to touch as human skin . . . Well, I closed the lid and shut my eyes, fell asleep, and when they woke me I was very ill. But I didn't die, as you see. What I meant by all that I don't know. There was no hope of winning you—you were simply a symbol of the hopelessness of ever getting out of the class I was born in.

JULIE: You put things very well, you know. Did you go to school?

JEAN: For a while. But I've read a lot of novels and been to the theatre. Besides, I've heard educated folk talking—that's what's taught me most.

JULIE: Do you stand round listening to what we're saying?

JEAN: Yes, of course. And I've heard quite a bit too. On the carriage box or rowing the boat. Once I heard you, Miss Julie, and one of your young lady friends . . .

JULIE: Oh! Whatever did you hear?

JEAN: Well, it wouldn't be nice to repeat it. And I must say I was pretty startled. I couldn't think where you had learnt such words. Perhaps, at bottom, there isn't as much difference between people as one's led to believe.

JULIE: How dare you! We don't behave as you do when we're engaged.

JEAN (looking hard at her): Are you sure? It's no use making out so innocent to me.

JULIE: The man I gave my love to was a rotter.

JEAN: That's what you always say—afterwards.

JULIE: Always?

JEAN: I think it must be always. I've heard the expression several times in similar circumstances.

JULIE: What circumstances?

JEAN: Like those in question. The last time . . .

JULIE (rising): Stop. I don't want to hear any more.

JEAN: Nor did *she*—curiously enough. May I go to bed now please?

JULIE (gently): Go to bed on Midsummer Eve?

JEAN: Yes. Dancing with that crowd doesn't really amuse me.

JULIE: Get the key of the boathouse and row me out on the lake. I want to see the sun rise.

JEAN: Would that be wise?

JULIE: You sound as though you're frightened for your reputation.

JEAN: Why not? I don't want to be made a fool of, nor to be sent packing without a character when

I'm trying to better myself. Besides, I have Kristin to consider.

JULIE: So now it's Kristin.

JEAN: Yes, but it's you I'm thinking about too. Take my advice and go to bed.

JULIE: Am I to take orders from you?

JEAN: Just this once, for your own sake. Please. It's very late and sleepiness goes to one's head and makes one rash. Go to bed. What's more, if my ears don't deceive me, I hear people coming this way. They'll be looking for me, and if they find us here, you're done for.

(The CHORUS approaches, singing. During the following dialogue the song is heard in snatches, and in full when the peasants enter.)

> Out of the wood two women came,
> Tridiri-ralla, tridiri-ra.
> The feet of one were bare and cold,
> Tridiri-ralla-la.
>
> The other talked of bags of gold,
> Tridiri-ralla, tridiri-ra.
> But neither had a sou to her name,
> Tridiri-ralla-la.
>
> The bridal wreath I give to you,
> Tridiri-ralla, tridiri-ra.
> But to another I'll be true,
> Tridiri-ralla-la.

JULIE: I know our people and I love them, just as they do me. Let them come. You'll see.

JEAN: No, Miss Julie, they don't love you. They take your food, then spit at it. You must believe me. Listen to them, just listen to what they're singing . . . No, don't listen.

JULIE (listening): What are they singing?

JEAN: They're mocking—you and me.

JULIE: Oh no! How horrible! What cowards!

JEAN: A pack like that's always cowardly. But against such odds there's nothing we can do but run away.

JULIE: Run away? Where to? We can't get out and we can't go into Kristin's room.

JEAN: Into mine then. Necessity knows no rules. And you can trust me. I really am your true and devoted friend.

JULIE: But supposing . . . supposing they were to look for you in there?

JEAN: I'll bolt the door, and if they try to break in I'll shoot. Come on (pleading) Please come.

JULIE (*tensely*): Do you promise . . . ?

JEAN: I swear!

(JULIE *goes quickly into his room and he excitedly follows her. Led by the fiddler, the peasants enter in festive attire with flowers in their hats. They put a barrel of beer and a keg of spirits, garlanded with leaves, on the table, fetch glasses and begin to carouse. The scene becomes a ballet. They form a ring and dance and sing and mime: "Out of the wood two women came." Finally they go out, still singing.* JULIE *comes in alone. She looks at the havoc in the kitchen, wrings her hands, then takes out her powder puff and powders her face.* JEAN *enters in high spirits.*)

JEAN: Now you see! And you heard, didn't you? Do you still think it's possible for us to stay here?

JULIE: No, I don't. But what can we do?

JEAN: Run away. Far away. Take a journey.

JULIE: Journey? But where to?

JEAN: Switzerland. The Italian lakes. Ever been there?

JULIE: No. Is it nice?

JEAN: Ah! Eternal summer, oranges, evergreens . . . ah!

JULIE: But what would we do there?

JEAN: I'll start a hotel. First-class accommodation and first-class customers.

JULIE: Hotel?

JEAN: There's life for you. New faces all the time, new languages—no time for nerves or worries, no need to look for something to do—work rolling up of its own accord. Bells ringing night and day, trains whistling, buses coming and going, and all the time gold pieces rolling on to the counter. There's life for you!

JULIE: For *you*. And I?

JEAN: Mistress of the house, ornament of the firm. With your looks, and your style . . . oh, it's bound to be a success! Terrific! You'll sit like a queen in the office and set your slaves in motion by pressing an electric button. The guests will file past your throne and nervously lay their treasure on your table. You've no idea the way people tremble when they get their bills. I'll salt the bills and you'll sugar them with your sweetest smiles. Ah, let's get away from here! (*produces a time-table*) At once, by the next train. We shall be at Malmö at six-thirty, Hamburg eight-forty next morning, Frankfurt-Basle the

following day, and Como by the St. Gothard pass in—let's see—three days. Three days!

JULIE: That's all very well. But Jean, you must give me courage. Tell me you love me. Come and take me in your arms.

JEAN (*reluctantly*): I'd like to, but I daren't. Not again in this house. I love you—that goes without saying. You can't doubt that, Miss Julie, can you?

JULIE (*shyly, very feminine*): Miss? Call me Julie. There aren't any barriers between us now. Call me Julie.

JEAN (*uneasily*): I can't. As long as we're in this house, there *are* barriers between us. There's the past and there's the Count. I've never been so servile to anyone as I am to him. I've only got to see his gloves on a chair to feel small. I've only to hear his bell and I shy like a horse. Even now, when I look at his boots, standing there so proud and stiff, I feel my back beginning to bend. (*kicks the boots*) It's those old, narrow-minded notions drummed into us as children . . . but they can soon be forgotten. You've only got to get to another country, a republic, and people will bend themselves double before my porter's livery. Yes, double they'll bend themselves, but I shan't. I wasn't born to bend. I've got guts, I've got character, and once I reach that first branch, you'll watch me climb. Today I'm valet, next year I'll be proprietor, in ten years I'll have made a fortune, and then I'll go to Romania, get myself decorated and I may, I only say *may*, mind you, end up as a Count.

JULIE (*sadly*): That would be very nice.

JEAN: You see in Romania one can buy a title, and then you'll be a Countess after all. My Countess.

JULIE: What do I care about all that? I'm putting those things behind me. Tell me you love me, because if you don't . . . if you don't, what am I?

JEAN: I'll tell you a thousand times over—later. But not here. No sentimentality now or everything will be lost. We must consider this thing calmly like reasonable people. (*takes a cigar, cuts and lights it*) You sit down there and I'll sit here and we'll talk as if nothing has happened.

JULIE: My God, have you no feelings at all?

JEAN: Nobody has more. But I know how to control them.

JULIE: A short time ago you were kissing my shoe. And now . . .

JEAN (*harshly*): Yes, that was then. Now we have something else to think about.

JULIE: Don't speak to me so brutally.

JEAN: I'm not. Just sensibly. One folly's been committed, don't let's have more. The Count will be back at any moment and we've got to settle our future before that. Now, what do you think of my plans? Do you approve?

JULIE: It seems a very good idea—but just one thing. Such a big undertaking would need a lot of capital. Have you got any?

JEAN (*chewing his cigar*): I certainly have. I've got my professional skill, my wide experience and my knowledge of foreign languages. That's capital worth having, it seems to me.

JULIE: But it won't buy even one railway ticket.

JEAN: Quite true. That's why I need a backer to advance some ready cash.

JULIE: How could you get that at a moment's notice?

JEAN: You must get it, if you want to be my partner.

JULIE: I can't. I haven't any money of my own. (*pause*)

JEAN: Then the whole thing's off.

JULIE: And . . . ?

JEAN: We go on as we are.

JULIE: Do you think I'm going to stay under this roof as your mistress? With everyone pointing at me. Do you think I can face my father after this? No. Take me away from here, away from this shame, this humiliation. Oh my God, what have I done? My God, my God! (*weeps*)

JEAN: So that's the tune now, is it? What have you done? Same as many before you.

JULIE (*hysterically*): And now you despise me. I'm falling, I'm falling.

JEAN: Fall as far as me and I'll lift you up again.

JULIE: Why was I so terribly attracted to you? The weak to the strong, the falling to the rising? Or was it love? Is that love? Do you know what love is?

JEAN: Do I? You bet I do. Do you think I never had a girl before?

JULIE: The things you say, the things you think!

JEAN: That's what life's taught me, and that's what I am. It's no good getting hysterical or giving yourself airs. We're both in the same boat now. Here, my dear girl, let me give you a glass of something special. (*opens the drawer, takes out the bottle of wine and fills two used glasses*)

JULIE: Where did you get that wine?

JEAN: From the cellar.

JULIE: My father's burgundy.

JEAN: Why not, for his son-in-law?

JULIE: And I drink beer.

JEAN: That only shows your taste's not so good as mine.

JULIE: Thief!

JEAN: Are you going to tell on me?

JULIE: Oh God! The accomplice of a petty thief! Was I blind drunk? Have I dreamt this whole night? Midsummer Eve, the night for innocent merry-making.

JEAN: Innocent, eh?

JULIE: Is anyone on earth as wretched as I am now?

JEAN: Why should *you* be? After such a conquest. What about Kristin in there? Don't you think she has any feelings?

JULIE: I did think so, but I don't any longer. No. A menial is a menial . . .

JEAN: And a whore is a whore.

JULIE (*falling to her knees, her hands clasped*): O God in heaven, put an end to my miserable life! Lift me out of this filth in which I'm sinking. Save me! Save me!

JEAN: I must admit I'm sorry for you. When I was in the onion bed and saw you up there among the roses, I . . . yes, I'll tell you now . . . I had the same dirty thoughts as all boys.

JULIE: You, who wanted to die because of me?

JEAN: In the oats-bin? That was just talk.

JULIE: Lies, you mean.

JEAN (*getting sleepy*): More or less. I think I read a story in some paper about a chimney-sweep who shut himself up in a chest full of lilac because he'd been summonsed for not supporting some brat . . .

JULIE: So this is what you're like.

JEAN: I had to think up something. It's always the fancy stuff that catches the women.

JULIE: Beast!

JEAN: *Merde!*

JULIE: Now you have seen the falcon's back.

JEAN: Not exactly its *back*.

JULIE: I was to be the first branch.

JEAN: But the branch was rotten.

JULIE: I was to be a hotel sign.

JEAN: And I the hotel.

JULIE: Sit at your counter, attract your clients and cook their accounts.

JEAN: I'd have done that myself.

JULIE: That any human being can be so steeped in filth!

JEAN: Clean it up then.

JULIE: Menial! Lackey! Stand up when I speak to you.

JEAN: Menial's whore, lackey's harlot, shut your mouth and get out of here! Are you the one to lecture me for being coarse? Nobody of my kind would ever be as coarse as you were tonight. Do you think any servant girl would throw herself at a man that way? Have you ever seen a girl of my class asking for it like that? I haven't. Only animals and prostitutes.

JULIE (*broken*): Go on. Hit me, trample on me—it's all I deserve. I'm rotten. But help me! If there's any way out at all, help me.

JEAN (*more gently*): I'm not denying myself a share in the honour of seducing you, but do you think anybody in my place would have dared look in your direction if you yourself hadn't asked for it? I'm still amazed . . .

JULIE: And proud.

JEAN: Why not? Though I must admit the victory was too easy to make me lose my head.

JULIE: Go on hitting me.

JEAN (*rising*): No. On the contrary I apologise for what I've said. I don't hit a person who's down—least of all a woman. I can't deny there's a certain satisfaction in finding that what dazzled one below was just moonshine, that that falcon's back is grey after all, that there's powder on the lovely cheek, that polished nails can have black tips, that the handkerchief is dirty although it smells of scent. On the other hand it hurts to find that what I was struggling to reach wasn't high and isn't real. It hurts to see you fallen so low you're far lower than your own cook. Hurts like when you see the last flowers of summer lashed to pieces by rain and turned to mud.

JULIE: You're talking as if you're already my superior.

JEAN: I am. I might make you a Countess, but you could never make me a Count, you know.

JULIE: But I am the child of a Count, and you could never be that.

JEAN: True, but I might be the father of Counts if . . .

JULIE: You're a thief. I'm not.

JEAN: There are worse things than being a thief— much lower. Besides, when I'm in a place I regard myself as a member of the family to some extent, as one of the children. You don't call it stealing when children pinch a berry from overladen bushes. (*his passion is roused again*) Miss Julie, you're a glorious woman, far too good for a man like me. You were carried away by some kind of madness, and now you're trying to cover up your mistake by persuading yourself you're in love with me. You're not, although you may find me physically attractive, which means your love's no better than mine. But I wouldn't be satisfied with being nothing but an animal for you, and I could never make you love me.

JULIE: Are you sure?

JEAN: You think there's a chance? Of my loving you, yes, of course. You're beautiful, refined—(*takes her hand*)—educated, and you can be nice when you want to be. The fire you kindle in a man isn't likely to go out. (*puts his arm round her*) You're like mulled wine, full of spices, and your kisses . . .

(*He tries to pull her to him, but she breaks away.*)

JULIE: Let go of me! You won't win me that way.

JEAN: Not that way, how then? Not by kisses and fine speeches, not by planning the future and saving you from shame? How then?

JULIE: How? How? I don't know. There isn't any way. I loathe you—loathe you as I loathe rats, but I can't escape from you.

JEAN: Escape with me.

JULIE (*pulling herself together*): Escape? Yes, we must escape. But I'm so tired. Give me a glass of wine.

(*He pours it out. She looks at her watch.*)

First we must talk. We still have a little time.

(*Empties the glass and holds it out for more.*)

JEAN: Don't drink like that. You'll get tipsy.

JULIE: What's that matter?

JEAN: What's it matter? It's vulgar to get drunk. Well, what have you got to say?

JULIE: We've got to run away, but we must talk first—or rather, I must, for so far you've done all the talking. You've told me about your life, now I want to tell you about mine, so that we really know each other before we begin this journey together.

JEAN: Wait. Excuse my saying so, but don't you think you may be sorry afterwards if you give away your secrets to me?

JULIE: Aren't you my friend?

JEAN: On the whole. But don't rely on me.

JULIE: You can't mean that. But anyway everyone knows my secrets. Listen. My mother wasn't well-born; she came of quite humble people, and was brought up with all those new ideas of sex-equality and women's rights and so on. She thought marriage was quite wrong. So when my father proposed to her, she said she would never become his *wife* . . . but in the end she did. I came into the world, as far as I can make out, against my mother's will, and I was left to run wild, but I had to do all the things a boy does—to prove women are as good as men. I had to wear boys' clothes; I was taught to handle horses—and I wasn't allowed in the dairy. She made me groom and harness and go out hunting; I even had to try to plough. All the men on the estate were given the women's jobs, and the women the men's, until the whole place went to rack and ruin and we were the laughing-stock of the neighborhood. At last my father seems to have come to his senses and rebelled. He changed everything and ran the place his own way. My mother got ill—I don't know what was the matter with her, but she used to have strange attacks and hide herself in the attic or the garden. Sometimes she stayed out all night. Then came the great fire which you have heard people talking about. The house and the stables and the barns—the whole place burnt to the ground. In very suspicious circumstances. Because the accident happened the very day the insurance had to be renewed, and my father had sent the new premium, but through some carelessness of the messenger it arrived too late. (*refills her glass and drinks*)

JEAN: Don't drink any more.

JULIE: Oh, what does it matter? We were destitute and had to sleep in the carriages. My father didn't know how to get money to rebuild, and then my mother suggested he should borrow from an old friend of hers, a local brick manufacturer. My father got the loan and, to his surprise, without having to pay interest. So the place was rebuilt. (*drinks*) Do you know who set fire to it?

JEAN: Your lady mother.

JULIE: Do you know who the brick manufacturer was?

JEAN: Your mother's lover?

JULIE: Do you know whose the money was?

JEAN: Wait . . . no, I don't know that.

JULIE: It was my mother's.

JEAN: In other words the Count's, unless there was a settlement.

JULIE: There wasn't any settlement. My mother had a little money of her own which she didn't want my father to control, so she invested it with her—friend.

JEAN: Who grabbed it.

JULIE: Exactly. He appropriated it. My father came to know all this. He couldn't bring an action, couldn't pay his wife's lover, nor prove it was his wife's money. That was my mother's revenge because he made himself master in his own house. He nearly shot himself then—at least there's a rumor he tried and didn't bring it off. So he went on living, and my mother had to pay dearly for what she'd done. Imagine what those five years were like for me. My natural sympathies were with my father, yet I took my mother's side, because I didn't know the facts. I'd learnt from her to hate and distrust men— you know how she loathed the whole male sex. And I swore to her I'd never become the slave of any man.

JEAN: And so you got engaged to that attorney.

JULIE: So that he should be my slave.

JEAN: But he wouldn't be.

JULIE: Oh yes, he wanted to be, be he didn't have the chance. I got bored with him.

JEAN: Is that what I saw—in the stable-yard?

JULIE: What did you see?

JEAN: What I saw was him breaking off the engagement.

JULIE: That's a lie. It was I who broke it off. Did he say it was him? The cad.

JEAN: He's not a cad. Do you hate men, Miss Julie?

JULIE: Yes . . . most of the time. But when that weakness comes, oh . . . the shame!

JEAN: Then do you hate me?

JULIE: Beyond words. I'd gladly have you killed like an animal.

JEAN: Quick as you'd shoot a mad dog, eh?

JULIE: Yes.

JEAN: But there's nothing here to shoot with—and there isn't a dog. So what do we do now?

JULIE: Go abroad.

JEAN: To make each other miserable for the rest of our lives?

JULIE: No, to enjoy ourselves for a day or two, for a week, for as long as enjoyment lasts, and then—to die . . .

JEAN: Die? How silly! I think it would be far better to start a hotel.

JULIE (*without listening*): . . . die on the shores of Lake Como, where the sun always shines and at Christmas time there are green trees and glowing oranges.

JEAN: Lake Como's a rainy hole and I didn't see any oranges outside the shops. But it's a good place for tourists. Plenty of villas to be rented by—er—honeymoon couples. Profitable business that. Know why? Because they all sign a lease for six months and all leave after three weeks.

JULIE (*naïvely*): After three weeks? Why?

JEAN: They quarrel, of course. But the rent has to be paid just the same. And then it's let again. So it goes on and on, for there's plenty of love although it doesn't last long.

JULIE: You don't want to die with me?

JEAN: I don't want to die at all. For one thing I like living and for another I consider suicide's a sin against the Creator who gave us life.

JULIE: You believe in God—*you*?

JEAN: Yes, of course. And I go to church every Sunday. Look here, I'm tired of all this. I'm going to bed.

JULIE: Indeed! And do you think I'm going to leave things like this? Don't you know what you owe the woman you've ruined?

JEAN (*taking out his purse and throwing a silver coin on the table*): There you are. I don't want to be in anybody's debt.

JULIE (*pretending not to notice the insult*): Don't you know what the law is?

JEAN: There's no law unfortunately that punishes a woman for seducing a man.

JULIE: But can you see anything for it but to go abroad, get married and then divorce?

JEAN: What if I refuse this *mésalliance*?

JULIE: *Mésalliance*?

JEAN: Yes, for me. I'm better bred than you, see! Nobody in my family committed arson.

JULIE: How do you know?

JEAN: Well, you can't prove otherwise, because we haven't any family records outside the Registrar's office. But I've seen your family tree in that book on the drawing-room table. Do you know who the founder of your family was? A miller who let his wife sleep with the King one night during the Danish war. I haven't any ancestors like that. I haven't any ancestors at all, but I might become one.

JULIE: This is what I get for confiding in someone so low, for sacrificing my family honor . . .

JEAN: Dishonor! Well, I told you so. One shouldn't drink, because then one talks. And one shouldn't talk.

JULIE: Oh, how ashamed I am, how bitterly ashamed! If at least you loved me!

JEAN: Look here—for the last time—what do you want? Am I to burst into tears? Am I to jump over your riding whip? Shall I kiss you and carry you off to Lake Como for three weeks, after which . . . What am I to do? What do you want? This is getting unbearable, but that's what comes of playing around with women. Miss Julie, I can see how miserable you are; I know you're going through hell, but I don't understand you. We don't have scenes like this; we don't go in for hating each other. We make love for fun in our spare time, but we haven't all day and all night for it like you. I think you must be ill. I'm sure you're ill.

JULIE: Then you must be kind to me. You sound almost human now.

JEAN: Well, be human yourself. You spit at me, then won't let me wipe it off—on you.

JULIE: Help me, help me! Tell me what to do, where to go.

JEAN: Jesus, as if I knew!

JULIE: I've been mad, raving mad, but there must be a way out.

JEAN: Stay here and keep quiet. Nobody knows anything.

JULIE: I can't. People do know. Kristin knows.

JEAN: They don't know and they wouldn't believe such a thing.

JULIE (*hesitating*): But—it might happen again.

JEAN: That's true.

JULIE: And there might be—consequences.

JEAN (*in panic*): Consequences! Fool that I am I never thought of that. Yes, there's nothing for it but to go. At once. I can't come with you. That would be a complete give-away. You must go alone—abroad—anywhere.

JULIE: Alone? Where to? I can't.

JEAN: You must. And before the Count gets back. If you stay, we know what will happen. Once you've sinned you feel you might as well go on, as the harm's done. Then you get more and more reckless and in the end you're found out. No. You must go abroad. Then write to the Count and tell him everything, except that it was me. He'll never guess that—and I don't think he'll want to.

JULIE: I'll go if you come with me.

JEAN: Are you crazy, woman? "Miss Julie elopes with valet." Next day it would be in the headlines, and the Count would never live it down.

JULIE: I can't go. I can't stay. I'm so tired, so completely worn out. Give me orders. Set me going. I can't think any more, can't act . . .

JEAN: You see what weaklings you are. Why do you give yourselves airs and turn up your noses as if you're the lords of creation? Very well, I'll give you your orders. Go upstairs and dress. Get money for the journey and come down here again.

JULIE (softly): Come up with me.

JEAN: To your room? Now you've gone crazy again. (hesitates a moment) No! Go along at once. (takes her hand and pulls her to the door)

JULIE (as she goes): Speak kindly to me, Jean.

JEAN: Orders always sound unkind. Now you know. Now you know.

(Left alone, JEAN sighs with relief, sits down at the table, takes out a note-book and pencil and adds up figures, now and then aloud. Dawn begins to break. KRISTIN enters dressed for church, carrying his white dickey and tie.)

KRISTIN: Lord Jesus, look at the state the place is in! What have you been up to? (turns out the lamp)

JEAN: Oh, Miss Julie invited the crowd in. Did you sleep through it? Didn't you hear anything?

KRISTIN: I slept like a log.

JEAN: And dressed for church already.

KRISTIN: Yes, you promised to come to Communion with me today.

JEAN: Why, so I did. And you've got my bib and tucker, I see. Come on then. (Sits. KRISTIN begins to put his things on. Pause. Sleepily.) What's the lesson today?

KRISTIN: It's about the beheading of John the Baptist, I think.

JEAN: That's sure to be horribly long. Hi, you're choking me! Oh Lord, I'm so sleepy, so sleepy!

KRISTIN: Yes, what have you been doing up all night? You look absolutely green.

JEAN: Just sitting here talking with Miss Julie.

KRISTIN: She doesn't know what's proper, that one. (pause)

JEAN: I say, Kristin.

KRISTIN: What?

JEAN: It's queer really, isn't it, when you come to think of it? Her.

KRISTIN: What's queer?

JEAN: The whole thing. (pause)

KRISTIN (looking at the half-filled glasses on the table): Have you been drinking together too?

JEAN: Yes.

KRISTIN: More shame you. Look me straight in the face.

JEAN: Yes.

KRISTIN: Is it possible? Is it possible?

JEAN (after a moment): Yes, it is.

KRISTIN: Oh! This I would never have believed. How low!

JEAN: You're not jealous of her, surely?

KRISTIN: No, I'm not. If it had been Clara or Sophie I'd have scratched your eyes out. But not of her. I don't know why; that's how it is though. But it's disgusting.

JEAN: You're angry with her then.

KRISTIN: No. With you. It was wicked of you, very, very wicked. Poor girl. And, mark my words, I won't stay here any longer now—in a place where one can't respect one's employers.

JEAN: Why should one respect them?

KRISTIN: You should know since you're so smart. But you don't want to stay in the service of people who aren't respectable, do you? I wouldn't demean myself.

JEAN: But it's rather a comfort to find out they're no better than us.

KRISTIN: I don't think so. If they're no better there's nothing for us to live up to. Oh and think of the Count! Think of him. He's been through so much already. No, I won't stay in the place any longer. A fellow like you too! If it had been that attorney now or somebody of her own class . . .

JEAN: Why, what's wrong with . . .

KRISTIN: Oh, you're all right in your own way, but when all's said and done there is a difference between one class and another. No, this is something I'll never be able to stomach. That our young lady who was so proud and so down on men you'd never believe she'd let one come near her should go and give herself to one like you. She who wanted to have poor Diana shot for running after the lodge-keeper's pug. No, I must say . . .! Well, I won't stay here any longer. On the twenty-fourth of October I quit.

JEAN: And then?

KRISTIN: Well, since you mention it, it's about time you began to look around, if we're ever going to get married.

JEAN: But what am I to look for? I shan't get a place like this when I'm married.

KRISTIN: I know you won't. But you might get a job as porter or caretaker in some public institution. Government rations are small but sure, and there's a pension for the widow and children.

JEAN: That's all very fine, but it's not in my line to start thinking at once about dying for my wife and children. I must say I had rather bigger ideas.

KRISTIN: You and your ideas! You've got obligations too, and you'd better start thinking about them.

JEAN: Don't *you* start pestering me about obligations. I've had enough of that. (*listens to a sound upstairs*) Anyway we've plenty of time to work things out. Go and get ready now and we'll be off to church.

KRISTIN: Who's that walking about upstairs?

JEAN: Don't know—unless it's Clara.

KRISTIN (*going*): You don't think the Count could have come back without our hearing him?

JEAN (*scared*): The Count? No, he can't have. He'd have rung for me.

KRISTIN: God help us! I've never known such goings on.

(*Exit. The sun has now risen and is shining on the treetops. The light gradually changes until it slants in through the windows.* JEAN *goes to the door and beckons.* JULIE *enters in travelling clothes, carrying a small bird-cage covered with a cloth, which she puts on a chair.*)

JULIE: I'm ready.

JEAN: Hush! Kristin's up.

JULIE (*in a very nervous state*): Does she suspect anything?

JEAN: Not a thing. But, my God, what a sight you are!

JULIE: Sight? What do you mean?

JEAN: You're white as a corpse and—pardon me—your face is dirty.

JULIE: Let me wash then. (*goes to a sink and washes her face and hands*) There. Give me a towel. Oh! The sun is rising!

JEAN: And that breaks the spell.

JULIE: Yes. The spell of Midsummer Eve . . . But listen, Jean. Come with me. I've got the money.

JEAN (*skeptically*): Enough?

JULIE: Enough to start with. Come with me. I can't

travel alone today. It's Midsummer Day, remember. I'd be packed into a suffocating train among crowds of people who'd all stare at me. And it would stop at every station while I yearned for wings. No, I can't do that, I simply can't. There will be memories too; memories of Midsummer Days when I was little. The leafy church—birch and lilac—the gaily spread dinner table, relatives, friends—evening in the park—dancing and music and flowers and fun. Oh, however far you run away—there'll always be memories in the baggage car—and remorse and guilt.

JEAN: I will come with you, but quickly now then, before it's too late. At once.

JULIE: Put on your things. (*picks up the cage*)

JEAN: No luggage mind. That would give us away.

JULIE: No, only what we can take with us in the carriage.

JEAN (*fetching his hat*): What on earth have you got there? What is it?

JULIE: Only my greenfinch. I don't want to leave it behind.

JEAN: Well, I'll be damned! We're to take a bird-cage along, are we? You're crazy. Put that cage down.

JULIE: It's the only thing I'm taking from my home. The only living creature who cares for me since Diana went off like that. Don't be cruel. Let me take it.

JEAN: Put that cage down, I tell you—and don't talk so loud. Kristin will hear.

JULIE: No, I won't leave it in strange hands. I'd rather you killed it.

JEAN: Give the little beast here then and I'll wring its neck.

JULIE: But don't hurt it, don't . . . no, I can't.

JEAN: Give it here. I *can*.

JULIE (*taking the bird out of the cage and kissing it*): Dear little Serena, must you die and leave your mistress?

JEAN: Please don't make a scene. It's *your* life and future we're worrying about. Come on, quick now!

(*He snatches the bird from her, puts it on a board, picks up a chopper, and kills the bird.* JULIE *turns away.*)

You should have learnt how to kill chickens instead of target-shooting. Then you wouldn't faint at a drop of blood.

JULIE (*screaming*): Kill me too! Kill me! You who can butcher an innocent creature without a quiver. Oh, how I hate you, how I loathe you! There is blood between us now. I curse the hour I first saw you. I curse the hour I was conceived in my mother's womb.

JEAN: What's the use of cursing. Let's go.

JULIE: (*going to the chopping-block as if drawn against her will*) No, I won't go yet. I can't . . . I must look. Listen! There's a carriage. (*listens without taking her eyes off the board and chopper*) You don't think I can bear the sight of blood. You think I'm so weak. Oh, how I should like to see your blood and your brains on a chopping-block! I'd like to see the whole of your sex swimming like that in a sea of blood. I think I could drink out of your skull, bathe my feet in your broken breast and eat your heart roasted whole. You think I'm weak. You think I love you, that my womb yearned for your seed and I want to carry your offspring under my heart and nourish it with my blood. You think I want to bear your child and take your name. By the way, what is your name? I've never heard your surname. I don't suppose you've got one. I should be "Mrs. Hovel" or "Madam Dunghill." You dog wearing my collar, you lackey with my crest on your buttons! I share you with my cook; I'm my own servant's rival! Oh! Oh! Oh! . . . You think I'm a coward and will run away. No, now I'm going to stay—and let the storm break. My father will come back . . . find his desk broken open . . . his money gone. Then he'll ring that bell—twice for the valet—and then he'll send for the police—and I shall tell everything. Everything. Oh how wonderful to make an end of it all—a real end! He has a stroke and dies and that's the end of all of us. Just peace and quietness . . . eternal rest. The coat of arms broken on the coffin and the Count's line extinct . . . But the valet's line goes on in an orphanage, wins laurels in the gutter and ends in jail.

JEAN: There speaks the noble blood! Bravo, Miss Julie. But now, don't let the cat out of the bag.

(KRISTIN *enters dressed for church, carrying a prayer-book.* JULIE *rushes to her and flings herself into her arms for protection.*)

JULIE: Help me, Kristin! Protect me from this man!

KRISTIN (*unmoved and cold*): What goings-on for a feast day morning! (*sees the board*) And what a filthy mess. What's it all about? Why are you screaming and carrying on so?

JULIE: Kristin, you're a woman and my friend. Beware of that scoundrel!

JEAN (*embarrassed*): While you ladies are talking things over, I'll go and shave. (*slips into his room*)

JULIE: You must understand. You must listen to me.

KRISTIN: I certainly don't understand such loose ways. Where are you off to in those traveling clothes? And he had his hat on, didn't he, eh?

JULIE: Listen, Kristen. Listen, I'll tell you everything.

KRISTIN: I don't want to know anything.

JULIE: You must listen.

KRISTIN: What to? Your nonsense with Jean? I don't care a rap about that; it's nothing to do with me. But if you're thinking of getting him to run off with you, we'll soon put a stop to that.

JULIE (*very nervously*): Please try to be calm, Kristin, and listen. I can't stay here, nor can Jean—so we must go abroad.

KRISTIN: Hm, hm!

JULIE (*brightening*): But you see, I've had an idea. Supposing we all three go—abroad—to Switzerland and start a hotel together . . . I've got some money, you see . . . and Jean and I could run the whole thing—and I thought you would take charge of the kitchen. Wouldn't that be splendid? Say yes, do. If you come with us everything will be fine. Oh do say yes! (*puts her arms round* KRISTIN)

KRISTIN (*cooly thinking*): Hm, hm.

JULIE (*presto tempo*): You've never travelled, Kristin. You should go abroad and see the world. You've no idea how nice it is travelling by train—new faces all the time and new countries. On our way through Hamburg we'll go to the zoo—you'll love that—and we'll go to the theatre and the opera too . . . and when we get to Munich there'll be the museums, dear, and pictures by Rubens and Raphael—the great painters, you know . . . You've heard of Munich, haven't you? Where King Ludwig lived—you know, the king who went mad . . . We'll see his castles—some of his castles are still just like in fairy-tales . . . and from there it's not far to Switzerland—and the Alps. Think of the Alps, Kristin dear, covered with snow in the middle of summer . . . and there are oranges there and trees that are green the whole year round . . .

(JEAN *is seen in the door of his room, sharpening his razor on a strop which he holds with his teeth and his left hand. He listens to the talk with satisfaction and now and then nods approval.* JULIE *continues, tempo prestissimo.*)

> And then we'll get a hotel . . . and I'll sit at the desk, while Jean receives the guests and goes out marketing and writes letters . . . There's life for you! Trains whistling, buses driving up, bells ringing upstairs and downstairs . . . and I shall make out the bills—and I shall cook them too . . . you've no idea how nervous travellers are when it comes to paying their bills. And you—you'll sit like a queen in the kitchen . . . of course there won't be any standing at the stove for you. You'll always have to be nicely dressed and ready to be seen, and with your looks—no, I'm not flattering you—one fine day you'll catch yourself a husband . . . some rich Englishman, I shouldn't wonder—they're the ones who are easy—(*slowing down*)—to catch . . . and then we'll get rich and build ourselves a villa on Lake Como . . . of course it rains there a little now and then—but—(*dully*)—the sun must shine there too sometimes—even though it seems gloomy—and if not—then we can come home again—come back—(*pause*)—here—or somewhere else . . .

KRISTIN: Look here, Miss Julie, do you believe all that yourself?

JULIE (*exhausted*): Do I believe it?

KRISTIN: Yes.

JULIE (*wearily*): I don't know. I don't believe anything any more. (*sinks down on the bench; her head in her arms on the table*) Nothing. Nothing at all.

KRISTIN: (*turning to* JEAN): So you meant to beat it, did you?

JEAN (*disconcerted, putting the razor on the table*): Beat it? What are you talking about? You've heard Miss Julie's plan, and though she's tired now with being up all night, it's a perfectly sound plan.

KRISTIN: Oh, is it? If you thought I'd work for that . . .

JEAN (*interrupting*): Kindly use decent language in front of your mistress. Do you hear?

KRISTIN: Mistress?

JEAN: Yes.

KRISTIN: Well, well, just listen to that!

JEAN: Yes, it would be a good thing if you did listen and talked less. Miss Julie is your mistress and what's made you lose your respect for her now ought to make you feel the same about yourself.

KRISTIN: I've always had enough self-respect—

JEAN: To despise other people.

KRISTIN: —not to go below my own station. Has the Count's cook ever gone with the groom or the swineherd? Tell me that.

JEAN: No, you were lucky enough to have a high-class chap for your beau.

KRISTIN: High-class all right—selling the oats out of the Count's stable.

JEAN: You're a fine one to talk—taking a commission on the groceries and bribes from the butcher.

KRISTIN: What the devil . . .?

JEAN: And now you can't feel any respect for your employers. You, you!

KRISTIN: Are you coming to church with me? I should think you need a good sermon after your fine deeds.

JEAN: No, I'm not going to church today. You can go alone and confess your own sins.

KRISTIN: Yes, I'll do that and bring back enough forgiveness to cover yours too. The Saviour suffered and died on the cross for all our sins, and if we go to Him with faith and a penitent heart, He takes all our sins upon Himself.

JEAN: Even grocery thefts?

JULIE: Do you believe that, Kristin?

KRISTIN: That is my living faith, as sure as I stand here. The faith I learnt as a child and have kept ever since, Miss Julie. "But where sin abounded, grace did much more abound."

JULIE: Oh, if I had your faith! Oh, if . . .

KRISTIN: But you see you can't have it without God's special grace, and it's not given to all to have that.

JULIE: Who is it given to then?

KRISTIN: That's the great secret of the workings of grace, Miss Julie. God is no respecter of persons, and with Him the last shall be first . . .

JULIE: Then I suppose He does respect the last.

KRISTIN (*continuing*): . . . and it is easier for a camel to go through the eye of a needle than for a rich man to enter into the kingdom of God. That's how it is, Miss Julie. Now I'm going—alone, and on my way I shall tell the groom not to let any of the horses out, in case anyone should want to leave before the Count gets back. Good-bye.

(*Exit*)

JEAN: What a devil! And all on account of a green-finch.

JULIE (*wearily*): Never mind the greenfinch. Do you see any way out of this, any end to it?

JEAN (*pondering*): No.

JULIE: If you were in my place, what would you do?

JEAN: In your place? Wait a bit. If I was a woman—a lady of rank who had—fallen. I don't know. Yes, I do know now.

JULIE (*picking up the razor and making a gesture*): This?

JEAN: Yes. But *I* wouldn't do it, you know. There's a difference between us.

JULIE: Because you're a man and I'm a woman? What is the difference?

JEAN: The usual difference—between man and woman.

JULIE (*holding the razor*): I'd like to. But I can't. My father couldn't either, that time he wanted to.

JEAN: No, he didn't want to. He had to be revenged first.

JULIE: And now my mother is revenged again, through me.

JEAN: Didn't you ever love your father, Miss Julie?

JULIE: Deeply, but I must have hated him too—unconsciously. And he let me be brought up to despise my own sex, to be half woman, half man. Whose fault is what's happened? My father's, my mother's or my own? My own? I haven't anything that's my own. I haven't one single thought that I didn't get from my father, one emotion that didn't come from my mother, and as for this last idea—about all people being equal—I got that from him, my fiancé—that's why I call him a cad. How can it be my fault? Push the responsibility on to Jesus, like Kristin does? No, I'm too proud and—thanks to my father's teaching—too intelligent. As for all that about a rich person not being able to get into heaven, it's just a lie, but Kristin, who has money in the savings bank, will certainly not get in. Whose fault is it? What does it matter whose fault it is? In any case I must take the blame and bear the consequences.

JEAN: Yes, but . . . (*There are two sharp rings on the bell.* JULIE *jumps to her feet.* JEAN *changes into his livery.*) The Count is back. Supposing Kristin .

. . (*Goes to the speaking-tube, presses it and listens.*)

JULIE: Has he been to his desk yet?

JEAN: This is Jean, sir. (*listens*) Yes, sir. (*listens*) Yes, sir, very good sir. (*listens*) At once, sir? (*listens*) Very good, sir. In half an hour.

JULIE (*in panic*): What did he say? My God, what did he say?

JEAN: He ordered his boots and his coffee in half an hour.

JULIE: Then there's half an hour . . . Oh, I'm so tired! I can't do anything. Can't be sorry, can't run away, can't stay, can't live—can't die. Help me. Order me, and I'll obey like a dog. Do me this last service—save my honor, save his name. You know what I ought to do, but haven't the strength to do. Use your strength and order me to do it.

JEAN: I don't know why—I can't now—I don't understand . . . It's just as if this coat made me—I can't give you orders—and now that the Count has spoken to me—I can't quite explain, but . . . well, that devil of a lackey is bending my back again. I believe if the Count came down now and ordered me to cut my throat, I'd do it on the spot.

JULIE: Then pretend you're him and I'm you. You did some fine acting before, when you knelt to me and played the aristocrat. Or . . . Have you ever seen a hypnotist at the theatre? (*he nods*) He says to the person "Take the broom," and he takes it. He says "Sweep," and he sweeps . . .

JEAN: But the person has to be asleep.

JULIE (*as if in a trance*): I'm asleep already . . . the whole room has turned to smoke—and you look like a stove—a stove like a man in black with a tall hat—your eyes are glowing like coals when the fire is low—and your face is a white patch like ashes.

(*The sunlight has now reached the floor and lights up* JEAN.)

How nice and warm it is!

(*She holds out her hands as though warming them at a fire.*)

And so light—and so peaceful.

JEAN (*putting the razor in her hand*): Here is the broom. Go now while it's light—out to the barn—and . . . (*whispers in her ear*)

JULIE (*waking*): Thank you. I am going now—to rest.

But just tell me that even the first can receive the gift of grace.

JEAN: The first? No, I can't tell you that. But wait . . . Miss Julie, I've got it! You aren't one of the first any longer. You're one of the last.

JULIE: That's true. I'm one of the very last. I *am* the last. Oh! . . . But now I can't go. Tell me again to go.

JEAN: No, I can't now either. I can't.

JULIE: And the first shall be last.

JEAN: Don't think, don't think. You're taking my strength away too and making me a coward. What's that? I thought I saw the bell move . . . To be so frightened of a bell! Yes, but it's not just a bell. There's somebody behind it—a hand moving it—and something else moving the hand—and if you stop your ears—if you stop your ears—yes, then it rings louder than ever. Rings and rings until you answer—and then it's too late. Then the police come and . . . and . . .

(*The bell rings twice loudly.* JEAN *flinches, then straightens himself up.*)

It's horrible. But there's no other way to end it . . . Go!

(JULIE *walks firmly out through the door.*)

CURTAIN

6 THE THREE SISTERS

Anton Chekhov
1901

The Three Sisters is a very difficult play to read correctly; on the surface it seems to be a dismal recounting of repeated human failure and despair, and such a surface reading may uncover little of the excitement one expects from dramatic literature. But, of all plays, this is one that cannot simply be understood "on the surface." The true interplay of the three sisters and their friends takes place well beneath that surface—in the psychological arena that Konstantin Stanislavski, the play's first director, called the "subtext."

What one must remember when reading *The Three Sisters* is that each of the play's four acts is, in some sense, a party; and that the characters in the play, despite their multifarious problems and misadventures, are working very hard, like most average people, simply to have a good time. In their efforts, they joke, they laugh, they make music, they make conversation, they make love—and, for the most part, they actually succeed in enjoying themselves! It is the areas in which they *don't* succeed that Chekhov works his greatest effects, but one must be mindful of the background of jollity and good spirits that forms the lifeline of the sisters' society, and creates the dramatic contrast that makes the suffering poignant. A good stage production can bring this out quite clearly (good produc-

tions of Chekhov's plays are often hilariously entertaining), but the reader of the printed text may have to work somewhat harder than usual to see the joyous liveliness that serves to set off the characters' final failures.

Chekhov (1860–1904) graduated as a doctor from Moscow University, but began writing short stories and plays while still a student; his work reflects a deep, almost clinical understanding of the exquisite details of human feeling, and a sure knowledge of the intricacies of personal relationships. His characters suffer not so much from great tragic crises, but from daily anxieties, boredom, the constant threat of humiliation, and an acute inability to master what comes out of their mouths. Chekhov's plays are not narrated; they are written in the language and syntax of ordinary conversation, and are filled with the familiar stunted speeches, hastily withdrawn utterances, forced laughs, failed jokes, broken sentences, and oddly occasioned sighs, sobs, silences, whistles, and hums that frequently substitute for more rational discourse. Chekhov deals with awkward embarrassment and interpersonal manipulation in a way that makes an audience cringe with recognition; his plays touch us because they force us to realize the frailty of the images we hold of ourselves, and the pathetic weakness of our efforts to control moment-to-moment existence.

But his plays are funny. Chekhov insisted on humor, even over the objections of Stanislavski. When, for example, Vershinin and Tusenbach "philosophize" in the living room, they are not really wrestling with the problems of Russian survival. Instead, they are courting their ladies (and each other) with a competitive battle of wits and intelligence: they are, in other words, showing off. That this level of energy, enthusiasm, and excitement is not immediately apparent to the reader has caused Chekhov's literary popularity to suffer; the reader of this volume is urged to see this play as a series not of laments but of lively and dramatic encounters, where the final failures (for example, of the sisters to go to Moscow) are always balanced by the awkward energy of the characters' passionate advances.

It is on stage, of course, where Chekhov shines; his works are the most frequently performed of all Russian dramas, and his dramatic characters offer brilliant opportunities to the actors who seek to embody them. It is said that Russians attend productions of *The Three Sisters* as if visiting the three sisters themselves; the characters of this play have a reality for theatre enthusiasts, Russian and otherwise, that is all but palpable. When Chekhov's characters are seen to have the vitality of real human beings, their ultimate defeats do not depress us, but give us the emotional satisfaction of making a profound connection, if often a sad one, with the deepest realities of human life. That can only enlighten us.

THE THREE SISTERS

CAST OF CHARACTERS

ANDREY SERGEYEVITCH PROZOROV

NATALYA IVANOVNA, *also called* NATASHA, *his fiancée, afterwards his wife*

OLGA ⎫

MASHA ⎬ *his sisters*

IRINA ⎭

FYODOR ILYITCH KULIGIN, *a high-school teacher, husband of* MASHA

LIEUTENANT-COLONEL ALEXANDR IGNATYEVITCH VERSHININ, *Battery-Commander*

BARON NIKOLAY LVOVITCH TUSENBACH, *Lieutenant*

VASSILY VASSILYEVITCH SOLYONY, *Captain*

IVAN ROMANITCH TCHEBUTYKIN, *Army Doctor*

ALEXEY PETROVITCH FEDOTIK, *Second Lieutenant*

VLADIMIR KARLOVITCH RODDEY, *Second Lieutenant*

FERAPONT SPIRIDONITCH, *an old porter from the Rural Board*

ANFISA, *the nurse, an old woman of eighty*

SCENE: *The action takes place in a provincial town.*

ACT ONE

(*In the house of the* PROZOROVS. *A drawing-room with columns beyond which a large room is visible. Midday; it is bright and sunny. The table in the farther room is being laid for lunch.* OLGA, *in the dark-blue uniform of a girls' high-school teacher, is correcting exercise books, at times standing still and then walking up and down;* MASHA, *in a black dress, with her hat on her knee, is reading a book;* IRINA *in a white dress is standing plunged in thought.*)

OLGA: Father died just a year ago, on this very day—the fifth of May, your name-day, Irina. It was very cold, snow was falling. I felt as though I should not live through it; you lay fainting as though you were dead. But now a year has passed and we can think of it calmly; you are already in a white dress, your face is radiant. (*the clock strikes twelve*) The clock was striking then too (*a pause*). I remember the band playing and the firing at the cemetery as they carried the coffin. Though he was a general in command of a brigade, yet there weren't many people there. It was raining, though. Heavy rain and snow.

IRINA: Why recall it!

(BARON TUSENBACH, TCHEBUTYKIN *and* SOLYONY *appear near the table in the dining-room beyond the columns.*)

OLGA: It is warm today, we can have the windows open, but the birches are not in leaf yet. Father was given his brigade and came here with us from Moscow eleven years ago and I remember distinctly that in Moscow at this time, at the beginning of May, everything was already in flower; it was warm, and everything was bathed in sunshine. It's eleven years ago, and yet I remember it all as though we had left it yesterday. Oh, dear! I woke up this morning, I saw a blaze of sunshine. I saw the spring, and joy stirred in my heart. I had a passionate longing to be back at home again!

TCHEBUTYKIN: The devil it is!

TUSENBACH: Of course, it's nonsense.

(MASHA, *brooding over a book, softly whistles a song.*)

OLGA: Don't whistle, Masha. How can you! (*a pause*) Being all day in school and then at my lessons till the evening gives me a perpetual headache and thoughts as gloomy as though I were old. And really these four years that I have been at the high-school I have felt my strength and my youth oozing away from me every day. And only one yearning grows stronger and stronger. . . .

IRINA: To go back to Moscow. To sell the house, to make an end of everything here, and off to Moscow. . . .

OLGA: Yes! To Moscow, and quickly.

(TCHEBUTYKIN *and* TUSENBACH *laugh.*)

IRINA: Andrey will probably be a professor, he will not live here anyhow. The only difficulty is poor Masha.

OLGA: Masha will come and spend the whole summer in Moscow every year.

(MASHA *softly whistles a tune.*)

IRINA: Please God it will all be managed. (*looking out of window*) How fine it is today. I don't know why I feel so light-hearted! I remembered this morning that it was my name-day and at once I felt joyful and thought of my childhood when mother was living. And I was thrilled by such wonderful thoughts, such thoughts!

OLGA: You are radiant today and looking lovelier than usual. And Masha is lovely too. Andrey would be nice-looking, but he has grown too fat and that does not suit him. And I have grown older and ever so much thinner. I suppose it's because I get so cross with the girls at school. Today now I am free, I am at home, and my head doesn't ache and I feel younger than yesterday. I am only twenty-eight. . . . It's all quite right, it's all from God, but it seems to me that if I were married and sitting at home all day, it would be better (*a pause*). I should be fond of my husband.

TUSENBACH (*to* SOLYONY): You talk such nonsense, I am tired of listening to you. (*coming into the drawing-room*) I forgot to tell you, you will receive a visit today from Vershinin, the new commander of our battery (*sits down to the piano*).

OLGA: Well, I shall be delighted.

IRINA: Is he old?

TUSENBACH: No, nothing to speak of. Forty or forty-five at the most (*softly plays the piano*). He seems to be a nice fellow. He is not stupid, that's certain. Only he talks a lot.

IRINA: Is he interesting?

TUSENBACH: Yes, he is all right, only he has a wife, a mother-in-law and two little girls. And it's his second wife too. He is paying calls and telling everyone that he has a wife and two little girls. He'll tell you so too. His wife seems a bit crazy, with her hair in a long plait like a girl's, always talks in a high-flown style, makes philosophical reflections and frequently attempts to commit suicide, evidently to annoy her husband. I should have left a woman like that years ago, but he puts up with her and merely complains.

SOLYONY (*coming into the drawing-room with* TCHEBUTYKIN): With one hand I can only lift up half a hundred-weight, but with both hands I can lift up a hundredweight and a half or even a hundredweight and three-quarters. From that I conclude that two men are not only twice but three times as strong as one man, or even more. . . .

TCHEBUTYKIN (*reading the newspaper as he comes in*): For hair falling out . . . two ounces of naphthaline in half a bottle of spirit . . . to be dissolved and used daily . . . (*puts it down in his notebook*). Let's make a note of it! No, I don't want it . . . (*scratches it out*). It doesn't matter.

IRINA: Ivan Romanitch, dear Ivan Romanitch!

TCHEBUTYKIN: What is it, my child, my joy?

IRINA: Tell me, why is it I am so happy today? As though I were sailing with the great blue sky above me and big white birds flying over it. Why is it? Why?

TCHEBUTYKIN (*kissing both her hands, tenderly*): My white bird. . . .

IRINA: When I woke up this morning, got up and washed, it suddenly seemed to me as though everything in the world was clear to me and that I knew how one ought to live. Dear Ivan Romanitch, I know all about it. A man ought to work, to toil in the sweat of his brow, whoever he may be, and all the purpose and meaning of his life, his happiness, his ecstasies lie in that alone. How delightful to be a workman who gets up before dawn and breaks stones on the road, or a shepherd, or a schoolmaster teaching children, or an engine-driver. . . . Oh, dear! to say nothing of human beings, it would be better to be an ox, better to be a humble horse and work, than a young woman who wakes at twelve o'clock, then has coffee in bed, then spends two hours dressing. . . . Oh, how awful that is! Just as one has a craving for water in hot weather I have a craving for work. And if I don't get up early and work, give me up as a friend, Ivan Romanitch.

TCHEBUTYKIN (*tenderly*): I'll give you up, I'll give you up. . . .

OLGA: Father trained us to get up at seven o'clock. Now Irina wakes at seven and lies in bed at least till nine thinking. And she looks so serious! (*laughs*)

IRINA: You are used to thinking of me as a child and are surprised when I look serious. I am twenty!

TUSENBACH: The yearning for work, oh dear, how well I understand it! I have never worked in my life. I was born in cold, idle Petersburg, in a family that had known nothing of work or cares of any kind. I remember, when I came home from the school of cadets, a footman used to pull off my boots. I used to be troublesome, but my mother looked at me with reverential awe, and was surprised when other people did not do the same. I was guarded from work. But I doubt if they have succeeded in guarding me completely, I doubt it! The time is at hand, an avalanche is moving down upon us, a mighty clearing storm which is coming, is already near and will soon blow the laziness, the indifference, the distaste for work, the rotten boredom out of our society. I shall work, and in another twenty-five or thirty years every one will have to work. Every one!

TCHEBUTYKIN: I am not going to work.

TUSENBACH: You don't count.

SOLYONY: In another twenty-five years you won't be here, thank God. In two or three years you will kick the bucket, or I shall lose my temper and put a bullet through your head, my angel. (*pulls a scent-bottle out of his pocket and sprinkles his chest and hands*)

TCHEBUTYKIN (*laughs*): And I really have never done anything at all. I haven't done a stroke of work since I left the University, I have never read a book, I read nothing but newspapers . . . (*takes another newspaper out of his pocket*). Here . . . I know, for instance, from the newspapers that there was such a person as Dobrolyubov, but what he wrote, I can't say. . . . Goodness only knows. . . . (*a knock is heard on the floor from the storey below*) There . . . they are calling me downstairs, someone has come for me. I'll be back directly. . . . Wait a

minute . . . (*goes out hurriedly, combing his beard*).

IRINA: He's got something up his sleeve.

TUSENBACH: Yes, he went out with a solemn face, evidently he is just going to bring you a present.

IRINA: What a nuisance!

OLGA: Yes, it's awful. He is always doing something silly.

MASHA: By the sea-strand an oak-tree green . . . upon that oak a chain of gold . . . upon that oak a chain of gold (*gets up, humming softly*).

OLGA: You are not very cheerful today, Masha.

(MASHA, *humming, puts on her hat.*)

OLGA: Where are you going?

MASHA: Home.

IRINA: How queer! . . .

TUSENBACH: To go away from a name-day party!

MASHA: Never mind. . . . I'll come in the evening. Good-bye, my darling . . . (*kisses* IRINA). Once again I wish you, be well and happy. In old days, when father was alive. we always had thirty or forty officers here on name-days; it was noisy, but to-day there is only a man and a half, and it is as still as the desert. . . . I'll go. . . . I am in the blues to-day, I am feeling glum, so don't you mind what I say (*laughing through her tears*). We'll talk some other time, and so for now good-bye, darling, I am going. . . .

IRINA (*discontentedly*): Oh, how tiresome you are. . . .

OLGA (*with tears*): I understand you, Masha.

SOLYONY: If a man philosophizes, there will be philosophy or sophistry, anyway, but if a woman philosophizes, or two do it, then you may just snap your fingers!

MASHA: What do you mean to say by that, you terrible person?

SOLYONY: Nothing. He had not time to say "alack," before the bear was on his back (*a pause*).

MASHA (*to* OLGA, *angrily*): Don't blubber!

(*Enter* ANFISA *and* FERAPONT *carrying a cake.*)

ANFISA: This way, my good man. Come in, your boots are clean. (*to* IRINA) From the Rural Board, from Mihail Ivanitch Protopopov. . . . A cake.

IRINA: Thanks. Thank him (*takes the cake*).

FERAPONT: What?

IRINA (*more loudly*): Thank him from me!

OLGA: Nurse dear, give him some pie. Ferapont, go along, they will give you some pie.

FERAPONT: Eh?

ANFISA: Come along, Ferapont Spiridonitch, my good soul, come along . . . (*goes out with* FERAPONT).

MASHA: I don't like that Protopopov, that Mihail Potapitch or Ivanitch. He ought not to be invited.

IRINA: I did not invite him.

MASHA: That's a good thing.

(*Enter* TCHEBUTYKIN, *followed by an orderly with a silver samovar; a hum of surprise and displeasure.*)

OLGA (*putting her hands over her face*): A samovar! How awful! (*goes out to the table in the dining-room*)

IRINA: My dear Ivan Romanitch, what are you thinking about!

TUSENBACH (*laughs*): I warned you!

MASHA: Ivan Romanitch, you really have no conscience!

TCHEBUTYKIN: My dear girls, my darlings, you are all that I have, you are the most precious treasures I have on earth. I shall soon be sixty, I am an old man, alone in the world, a useless old man. . . . There is nothing good in me, except my love for you, and if it were not for you, I should have been dead long ago. . . . (*to* IRINA) My dear, my little girl, I've known you from a baby . . . I've carried you in my arms. . . . I loved your dear mother. . . .

IRINA: But why such expensive presents?

TCHEBUTYKIN (*angry and tearful*): Expensive presents. . . . Get along with you! (*to the orderly*) Take the samovar in there . . . (*mimicking*) Expensive presents . . . (*the orderly carries the samovar into the dining-room*)

ANFISA (*crossing the room*): My dears, a colonel is here, a stranger. . . . He has taken off his greatcoat, children, he is coming in here. Irinushka, you must be nice and polite, dear . . . (*as she goes out*) And it's time for lunch already . . . mercy on us. . . .

TUSENBACH: Vershinin, I suppose.

(*Enter* VERSHININ)

TUSENBACH: Colonel Vershinin.

VERSHININ (*to* MASHA *and* IRINA): I have the honor to introduce myself, my name is Vershinin. I am very, very glad to be in your house at last. How you have grown up! Aie-aie!

IRINA: Please sit down. We are delighted to see you.

VERSHININ (*with animation*): How glad I am, how glad I am! But there are three of you sisters. I remember—three little girls. I don't remember your faces, but that your father, Colonel Prozorov, had three little girls I remember perfectly, and saw them with my own eyes. How time passes! Hey-ho, how it passes!

TUSENBACH: Alexandr Ignatyevitch has come from Moscow.

IRINA: From Moscow? You have come from Moscow?

VERSHININ: Yes. Your father was in command of a battery there, and I was an officer in the same brigade. (*to* MASHA) Your face, now, I seem to remember.

IRINA: Olya! Olya! (*calls into the dining-room*) Olya, come!

(OLGA *comes out of the dining-room into the drawing-room.*)

IRINA: Colonel Vershinin is from Moscow, it appears.

VERSHININ: So you are Olga Sergeyevna, the eldest. . . . And you are Marya. . . . And you are Irina, the youngest. . . .

OLGA: You come from Moscow?

VERSHININ: Yes. I studied in Moscow. I began my service there, I served there for years, and at last I have been given a battery here—I have come here as you see. I don't remember you exactly, I only remember you were three sisters. I remember your father. If I shut my eyes, I can see him as though he were living. I used to visit you in Moscow. . . .

OLGA: I thought I remembered everyone, and now all at once . . .

VERSHININ: My name is Alexandr Ignatyevitch.

IRINA: Alexandr Ignatyevitch, you have come from Moscow. . . . What a surprise!

OLGA: We are going to move there, you know.

IRINA: We are hoping to be there by the autumn. It's our native town, we were born there. . . . In Old Basmanny Street . . . (*both laugh with delight*).

MASHA: To see some one from our own town unexpectedly! (*eagerly*) Now I remember! Do you remember, Olya, they used to talk of the "love-sick major"? You were a lieutenant at that time and were in love, and for some reason everyone called you "major" to tease you. . . .

VERSHININ (*laughs*): Yes, yes. . . . The love-sick major, that was it.

MASHA: You only had a moustache then. . . . Oh,

how much older you look! (*through tears*) how much older!

VERSHININ: Yes, when I was called the love-sick major I was young, I was in love. Now it's very different.

OLGA: But you haven't a single grey hair. You have grown older but you are not old.

VERSHININ: I am in my forty-third year, though. Is it long since you left Moscow?

IRINA: Eleven years. But why are you crying, Masha, you queer girl? . . . (*through her tears*) I shall cry too. . . .

MASHA: I am all right. And in which street did you live?

VERSHININ: In Old Basmanny.

OLGA: And that's where we lived too. . . .

VERSHININ: At one time I lived in Nyemetsky Street. I used to go from there to the Red Barracks. There is a gloomy-looking bridge on the way, where the water makes a noise. It makes a lonely man feel melancholy (*a pause*). And here what a broad, splendid river! A marvellous river!

OLGA: Yes, but it is cold. It's cold here and there are gnats. . . .

VERSHININ: How can you! You've such a splendid healthy Russian climate here. Forest, river . . . and birches here too. Charming, modest birches, I love them better than any other trees. It's nice to live here. The only strange thing is that the railway station is fifteen miles away . . . . And no one knows why it is so.

SOLYONY: I know why it is (*they all look at him*). Because if the station had been near it would not have been so far, and if it is far, it's because it is not near.

(*an awkward silence*)

TUSENBACH: He is fond of his joke, Vassily Vassilyevitch.

OLGA: Now I recall you, too. I remember.

VERSHININ: I knew your mother.

TCHEBUTYKIN: She was a fine woman, the Kingdom of Heaven be hers.

IRINA: Mother is buried in Moscow.

OLGA: In the Novo-Dyevitchy. . . .

MASHA: Would you believe it, I am already beginning to forget her face. So people will not remember us either . . . they will forget us.

VERSHININ: Yes. They will forget us. Such is our fate, there is no help for it. What seems to us serious, significant, very important, will one day be forgotten or will seem unimportant (*a pause*). And it's curious that we can't possibly tell what exactly will be considered great and important, and what will seem paltry and ridiculous. Did not the discoveries of Copernicus or Columbus, let us say, seem useless and ridiculous at first, while the nonsensical writings of some wiseacre seemed true? And it may be that our present life, which we accept so readily, will in time seem queer, uncomfortable, not sensible, not clean enough, perhaps even sinful. . . .

TUSENBACH: Who knows? Perhaps our age will be called a great one and remembered with respect. Now we have no torture-chamber, no executions, no invasions, but at the same time how much unhappiness there is!

SOLYONY (*in a high-pitched voice*): Chook, chook, chook. . . . It's bread and meat to the baron to talk about ideas.

TUSENBACH: Vassily Vassilyevitch, I ask you to let me alone . . . (*moves to another seat*). It gets boring, at last.

SOLYONY (*in a high-pitched voice*): Chook, chook, chook. . . .

TUSENBACH (*to* VERSHININ): The unhappiness which one observes now—there is so much of it—does indicate, however, that society has reached a certain moral level. . . .

VERSHININ: Yes, yes, of course.

TCHEBUTYKIN: You said just now, baron, that our age will be called great; but people are small all the same . . . (*gets up*). Look how small I am.

(*A violin is played behind the scenes.*)

MASHA: That's Andrey playing, our brother.

IRINA: He is the learned one of the family. We expect him to become a professor. Father was a military man, but his son has gone in for a learned career.

MASHA: It was father's wish.

OLGA: We have been teasing him today. We think he is a little in love.

IRINA: With a young lady living here. She will come in today most likely.

MASHA: Oh, how she dresses! It's not that her clothes are merely ugly or out of fashion, they are simply pitiful. A queer, gaudy, yellowish skirt with some sort of vulgar fringe and a red blouse. And her cheeks scrubbed till they shine! Andrey is not in love with her—I won't admit that, he has some taste anyway—it's simply for fun, he is teasing us, playing the fool. I heard yesterday that she is going to be married to Protopopov, the chairman of our Rural Board. And a very good thing too. . . . (*at the side door*) Andrey, come here, dear, for a minute!

(*Enter* ANDREY)

OLGA: This is my brother, Andrey Sergeyevitch.

VERSHININ: My name is Vershinin.

ANDREY: And mine is Prozorov (*mops his perspiring face*). You are our new battery commander?

OLGA: Only fancy, Alexandr Ignatyevitch comes from Moscow.

ANDREY: Really? Well, then, I congratulate you. My sisters will let you have no peace.

VERSHININ: I have had time to bore your sisters already.

IRINA: See what a pretty picture-frame Andrey has given me today! (*shows the frame*) He made it himself.

VERSHININ (*looking at the frame and not knowing what to say*): Yes . . . it is a thing . . .

IRINA: And that frame above the piano, he made that too!

(ANDREY *waves his hand in despair and moves away.*)

OLGA: He is learned, and he plays the violin, and he makes all sorts of things with the fretsaw. In fact he is good all round. Andrey, don't go! That's a way he has—he always tries to make off! Come here!

(MASHA *and* IRINA *take him by the arms and, laughing, lead him back.*)

MASHA: Come, come!

ANDREY: Leave me alone, please!

MASHA: How absurd he is! Alexandr Ignatyevitch used to be called the love-sick major at one time, and he was not a bit offended.

VERSHININ: Not in the least!

MASHA: And I should like to call you the love-sick violinist!

IRINA: Or the love-sick professor!

OLGA: He is in love! Andryusha is in love!

IRINA (*claps her hands*): Bravo, bravo! Encore! Andryusha is in love!

TCHEBUTYKIN (*comes up behind* ANDREY *and puts both arms round his waist*): Nature our hearts for love created! (*laughs, then sits down and reads the newspaper which he takes out of his pocket*)

ANDREY: Come that's enough, that's enough . . . (*mops his face*). I haven't slept all night and this morning I don't feel quite myself, as they say. I read till four o'clock and then went to bed, but it was no use. I thought of one thing and another, and then it gets light so early; the sun simply pours into my bedroom. I want while I am here during the summer to translate a book from the English. . . .

VERSHININ: You read English then?

ANDREY: Yes. Our father, the Kingdom of Heaven be his, oppressed us with education. It's absurd and silly, but it must be confessed I began to get fatter after his death, and I have grown too fat in one year, as though a weight had been taken off my body. Thanks to our father we all know English, French and German, and Irina knows Italian too. But what it cost us!

MASHA: In this town to know three languages is an unnecessary luxury! Not even a luxury, but an unnecessary encumbrance, like a sixth finger. We know a great deal that is unnecessary.

VERSHININ: What next! (*laughs*) You know a great deal that is unnecessary! I don't think there can be a town so dull and dismal that intelligent and educated people are unnecessary in it. Let us suppose that of the hundred thousand people living in this town, which is, of course, uncultured and behind the times, there are only three of your sort. It goes without saying that you cannot conquer the mass of darkness round you; little by little, as you go on living, you will be lost in the crowd. You will have to give in to it. Life will get the better of you, but still you will not disappear without a trace. After you there may appear perhaps six like you, then twelve and so on until such as you form a majority. In two or three hundred years life on earth will be unimaginably beautiful, marvellous. Man needs such a life and, though he hasn't it yet, he must have a presentiment of it, expect it, dream of it, prepare for it; for that he must see and know more than his father and grandfather (*laughs*). And you complain of knowing a great deal that's unnecessary.

MASHA (*takes off her hat*): I'll stay to lunch.

IRINA (*with a sigh*): All that really ought to be written down. . . .

(ANDREY *has slipped away unobserved.*)

TUSENBACH: You say that after many years life on

earth will be beautiful and marvellous. That's true. But in order to have any share, however far off, in it now one must be preparing for it, one must be working. . . .

VERSHININ (*gets up*): Yes. What a lot of flowers you have! (*looking round*) And delightful rooms. I envy you! I've been knocking about all my life from one wretched lodging to another, always with two chairs and a sofa and stoves which smoke. What I have been lacking all my life is just such flowers . . . (*rubs his hands*). But there, it's no use thinking about it!

TUSENBACH: Yes, we must work. I'll be bound you think the German is getting sentimental. But on my honor I am Russian and I can't even speak German. My father belonged to the Orthodox Church . . . (*a pause*).

VERSHININ (*walks about the stage*): I often think, what if one were to begin life over again, knowing what one is about! If one life, which has been already lived, were only a rough sketch so to say, and the second were the fair copy! Then, I fancy, every one of us would try before everything not to repeat himself, anyway he would create a different setting for his life; would have a house like this with plenty of light and masses of flowers. . . . I have a wife and two little girls, my wife is in delicate health and so on and so on, but if I were to begin life over again I would not marry. . . . No, no!

(*Enter* KULIGIN *in the uniform of a school-master*)

KULIGIN (*goes up to* IRINA): Dear sister, allow me to congratulate you on your name-day and with all my heart to wish you good health and everything else that one can desire for a girl of your age. And to offer you as a gift this little book (*gives her a book*). The history of our high-school for fifty years, written by myself. An insignificant little book, written because I had nothing better to do, but still you can read it. Good morning, friends. (*to* VERSHININ) My name is Kuligin, teacher in the high-school here. (*to* IRINA) In that book you will find a list of all who have finished their studies in our high-school during the last fifty years. *Feci quod potui, faciant meliora potentes* (*kisses* MASHA).

IRINA: Why, but you gave me a copy of this book at Easter.

KULIGIN (*laughs*): Impossible! If that's so, give it me back, or better still, give it to the Colonel. Please accept it, Colonel. Some day when you are bored you can read it.

VERSHININ: Thank you (*is about to take leave*). I am extremely glad to have made your acquaintance. . . .

OLGA: You are going? No, no!

IRINA: You must stay to lunch with us. Please do.

OLGA: Pray do!

VERSHININ (*bows*): I believe I have chanced on a name-day. Forgive me, I did not know and have not congratulated you . . . (*walks away with* OLGA *into the dining-room*)

KULIGIN: To-day, gentlemen, is Sunday, a day of rest. Let us all rest and enjoy ourselves each in accordance with our age and our position. The carpets should be taken up for the summer and put away till the winter. . . . Persian powder or naphthaline. . . . The Romans were healthy because they knew how to work and they knew how to rest, they had *mens sana in corpore sano*. Their life was moulded into a certain framework. Our headmaster says that the most important thing in every life is its framework. . . . What loses its framework, comes to an end—and it's the same in our everyday life. (*puts his arm round* MASHA's *waist, laughing*). Masha loves me. My wife loves me. And the window curtains, too, ought to be put away together with the carpets. . . . To-day I feel cheerful and in the best of spirits. Masha, at four o'clock this afternoon we have to be at the headmaster's. An excursion has been arranged for the teachers and their families.

MASHA: I am not going.

KULIGIN (*grieved*): Dear Masha, why not?

MASHA: We'll talk about it afterwards . . . (*angrily*) Very well, I will go, only let me alone, please . . . (*walks away*).

KULIGIN: And then we shall spend the evening at the headmaster's. In spite of the delicate state of his health, that man tries before all things to be sociable. He is an excellent, noble personality. A splendid man. Yesterday, after the meeting, he said to me, "I am tired, Fyodor Ilyitch, I am tired." (*looks at the clock, then at his watch*) Your clock is seven minutes fast. "Yes," he said, "I am tired."

(*Sounds of a violin behind the scenes*)

OLGA: Come to lunch, please. There's a pie!

KULIGIN: Ah, Olga, my dear Olga! Yesterday I was

working from early morning till eleven o'clock at night and was tired out, and to-day I feel happy (*goes up to the table in the dining-room*). My dear. . . .

TCHEBUTYKIN (*puts the newspaper in his pocket and combs his beard*): Pie? Splendid!

MASHA (*to* TCHEBUTYKIN, *sternly*): Only mind you don't drink to-day! Do you hear? It's bad for you to drink.

TCHEBUTYKIN: Oh, come, that's a thing of the past. It's two years since I got drunk. (*impatiently*) But there, my good girl, what does it matter!

MASHA: Anyway, don't you dare to drink. Don't dare. (*angrily, but so as not to be heard by her husband*) Again, damnation, take it, I am to be bored a whole evening at the headmaster's!

TUSENBACH: I wouldn't go if I were you. . . . It's very simple.

TCHEBUTYKIN: Don't go, my love.

MASHA: Oh, yes, don't go! . . . It's a damnable life, insufferable . . . (*goes to the dining-room*).

TCHEBUTYKIN (*following her*): Come, come . . .

SOLYONY (*going to the dining-room*): Chook, chook, chook. . . .

TUSENBACH: Enough, Vassily Vassilyevitch! Leave off!

SOLYONY: Chook, chook, chook. . . .

KULIGIN (*gaily*): Your health, Colonel! I am a schoolmaster and one of the family here. Masha's husband. . . . She is very kind, really, very kind.

VERSHININ: I'll have some of this dark-colored vodka . . . (*drinks*). To your health! (*to* OLGA) I feel so happy with all of you!

(*No one is left in the drawing-room but* IRINA *and* TUSENBACH.)

IRINA: Masha is in low spirits today. She was married at eighteen, when she thought him the cleverest of men. But now it's not the same. He is the kindest of men, but he is not the cleverest.

OLGA (*impatiently*): Andrey, do come!

ANDREY (*behind the scenes*): I am coming (*comes in and goes to the table*).

TUSENBACH: What are you thinking about?

IRINA: Nothing. I don't like that Solyony of yours, I am afraid of him. He keeps on saying such stupid things. . . .

TUSENBACH: He is a queer man. I am sorry for him and annoyed by him, but more sorry. I think he is shy. . . . When one is alone with him he is very intelligent and friendly, but in company he is rude, a bully. Don't go yet, let them sit down to the table. Let me be by you. What are you thinking of? (*a pause*) You are twenty, I am not yet thirty. How many years have we got before us, a long, long chain of days full of my love for you. . . .

IRINA: Nikolay Lvovitch, don't talk to me about love.

TUSENBACH (*not listening*): I have a passionate craving for life, for struggle, for work, and that craving is mingled in my soul with my love for you, Irina, and just because you are beautiful it seems to me that life too is beautiful! What are you thinking of?

IRINA: You say life is beautiful. . . . Yes, but what if it only seems so! Life for us three sisters has not been beautiful yet, we have been stifled by it as plants are choked by weeds. . . . I am shedding tears. . . . I mustn't do that (*hurriedly wipes her eyes and smiles*). I must work, I must work. The reason we are depressed and take such a gloomy view of life is that we know nothing of work. We come of people who despised work. . . .

(*Enter* NATALYA IVANOVNA; *she is wearing a pink dress with a green sash.*)

NATASHA: They are sitting down to lunch already. . . . I am late . . . (*steals a glance at herself in the glass and sets herself to rights*) I think my hair is all right. (*seeing* IRINA) Dear Irina Sergeyevna, I congratulate you! (*gives her a vigorous and prolonged kiss*) You have a lot of visitors, I really feel shy. . . . Good day, Baron!

OLGA (*coming into the drawing-room*): Well, here is Natalya Ivanovna! How are you, my dear? (*kisses her*)

NATASHA: Congratulations on the name-day. You have such a big party and I feel awfully shy. . . .

OLGA: Nonsense, we have only our own people. (*in an undertone, in alarm*) You've got on a green sash! My dear, that's not nice!

NATASHA: Why, is that a bad omen?

OLGA: No, it's only that it doesn't go with your dress . . . and it looks queer. . . .

NATASHA (*in a tearful voice*): Really? But you know it's not green exactly, it's more a dead color (*follows* OLGA *into the dining-room*).

(*In the dining-room they are all sitting down to lunch; there is no one in the drawing-room.*)

KULIGIN: I wish you a good husband, Irina. It's time for you to think of getting married.

TCHEBUTYKIN: Natalya Ivanovna, I hope we may hear of your engagement, too.

KULIGIN: Natalya Ivanovna has got a suitor already.

MASHA (*strikes her plate with her fork*): Ladies and gentlemen, I want to make a speech!

KULIGIN: You deserve three bad marks for conduct.

VERSHININ: How nice this cordial is! What is it made of?

SOLYONY: Beetles.

IRINA (*in a tearful voice*): Ugh, ugh! How disgusting.

OLGA: We are going to have roast turkey and apple pie for supper. Thank God I am at home all day and shall be at home in the evening. . . . Friends, won't you come this evening?

VERSHININ: Allow me to come too.

IRINA: Please do.

NATASHA: They don't stand on ceremony.

TCHEBUTYKIN: Nature our hearts for love created! (*laughs*)

ANDREY (*angrily*): Do leave off, I wonder you are not tird of it!

(FEDOTIK *and* RODDEY *come in with a big basket of flowers.*)

FEDOTIK: I say, they are at lunch already.

RODDEY (*speaking, loudly, with a lisp*): At lunch? Yes, they are at lunch already. . . .

FEDOTIK: Wait a minute (*takes a snapshot*). One! Wait another minute . . . (*takes another snapshot*). Two! Now it's ready. (*they take the basket and walk into the dining-room, where they are greeted noisily*).

RODDEY (*loudly*): My congratulations! I wish you everything, everything! The weather is delightful, perfectly magnificient. I've been out all the morning for a walk with the high-school boys. I teach them gymnastics.

FEDOTIK: You may move, Irina Sergeyevna, you may move (*taking a photograph*). You look charming today (*taking a top out of his pocket*). Here is a top, by the way. . . . It has a wonderful note. . . .

IRINA: How lovely!

MASHA: By the sea-shore an oak-tree green. . . . Upon that oak a chain of gold . . . (*complainingly*) Why do I keep saying that? That phrase has been haunting me all day. . . .

KULIGIN: Thirteen at table!

RODDEY (*loudly*): Surely you do not attach importance to such superstitions? (*laughter*)

KULIGIN: If there are thirteen at table, it means that someone present is in love. It's not you, Ivan Romanovitch, by any chance? (*laughter*)

TCHEBUTYKIN: I am an old sinner, but why Natalya Ivanovna is overcome, I can't imagine. . . .

(*Loud laughter;* NATASHA *runs out from the dining-room into the drawing-room followed by* ANDREY.)

ANDREY: Come, don't take any notice! Wait a minute . . . stop, I entreat you. . . .

NATASHA: I am ashamed. . . . I don't know what's the matter with me and they make fun of me. I know it's improper for me to leave the table like this, but I can't help it. . . . I can't . . . (*covers her face with her hands*).

ANDREY: My dear girl, I entreat you, I implore you, don't be upset. I asure you they are only joking, they do it in all kindness. My dear, my sweet, they are all kind, warm-hearted people and they are fond of me and of you. Come here to the window, here they can't see us . . . (*looks round*).

NATASHA: I am so unaccustomed to society! . . .

ANDREY: Oh youth, lovely, marvellous youth! My dear, my sweet, don't be so distressed! Believe me, believe me. . . . I feel so happy, my soul is full of love and rapture. . . . Oh, they can't see us, they can't see us! Why, why, I love you, when I first loved you—oh, I don't know. My dear, my sweet, pure one, be my wife! I love you, I love you . . . as I have never loved anyone . . . (*a kiss*).

(*Two officers come in and, seeing the pair kissing, stop in amazement.*)

CURTAIN

ACT TWO

(*The same scene as in the First Act. Eight o'clock in the evening. Behind the scenes in the street there is the faintly audible sound of a concertina. There is no light.* NATALYA IVANOVNA *enters in a dressing-gown, carrying a candle; she comes in and stops at the door leading to* ANDREY'S *room.*)

NATASHA: What are you doing, Andryusha? Reading? Never mind, I only just asked . . . (*goes and opens another door and, peeping into it, shuts it again*). Is there a light?

ANDREY (*enters with a book in his hand*): What is it, Natasha?

NATASHA: I was looking to see whether there was a light. . . . It's Carnival, the servants are not themselves; one has always to be on the lookout for fear something goes wrong. Last night at twelve o'clock I passed through the dining-room, and there was a candle left burning. I couldn't find out who had lighted it (*puts down the candle*). What's the time?

ANDREY (*looking at his watch*): A quarter past eight.

NATASHA: And Olga and Irina aren't in yet. They haven't come in. Still at work, poor dears! Olga is at the teachers' council and Irina at the telegraph office . . . (*sighs*). I was saying to your sister this morning, "Take care of yourself, Irina darling," said I. But she won't listen. A quarter past eight, you say? I am afraid our Bobik is not at all well. Why is he so cold? Yesterday he was feverish and today he is cold all over. . . . I am so anxious!

ANDREY: It's all right, Natasha. The boy is quite well.

NATASHA: We had better be careful about his food, anyway. I am anxious. And I am told that the mummers are going to be here for the Carnival at nine o'clock this evening. It would be better for them not to come, Andryusha.

ANDREY: I really don't know. They've been invited, you know.

NATASHA: Baby woke up this morning, looked at me, and all at once he gave a smile; so he knew me. "Good morning, Bobik!" said I. "Good morning, darling!" And he laughed. Children understand; they understand very well. So I shall tell them, Andryusha, not to let the carnival party come in.

ANDREY (*irresolutely*): That's for my sisters to say. It's for them to give orders.

NATASHA: Yes, for them too; I will speak to them. They are so kind . . . (*is going*). I've ordered junket for supper. The doctor says you must eat nothing but junket, or you will never get thinner (*stops*). Bobik is cold. I am afraid his room is chilly, perhaps. We ought to put him in a different room till the warm weather comes, anyway. Irina's room, for instance, is just right for a nursery: it's dry and the sun shines there all day. I must tell her; she might share Olga's room for the time. . . . She is never at home, anyway, except for the night. . . . (*a pause*). Andryusantchik, why don't you speak?

ANDREY: Nothing. I was thinking. . . . Besides, I have nothing to say.

NATASHA: Yes . . . what was it I meant to tell you? . . . Oh, yes; Ferapont has come from the Rural Board, and is asking for you.

ANDREY (*yawns*): Send him in.

(NATASHA *goes out;* ANDREY, *bending down to the candle which she has left behind, reads. Enter* FERAPONT; *he wears an old shabby overcoat, with the collar turned up, and has a scarf over his ears.*)

ANDREY: Good evening, my good man. What is it?

FERAPONT: The Chairman has sent a book and a paper of some sort here . . . (*gives the book and an envelope*).

ANDREY: Thanks. Very good. But why have you come so late? It is past eight.

FERAPONT: Eh?

ANDREY (*louder*): I say, you have come late. It is eight o'clock.

FERAPONT: Just so. I came before it was dark, but they wouldn't let me see you. The master is busy, they told me. Well, of course, if you are busy, I am in no hurry (*thinking that* AUDREY *has asked him a question*). Eh?

ANDREY: Nothing (*examines the book*). Tomorrow is Friday. We haven't a sitting, but I'll come all the same . . . and do my work. It's dull at home . . . (*a pause*). Dear old man, how strangely life changes and deceives one! Today I was so bored and had nothing to do, so I picked up this book—old university lectures—and I laughed. . . . Good heavens! I am the secretary of the Rural Board of which Protopopov is the chairman. I am the secretary, and the most I can hope for is to become a member of the Board! Me, a member of the local Rural Board, while I dream every night I am professor of the University of Moscow—a distinguished man, of whom all Russia is proud!

FERAPONT: I can't say, sir. . . . I don't hear well. . . .

ANDREY: If you did hear well, perhaps I should not talk to you. I must talk to somebody, and my wife does not understand me. My sisters I am somehow afraid of—I'm afraid they will laugh at me and make me ashamed. . . . I don't drink, I am not fond of restaurants, but how I should enjoy sitting at Tyestov's in Moscow at this moment, dear old chap!

FERAPONT: A contractor was saying at the Board the other day that there were some merchants in Moscow eating pancakes; one who ate forty, it seems, died. It was either forty or fifty, I don't remember.

ANDREY: In Moscow you sit in a huge room at a restaurant; you know no one and no one knows you, and at the same time you don't feel a stranger. . . . But here you know everyone and everyone knows you, and yet you are a stranger—a stranger. . . . A stranger, and lonely. . . .

FERAPONT: Eh? (*a pause*) And the same contractor says—maybe it's not true—that there's a rope stretched right across Moscow.

ANDREY: What for?

FERAPONT: I can't say, sir. The contractor said so.

ANDREY: Nonsense (*reads*). Have you ever been in Moscow?

FERAPONT (*after a pause*): No, never. It was not God's will I should (*a pause*). Am I to go?

ANDREY: You can go. Good-bye. (FERAPONT *goes out*) Good-bye (*reading*). Come tomorrow morning and take some papers here. . . . Go. . . . (*a pause*). He has gone (*a ring*). Yes, it is a business . . . (*stretches and goes slowly into his own room*).

(*Behind the scenes a Nurse is singing, rocking a baby to sleep. Enter* MASHA *and* VERSHININ. *While they are talking a maidservant is lighting a lamp and candles in the dining-room.*)

MASHA: I don't know (*a pause*). I don't know. Of course habit does a great deal. After father's death, for instance, it was a long time before we could get used to having no orderlies in the house. But apart from habit, I think it's a feeling of justice makes me say so. Perhaps it is not so in other places, but in our town the most decent, honorable, and well-bred people are all in the army.

VERSHININ: I am thirsty. I should like some tea.

MASHA (*glancing at the clock*): They will soon be bringing it. I was married when I was eighteen, and I was afraid of my husband because he was a teacher, and I had only just left school. In those days I thought him an awfully learned, clever, and important person. And now it is not the same, unfortunately. . . .

VERSHININ: Yes. . . . I see. . . .

MASHA: I am not speaking of my husband—I am used to him; but among civilians generally there are so many rude, ill-mannered, badly-brought-up people. Rudeness upsets and distresses me: I am unhappy when I see that a man is not refined, not gentle, not polite enough. When I have to be among the teachers, my husband's colleagues, it makes me quite miserable.

VERSHININ: Yes. . . . But, to my mind, it makes no difference whether they are civilians or military men—they are equally uninteresting, in this town anyway. It's all the same! If one listens to a man of the educated class here, civilian or military, he is worried to death by his wife, worried to death by his house, worried to death by his estate, worried to death by his horses. . . . A Russian is peculiarly given to exalted ideas, but why is it he always falls so short in life? Why?

MASHA: Why?

VERSHININ: Why is he worried to death by his children and by his wife? And why are his wife and children worried to death by him?

MASHA: You are rather depressed this evening.

VERSHININ: Perhaps. . . . I've had no dinner today, and had nothing to eat since the morning. My daughter is not quite well, and when my little girls are ill I am consumed by anxiety; my conscience reproaches me for having given them such a mother. Oh, if you had seen her today! She is a wretched creature! We began quarreling at seven o'clock in the morning, and at nine I slammed the door and went away (*a pause*). I never talk about it. Strange, it's only to you I complain (*kisses her hand*). Don't be angry with me. . . . Except for you I have no one—no one . . . (*a pause*).

MASHA: What a noise in the stove! Before father died there was howling in the chimney. There, just like that.

VERSHININ: Are you superstitious?

MASHA: Yes.

VERSHININ: That's strange (*kisses her hand*). You are a splendid, wonderful woman. Splendid! Wonderful! It's dark, but I see the light in your eyes.

MASHA (*moves to another chair*): It's lighter here.

VERSHININ: I love you—love, love. . . . I love your

eyes, your movements, I see them in my dreams. . . . Splendid, wonderful woman!

MASHA: (*laughing softly*): When you talk to me like that, for some reason I laugh, though I am frightened. . . . Please don't do it again . . . (*in an undertone*) You may say it, though; I don't mind . . . (*covers her face with her hands*). I don't mind. . . . Someone is coming. Talk of something else.

(IRINA *and* TUSENBACH *come in through the dining-room.*)

TUSENBACH: I've got a three-barrelled name. My name is Baron Tusenbach-Krone-Altschauer, but I belong to the Orthodox Church and am just as Russian as you. There is very little of the German left in me—nothing, perhaps, but the patience and perseverance with which I bore you. I see you home every evening.

IRINA: How tired I am!

TUSENBACH: And every day I will come to the telegraph office and see you home. I'll do it for ten years, for twenty years, till you drive me away . . . (*seeing* MASHA *and* VERSHININ, *delightedly*) Oh, it's you! How are you?

IRINA: Well, I am home at last. (*to* MASHA) A lady came just now to telegraph to her brother in Saratov that her son died today, and she could not think of the address. So she sent it without an address–simply to Saratov. She was crying. And I was rude to her for no sort of reason. Told her I had no time to waste. It was so stupid. Are the Carnival people coming tonight?

MASHA: Yes.

IRINA (*sits down in an arm-chair*): I must rest. I am tired.

TUSENBACH (*with a smile*): When you come from the office you seem so young, so forlorn . . . (*a pause*).

IRINA: I am tired. No, I don't like telegraph work, I don't like it.

MASHA: You've grown thinner . . . (*whistles*). And you look younger, rather like a boy in the face.

TUSENBACH: That's the way she does her hair.

IRINA: I must find some other job, this does not suit me. What I so longed for, what I dreamed of is the very thing that it's lacking in. . . . It is work without poetry, without meaning. . . . (*a knock on the floor*). There's the doctor knocking. . . . (*to* TUSENBACH) Do knock, dear. . . . I can't. . . . I am tired.

(TUSENBACH *knocks on the floor.*)

IRINA: He will come directly. We ought to do something about it. The doctor and our Andrey were at the Club yesterday and they lost again. I am told Andrey lost two hundred roubles.

MASHA (*indifferently*): Well, it can't be helped now.

IRINA: A fortnight ago he lost money, in December he lost money. I wish he'd make haste and lose everything, then perhaps we should go away from this town. My God, every night I dream of Moscow, it's perfect madness (*laughs*). We'll move there in June and there is still left February, March, April, May . . . almost half a year.

MASHA: The only thing is Natasha must not hear of his losses.

IRINA: I don't suppose she cares.

(TCHEBUTYKIN, *who has only just got off his bed—he has been resting after dinner—comes into the dining-room combing his beard, then sits down to the table and takes a newspaper out of his pocket.*)

MASHA: Here he is . . . has he paid his rent?

IRINA (*laughs*): No. Not a kopek for eight months. Evidently he has forgotten.

MASHA (*laughs*): How gravely he sits.

(*They all laugh; a pause.*)

IRINA: Why are you so quiet, Alexandr Ignatyevitch?

VERSHININ: I don't know. I am longing for tea. I'd give half my life for a glass of tea. I have had nothing to eat since the morning.

TCHEBUTYKIN: Irina Sergeyevna!

IRINA: What is it?

TCHEBUTYKIN: Come here. *Venez ici.* (IRINA *goes and sits down at the table*) I can't do without you. (IRINA *lays out the cards for patience*)

VERSHININ: Well, if they won't bring tea, let us discuss something.

TUSENBACH: By all means. What?

VERSHININ: What? Let us dream . . . for instance of the life that will come after us, in two or three hundred years.

TUSENBACH: Well? When we are dead, men will fly in balloons, change the fashion of their coats, will discover a sixth sense, perhaps, and develop it, but life will remain just the same, difficult, full of mysteries and happiness. In a thousand years man will sigh just the same, "Ah, how hard life is," and yet just as now he will be afraid of death and not want it.

VERSHININ (*after a moment's thought*): Well, I don't know. . . . It seems to me that everything on earth is bound to change by degrees and is already changing before our eyes. In two or three hundred, perhaps in a thousand years—the time does not matter—a new, happy life will come. We shall have no share in that life, of course, but we are living for it, we are working, well, yes, and suffering for it, we are creating it—and that alone is the purpose of our existence, and is our happiness, if you like.

(MASHA *laughs softly*).

TUSENBACH: What is it?

MASHA: I don't know. I've been laughing all day.

VERSHININ: I was at the same school as you were, I did not go to the Military Academy; I read a great deal, but I do not know how to choose my books, and very likely I read quite the wrong things, and yet the longer I live the more I want to know. My hair is turning grey, I am almost an old man, but I know so little, oh so little! But all the same I fancy that I do know and thoroughly grasp what is essential and matters most. And how I should like to make you see that there is no happiness for us, that there ought not to be and will not be. . . . We must work and work, and happiness is the portion of our remote descendants (*a pause*). If it is not for me, at least it is for the descendants of my descendants. . . .

(FEDOTIK *and* RODDEY *appear in the dining-room; they sit down and sing softly, playing the guitar.*)

TUSENBACH: You think it's no use even dreaming of happiness! But what if I am happy?

VERSHININ: No.

TUSENBACH (*flinging up his hands and laughing*): It is clear we don't understand each other. Well, how am I to convince you?

(MASHA *laughs softly.*)

TUSENBACH (*holds up a finger to her*): Laugh! (*to* VERSHININ) Not only in two or three hundred years but in a million years life will be just the same; it does not change, it remains stationary, following its own laws which we have nothing to do with or which, anyway, we shall never find out. Migratory birds, cranes for instance, fly backwards and forwards, and whatever ideas, great or small, stray through their minds, they will still go on flying just the same without knowing where or why. They fly and will continue to fly, however philosophic they may become; and it doesn't matter how philosophical they are so long as they go on flying. . . .

MASHA: But still there is a meaning?

TUSENBACH: Meaning. . . . Here it is snowing. What meaning is there in that? (*a pause*)

MASHA: I think man ought to have faith or ought to seek a faith, or else his life is empty, empty. . . . To live and not to understand why cranes fly; why children are born; why there are stars in the sky. . . . One must know what one is living for or else it is all nonsense and waste (*a pause*).

VERSHININ: And yet one is sorry that youth is over. . . .

MASHA: Gogol says: it's dull living in this world, friends!

TUSENBACH: And I say: it is difficult to argue with you, my friends, God bless you. . . .

TCHEBUTYKIN (*reading the newspaper*): Balzac was married at Berditchev.

(IRINA *hums softly.*)

TCHEBUTYKIN: I really must put that down in my book (*writes*). Balzac was married at Berditchev (*reads the paper*).

IRINA (*lays out the cards for patience, dreamily*): Balzac was married at Berditchev.

TUSENBACH: The die is cast. You know, Marya Sergeyevna, I've resigned my commission.

MASHA: So I hear. And I see nothing good in that. I don't like civilians.

TUSENBACH: Never mind . . . (*gets up*). I am not good-looking enough for a soldier. But that does not matter, though . . . I am going to work. If only for one day in my life, to work so that I come home at night tired out and fall asleep as soon as I get into bed . . . (*going into the dining-room*). Workmen must sleep soundly!

FEDOTIK (*to* IRINA): I bought these chalks for you just now as I passed the shop. . . . And this penknife. . . .

IRINA: You've got into the way of treating me as though I were little, but I am grown up, you know . . . (*takes the chalks and the penknife, joyfully*). How lovely!

FEDOTIK: And I bought a knife for myself . . . look . . . one blade, and another blade, a third, and this is for the ears, and here are scissors, and that's for cleaning the nails. . . .

RODDEY (*loudly*): Doctor, how old are you?

TCHEBUTYKIN: I? Thirty-two (*laughter*).

FEDOTIK: I'll show you another patience . . . (*lays out the cards*).

(*The samovar is brought in;* ANFISA *is at the samovar; a little later* NATASHA *comes in and is also busy at the table;* SOLYONY *comes in, and after greeting the others sits down at the table.*)

VERSHININ: What a wind there is!

MASHA: Yes. I am sick of the winter. I've forgotten what summer is like.

IRINA: It's coming out right, I see. We shall go to Moscow.

FEDOTIK: No, it's not coming out. You see, the eight is over the two of spades (*laughs*). So that means you won't go to Moscow.

TCHEBUTYKIN (*reads from the newspaper*): Tsi-tsi-kar. Smallpox is raging here.

ANFISA (*going up to* MASHA): Masha, come to tea, my dear. (*to* VERSHININ) Come, your honor . . . excuse me, sir, I have forgotten your name. . . .

MASHA: Bring it here, nurse, I am not going there.

IRINA: Nurse!

ANFISA: I am coming!

NATASHA (*to* SOLYONY): Little babies understand very well. "Good morning Bobik, good morning, darling," I said. He looked at me in quite a special way. You think I say that because I am a mother, but no, I assure you! He is an extraordinary child.

SOLYONY: If that child were mine, I'd fry him in a frying pan and eat him. (*takes his glass, comes into the drawing-room and sits down in a corner*)

NATASHA (*covers her face with her hands*): Rude, ill-bred man!

MASHA: Happy people don't notice whether it is winter or summer. I fancy if I lived in Moscow I should not mind what the weather was like.
. . .

VERSHININ: The other day I was reading the diary of a French minister written in prison. The minister was condemned for the Panama affair. With what enthusiasm and delight he describes the birds he sees from the prison window, which he never noticed before when he was a minister. Now that he is released, of course he notices birds no more than he did before. In the same way, you won't notice Moscow when you live in it. We have no happiness and never do have, we only long for it.

TUSENBACH (*takes a box from the table*): What has become of the sweets?

IRINA: Solyony has eaten them.

TUSENBACH: All?

ANFISA (*handing tea*): There's a letter for you, sir.

VERSHININ: For me? (*takes the letter*) From my daughter (*reads*). Yes, of course. . . . Excuse me, Marya Sergeyevna, I'll slip away. I won't have tea (*gets up in agitation*). Always these upsets.
. . .

MASHA: What is it? Not a secret?

VERSHININ (*in a low voice*): My wife has taken poison again. I must go. I'll slip off unnoticed. Horribly unpleasant it all is. (*kisses* MASHA's *hand*) My fine, dear, splendid woman. . . . I'll go this way without being seen . . . (*goes out*).

ANFISA: Where is he off to? I've just given him his tea. . . . What a man.

MASHA (*getting angry*): Leave off! Don't pester, you give one no peace . . . (*goes with her cup to the table*). You bother me, old lady.

ANFISA: Why are you so huffy? Darling!

(ANDREY's *voice:* "Anfisa!")

ANFISA (*mimicking*): Anfisa! he sits there. . . . (*goes out*).

MASHA (*by the table in the dining-room angrily*): Let me sit down! (*mixes the cards on the table*) You take up all the table with your cards. Drink your tea!

IRINA: How cross you are, Masha!

MASHA: If I'm cross, don't talk to me. Don't interfere with me.

TCHEBUTYKIN (*laughing*): Don't touch her, don't touch her!

MASHA: You are sixty, but you talk rot like a schoolboy.

NATASHA (*sighs*): Dear Masha, why make use of such expressions in conversation? With your attractive appearance I tell you straight out, you would be simply fascinating in a well-bred social circle if it were not for the things you say. *Je vous prie, pardonnez-moi, Marie, mais vous avez des manières un peu grossières.*

TUSENBACH (*suppressing a laugh*): Give me . . . give me . . . I think there is some brandy there.

NATASHA: *Il paraît que mon Bobik déjà ne dort pas,* he is awake. He is not well to-day. I must go to him, excuse me. . . . (*goes out*).

IRINA: Where has Alexandr Ignatyevitch gone?

MASHA: Home. Something queer with his wife again.

TUSENBACH (*goes up to* SOLYONY *with a decanter of brandy in his hand*): You always sit alone, thinking, and there's no making out what you think about. Come, let us make it up. Let us have a drink of brandy. (*they drink*) I shall have to play the piano all night, I suppose, play all sorts of trash. . . . Here goes!

SOLYONY: Why make it up? I haven't quarrelled with you.

TUSENBACH: You always make me feel as though something had gone wrong between us. You are a queer character, there's no denying that.

SOLYONY (*declaims*): I am strange, who is not strange! Be not wrath, Aleko!

TUSENBACH: I don't see what Aleko has got to do with it. . . .

SOLYONY: When I am *tête-à-tête* with somebody, I am all right, just like anyone else, but in company I am depressed, ill at ease and . . . say all sorts of idiotic things, but at the same time I am more conscientious and straightforward than many. And I can prove it . . .

TUSENBACH: I often feel angry with you, you are always attacking me when we are in company, and yet I somehow like you. Here goes, I am going to drink a lot today. Let's drink!

SOLYONY: Let us (*drinks*). I have never had anything against you Baron. But I have the temperament of Lermontov (*in a low voice*) In fact I am rather like Lermontov to look at . . . so I am told (*takes out scent-bottle and sprinkles scent on his hands*).

TUSENBACH: I have sent in my papers. I've had enough of it! I have been thinking of it for five years and at last I have come up to the scratch. I am going to work.

SOLYONY (*declaims*): Be not wrath, Aleko. . . . Forget, forget thy dreams. . . .

(*While they are talking* ANDREY *comes in quietly with a book and sits down by a candle.*)

TUSENBACH: I am going to work.

TCHEBUTYKIN (*coming into the drawing-room with* IRINA): And the food too was real Caucasian stuff: onion soup and for the meat course *tchehartma.* . . .

SOLYONY: *Tcheremsha* is not meant at all, it's a plant rather like our onion.

TCHEBUTYKIN: No, my dear soul. It's not onion, but mutton roasted in a special way.

SOLYONY: But I tell you that *tcheremsha* is an onion.

TCHEBUTYKIN: And I tell you that *tchehartma* is mutton.

SOLYONY: And I tell you that *tcheremsha* is an onion.

TCHEBUTYKIN: What's the use of my arguing with you? You have never been to the Caucasus or eaten *tchehartma.*

SOLYONY: I haven't eaten it because I can't bear it. *Tcheremsha* smells like garlic.

ANDREY (*imploringly*): That's enough! Please!

TUSENBACH: When are the Carnival party coming?

IRINA: They promised to come at nine, so they will be here directly.

TUSENBACH (*embraces* ANDREY *and sings*): "Oh my porch, oh my new porch . . ."

ANDREY (*dances and sings*): "With posts of maple wood . . ."

TCHEBUTYKIN (*dances*): "And lattice work complete . . ." (*laughter*).

TUSENBACH (*kisses* ANDREY): Hang it all, let us have a drink. Andryusha, let us drink to our everlasting friendship. I'll go to the University when you do, Andryusha.

SOLYONY: Which? There are two universities in Moscow.

ANDREY: There is only one university in Moscow.

SOLYONY: I tell you there are two.

ANDREY: There may be three for aught I care. So much the better.

SOLYONY: There are two universities in Moscow! (*a murmur and hisses*) There are two universities in Moscow: the old one and the new one. And if you don't care to hear, if what I say irritates you, I can keep quiet. I can even go into another room (*goes out at one of the doors*).

TUSENBACH: Bravo, bravo! (*laughs*) Friends begin, I'll sit down and play! Funny fellow that Solyony. . . . (*sits down to the piano and plays a waltz*)

MASHA (*dances a waltz alone*): The baron is drunk, the baron is drunk, the baron is drunk.

(*Enter* NATASHA)

NATASHA (*to* TCHEBUTYKIN): Ivan Romanitch! (*says something to* TCHEBUTYKIN *then goes out softly.* TCHEBUTYKIN *touches* TUSENBACH *on the shoulder and whispers something to him.*)

IRINA: What is it?

TCHEBUTYKIN: It's time we were going. Good night.

TUSENBACH: Good night. It's time to be going.

IRINA: But I say . . . what about the Carnival party?

ANDREY (*with embarrassment*): They won't be coming. You see, dear, Natasha says Bobik is not well, and so . . . In fact I know nothing about it, and don't care either.

IRINA (*shrugs her shoulders*): Bobik is not well!

MASHA: Well, it's not the first time we've had to lump it! If we are turned out, we must go. (*to* IRINA) It's not Bobik that is ill, but she is a bit . . . (*taps her forehead with her finger*). Petty, vulgar creature!

(ANDREY *goes by door on right to his own room,* TCHEBU-TYKIN *following him; they are saying good-bye in the dining-room.*)

FEDOTIK: What a pity! I was meaning to spend the evening, but of course if the child is ill . . . I'll bring him a toy to-morrow.

RODDEY (*loudly*): I had a nap today after dinner on purpose, I thought I would be dancing all night. . . . Why, it's only nine o'clock.

MASHA: Let us go into the street; there we can talk. We'll decide what to do.

(*Sounds of "Good-bye! Good night!" The good-humored laugh of* TUSENBACH *is heard. All go out.* ANFISA *and the maidservant clear the table and put out the light. There is the sound of the nurse singing.* ANDREY, *in his hat and coat, and* TCHEBUTYKIN *come in quietly.*)

TCHEBUTYKIN: I never had time to get married, because life has flashed by like lightning and because I was passionately in love with your mother, who was married.

ANDREY: One shouldn't get married. One shouldn't, because it's boring.

TCHEBUTYKIN: That's all very well, but what about loneliness? Say what you like, it's a dreadful thing to be lonely, my dear boy. . . . But no matter, though!

ANDREY: Let's make haste and go.

TCHEBUTYKIN: What's the hurry? We have plenty of time.

ANDREY: I am afraid my wife may stop me.

TCHEBUTYKIN: Oh!

ANDREY: I am not going to play today, I shall just sit and look on. I don't feel well. . . . What am I to do, Ivan Romanitch, I am so short of breath?

TCHEBUTYKIN: It's no use asking me! I don't remember, dear boy. . . . I don't know. . . .

ANDREY: Let us go through the kitchen. (*they go out*)

(*A ring, then another ring; there is a sound of voices and laughter.*)

IRINA (*enters*): What is it?

ANFISA (*in a whisper*): The mummers, all dressed up (*a ring*).

IRINA: Nurse, dear, say there is no one at home. They must excuse us.

(ANFISA *goes out.* IRINA *walks about the room in hesitation; she is excited. Enter* SOLYONY.)

SOLYONY (*in perplexity*): No one here. . . . Where are they all?

IRINA: They have gone home.

SOLYONY: How queer. Are you alone here?

IRINA: Yes (*a pause*). Good night.

SOLYONY: I behaved tactlessly, without sufficient restraint just now. But you are not like other people, you are pure and lofty, you see the truth. You alone can understand me. I love you, I love you deeply, infinitely.

IRINA: Good night! You must go.

SOLYONY: I can't live without you (*following her*). Oh, my bliss! (*through his tears*) Oh, happiness! Those glorious, exquisite, marvellous eyes such as I have never seen in any other woman.

IRINA (*coldly*): Don't, Vassily Vassilyitch!

SOLYONY: For the first time I am speaking of love to you, and I feel as though I were not on earth but on another planet (*rubs his forehead*). But there, it does not matter. There is no forcing kindness, of course. . . . But there must be no happy rivals. . . . There must not. . . . I swear by all that is sacred I will kill any rival. . . . O exquisite being!

(NATASHA *passes with a candle.*)

NATASHA (*peeps in at one door, then at another, and passes by the door that leads to her husband's room*): Andrey is there. Let him read. Excuse me, Vassily Vassilyitch, I did not know you were here, and I am in my dressing-gown. . . .

SOLYONY: I don't care. Good-bye! (*goes out*)

NATASHA: You are tired, my poor, dear little girl! (*kisses* IRINA). You ought to go to bed earlier. . . .

IRINA: Is Bobik asleep?

NATASHA: He is asleep, but not sleeping quietly. By the way, dear, I keep meaning to speak to you, but either you are out or else I haven't the time. . . . I think Bobik's nursery is cold and damp. And your room is so nice for a baby. My sweet, my dear, you might move for a time into Olya's room!

IRINA (*not understanding*): Where?

(*The sound of a three-horse sledge with bells driving up to the door.*)

NATASHA: You would be in the same room with Olya, and Bobik in your room. He is such a poppet. I said to him today, "Bobik, you are mine, you are mine!" and he looked at me with his funny little eyes. (*a ring*) That must be Olya. How late she is!

(*The maid comes up to* NATASHA *and whispers in her ear.*)

NATASHA: Protopopov? What a queer fellow he is! Protopopov has come, and asks me to go out with him in his sledge (*laughs*). How strange men are! . . . (*a ring*) Somebody has come. I might go for a quarter of an hour. . . . (*to the maid*) Tell him I'll come directly. (*a ring*) You hear . . . it must be Olya (*goes out*).

(*The maid runs out;* IRINA *sits lost in thought;* KULIGIN, OLGA *and* VERSHININ *come in*).

KULIGIN: Well, this is a surprise! They said they were going to have an evening party.

VERSHININ: Strange! And when I went away half an hour ago they were expecting the Carnival people. . . .

IRINA: They have all gone.

KULIGIN: Has Masha gone too? Where has she gone? And why is Protopopov waiting below with his sledge? Whom is he waiting for?

IRINA: Don't ask questions. . . . I am tired.

KULIGIN: Oh, you little cross-patch. . . .

OLGA: The meeting is only just over. I am tired out. Our headmistress is ill and I have to take her place. Oh, my head, my head does ache; oh, my head! (*sits down*) Andrey lost two hundred roubles yesterday at cards. . . . The whole town is talking about it. . . .

KULIGIN: Yes, I am tired out by the meeting too (*sits down*).

VERSHININ: My wife took it into her head to give me a fright, she nearly poisoned herself. It's all right now, and I'm glad, it's a relief. . . . So we are to go away? Very well, then, I will say good night. Fyodor Ilyitch, let us go somewhere together! I can't stay at home, I absolutely can't. . . . Come along!

KULIGIN: I am tired. I am not coming (*gets up*). I am tired. Has my wife gone home?

IRINA: I expect so.

KULIGIN (*kisses* IRINA's *hand*): Good-bye! I have all day tomorrow and next day to rest. Good night! (*going*) I do want some tea. I was reckoning on spending the evening in pleasant company. . . . *O fallacem hominum spem!* . . . Accusative of exclamation.

VERSHININ: Well, then, I must go alone (*goes out with* KULIGIN, *whistling*).

OLGA: My head aches, oh how my head aches. . . . Andrey has lost at cards. . . . The whole town is talking about it. . . . I'll go and lie down (*is going*). Tomorrow I shall be free. . . . Oh, goodness, how nice that is! Tomorrow I am free, and the day after I am free. . . . My head does ache, oh, my head . . . (*goes out*).

IRINA (*alone*): They have all gone away. There is no one left.

(*A concertina plays in the street; the nurse sings.*)

NATASHA (*in a fur cap and coat crosses the dining-room, followed by the maid*): I shall be back in half an hour. I shall only go a little way (*goes out*).

IRINA (*left alone, in dejection*): Oh, to go to Moscow, to Moscow!

CURTAIN

ACT THREE

(*The Bedroom of* OLGA *and* IRINA. *On left and right beds with screens round them. Past two o'clock in the night. Behind the scenes a bell is ringing on account of a fire in the town, which has been going on for some time. It can be seen that no one in the house has gone to bed yet. On the sofa* MASHA *is lying, dressed as usual in black. Enter* OLGA *and* ANFISA.)

ANFISA: They are sitting below, under the stairs. . . . I said to them, "Come upstairs; why, you mustn't stay there"—they only cried. "We don't know where father is," they said. "What if he is burnt!" What an idea! And the poor souls in the yard . . . they are all undressed too.

OLGA (*taking clothes out of the cupboard*): Take this grey dress . . . and this one . . . and the blouse too . . . and that skirt, nurse. . . . Oh, dear, what a dreadful thing! Kirsanov Street is burnt to the ground, it seems. . . . Take this . . . take this . . . (*throws clothes into her arms*). The Vershinins have had a fright, poor things. . . . Their house was very nearly burnt. Let them stay the night here . . . we can't let them go home. . . . Poor Fedotik has had everything burnt, he has not a thing left. . . .

ANFISA: You had better call Ferapont, Olya darling, I can't carry it all.

OLGA (*rings*): No one will answer the bell (*at the door*). Come here, whoever is there!

(*Through the open door can be seen a window red with fire; the fire brigade is heard passing the house*).

How awful it is! And how sickening!

(*Enter* FERAPONT)

OLGA: Here take these, carry them downstairs. . . . The Kolotilin young ladies are downstairs . . . give it to them . . . and give this too.

FERAPONT: Yes, miss. In 1812 Moscow was burnt too. . . . Mercy on us! The French marvelled.

OLGA: You can go now.

FERAPONT: Yes, miss (*goes out*).

OLGA: Nurse darling, give them everything. We don't want anything, give it all to them. . . . I am tired, I can hardly stand on my feet. . . . We mustn't let the Vershinins go home. . . . The little girls can sleep in the drawing-room, and Alexandr Ignatyevitch down below at the baron's. . . . Fedotik can go to the baron's, too, or sleep in our dining-room. . . . As ill-luck will have it, the doctor is drunk, frightfully drunk, and no one can be put in his room. And Vershinin's wife can be in the drawing-room too.

ANFISA (*wearily*): Olya darling, don't send me away; don't send me away!

OLGA: That's nonsense, nurse. No one is sending you away.

ANFISA (*lays her head on* OLGA's *shoulder*): My own, my treasure, I work, I do my best. . . . I'm getting weak, everyone will say "Be off!" And where am I to go? Where? I am eighty. Eighty-one.

OLGA: Sit down, nurse darling. . . . You are tired, poor thing . . . (*makes her sit down*). Rest, dear good nurse. . . . How pale you are!

(*Enter* NATASHA)

NATASHA: They are saying we must form a committee at once for the assistance of those whose houses have been burnt. Well, that's a good idea. Indeed, one ought always to be ready to help the poor, it's the duty of the rich. Bobik and baby Sophie are both asleep, sleeping as though nothing were happening. There are such a lot of people everywhere, wherever one goes, the house is full. There is influenza in the town now; I am so afraid the children may get it.

OLGA (*not listening*): In this room one does not see the fire, it's quiet here.

NATASHA: Yes . . . my hair must be untidy (*in front of the looking-glass*). They say I have grown fatter . . . but it's not true! Not a bit! Masha is asleep, she is tired out, poor dear. . . . (*to* ANFISA *coldly*) Don't dare to sit down in my presence! Get up! Go out of the room!

(ANFISA *goes out; a pause.*)

Why you keep that old woman, I can't understand!

OLGA (*taken aback*): Excuse me, I don't understand either. . . .

NATASHA: She is no use here. She is a peasant; she ought to be in the country. . . . You spoil people! I like order in the house! There ought to be no useless servants in the house. (*strokes her cheek*) You are tired, poor darling. Our headmistress is tired! When baby Sophie is a big girl and goes to the high-school, I shall be afraid of you.

OLGA: I shan't be headmistress.

NATASHA: You will be elected, Olya. That's a settled thing.

OLGA: I shall refuse. I can't. . . . It's too much for me . . . (*drinks water*). You were so rude to nurse just now. . . . Excuse me, I can't endure it. . . . It makes me feel faint.

NATASHA (*perturbed*): Forgive me, Olya; forgive me. . . . I did not mean to hurt your feelings.

(MASHA *gets up, takes her pillow, and goes out in a rage*.)

OLGA: You must understand, my dear, it may be that we have been strangely brought up, but I can't endure it. . . . Such an attitude oppresses me, it makes me ill. . . . I feel simply unnerved by it. . . .

NATASHA: Forgive me; forgive me . . . (*kisses her*).

OLGA: The very slightest rudeness, a tactless word, upsets me. . . .

NATASHA: I often say too much, that's true, but you must admit, dear, that she might just as well be in the country.

OLGA: She has been thirty years with us.

NATASHA: But now she can't work! Either I don't understand, or you won't understand me. She is not fit for work. She does nothing but sleep or sit still.

OLGA: Well, let her sit still.

NATASHA (*surprised*): How, sit still? Why, she is a servant. (*through tears*) I don't understand you, Olya. I have a nurse to look after the children as well as a wet nurse for baby, and we have a housemaid and a cook, what do we want that old woman for? What's the use of her?

(*The alarm bell rings behind the scenes.*)

OLGA: This night has made me ten years older.

NATASHA: We must come to an understanding, Olya. You are at the high-school, I am at home; you are teaching while I look after the house, and if I say anything about the servants, I know what I'm talking about; I do know what I am talking about. . . . And that old thief, that old hag . . . (*stamps*), that old witch shall clear out of the house tomorrow! . . . I won't have people annoy me! I won't have it! (*feeling that she has gone too far*) Really, if you don't move downstairs, we shall always be quarrelling. It's awful.

(*Enter* KULIGIN)

KULIGIN: Where is Masha? It's time to be going home. The fire is dying down, so they say (*stretches*). Only one part of the town has been burnt, and yet there was a wind; it seemed at first as though the whole town would be destroyed (*sits down*). I am exhausted. Olya, my dear . . . I often think if it had not been for Masha I should have married you. You are so good. . . . I am tired out (*listens*).

OLGA: What is it?

KULIGIN: It is unfortunate the doctor should have a drinking bout just now; he is helplessly drunk. Most unfortunate (*gets up*). Here he comes, I do believe. . . . Do you hear? Yes, he is coming this way . . . (*laughs*). What a man he is, really. . . . I shall hide (*goes to the cupboard and stands in the corner*). Isn't he a ruffian!

OLGA: He has not drunk for two years and now he has gone and done it . . . (*walks away with* NATASHA *to the back of the room*).

(TCHEBUTYKIN *comes in; walking as though sober without staggering, he walks across the room, stops, looks around; then goes up to the washing-stand and begins to wash his hands.*)

TCHEBUTYKIN (*morosely*): The devil take them all . . . damn them all. They think I am a doctor, that I can treat all sorts of complaints, and I really know nothing about it, I have forgotten all I did know, I remember nothing, absolutely nothing. (OLGA *and* NATASHA *go out unnoticed by him.*) The devil take them. Last Wednesday I treated a woman at Zasyp—she died, and it's my fault that she died. Yes . . . I did know something twenty-five years ago, but now I remember nothing, nothing. Perhaps I am not a man at all but only pretend to have arms and legs and head; perhaps I don't exist at all and only fancy that I walk about eat and sleep (*weeps*). Oh, if only I did not exist! (*leaves off weeping, morosely*) I don't care! I don't care a scrap! (*a pause*) Goodness knows. . . . The day before yesterday there was a conversation at the club: they talked about Shakespeare, Voltaire. . . . I have read nothing, nothing at all, but I looked as though I had read them. And the others did the same as I did. The vulgarity! The meanness! And that woman I killed on Wednesday came back to my mind . . . and it all came back to my mind and everything seemed nasty, disgusting and all awry in my soul. . . . I went and got drunk. . . .

(*Enter* IRINA, VERSHININ *and* TUSENBACH; TUSENBACH *is wearing a fashionable new civilian suit.*)

IRINA: Let us sit here. No one will come here.

VERSHININ: If it had not been for the soldiers, the whole town would have been burnt down. Splendid fellows! (*rubs his hands with pleasure*) They are first-rate men! Splendid fellows!

KULIGIN (*going up to them*): What time is it?

TUSENBACH: It's past three. It's getting light already.

IRINA: They are all sitting in the dining-room. No one seems to think of going. And that Solyony of yours is sitting there too. . . . (*to* TCHEBUTYKIN) You had better go to bed, doctor.

TCHEBUTYKIN: It's all right. . . . Thank you! (*combs his beard*)

KULIGIN (*laughs*): You are a bit fuddled, Ivan Romanitch! (*slaps him on the shoulder*) Bravo! *In vino veritas*, the ancients used to say.

TUSENBACH: Everyone is asking me to get up a concert for the benefit of the families whose houses have been burnt down.

IRINA: Why, who is there? . . .

TUSENBACH: We could get it up, if we wanted to. Marya Sergeyevna plays the piano splendidly, to my thinking.

KULIGIN: Yes, she plays splendidly.

IRINA: She has forgotten. She has not played for three . . . or four years.

TUSENBACH: There is absolutely no one who understands music in this town, not one soul, but I do understand and on my honor I assure you that Marya Sergeyevna plays magnificently, almost with genius.

KULIGIN: You are right, Baron. I am very fond of her; Masha, I mean. She is a good sort.

TUSENBACH: To be able to play so gloriously and to know that no one understands you!

KULIGIN (*sighs*): Yes. . . . But would it be suitable for her to take part in a concert? (*a pause*) I know nothing about it, my friends. Perhaps it would be all right. There is no denying that our director is a fine man, indeed a very fine man, very intelligent, but he has such views. . . . Of course it is not his business, still if you like I'll speak to him about it.

(TCHEBUTYKIN *takes up a china clock and examines it.*)

VERSHININ: I got dirty all over at the fire. I am a sight (*a pause*). I heard a word dropped yesterday about our brigade being transferred ever so far away. Some say to Poland, and others to Tchita.

TUSENBACH: I've heard something about it too. Well! The town will be a wilderness then.

IRINA: We shall go away too.

TCHEBUTYKIN (*drops the clock, which smashes*): To smithereens!

KULIGIN (*picking up the pieces*): To smash such a valuable thing—oh, Ivan Romanitch, Ivan Romanitch! I should give you minus zero for conduct!

IRINA: That was mother's clock.

TCHEBUTYKIN: Perhaps. . . . Well, if it was hers, it was. Perhaps I did not smash it, but it only seems as though I had. Perhaps it only seems to us that we exist, but really we are not here at all. I don't know anything—nobody knows anything. (*by the door*) What are you staring at? Natasha has got a little affair on with Protopopov, and you don't see it . . . You sit here and see nothing, while Natasha has a little affair on with Protopopov . . . (*sings*). May I offer you this date? . . . (*goes out*)

VERSHININ: Yes . . . (*laughs*) How very queer it all is, really! (*a pause*) When the fire began I ran home as fast as I could. I went up and saw our house was safe and sound and out of danger, but my little girls were standing in the doorway in their nightgowns; their mother was nowhere to be seen, people were bustling about, horses and dogs were running about, and my children's faces were full of alarm, horror, entreaty, and I don't know what; it wrung my heart to see their faces. My God, I thought, what more have these children to go through in the long years to come! I took their hands and ran along with them, and could think of nothing else but what more they would have to go through in this world! (*a pause*) When I came to your house I found their mother here, screaming, angry.

(MASHA *comes in with the pillow and sits down on the sofa.*)

VERSHININ: And while my little girls were standing in the doorway in their nightgowns and the street was red with the fire, and there was a fearful noise, I thought that something like it used to happen years ago when the enemy would suddenly make a raid and begin plundering and burning. . . . And yet, in reality, what a difference there is between what is now and has been in the past! And when a little more time has passed—another two or three hundred years—people will look at our present manner of life with horror and derision, and everything of today will seem awkward and heavy, and very strange and uncomfortable. Oh, what a wonderful life that will be—what a wonderful life!

(*laughs*) Forgive me, here I am airing my theories again! Allow me to go on. I have such a desire to talk about the future. I am in the mood (*a pause*). It's as though everyone were asleep. And so, I say, what a wonderful life it will be! Can you only imagine? . . . Here there are only three of your sort in the town now, but in generations to come there will be more and more and more; and the time will come when everything will be changed and be as you would have it; they will live in your way, and later on you too will be out of date—people will be born who will be better than you. . . . (*laughs*). I am in such a strange state of mind today. I have a fiendish longing for life . . . (*sings*). Young and old are bound by love, and precious are its pangs . . . (*laughs*).

MASHA: Tram-tam-tam!

VERSHININ: Tam-tam!

MASHA: Tra-ra-ra?

VERSHININ: Tra-ta-ta! (*laughs*)

(*Enter* FEDOTIK)

FEDOTIK (*dances*): Burnt to ashes! Burnt to ashes! Everything I had in the world (*laughter*).

IRINA: A queer thing to joke about. Is everything burnt?

FEDOTIK (*laughs*): Everything I had in the world. Nothing is left. My guitar is burnt, and the camera and all my letters. . . . And the note-book I meant to give you—that's burnt too.

(*Enter* SOLYONY)

IRINA: No; please go, Vassily Vassilyitch. You can't stay here.

SOLYONY: How is it the baron can be here and I can't?

VERSHININ: We must be going, really. How is the fire?

SOLYONY: They say it is dying down. No, I really can't understand why the baron may be here and not I (*takes out a bottle of scent and sprinkles himself*).

VERSHININ: Tram-tam-tam!

MASHA: Tram-tam!

VERSHININ (*laughs, to* SOLYONY): Let us go into the dining-room.

SOLYONY: Very well; we'll make a note of it. I might explain my meaning further, but I fear I may provoke the geese . . . (*looking at* TUSENBACH). Chook, chook, chook! . . . (*goes out with* VERSHININ *and* FEDOTIK)

IRINA: How that horrid Solyony has made the room smell of tobacco! . . . (*in surprise*) The baron is asleep! Baron, baron!

TUSENBACH (*waking up*): I am tired, though. . . . The brickyard. I am not talking in my sleep. I really am going to the brickyard directly, to begin work. . . . I'ts nearly settled. (*to* IRINA, *tenderly*) You are so pale and lovely and fascinating. . . . It seems to me as though your paleness sheds a light through the dark air . . . . You are melancholy; you are disatisfied with life. . . . Ah, come with me; let us go and work together!

MASHA: Nikolay Lvovitch, do go!

TUSENBACH (*laughing*): Are you here? I didn't see you . . . (*kisses* IRINA*'s hand*). Good-bye, I am going. . . . I look at you now, and I remember as though it were long ago how on your name-day you talked of the joy of work, and were so gay and confident. . . . And what a happy life I was dreaming of then! What has become of it? (*kisses her hand*) There are tears in your eyes. Go to bed, it's getting light . . . it is nearly morning. . . . If it were granted to me to give my life for you!

MASHA: Nikolay Lvovitch, do go! Come, really. . . .

TUSENBACH: I am going (*goes out*).

MASHA (*lying down*): Are you asleep, Fyodor?

KULIGIN: Eh?

MASHA: You had better go home.

KULIGIN: My darling Masha, my precious girl! . . .

IRINA: She is tired out. Let her rest, Fedya.

KULIGIN: I'll go at once. . . . My dear, charming wife! . . . I love you, my only one! . . .

MASHA (*angrily*): Amo, amas, amat; amamus, amatis, amant.

KULIGIN (*laughs*): Yes, really she is wonderful. You have been my wife for seven years, and it seems to me as though we were only married yesterday. Honor bright! Yes, really you are a wonderful woman! I am content, I am content, I am content!

MASHA: I am bored, I am bored, I am bored! . . . (*gets up and speaks, sitting down*) And there's something I can't get out of my head. . . . It's simply revolting. It sticks in my head like a nail; I must speak of it. I mean about Andrey. . . . He has mortgaged this house in the bank and his wife has grabbed all the money, and you know the house does not belong to him alone, but to us four! He ought to know that, if he is a decent man.

KULIGIN: Why do you want to bother about it, Masha? What is it to you? Andryusha is in debt all round, so there it is.

MASHA: It's revolting, anyway (*lies down*).

KULIGIN: We are not poor. I work—I go to the high-school, and then I give private lessons. . . . I do my duty. . . . There's no nonsense about me. *Omnia mea mecum porto*, as the saying is.

MASHA: I want nothing, but it's the injustice that revolts me (*a pause*). Go, Fyodor.

KULIGIN (*kisses her*): You are tired, rest for half an hour, and I'll sit and wait for you. . . . Sleep . . . (*goes*). I am content, I am content, I am content (*goes out*).

IRINA: Yes, how petty our Andrey has grown, how dull and old he has become beside that woman! At one time he was working to get a professorship and yesterday he was boasting of having succeeded at last in becoming a member of the Rural Board. He is a member, and Protopopov is chairman. . . . The whole town is laughing and talking of it and he is the only one who sees and knows nothing. . . . And here everyone has been running to the fire while he sits still in his room and takes no notice. He does nothing but play his violin . . . (*nervously*). Oh, it's awful, awful, awful! (*weeps*) I can't bear it any more, I can't! I can't, I can't!

(OLGA *comes in and begins tidying up her table.*)

IRINA (*sobs loudly*): Turn me out, turn me out, I can't bear it any more!

OLGA (*alarmed*): What is it? What is it, darling?

IRINA (*sobbing*): Where? Where has it all gone? Where is it? Oh, my God, my God! I have forgotten everything, everything . . . everything is in a tangle in my mind. . . . I don't remember the Italian for window or ceiling . . . I am forgetting everything; every day I forget something more and life is slipping away and will never come back, we shall never, never go to Moscow. . . . I see that we shan't go. . . .

OLGA: Darling, darling. . . .

IRINA (*restraining herself*): Oh, I am wretched. . . . I can't work, I am not going to work. I have had enough of it, enough of it! I have been a telegraph clerk and now I have a job in the town council and I hate and despise every bit of the work they give me. . . . I am nearly twenty-four, I have been working for years, my brains are drying up, I am getting thin and old and ugly and there is nothing, nothing, not the slightest satisfaction, and time is passing and one feels that one is moving away from a real, fine life, moving farther and farther away and being drawn into the depths. I am in despair and I don't know how it is I am alive and have not killed myself yet. . . .

OLGA: Don't cry, my child, don't cry. It makes me miserable.

IRINA: I am not crying, I am not crying. . . . It's over. . . . There, I am not crying now. I won't . . . I won't.

OLGA: Darling, I am speaking to you as a sister, as a friend, if you care for my advice, marry the baron!

(IRINA *weeps.*)

OLGA (*softly*): You know you respect him, you think highly of him. . . . It's true he is ugly, but he is such a thoroughly nice man, so good. . . . One doesn't marry for love, but to do one's duty . . . . That's what I think, anyway, and I would marry without love. Whoever proposed to me I would marry him, if only he were a good man. . . . I would even marry an old man. . . .

IRINA: I kept expecting we should move to Moscow and there I should meet my real one. I've been dreaming of him, loving him. . . . But it seems that was all nonsense, nonsense. . . .

OLGA (*puts her arms round her sister*): My darling, lovely sister, I understand it all; when the baron left the army and came to us in a plain coat, I thought he looked so ugly that it positively made me cry. . . . He asked me. "Why are you crying?" How could I tell him! But if God brought you together I should be happy. That's a different thing, you know, quite different.

(NATASHA *with a candle in her hand walks across the stage from door on right to door on left without speaking.*)

MASHA (*sits up*): She walks about as though it were she had set fire to the town.

OLGA: Masha, you are silly. The very silliest of the family, that's you. Please forgive me (*a pause*).

MASHA: I want to confess my sins, dear sisters. My soul is yearning. I am going to confess to you and never again to anyone. . . . I'll tell you this minute (*softly*). It's my secret, but you must know everything. . . . I can't be silent . . . (*a pause*). I am in love, I am in love. . . . I love that man. . . . You have just seen him. . . . Well, I may as well say it straight out. I love Vershinin.

OLGA (*going behind her screen*): Leave off. I don't hear anyway.

MASHA: But what am I to do? (*clutches her head*) At first I thought him queer . . . then I was sorry for him . . . then I came to love him . . . to love him with his voice, his words, his misfortunes, his two little girls. . . .

OLGA (*behind the screen*): I don't hear you anyway. Whatever silly things you say I shan't hear them.

MASHA: Oh, Olya, you are silly. I love him—so that's my fate. It means that that's my lot. . . . And he loves me. . . . It's all dreadful. Yes? Is it wrong? (*takes* IRINA *by the hand and draws her to herself*) Oh, my darling. . . . How are we going to live our lives, what will become of us? . . . When one reads a novel it all seems stale and easy to understand, but when you are in love yourself you see that one one knows anything and we all have to settle things for ourselves. . . . My darling, my sister. . . . I have confessed it to you, now I'll hold my tongue. . . . I'll be like Gogol's madman . . . silence . . . silence. . . .

(*Enter* ANDREY *and after him* FERAPONT)

ANDREY (*angrily*): What do you want? I can't make it out.

FERAPONT (*in the doorway, impatiently*): I've told you ten times already, Andrey Sergeyevitch.

ANDREY: In the first place I am not Andrey Sergeyevitch, but your honor, to you!

FERAPONT: The firemen ask leave, your honor, to go through the garden on their way to the river. Or else they have to go round and round, an awful nuisance for them.

ANDREY: Very good. Tell them, very good. (FERAPONT *goes out*). I am sick of them. Where is Olya? (OLGA *comes from behind the screen*) I've come to ask you for the key of the cupboard, I have lost mine. You've got one, it's a little key.

(OLGA *gives him the key in silence;* IRINA *goes behind her screen; a pause.*)

ANDREY: What a tremendous fire! Now it's begun to die down. Hang it all, that Ferapont made me so cross I said something silly to him. Your

honor . . . (*a pause*). Why don't you speak, Olya? (*a pause*) It's time to drop this foolishness and sulking all about nothing. . . . You are here, Masha, and you too, Irina—very well, then, let us have things out thoroughly, once for all. What have you against me? What is it?

OLGA: Leave off, Andryusha. Let us talk tomorrow (*nervously*). What an agonising night!

ANDREY (*greatly confused*): Don't excite yourself. I ask you quite coolly, what have you against me? Tell me straight out.

(VERSHININ's *voice:* "Tram-tam-tam!")

MASHA (*standing up, loudly*): Tra-ta-ta! (*to* OLGA) Good night, Olya, God bless you . . . (*goes behind the screen and kisses* IRINA) Sleep well. . . . Good night, Andrey. You'd better leave them now, they are tired out . . . you can go into things tomorrow (*goes out*).

OLGA: Yes, really, Andryusha, let us put it off till tomorrow . . . (*goes behind her screen*). It's time we were in bed.

ANDREY: I'll say what I have to say and then go. Directly. . . . First, you have something against Natasha, my wife, and I've noticed that from the very day of my marriage. Natasha is a splendid woman, conscientious, straightfoward and honorable—that's my opinion! I love and respect my wife, do you understand? I respect her, and I insist on other people respecting her too. I repeat, she is a conscientious, honorable woman, and all your disagreements are simply caprice, or rather the whims of old maids. Old maids never like and never have liked their sisters-in-law—that's the rule (*a pause*). Secondly, you seem to be cross with me for not being a professor, not working at something learned. But I am in the service of the Zemstvo, I am a member of the Rural Board, and I consider this service just as sacred and elevated as the service of learning. I am a member of the Rural Board and I am proud of it, if you care to know . . . (*a pause*). Thirdly . . . there's something else I have to say. . . . I have mortgaged the house without asking your permission . . . . For that I am to blame, yes, and I ask your pardon for it. I was driven to it by my debts . . . thirty-five thousand. . . . I am not gambling now—I gave up cards long ago; but the chief thing I can say in self-defence is that you are, so to say, of the privileged sex—you get a pension . . . while I had not . . . my wages, so to speak . . . (*a pause*).

KULIGIN (*at the door*): Isn't Masha here? (*perturbed*) Where is she? It's strange . . . (*goes out*).

ANDREY: They won't listen. Natasha is an excellent, conscientious woman (*paces up and down the stage in silence, then stops*). When I married her, I thought we should be happy . . . happy, all of us. . . . But, my God! (*weeps*) Dear sisters, darling sisters, you must not believe what I say, you musn't believe it . . . (*goes out*).

KULIGIN (*at the door, uneasily*): Where is Masha? Isn't Masha here? How strange! (*goes out*)

(*The firebell rings in the street. The stage is empty.*)

IRINA (*behind the screen*): Olya! Who is that knocking on the floor?

OLGA: It's the doctor, Ivan Romanitch. He is drunk.

IRINA: What a troubled night! (*a pause*) Olya! (*peeps out from behind the screen*) Have you heard? The brigade is going to be taken away; they are being transferred to some place very far off.

OLGA: That's only a rumor.

IRINA: Then we shall be alone. . . . Olya!

OLGA: Well?

IRINA: My dear, my darling, I respect the baron, I think highly of him, he is a fine man—I will marry him, I consent, only let us go to Moscow! I entreat you, do let us go! There's nothing in the world better than Moscow! Let us go Olya! Let us go!

CURTAIN

ACT FOUR

(*Old garden of the* PROZOROV's *house. A long avenue of fir trees, at the end of which is a view of the river. On the farther side of the river there is a wood. On the right the verandah of the house; on the table in it are bottles and glasses; evidently they have just been drinking champagne. It is twelve o'clock in the day. People pass occasionally from the street across the garden to the river; five soldiers pass rapidly.* TCHEBU-TYKIN, *in an affable mood, which persists throughout the act, is sitting in an easy chair in the garden, waiting to be summoned; he is wearing a military cap and has a stick.* IRINA, KULIGIN *with a decoration on his breast and with no moustache, and* TUSENBACH, *standing on the verandah, are saying good-bye to* FEDOTIK *and* RODDEY, *who are going down the steps; both officers are in marching uniform.*)

TUSENBACH (*kissing* FEDOTIK): You are a good fellow; we've got on so happily together. (*kisses* RODDEY) Once more. . . . Good-bye, my dear boy. . . .

IRINA: Till we meet again!

FEDOTIK: No, it's good-bye for good; we shall never meet again.

KULIGIN: Who knows! (*wipes his eyes, smiles*) Here I am crying too.

IRINA: We shall meet some day.

FERAPONT: In ten years, or fifteen perhaps? But then we shall scarcely recognise each other—we

shall greet each other coldly . . . (*takes a snapshot*) Stand still. . . . Once more, for the last time.

RODDEY (*embraces* TUSENBACH): We shall not see each other again. . . . (*kisses* IRINA's *hand*) Thank you for everything, everything. . . .

FEDOTIK (*with vexation*): Oh, do wait!

TUSENBACH: Please God we shall meet again. Write to us. Be sure to write to us.

RODDEY (*taking a long look at the garden*): Good-bye, trees! (*shouts*) Halloo! (*a pause*) Good-bye, echo!

KULIGIN: I shouldn't wonder if you get married in Poland. . . . Your Polish wife will clasp you in her arms and call you *kochany!* (*laughs*)

FEDOTIK (*looking at his watch*): We have less than an hour. Of our battery only Solyony is going on the barge; we are going with the rank and file. Three divisions of the battery are going to-day and three more tomorrow—and peace and quiet will descend upon the town.

TUSENBACH: And dreadful boredom too.

RODDEY: And where is Marya Sergeyevna?

KULIGIN: Masha is in the garden.

FEDOTIK: We must say good-bye to her.

RODDEY: Good-bye. We must go, or I shall begin to cry . . . (*hurriedly embraces* TUSENBACH *and* KULIGIN *and kisses* IRINA's *hand*) We've had a splendid time here.

FEDOTIK (*to* KULIGIN): This is a little souvenir for you

. . . a note-book with a pencil. . . . We'll go down here to the river . . . (*as they go away both look back*)

RODDEY (*shouts*): Halloo-oo!

KULIGIN (*shouts*): Good-bye!

(RODDEY *and* FEDOTIK *meet* MASHA *in the background and say good-bye to her; she walks away with them.*)

IRINA: They've gone . . . (*sits down on the bottom step of the verandah*).

TCHEBUTYKIN: They have forgotten to say good-bye to me.

IRINA: And what were you thinking about?

TCHEBUTYKIN: Why, I somehow forget, too. But I shall see them again soon, I am setting off tomorrow. Yes . . . I have one day more. In a year I shall be on the retired list. Then I shall come here again and shall spend the rest of my life near you. . . . There is only one year now before I get my pension. (*puts a newspaper into his pocket and takes out another*) I shall come here to you and arrange my life quite differently. . . . I shall become such a quiet . . . God-fearing . . . well-behaved person.

IRINA: Well, you do need to arrange your life differently, dear Ivan Romanitch. You certainly ought to somehow.

TCHEBUTYKIN: Yes, I feel it. (*softly hums*) "Tarara-boom-dee-ay—Tarara-boom-dee-ay."

KULIGIN: Ivan Romanitch is incorrigible! Incorrigible!

TCHEBUTYKIN: You ought to take me in hand. Then I should reform.

IRINA: Fyodor has shaved off his moustache. I can't bear to look at him!

KULIGIN: Why, what's wrong?

TCHEBUTYKIN: I might tell you what your countenance looks like now, but I really can't.

KULIGIN: Well! It's the thing now, *modus vivendi*. Our headmaster is clean-shaven and now I am second to him I have taken to shaving too. Nobody likes it, but I don't care. I am content. With moustache or without moustache I am equally content (*sits down*).

(*In the background* ANDREY *is wheeling a baby asleep in a perambulator.*)

IRINA: Ivan Romanitch, darling, I am dreadfully uneasy. You were on the boulevard yesterday, tell me what was it that happened?

TCHEBUTYKIN: What happened? Nothing. Nothing much (*reads the newspaper*). It doesn't matter!

KULIGIN: The story is that Solyony and the baron met yesterday on the boulevard near the theatre. . . .

TUSENBACH: Oh, stop it! Really . . . (*with a wave of his hand walks away into the house*).

KULIGIN: Near the theatre. . . . Solyony began pestering the baron and he couldn't keep his temper and said something offensive. . . .

TCHEBUTYKIN: I don't know. It's all nonsense.

KULIGIN: A teacher at a divinity school wrote "nonsense" at the bottom of an essay and the pupil puzzled over it thinking it was a Latin word . . . (*laughs*). It was fearfully funny. . . . They say Solyony is in love with Irina and hates the baron. . . . That's natural. Irina is a very nice girl.

(*From the background behind the scenes,* "Aa-oo! Halloo!")

IRINA (*starts*): Everything frightens me somehow today (*a pause*). All my things are ready, after dinner I shall send off my luggage. The baron and I are to be married to-morrow, to-morrow we go to the brickyard and the day after that I shall be in the school. A new life is beginning. God will help me! How will it fare with me? When I passed my exam as a teacher I felt so happy, so blissful, that I cried . . . (*a pause*). The cart will soon be coming for my things. . . .

KULIGIN: That's all very well, but it does not seem serious. It's all nothing but ideas and very little that is serious. However, I wish you success with all my heart.

TCHEBUTYKIN (*moved to tenderness*): My good, delightful darling. . . . My heart of gold. . . .

KULIGIN: Well, today the officers will be gone and everything will go on in the old way. Whatever people may say, Masha is a true, good woman. I love her dearly and am thankful for my lot! . . . People have different lots in life. . . . There is a man called Kozyrev serving in the Excise here. He was at school with me, but he was expelled from the fifth form because he could never understand *ut consecutivum*. Now he is frightfully poor and ill, and when I meet him I say, "How are you, *ut consecutivum*?" "Yes," he says, "just so—*consecutivum*" . . . and then he coughs. . . . Now I have always been successful, I am fortunate, I have even got the order of the Stanislav of the second degree and I am teaching others that *ut consecutivum*. Of course I am clever, cleverer than very many people, but happiness does not lie in that . . . (*a pause*).

(*In the house the "Maiden's Prayer" is played on the piano.*)

IRINA: Tomorrow evening I shall not be hearing that "Maiden's Prayer," I shan't be meeting Protopopov . . . (*a pause*). Protopopov is sitting there in the drawing-room; he has come again to-day. . . .

KULIGIN: The headmistress has not come yet?

IRINA: No. They have sent for her. If only you knew how hard it is for me to live here alone, without Olya. . . . Now that she is headmistress and lives at the high-school and is busy all day long, I am alone, I am bored, I have nothing to do, and I hate the room I live in. . . . I have made up my mind, since I am not fated to be in Moscow, that so it must be. It must be destiny. There is no help for it. . . . It's all in God's hands, that's the truth. When Nikolay Lvovitch made me an offer again . . . I thought it over and made up my mind. . . . He is a good man, it's wonderful really how good he is. . . . And I suddenly felt as though my soul had grown wings, my heart felt so light and again I longed for work, work. . . . Only something happened yesterday, there is some mystery hanging over me.

TCHEBUTYKIN: Nonsense.

NATASHA (*at the window*): Our headmistress!

KULIGIN: The headmistress has come. Let us go in (*goes into the house with* IRINA).

TCHEBUTYKIN (*reads the newspaper, humming softly*): "Tarara-boom-dee-ay."

(MASHA *approaches; in the background* ANDREY *is pushing the perambulator.*)

MASHA: Here he sits, snug and settled.

TCHEBUTYKIN: Well, what then?

MASHA (*sits down*): Nothing . . . (*a pause*). Did you love my mother?

TCHEBUTYKIN: Very much.

MASHA: And did she love you?

TCHEBUTYKIN (*after a pause*): That I don't remember.

MASHA: Is my man here? It's just like our cook Marfa used to say about her policeman: is my man here?

TCHEBUTYKIN: Not yet.

MASHA: When you get happiness by snatches, by little bits, and then lose it, as I am losing it, by degrees one grows coarse and spiteful . . . (*points to her bosom*) I'm boiling here inside . . . (*looking at* ANDREY, *who is pushing the perambulator*) Here is our Andrey. . . . All our hopes are shattered. Thousands of people raised the bell, a lot of money and of labor was spent on it, and it suddenly fell and smashed. All at once, for no reason whatever. That's just how it is with Andrey. . . .

ANDREY: When will they be quiet in the house? There is such a noise.

TCHEBUTYKIN: Soon (*looks at his watch*). My watch is an old-fashioned one with a repeater . . . (*winds his watch, it strikes*). The first, the second, and the fifth batteries are going at one o'clock (*a pause*). And I am going tomorrow.

ANDREY: For good?

TCHEBUTYKIN: I don't know. Perhaps I shall come back in a year. Though goodness knows. . . . It doesn't matter one way or another.

(*There is the sound of a harp and violin being played far away in the street.*)

ANDREY: The town will be empty. It's as though one put an extinguisher over it (*a pause*). Something happened yesterday near the theatre; everyone is talking of it, and I know nothing about it.

TCHEBUTYKIN: It was nothing. Foolishness. Solyony began annoying the baron and he lost his temper and insulted him, and it came in the end to Solyony's having to challenge him (*looks at his watch*). It's time, I fancy. . . . It was to be at half-past twelve in the Crown forest that we can see from here beyond the river . . . Piff-paff! (*laughs*) Solyony imagines he is a Lermontov and even writes verses. Joking apart, this is his third duel.

MASHA: Whose?

TCHEBUTYKIN: Solyony's.

MASHA: And the baron's?

TCHEBUTYKIN: What about the baron? (*a pause*)

MASHA: My thoughts are in a muddle. . . . Anyway, I tell you, you ought not to let them do it. He may wound the baron or even kill him.

TCHEBUTYKIN: The baron is a very good fellow, but one baron more or less in the world, what does it matter? Let them! It doesn't matter. (*beyond *the garden a shout of* "Aa-oo! Halloo!") You can wait. That is Skvortsov, the second, shouting. He is in a boat (*a pause*).

ANDREY: In my opinion to take part in a duel, or to be present at it even in the capacity of a doctor, is simply immoral.

TCHEBUTYKIN: That only seems so. . . . We are not real, nothing in the world is real, we don't exist, but only seem to exist. . . . Nothing matters!

MASHA: How they keep on talking, talking all day long (*goes*). To live in such a climate, it may snow any minute, and then all this talk on the top of it (*stops*). I am not going indoors, I can't go in there. . . . When Vershinin comes, tell me . . . (*goes down the avenue*). And the birds are already flying south . . . (*looks up*). Swans or geese. . . . Darlings, happy things. . . . (*goes out*).

ANDREY: Our house will be empty. The officers are going, you are going, Irina is getting married, and I shall be left in the house alone.

TCHEBUTYKIN: What about your wife?

(*Enter* FERAPONT *with papers*)

ANDREY: A wife is a wife. She is a straightforward, upright woman, good-natured, perhaps, but for all that there is something in her which makes her no better than some petty, blind, hairy animal. Anyway she is not a human being. I speak to you as to a friend, the one man to whom I can open my soul. I love Natasha, that is so, but sometimes she seems to me wonderfully vulgar, and then I don't know what to think, I can't account for my loving her or, anyway, having loved her.

TCHEBUTYKIN (*gets up*): I am going away tomorrow, my boy, perhaps we shall never meet again, so this is my advice to you. Put on your cap, you know, take your stick and walk off . . . walk off and just go, go without looking back. And the farther you go, the better (*a pause*). But do as you like! It doesn't matter. . . .

(SOLYONY *crosses the stage in the background with two officers; seeing* TCHEBUTYKIN *he turns towards him; officers walk on.*)

SOLYONY: Doctor, it's time! It's half-past twelve (*greets* ANDREY).

TCHEBUTYKIN: Directly. I am sick of you all. (*to* ANDREY) If anyone asks for me, Andryusha, say I'll be back directly . . . (*sighs*). Oho-ho-ho!

SOLYONY: He had not time to say alack before the bear was on his back (*walks away with the doctor*). Why are you croaking, old chap?

TCHEBUTYKIN: Come!

SOLYONY: How do you feel?

TCHEBUTYKIN (*angrily*): Like a pig in clover.

SOLYONY: The old chap need not excite himself. I won't do anything much, I'll only shoot him like a snipe (*takes out scent and sprinkles his hands*). I've used a whole bottle today, and still they smell. My hands smell like a corpse (*a pause*). Yes. . . . Do you remember the poem? "And, restless, seeks the stormy ocean, as though in tempest there were peace." . . .

TCHEBUTYKIN: Yes. He had not time to say alack before the bear was on his back (*Goes out with* SOLYONY. *Shouts are heard:* "Halloo! Oo-oo!" ANDREY *and* FERAPONT *come in*).

FERAPONT: Papers for you to sign. . . .

ANDREY (*nervously*): Let me alone! Let me alone! I entreat you! (*Walks away with the perambulator*)

FERAPONT: That's what the papers are for—to be signed (*retires into the background*).

(*Enter* IRINA *and* TUSENBACH *wearing a straw hat;* KULIGIN *crosses the stage shouting* "Aa-oo, Masha, aa-oo!")

TUSENBACH: I believe that's the only man in the town who is glad that the officers are going away.

IRINA: That's very natural (*a pause*). Our town will be empty now.

TUSENBACH: Dear, I'll be back directly.

TCHEBUTYKIN: Where are you going?

TUSENBACH: I must go into the town, and then . . . to see my comrades off.

IRINA: That's not true. . . . Nikolay, why are you so absent-minded today? (*a pause*) What happened yesterday near the theatre?

TUSENBACH (*with a gesture of impatience*): I'll be here in an hour and with you again (*kisses her hands*). My beautiful one . . . (*looks into her face*). For five years now I have loved you and still I can't get used to it, and you seem to me more and more lovely. What wonderful, exquisite hair! What eyes! I shall carry you off tomorrow, we will work, we will be rich, my dreams will come true. You shall be happy. There is only one thing, one thing: you don't love me!

IRINA: That's not in my power! I'll be your wife and be faithful and obedient, but there is no love, I can't help it (*weeps*). I've never been in love in my life! Oh, I have so dreamed of love, I've been dreaming of it for years, day and night, but my soul is like a wonderful piano of which the key has been lost (*a pause*). You look uneasy.

TUSENBACH: I have not slept all night. There has never been anything in my life so dreadful that it could frighten me, and only that lost key frets at my heart and won't let me sleep. . . . Say something to me . . . (*a pause*). Say something to me. . . .

IRINA: What? What am I to say to you? What?

TUSENBACH: Anything.

IRINA: There, there! (*a pause*)

TUSENBACH: What trifles, what little things suddenly *à propos* of nothing acquire importance in life! One laughs at them as before, thinks them nonsense, but still one goes on and feels that one has not the power to stop. Don't let us talk about it! I am happy. I feel as though I were seeing these pines, these maples, these birch trees for the first time in my life, and they all seem to be looking at me with curiosity and waiting. What beautiful trees, and, really, how beautiful life ought to be under them! (*a shout of* "Halloo! Aa-oo!") I must be off; it's time. . . . See, that tree is dead, but it waves in the wind with the others. And so it seems to me that if I die I shall still have part in life, one way or another. Good-bye, my darling . . . (*kisses her hands*). Those papers of yours you gave me are lying under the calendar on my table.

IRINA: I am coming with you.

TUSENBACH (*in alarm*): No, no! (*goes off quickly, stops in the avenue*) Irina!

IRINA: What is it?

TUSENBACH (*not knowing what to say*): I didn't have any coffee this morning. Ask them to make me some (*goes out quickly*).

(IRINA *stands lost in thought, then walks away into the background of the scene and sits down on the swing. Enter* ANDREY *with the perambulator, and* FERAPONT *comes into sight.*)

FERAPONT: Andrey Sergeyevitch, the papers aren't mine; they are Government papers. I didn't invent them.

ANDREY: Oh, where is it all gone? What has become of my past, when I was young, gay, and clever, when my dreams and thoughts were exquisite, when my present and my past were lighted up

by hope? Why on the very threshold of life do we become dull, grey, uninteresting, lazy, indifferent, useless, unhappy? . . . Our town has been going on for two hundred years—there are a hundred thousand people living in it; and there is not one who is not like the rest, not one saint in the past, or the present, not one man of learning, not one artist, not one man in the least remarkable who could inspire envy or a passionate desire to imitate him. . . . They only eat, drink, sleep, and then die . . . others are born, and they also eat and drink and sleep, and not to be bored to stupefaction they vary their lives by nasty gossip, vodka, cards, litigation; and the wives deceive their husbands, and the husbands tell lies and pretend that they see and hear nothing, and an overwhelmingly vulgar influence weighs upon the children, and the divine spark is quenched in them and they become the same sort of pitiful, dead creatures, all exactly alike, as their fathers and mothers. . . . (*to* FERAPONT, *angrily*) What do you want?

FERAPONT: Eh? There are papers to sign.

ANDREY: You bother me!

FERAPONT (*handing him the papers*): The porter from the local treasury was saying just now that there was as much as two hundred degrees of frost in Petersburg this winter.

ANDREY: The present is hateful, but when I think of the future, it is so nice! I feel so light-hearted, so free. A light dawns in the distance, I see freedom. I see how I and my children will become free from sloth, from kvass, from goose and cabbage, from sleeping after dinner, from mean, parasitic living. . . .

FERAPONT: He says that two thousand people were frozen to death. The people were terrified. It was either in Petersburg or Moscow, I don't remember.

ANDREY (*in a rush of tender feeling*): My dear sisters, my wonderful sisters! (*through tears*) Masha, my sister!

NATASHA (*in the window*): Who is talking so loud out there? Is that you, Andryusha? You will wake baby Sophie. *Il ne faut pas faire de bruit, la Sophie est dormée déjà. Vous êtes un ours.* (*getting angry*) If you want to talk, give the perambulator with the baby to somebody else. Ferapont, take the perambulator from the master!

FERAPONT: Yes, ma'am (*takes the pram*).

ANDREY (*in confusion*): I am talking quietly.

NATASHA (*petting her child, inside the room*): Bobik! Naughty Bobik! Little rascal!

ANDREY (*looking through the papers*): Very well, I'll look through them and sign what wants signing, and then you can take them back to the Board. . . . (*Goes into the house reading the papers;* FERAPONT *pushes the pram farther into the garden.*)

NATASHA (*speaking indoors*): Bobik, what is mamma's name? Darling, darling! And who is this? This is auntie Olya. Say to auntie, "Good morning, Olya!"

(*Two wandering musicians, a man and a girl, enter and play a violin and a harp; from the house enter* VERSHININ *with* OLGA *and* ANFISA, *and stand for a minute listening in silence;* IRINA *comes up.*)

OLGA: Our garden is like a public passage; they walk and ride through. Nurse, give those people something.

ANFISA (*gives money to the musicians*): Go away, and God bless you, my dear souls! (*the musicians bow and go away*) Poor things. People don't play if they have plenty to eat. (*to* IRINA) Good morning, Irisha! (*kisses her*) Aye, aye, my little girl, I am having a time of it! Living in the high-school, in a government flat, with dear Olya—that's what the Lord has vouchsafed me in my old age! I have never lived so well in my life, sinful woman that I am. . . . It's a big flat, and I have a room to myself and a bedstead. All at the government expense. I wake up in the night and, O Lord, Mother of God, there is no one in the world happier than I!

VERSHININ (*looks at his watch*): We are just going, Olga Sergeyevna. It's time to be off (*a pause*). I wish you everything, everything. . . . Where is Marya Sergeyevna?

IRINA: She is somewhere in the garden. . . . I'll go and look for her.

VERSHININ: Please be so good. I am in a hurry.

ANFISA: I'll go and look for her too. (*shouts*) Mashenka, aa-oo! (*goes with* IRINA *into the farther part of the garden*) Aa-oo! Aa-oo!

VERSHININ: Everything comes to an end. Here we are parting (*looks at his watch*). The town has given us something like a lunch; we have been drinking champagne, the mayor made a speech. I ate and listened, but my heart was here, with you all . . . (*looks round the garden*). I've grown used to you. . . .

OLGA: Shall we ever see each other again?

VERSHININ: Most likely not (*a pause*). My wife and two little girls will stay here for another two months; please, if anything happens, if they need anything . . .

OLGA: Yes, yes, of course. Set your mind at rest (*a pause*). By tomorrow there won't be a soldier in the town—it will all turn into a memory, and of course for us it will be like beginning a new life . . . (*a pause*). Nothing turns out as we would have it. I did not want to be a headmistress, and yet I am. It seems we are not to live in Moscow. . . .

VERSHININ: Well. . . . Thank you for everything. . . . Forgive me if anything was amiss. . . . I have talked a great deal: forgive me for that too—don't remember evil against me.

OLGA (*wipes her eyes*): Why doesn't Masha come?

VERSHININ: What else am I to say to you at parting? What am I to theorise about? . . . (*laughs*) Life is hard. It seems to many of us blank and hopeless; but yet we must admit that it goes on getting clearer and easier, and it looks as though the time were not far off when it will be full of happiness (*looks at his watch*). It's time for me to go! In old days men were absorbed in wars, filling all their existence with marches, raids, victories, but now all that is a thing of the past, leaving behind it a great void which there is so far nothing to fill: humanity is searching for it passionately, and of course will find it. Ah, if only it could be quickly! (*a pause*) If, don't you know, industry were united with culture and culture with industry . . . (*looks at his watch*) But, I say, it's time for me to go. . . .

OLGA: Here she comes.

(MASHA *comes in.*)

VERSHININ: I have come to say good-bye. . . .

(OLGA *moves a little away to leave them free to say good-bye.*)

MASHA (*looking into his face*): Good-bye . . . (*a prolonged kiss*).

OLGA: Come, come. . . .

(MASHA *sobs violently.*)

VERSHININ: Write to me. . . . Don't forget me! Let me go! . . . Time is up! . . . Olga Sergeyevna, take her, I must . . . go . . . I am late . . . (*Much moved, kisses* OLGA's *hands; then again embraces* MASHA *and quickly goes off.*)

OLGA: Come, Masha! Leave off, darling.

(*Enter* KULIGIN)

KULIGIN (*embarrassed*): Never mind, let her cry—let her. . . . My good Masha, my dear Masha! . . . You are my wife, and I am happy, anyway. . . . I don't complain: I don't say a word of blame. . . . Here Olya is my witness. . . . We'll begin the old life again, and I won't say one word, not a hint. . . .

MASHA (*restraining her sobs*): By the sea-strand an oak-tree green. . . . Upon that oak a chain of gold. . . . Upon that oak a chain of gold. . . . I am going mad. . . . By the sea-strand . . . an oak-tree green. . . .

OLGA: Calm yourself, Masha. . . . Calm yourself . . . . Give her some water.

MASHA: I am not crying now. . . .

KULIGIN: She is not crying now . . . she is good. . . .

(*The dim sound of a far-away shot.*)

MASHA: By the sea-strand an oak-tree green, upon that oak a chain of gold. . . . The cat is green . . . the oak is green. . . . I am mixing it up . . . (*drinks water*). My life is a failure. . . . I want nothing now. . . . I shall be calm directly. . . . It doesn't matter. . . . What does "strand" mean? Why do these words haunt me? My thoughts are in a tangle.

(*Enter* IRINA)

OLGA: Calm yourself, Masha. Come, that's a good girl. Let us go indoors.

MASHA (*angrily*): I am not going in. Let me alone! (*sobs, but at once checks herself*) I don't go into that house now and I won't.

IRINA: Let us sit together, even if we don't say anything. I am going away tomorrow, you know . . . (*a pause*).

KULIGIN: I took a false beard and moustache from a boy in the third form yesterday, just look . . . (*puts on the beard and moustache*). I look like the German teacher . . . (*laughs*). Don't I? Funny creatures, those boys.

MASHA: You really do look like the German teacher.

OLGA (*laughs*): Yes.

(MASHA *weeps.*)

IRINA: There, Masha!

KULIGIN: Awfully like. . . .

(*Enter* NATASHA)

NATASHA (*to the maid*): What? Mr. Protopopov will sit with Sophie, and let Andrey Sergeyitch wheel Bobik up and down. What a lot there is to do with children . . . (*to* IRINA) Irina, you are going away tomorrow, what a pity. Do stay just another week. (*Seeing* KULIGIN *utters a shriek; the latter laughs and takes off the beard and moustache.*) Well, what next, you gave me such a fright! (*to* IRINA) I am used to you and do you suppose that I don't feel parting with you? I shall put Andrey with his violin into your room—let him saw away there!—and we will put baby Sophie in his room. Adorable, delightful baby! Isn't she a child! To-day she looked at me with such eyes and said "Mamma"!

KULIGIN: A fine child, that's true.

NATASHA: So tomorrow I shall be all alone here (*sighs*). First of all I shall have this avenue of fir trees cut down, and then that maple. . . . It looks so ugly in the evening. . . . (*to* IRINA) My dear, that sash does not suit you at all. . . . It's in bad taste. You want something light. And then I shall have flowers, flowers planted everywhere, and there will be such a scent. . . . (*severely*) Why is there a fork lying about on that seat? (*going into the house, to the maid*) Why is there a fork lying about on this seat. I ask you? (*shouts*) Hold your tongue!

KULIGIN: She is at it!

(*Behind the scenes the band plays a march; they all listen.*)

OLGA: They are going.

(*Enter* TCHEBUTYKIN)

MASHA: Our people are going. Well . . . a happy journey to them! (*to her husband*) We must go home. . . . Where are my hat and cape?

KULIGIN: I took them into the house . . . I'll get them directly. . . .

OLGA: Yes, now we can go home, it's time.

TCHEBUTYKIN: Olga Sergeyevna!

OLGA: What is it? (*a pause*) What?

TCHEBUTYKIN: Nothing. . . . I don't know how to tell you. (*whispers in her ear*)

OLGA (*in alarm*): It can't be!

TCHEBUTYKIN: Yes . . . such a business. . . . I am so worried and worn out. I don't want to say another word. . . . (*with vexation*). But there, it doesn't matter!

MASHA: What has happened?

OLGA (*pushes her arms round* IRINA): This is a terrible day. . . . I don't know how to tell you, my precious. . . .

IRINA: What is it? Tell me quickly, what is it? For God's sake! (*cries*)

TCHEBUTYKIN: The baron has just been killed in a duel.

IRINA (*weeping quietly*): I knew, I knew. . . .

TCHEBUTYKIN (*in the background of the scene sits down on a garden seat*): I am worn out . . . (*takes a newspaper out of his pocket*). Let them cry. . . . (*sings softly*) "Tarara-boom-dee-ay" . . . It doesn't matter.

(*The three sisters stand with their arms round one another.*)

MASHA: Oh, listen to that band! They are going away from us; one has gone altogether, gone forever. We are left alone to begin our life over again . . . . We've got to live . . . we've got to live. . .

IRINA (*lays her head on* OLGA's *bosom*): A time will come when everyone will know what all this is for, why there is this misery; there will be no mysteries and, meanwhile, we have got to live . . . we have got to work, only to work! Tomorrow I shall go alone; I shall teach in the school, and I will give all my life to those to whom it may be of use. Now it's autumn; soon winter will come and cover us with snow, and I will work, I will work.

OLGA (*embraces both her sisters*): The music is so gay, so confident, and one longs for life! O my god! Time will pass, and we shall go away for ever, and we shall be forgotten, our faces will be forgotten, our voices, and how many there were of us; but our sufferings will pass into joy for those who will live after us, happiness and peace will be established upon earth, and they will remember kindly and bless those who have lived before. Oh, dear sisters, our life is not ended yet. We shall live! The music is so gay, so joyful, and it seems as though a little more and we shall know what we are living for, why we are suffering. . . . If we only knew—if we only knew!

(*The music grows more and more subdued;* KULIGIN *cheerful and smiling, brings the hat and cape;* ANDREY *pushes the perambulator in which* BOBIK *is sitting.*)

TCHEBUTYKIN (*humming softly*): "Tarara-boom-dee-ay!" (*reads his paper*) It doesn't matter, it doesn't matter.

OLGA: If we only knew, if we only knew!

CURTAIN

7 HAPPY DAYS

Samuel Beckett
1961

It would be impossible to overestimate the impact of Samuel Beckett's *Waiting for Godot*, which appeared first in Paris in 1953, and then in New York in 1957. *Godot* revolutionized the theatre by opening up a new range of possibilities, by reexamining what the theatre could do and be. However, simply to consider that play, and the rest of Beckett's work, as the foundation of a theatrical style—the "theatre of the absurd"—would be wrong, for it would "pigeonhole" the work of a writer who many consider to be the most significant of modern times.

Beckett (1906–) was born and schooled in Ireland. He moved to Paris in 1928 and has lived there, for the most part, ever since, writing many of his works initially in French (but not *Happy Days*) and translating them into his native English. Influenced early in his literary career by his friend and fellow countryman, James Joyce, Beckett's first publication (in 1929) was a discussion of Joyce's *Finnegan's Wake*, then in progress; Beckett's own first published fictional pieces, highly regarded by an avant-garde coterie, bore the powerful influence of his admired Irish colleague. Since the 1940s, however, Beckett's work has become highly individual and unique, and his reputation, both as a novelist and playwright, has grown accordingly. The body of published critical literature on Beckett's work is huge—certainly greater than on any other dramatist besides Shakespeare.

Beckett began his dramatic work (which is generally his most admired) shortly after World War II; his *Godot* gained him literary fame, and his following stage plays of the 1950s and 1960s—*Endgame*, *Krapp's Last Tape*, *Happy Days*, and *Play*—earned him a worldwide reputation, which has been kept alive through the 1970s and 1980s by a series of intensely provocative shorter plays: *Not I*, *Footfalls*, *Rockaby*, and *Ohio Impromptu*.

Beckett's work, particularly in the later period, is complex and difficult; he writes about fundamental human confusion and ignorance, and he writes about confusion "from the inside." His plays do not open themselves up for simple explanations nor immediately useful maxims, because life's lack of simple explanations and useful maxims form his basic subject. His characters are typically at the end of their lives, trying—failing—to make sense of their vacant inner and outer landscapes. Their confusion tends to become ours—as reader, as audience, as human being. One of the great joys of reading or seeing Beckett's work lies in penetrating this confusion; the depth of Beckett's art will prove immensely rewarding to the patient and careful reader/spectator.

Happy Days is probably Beckett's most immediately accessible play; once we accept the unexplained fact that Winnie is buried in sand, the play makes as much logical sense as most human struggles against daunting predicaments. Like all of Beckett's early plays, it is both sad and funny, and at some points *wildly* funny. It is also quite obviously absurd, both in our common understanding of that word and in the general philosophic sense, which is the condition, first defined by Albert Camus, in which characters seek victories they know are impossible to achieve. For Camus the "absurd man" was best exemplified by the myth of Sisyphus, the Greek demigod whose punishment was to push a stone eternally up a mountain—only to have the stone eternally fall down the other side. Winnie is an "absurd hero," compelled to rationalize the world (even in "happy" terms), and yet deeply aware of the impossibility of understanding it, as the earth continues to swallow her up. And while the "happiness" of the play is meant to be ironic, the notion of the "absurd hero" is important; for while the search for final knowledge is an absurd one, the searcher is, in Camus' view, both happy and heroic for trying. By the end of *Happy Days* we admire—maybe even love—Winnie's wit and courage, which is the primary reason for the continuing success of this play in the theatre. Not only Beckett's most accessible play, *Happy Days* has enjoyed a great revival in the 1980s, and may ultimately prove to be his most enduring work.

HAPPY DAYS

CAST OF CHARACTERS

WINNIE, *a woman about fifty*

WILLIE, *a man about sixty*

ACT ONE

Expanse of scorched grass rising centre to low mound. Gentle slopes down to front and either side of stage. Back an abrupter fall to stage level. Maximum of simplicity and symmetry.

Blazing light.

Very pompier trompe-l'oeil backcloth to represent unbroken plain and sky receding to meet in far distance.

Imbedded up to above her waist in exact centre of mound, WINNIE. *About fifty, well preserved, blond for preference, plump, arms and shoulders bare, low bodice, big bosom, pearl necklet. She is discovered sleeping, her arms on the ground before her, her head on her arms. Beside her on ground to her left a capacious black bag, shopping variety, and to her right a collapsible collapsed parasol, beak of handle emerging from sheath.*

To her right and rear, lying asleep on ground, hidden by mound, WILLIE.

Long pause. A bell rings piercingly, say ten seconds, stops. She does not move. Pause. Bell more piercingly, say five seconds. She wakes. Bell stops. She raises her head, gazes front. Long pause. She straightens up, lays her hands flat on ground, throws back her head and gazes at zenith. Long pause.

WINNIE (*gazing at zenith*): Another heavenly day. (*Pause. Head back level, eyes front, pause. She clasps hands to breast, closes eyes. Lips move in inaudible prayer, say ten seconds. Lips still. Hands remain clasped. Low.*) For Jesus Christ sake Amen. (*Eyes open, hands unclasp, return to mound. Pause. She clasps hands to breast again, closes eyes, lips move again in inaudible addendum, say five seconds. Low.*) World without end Amen. (*Eyes open, hands unclasp, return to mound. Pause.*) Begin, Winnie. (*Pause.*) Begin your day, Winnie. (*Pause. She turns to bag, rummages in it without moving it from its place, brings out toothbrush, rummages again, brings out flat tube of toothpaste, turns back front, unscrews cap of tube, lays cap on ground, squeezes with difficulty small blob of paste on brush, holds tube in one hand and brushes teeth with other. She turns modestly aside and back to her right to spit out behind mound. In this position her eyes rest on* WILLIE. *She spits out. She cranes a little further back and down. Loud.*) Hoo-oo! (*Pause. Louder.*) Hoo-oo! (*Pause. Tender smile as she turns back front, lays down brush.*) Poor Willie—(*examines tube, smile off*)—running out—(*looks for cap*)—ah well—(*finds cap*)—can't be helped—(*screws on cap*)—just one of those old things—(*lays down tube*)—another of those old things—(*turns towards bag*)—just can't be cured—(*rummages in bag*)—cannot be cured—(*brings out small mirror, turns back front*)—ah yes—(*inspects teeth in mirror*)—poor dear Willie—(*testing upper front teeth with thumb, indistinctly*)—good Lord!—(*pulling back upper lip to inspect gums, do.[1]*)—good God!—(*pulling back corner of mouth, mouth open, do.*)—ah well—(*other corner, do.*)—no worse—(*abandons inspection, normal speech*)—no better, no worse—(*lays down mirror*)—no change—(*wipes fingers on*

---

1. do. = ditto.

grass)—no pain—(*looks for toothbrush*)—hardly any—(*takes up toothbrush*)—great thing that—(*examines handle of brush*)—nothing like it—(*examines handle, reads*—pure . . . what?—(*pause*)—what?—(*lays down brush*)—ah yes—(*turns towards bag*)—poor Willie—(*rummages in bag*)—no zest—(*rummages*)—for anything—(*brings out spectacles in case*)—no interest—(*turns back front*)—in life—(*takes spectacles from case*)—poor dear Willie—(*lays down case*)—sleep forever—(*opens spectacles*)—marvellous gift—(*puts on spectacles*)—nothing to touch it—(*looks for toothbrush*)—in my opinion—(*takes up toothbrush*)—always said so—(*examines handle of brush*)—wish I had it—(*examines handle, reads*)—genuine . . . pure . . . what?—(*lays down brush*)—blind next—(*takes off spectacles*)—ah well—(*lays down spectacles*)—seen enough—(*feels in bodice for handkerchief*)—I suppose—(*takes out folded handkerchief*)—by now—(*shakes out handkerchief*)—what are those wonderful lines—(*wipes one eye*)—woe woe is me—(*wipes the other*)—to see what I see—(*looks for spectacles*)—ah yes—(*takes up spectacles*)—wouldn't miss it—(*starts polishing spectacles, breathing on lenses*)—or would I?—(*polishes*)—holy light—(*polishes*)—bob up out of dark—(*polishes*)—blaze of hellish light. (*Stops polishing, raises face to sky, pause, head back level, resumes polishing, stops polishing, cranes back to her right and down.*) Hoo-oo! (*Pause. Tender smile as she turns back front and resumes polishing. Smile off.*) Marvellous gift—(*stops polishing, lays down spectacles*)—wish I had it—(*folds handkerchief*)—ah well—(*puts handkerchief back in bodice*)—can't complain—(*looks for spectacles*)—no no—(*takes up spectacles*)—mustn't complain—(*holds up spectacles, looks through lens*)—so much to be thankful for—(*looks through other lens*)—no pain—(*puts on spectacles*)—hardly any—(*looks for toothbrush*)—wonderful thing that—(*takes up toothbrush*)—nothing like it—(*examines handle of brush*)—slight headache sometimes—(*examines handle, reads*)—guaranteed . . . genuine . . . pure . . . what?—(*looks closer*)—genuine pure . . . —(*takes handkerchief from bodice*)—ah yes—(*shakes out handkerchief*)—occasional mild mi-

graine—(*starts wiping handle of brush*)—it comes—(*wipes*)—and then goes—(*wiping mechanically*)—ah yes—(*wiping*)—many mercies—(*wiping*)—great mercies—(*stops wiping, fixed lost gaze, brokenly*)—prayers perhaps not for naught—(*pause, do.*)—first thing—(*pause, do.*)—last thing—(*head down, resumes wiping, stops wiping, head up, calmed, wipes eyes, folds handkerchief, puts it back in bodice, examines handle of brush, reads*)—fully guaranteed . . . geniune pure . . . —(*looks closer*)—genuine pure . . . (*Takes off spectacles, lays them and brush down, gazes before her.*) Old things. (*Pause.*) Old eyes. (*Long pause.*) On, Winnie. (*She casts about her, sees parasol, considers it at length, takes it up and develops from sheath a handle of surprising length. Holding butt of parasol in right hand she cranes back and down to her right to hang over* WILLIE). Hoo-oo! (*Pause.*) Willie! (*Pause.*) Wonderful gift. (*She strikes down at him with beak of parasol.*) Wish I had it. (*She strikes again. The parasol slips from her grasp and falls behind mound. It is immediately restored to her by* WILLIE's *invisible hand.*) Thank you, dear. (*She transfers parasol to left hand, turns back front and examines right palm.*) Damp. (*Returns parasol to right hand, examines left palm.*) Ah well, no worse. (*Head up, cheerfully.*) No better, no worse, no change. (*Pause. Do.*) No pain. (*Cranes back to look down at* WILLIE, *holding parasol by butt as before.*) Don't go off on me again now dear will you please, I may need you. (*Pause.*) No hurry, no hurry, just don't curl up on me again. (*Turns back front, lays down parasol, examines palms together, wipes them on grass.*) Perhaps a shade off colour just the same. (*Turns to bag, rummages in it, brings out revolver, holds it up, kisses it rapidly, puts it back, rummages, brings out almost empty bottle of red medicine, turns back front, looks for spectacles, puts them on, reads label.*) Loss of spirits . . . lack of keenness . . . want of appetite . . . infants . . . children . . . adults . . . six level . . . tablespoonfuls daily—(*head up, smile*)—the old style!—(*smile off, head down, reads*)—daily . . . before and after . . . meals . . . instantaneous . . . (*looks closer*) . . . improvement. (*Takes off spectacles, lays them down, holds up bottle at arm's length to see level, unscrews cap, swigs it off head well back, tosses cap and bottle away in* WILLIE's *direction. Sound of breaking glass.*) Ah that's better! (*Turns to bag, rummages in it, brings out lipstick, turns back front, examines lipstick.*) Running out. (*Looks for spectacles.*) Ah well. (*Puts on spectacles, looks for mirror.*) Mustn't complain. (*Takes up mirror, starts doing lips.*) What is that wonderful line? (*Lips.*) Oh fleeting joys—(*lips*)—oh something lasting woe. (*Lips. She is interrupted by disturbance from* WILLIE. *He is sitting up. She lowers lipstick and mirror and cranes back and down to look at him. Pause. Top back of* WILLIE's *bald head, trickling blood, rises to view above slope, comes to rest.* WINNIE *pushes up her spectacles. Pause. His hand appears with handkerchief, spreads it on skull, disappears. Pause. The hand appears with boater, club ribbon, settles it on head, rakish angle, disappears. Pause.* WINNIE *cranes a little further back and down.*) Slip on your drawers, dear, before you get singed. (*Pause.*) No? (*Pause.*) Oh I see, you still have some of that stuff left. (*Pause.*) Work it well in, dear. (*Pause.*) Now the other. (*Pause. She turns back front, gazes before her. Happy expression.*) Oh this is going to be another happy day! (*Pause. Happy expression off. She pulls down spectacles and resumes lips.* WILLIE *opens newspaper, hands invisible. Tops of yellow sheets appear on either side of his head.* WINNIE *finishes lips, inspects them in mirror held a little further away.*) Ensign crimson. (WILLIE *turns page.* WINNIE *lays down lipstick and mirror, turns towards bag.*) Pale flag.

WILLIE *turns page.* WINNIE *rummages in bag, brings out small, ornate, brimless hat with crumpled feather, turns back front, straightens hat, smooths feather, raises it towards head, arrests gesture as* WILLIE *reads.*

WILLIE: His Grace and Most Reverend Father in God Dr Carolus Hunter dead in tub.

Pause.

WINNIE (*gazing front, hat in hand, tone of fervent reminiscence*): Charlie Hunter! (*Pause.*) I close my eyes—(*she takes off spectacles and does so, hat in one hand, spectacles in other,* WILLIE *turns page*)—and am sitting on his knees again, in the back garden at Borough Green, under the horse-beech. (*Pause. She opens eyes, puts on*

spectacles, fiddles with hat.) Oh the happy memories!

Pause. She raises hat towards head, arrests gesture as WILLIE *reads.*

WILLIE: Opening for smart youth.

Pause. She raises hat towards head, arrests gesture, takes off spectacles, gazes front, hat in one hand, spectacles in other.

WINNIE: My first ball! (*Long pause.*) My second ball! (*Long pause. Closes eyes.*) My first kiss! (*Pause.* WILLIE *turns page.* WINNIE *opens eyes.*) A Mr Johnson, or Johnston, or perhaps I should say Johnstone. Very bushy moustache, very tawny. (*Reverently.*) Almost ginger! (*Pause.*) Within a toolshed, though whose I cannot conceive. We had no toolshed and he most certainly had no toolshed. (*Closes eyes.*) I see the piles of pots. (*Pause.*) The tangles of bast. (*Pause.*) The shadows deepening among the rafters.

Pause. She opens eyes, puts on spectacles, raises hat towards head, arrests gesture as WILLIE *reads.*

WILLIE: Wanted bright boy.

Pause. WINNIE *puts on hat hurriedly, looks for mirror.* WILLIE *turns page.* WINNIE *takes up mirror, inspects hat, lays down mirror, turns towards bag. Paper disappears.* WINNIE *rummages in bag, brings out magnifying-glass, turns back front, looks for toothbrush. Paper reappears, folded, and begins to fan* WILLIE's *face, hand invisible.* WINNIE *takes up toothbrush and examines handle through glass.*

WINNIE: Full guaranteed . . . (WILLIE *stops fanning*) . . . genuine pure . . . (*Pause.* WILLIE *resumes fanning.* WINNIE *looks closer, reads.*) Fully guaranteed . . . WILLIE *stops fanning*) . . . genuine pure . . . (*Pause.* WILLIE *resumes fanning.* WINNIE *lays down glass and brush, takes handkerchief from bodice, takes off and polishes spectacles, puts on spectacles, looks for glass, takes up and polishes glass, lays down glass, looks for brush, takes up brush and wipes handle, lays down brush, puts handkerchief back in bodice, looks for glass, takes up glass, looks for brush, takes up brush and examines handle through glass.*) Fully guaranteed . . . (WILLIE *stops fanning*) . . . genuine pure . . . (*pause,* WILLIE *resumes fanning*) . . . hog's (WILLIE *stops fanning, pause*)

. . . setae. (*Pause.* WINNIE *lays down glass and brush, paper disappears,* WINNIE *takes off spectacles, lays them down, gazes front.*) Hog's setae. (*Pause.*) That is what I find so wonderful, that not a day goes by—(*smile*)—to speak in the old style—(*smile off*)—hardly a day, without some addition to one's knowledge however trifling, the addition I mean, provided one takes the pains. (WILLIE'S *hand reappears with a postcard which he examines close to eyes.*) And if for some strange reason no further pains are possible, why then just close the eyes—(*she does so*)—and wait for the day to come—(*opens eyes*)—the happy day to come when flesh melts at so many degrees and the night of the moon has so many hundred hours. (*Pause.*) That is what I find so comforting when I lose heart and envy the brute beast. (*Turning towards* WILLIE.) I hope you are taking in—(*She sees postcard, bends lower.*) What is that you have there, Willie, may I see? (*She reaches down with hand and* WILLIE *hands her card. The hairy forearm appears above slope, raised in gesture of giving, the hand open to take back, and remains in this position till card is returned.* WINNIE *turns back front and examines card.*) Heavens what are they up to! (*She looks for spectacles, puts them on and examines card.*) No but this is just genuine pure filth! (*Examines card.*) Make any nice-minded person want to vomit! (*Impatience of* WILLIE'S *fingers. She looks for glass, takes it up and examines card through glass. Long pause.*) What does that creature in the background think he's doing? (*Looks closer.*) Oh no really! (*Impatience of fingers. Last long look. She lays down glass, takes edge of card between right forefinger and thumb, averts head, takes nose between left forefinger and thumb.*) Pah! (*Drops card.*) Take it away! (WILLIE'S *arm disappears. His hand reappears immediately, holding card.* WINNIE *takes off spectacles, lays them down, gazes before her. During what follows* WILLIE *continues to relish card, varying angles and distance from his eyes.*) Hog's setae. (*Puzzled expression.*) What exactly is a hog? (*Pause. Do.*) A sow of course I know, but a hog . . . (*Puzzled expression off.*) Oh well what does it matter, that is what I always say, it will come back, that is what I find so wonderful, all comes back. (*Pause.*) All? (*Pause.*) No, not all. (*Smile.*) No No. (*Smile off.*) Not quite. (*Pause.*) A part.

(*Pause.*) Floats up, one fine day, out of the blue. (*Pause.*) That is what I find so wonderful. (*Pause. She turns towards bag. Hand and card disappear. She makes to rummage in bag, arrests gesture.*) No. (*She turns back front. Smile.*) No no. (*Smile off.*) Gently Winnie. (*She gazes front.* WILLIE'S *hand reappears, takes off hat, disappears with hat.*) What then? (*Hand reappears, takes handerchief from skull, disappears with handkerchief. Sharply, as to one not paying attention.*) Winnie! (WILLIE *bows head out of sight.*) What *is* the alternative? (*Pause.*) What *is* the al—(WILLIE *blows nose loud and long, head and hands invisible. She turns to look at him. Pause. Head reappears. Pause. Hand reappears with handkerchief, spreads it on skull, disappears. Pause. Hand reappears with boater, settles it on head, rakish angle, disappears. Pause.*) Would I had let you sleep on. (*She turns back front. Intermittent plucking at grass, head up and down, to animate following.*) Ah yes, if only I could bear to be alone, I mean prattle away with not a soul to hear. (*Pause.*) Not that I flatter myself you hear much, no Willie, God forbid. (*Pause.*) Days perhaps when you hear nothing. (*Pause.*) But days too when you answer. (*Pause.*) So that I may say at all times, even when you do not answer and perhaps hear nothing, Something of this is being heard, I am not merely talking to myself, that is in the wilderness, a thing I could never bear to do—for any length of time. (*Pause.*) That is what enables me to go on, go on talking that is. (*Pause.*) Whereas if you were to die—(*smile*)—to speak in the old style—(*smile off*)—or go away and leave me, then what would I do, what *could* I do, all day long, I mean between the bell for waking and the bell for sleep? (*Pause.*) Simply gaze before me with compressed lips. (*Long pause while she does so. No more plucking.*) Not another word as long as I drew breath, nothing to break the silence of this place. (*Pause.*) Save possibly, now and then, every now and then, a sigh into my looking-glass. (*Pause.*) Or a brief . . . gale of laughter, should I happen to see the old joke again. (*Pause. Smile appears, broadens and seems about to culminate in laugh when suddenly replaced by expression of anxiety.*) My hair! (*Pause.*) Did I brush and comb my hair? (*Pause.*) I may have done. (*Pause.*) Normally I do. (*Pause.*) There is so little one *can* do.

(*Pause.*) One does it all. (*Pause.*) All one can. (*Pause.*) Tis only human. (*Pause.*) Human nature. (*She begins to inspect mound, looks up.*) Human weakness. (*She resumes inspection of mound, looks up.*) Natural weakness. (*She resumes inspection of mound.*) I see no comb. (*Inspect.*) Nor any hairbrush. (*Looks up. Puzzled expression. She turns to bag, rummages in it.*) The comb is here. (*Back front. Puzzled expression. Back to bag. Rummages.*) The brush is here. (*Back front. Puzzled expression.*) Perhaps I put them back, after use. (*Pause. Do.*) But normally I do not put things back, after use, no, I leave them lying about and put them back all together, at the end of the day. (*Smile.*) To speak in the old style. (*Pause.*) The sweet old style. (*Smile off.*) And yet . . . I seem . . . to remember . . . (*Suddenly careless.*) Oh well, what does it matter, that is what I always say, I shall simply brush and comb them later on, purely and simply, I have the whole—(*Pause. Puzzled.*) Them? (*Pause.*) Or it? (*Pause.*) Brush and comb it? (*Pause.*) Sounds improper somehow. (*Pause. Turning a little towards* WILLIE.) What would you say, Willie? (*Pause. Turning a little further.*) What would you say, Willie, speaking of your hair, them or it? (*Pause.*) The hair on your head, I mean. (*Pause. Turning a little further.*) The hair on your head, Willie, what would you say speaking of the hair on your head, them or it?

Long pause.

WILLIE: It.

WINNIE (*turning back front, joyful*): Oh you are going to talk to me today, this is going to be a happy day! (*Pause. Joy off.*) Another happy day. (*Pause.*) Ah well, where was I, my hair, yes, later on, I shall be thankful for it later on. (*Pause.*) I have my—(*raises hands to hat*)—yes, on, my hat on—(*lower hands*)—I cannot take it off now. (*Pause.*) To think there are times one cannot take off one's hat, not if one's life were at stake. Times one cannot put it on, times one cannot take it off. (*Pause.*) How often I have said, Put on your hat now, Winnie, there is nothing else for it, take off your hat now, Winnie, like a good girl, it will do you good, and did not. (*Pause.*) Could not. (*Pause. She raises hand, frees a strand of hair from under hat, draws it towards eye, squints at it, lets it go,

hand down.*) Golden you called it, that day, when the last guest was gone—(*hand up in gesture of raising a glass*)—to your golden . . . may it never . . . (*voice breaks*) . . . may it never . . . (*Hand down. Head down. Pause. Low.*) That day. (*Pause. Do.*) What day? (*Pause. Head up. Normal voice.*) What now? (*Pause.*) Words fail, there are times when even they fail. (*Turning a little towards* WILLIE.) Is that not so, Willie? (*Pause. Turning a little further.*) Is not that so, Willie, that even words fail, at times? (*Pause. Back front.*) What is one to do then, until they come again? Brush and comb the hair, if it has not been done, or if there is some doubt, trim the nails if they are in need of trimming, these things tide one over. (*Pause.*) That is what I mean. (*Pause.*) That is all I mean. (*Pause.*) That is what I find so wonderful, that not a day goes by—(*smile*)—to speak in the old style—(*smile off*)—without some blessing—(WILLIE *collapses behind slope, his head disappears,* WINNIE *turns towards event*)—in disguise. (*She cranes back and down.*) Go back into your hole now, Willie, you've exposed yourself enough. (*Pause.*) Do as I say, Willie, don't lie sprawling there in this hellish sun, go back into your hole. (*Pause.*) Go on now, Willie. (WILLIE *invisible starts crawling left towards hole.*) That's the man. (*She follows his progress with her eyes.*) Not head first, stupid, how are you going to turn? (*Pause.*) That's it . . . right round . . . now . . . back in. (*Pause.*) Oh I know it is not easy, dear, crawling backwards, but it is rewarding in the end. (*Pause.*) You have left your vaseline behind. (*She watches as he crawls back for vaseline.*) The lid! (*She watches as he crawls back towards hole. Irritated.*) Not head first, I tell you! (*Pause.*) More to the right. (*Pause.*) The *right*, I said. (*Pause. Irritated.*) Keep your tail down, can't you! (*Pause.*) Now. (*Pause.*) There! (*All these directions loud. Now in her normal voice, still turned towards him.*) Can you hear me? (*Pause.*) I beseech you, Willie, just yes or no, can you hear me, just yes or nothing.

Pause.

WILLIE: Yes.

WINNIE (*turning front, same voice*): And now?

WILLIE (*irritated*): Yes.

WINNIE (*less loud*): And now?

WILLIE (*more irritated*): Yes.

WINNIE (*still less loud*): And now? (*A little louder.*) And now?

WILLIE (*violently*): Yes!

WINNIE (*same voice*): Fear no more the heat o' the sun. (*Pause.*) Did you hear that?

WILLIE (*irritated*): Yes.

WINNIE (*same voice*): What? (*Pause.*) What?

WILLIE (*more irritated*): Fear no more.

Pause.

WINNIE (*same voice*): No more what? (*Pause.*) Fear no more what?

WILLIE (*violently*): Fear no more!

WINNIE (*normal voice, gabbled*): Bless you Willie I do appreciate your goodness I know what an effort it costs you, now you may relax I shall not trouble you again unless I am obliged to, by that I mean unless I come to the end of my own resources which is most unlikely, just to know that in theory you can hear me even though in fact you don't is all I need, just to feel you there within earshot and conceivably on the qui vive is all I ask, not to say anything I would not wish you to hear or liable to cause you pain, not to be just babbling away on trust as it is were not knowing and something gnawing at me. (*Pause for breath.*) Doubt. (*Places index and second finger on heart area, moves them about, brings them to rest.*) Here. (*Moves them slightly.*) Abouts. (*Hand away.*) Oh no doubt the time will come when before I can utter a word I must make sure you heard the one that went before and then no doubt another come another time when I must learn to talk to myself a thing I could never bear to do such wilderness. (*Pause.*) Or gaze before me with compressed lips. (*She does so.*) All day long. (*Gaze and lips again.*) No. (*Smile.*) No no. (*Smile off.*) There is of course the bag. (*Turns towards it.*) There will always be the bag. (*Back front.*) Yes, I suppose so. (*Pause.*) Even when you are gone, Willie.

(*She turns a little towards him.*) You *are* going, Willie, aren't you? (*Pause. Louder.*) You *will* be going soon, Willie, won't you? (*Pause. Louder.*) Willie! (*Pause. She cranes back and down to look at him.*) So you have taken off your straw, that is wise. (*Pause.*) You do look snug, I must say, with your chin on your hands and the old blue eyes like saucers in the shadows. (*Pause.*) Can you see me from there I wonder, I still wonder. (*Pause.*) No? (*Back front.*) Oh I know it does not follow when two are gathered together—(*faltering*)—in this way—(*normal*)—that because one sees the other the other sees the one, life has taught me that . . . too. (*Pause.*) Yes, life I suppose, there is no other word. (*She turns a litle towards him.*) Could you see me, Willie, do you think, from where you are, if you were to raise your eyes in my direction? (*Turns a little further.*) Lift up your eyes to me, Willie, and tell me can you see me, do that for me, I'll lean back as far as I can. (*Does so. Pause.*) No? (*Pause.*) Well never mind. (*Turns back painfully front.*) The earth is very tight today, can it be I have put on flesh, I trust not. (*Pause. Absently, eyes lowered.*) The great heat possibly. (*Starts to pat and stroke ground.*) All thing expanding, some more than others. (*Pause. Patting and stroking.*) Some less. (*Pause. Do.*) Oh I can well imagine what is passing through your mind, it is not enough to have to listen to the woman, now I must look at her as well. (*Pause. Do.*) Well it is very understandable. (*Pause. Do.*) Most understandable. (*Pause. Do.*) One does not appear to be asking a great deal, indeed at times it would seem hardly possible—(*voice breaks, falls to a murmur*)—to ask less—of a fellow-creature—to put it mildly—whereas actually—when you think about it—look into your heart—see the other—what he needs—peace—to be left in peace—then perhaps the moon—all this time—asking for the moon. (*Pause. Stroking hand suddenly still. Lively.*) Oh I say, what have we here? (*Bending head to ground, incredulous.*) Looks like life of some kind! (*Looks for spectacles, puts them on, bends closer. Pause.*) An emmet! (*Recoils. Shrill.*) Willie, an emmet, a live emmet! (*Seizes magnifying-glass, bends to ground again, inspects through glass.*) Where's it gone? (*Inspects.*) Ah! (*Follows its progress through grass.*) Has like a little white ball in its arms. (*Follows progress. Hand still. Pause.*) It's gone in. (*Continues a moment to gaze at spot through glass, then slowly straightens up, lays down glass, takes off spectacles and gazes before her, spectacles in hand. Finally.*) Like a little white ball.

Long pause. Gesture to lay down spectacles.
WILLIE: Eggs.

WINNIE (*arresting gesture*): What?

Pause.

WILLIE: Eggs. (*Pause. Gesture to lay down glasses.*) Formication.

WINNIE (*arresting gesture*): What?

Pause.

WILLIE: Formication.

Pause. She lays down spectacles, gazes before her. Finally.

WINNIE (*murmur*). God. (*Pause.* WILLIE *laughs quietly. After a moment she joins in. They laugh quietly together.* WILLIE *stops. She laughs on a moment alone.* WILLIE *joins in. They laugh together. She stops.* WILLIE *laughs on a moment alone. He stops. Pause. Normal voice.*) Ah well what a joy in any case to hear you laugh again, Willie, I was convinced I never would, you never would. (*Pause.*) I suppose some people might think us a trifle irreverent, but I doubt it. (*Pause.*) How can one better magnify the Almighty than by sniggering with him at his little jokes, particularly the poorer ones? (*Pause.*) I think you would back me up there, Willie. (*Pause.*) Or were we perhaps diverted by two quite different things? (*Pause.*) Oh well, what does it matter, that is what I always say, so long as one . . . you know . . . what is that wonderful line . . . laughing wild . . . something something laughing wild amid severest woe. (*Pause.*) And now? (*Long pause.*) Was I lovable once, Willie? (*Pause.*) Was I ever lovable? (*Pause.*) Do not misunderstand my question, I am not asking you if you loved me, we know all about that, I am asking you if you found me lovable—at one stage. (*Pause.*) No? (*Pause.*) You can't? (*Pause.*) Well I admit it is a teaser. And you have done more than your bit already, for the time being,

just lie back now and relax, I shall not trouble you again unless I am compelled to, just to know you are there within hearing and conceivably on the semi-alert is . . . er . . . paradise enow. (*Pause.*) The day is now well advanced. (*Smile.*) To speak in the old style. (*Smile off.*) And yet it is perhaps a little soon for my song. (*Pause.*) To sing too soon is a great mistake, I find. (*Turning towards bag.*) There is of course the bag. (*Looking at bag.*) The bag. (*Back front.*) Could I enumerate its contents? (*Pause.*) No. (*Pause.*) Could I, if some kind person were to come along and ask, What all have you got in that big black bag, Winnie? give an exhaustive answer? (*Pause.*) No. (*Pause.*) The depths in particular, who knows what treasures. (*Pause.*) What comforts. (*Turns to look at bag.*) Yes, there is the bag. (*Back front.*) But something tells me, Do no overdo the bag, Winnie, make use of it of course, let it help you . . . along, when stuck, by all means, but cast your mind forward, something tells me, cast your mind forward, Winnie, to the time when words must fail—(*she closes eyes, pause, opens eyes*)—and do not overdo the bag. (*Pause. She turns to look at bag.*) Perhaps just one quick dip. (*She turns back front, closes eyes, throws out left arm, plunges hand in bag and brings out revolver. Disgusted.*) You again! (*She opens eyes, brings revolver front and contemplates it. She weighs it in her palm.*) You'd think the weight of this thing would bring it down among the . . . last rounds. But no. It doesn't. Ever uppermost, like Browning. (*Pause.*) Brownie . . . (*Turning a little towards* WILLIE.) Remember Brownie, Willie? (*Pause.*) Remember how you used to keep on at me to take it away from you? Take it away, Winnie, take it away, before I put myself out of my misery. (*Back front. Derisive.*) *Your* misery! (*To revolver.*) Oh I suppose it's a comfort to know you're there, but I'm tired of you. (*Pause.*) I'll leave you out, that's what I'll do. (*She lays revolver on ground to her right.*) There, that's your home from this day out. (*Smile.*) The old style! (*Smile off.*) And now? (*Long pause.*) Is gravity what it was, Willie, I fancy not. (*Pause.*) Yes, the feeling more and more that if I were not held—(*gesture*)—in this way, I would simply float up into the blue. (*Pause.*) And that perhaps some day the earth will yield and let me go, the pull is so great, yes, crack all round me and let me out. (*Pause.*) Don't you ever have that feeling, Willie, of being sucked up? (*Pause.*) Don't you have to cling on sometimes, Willie? (*Pause. She turns a little towards him.*) Willie.

Pause.

WILLIE: *Sucked* up?

WINNIE: Yes love, up into the blue, like gossamer. (*Pause.*) No? (*Pause.*) You don't? (*Pause.*) Ah well, natural laws, natural laws, I suppose it's like everything else, it all depends on the creature you happen to be. All I can say is for my part is that for me they are not what they were when I was young and . . . foolish and . . . (*faltering, head down*) . . . beautiful . . . possibly . . . lovely . . . in a way . . . to look at. (*Pause. Head up.*) Forgive me, Willie, sorrow keeps breaking in. (*Normal voice.*) Ah well what a joy in any case to know you are there, as usual, and perhaps awake, and perhaps taking all this in, some of all this, what a happy day for me . . . it will have been. (*Pause.*) So far. (*Pause.*) What a blessing nothing grows, imagine if all this stuff were to start growing. (*Pause.*) Imagine. (*Pause.*) Ah yes, great mercies. (*Long pause.*) I can say no more. (*Pause.*) For the moment. (*Pause. Turns to look at bag. Back front. Smile.*) No no. (*Smile off. Looks at parasol.*) I suppose I might—(*takes up parasol*)—yes, I suppose I might . . . hoist this thing now. (*Begins to unfurl it. Following punctuated by mechanical difficulties overcome.*) One keeps putting off—putting up—for fear of putting up—too soon—and the day goes by—quite by—without one's having put up—at all. (*Parasol now fully open. Turned to her right she twirls it idly this way and that.*) Ah yes, so little to say, so little to do, and the fear so great, certain days, of finding oneself . . . left, with hours still to run, before the bell for sleep, and nothing more to say, nothing more to do, that the days go by, certain days go by, quite by, the bell goes, and little or nothing said, little or nothing done. (*Raising parasol.*) That is the danger. (*Turning front.*) To be guarded against. (*She gazes front, holding up parasol with right hand. Maximum pause.*) I used to perspire freely. (*Pause.*) Now hardly at all. (*Pause.*) The heat is much greater. (*Pause.*) The perspiration much less. (*Pause.*) That is what I find so wonderful. (*Pause.*) The way man adapts himself. (*Pause.*) To changing conditions. (*She transfers parasol to left hand. Long pause.*) Holding up wearies the arm. (*Pause.*) Not if one is going along. (*Pause.*) Only if one is at rest. (*Pause.*) That is a curious observation. (*Pause.*) I hope you heard that, Willie, I should be grieved to think you had not heard that. (*She takes parasol in both hands. Long pause.*) I am weary, holding it up, and I cannot put it down. (*Pause.*) I am worse off with it up than with it down, and I cannot put it down. (*Pause.*) Reason says, Put it down, Winnie, it is not helping you, put the thing down and get on with something else. (*Pause.*) I cannot. (*Pause.*) I cannot move. (*Pause.*) No, something must happen, in the world, take place, some change, I cannot, if I am to move again. (*Pause.*) Willie. (*Mildly.*) Help. (*Pause.*) No? (*Pause.*) Bid me put this thing down, Willie, I would obey you instantly, as I have always done, honoured and obeyed. (*Pause.*) Please, Willie. (*Mildly.*) For pity's sake. (*Pause.*) No? (*Pause.*) You can't? (*Pause.*) Well I don't blame you, no, it would ill become me, who cannot move, to blame my Willie because he cannot speak. (*Pause.*) Fortunately I am in tongue again. (*Pause.*) That is what I find so wonderful, my two lamps, when one goes out the other burns brighter. (*Pause.*) Oh yes, great mercies. (*Maximum pause. The parasol goes on fire. Smoke, flames if feasible. She sniffs, looks up, throws parasol to her right behind mound, cranes back to watch it burning. Pause.*) Ah earth you old extinguisher. (*Back front.*) I presume this has occurred before, though I cannot recall it. (*Pause.*) Can you, Willie? (*Turns a little towards him.*) Can you recall this having occurred before? (*Pause. Cranes back to look at him.*) Do you know what has occurred, Willie? (*Pause.*) Have you gone off on me again? (*Pause.*) I do not ask if you are alive to all that is going on, I merely ask if you have not gone off on me again. (*Pause.*) Your eyes appear to be closed, but that has no particular significance we know. (*Pause.*) Raise a finger, dear, will you please, if you are not quite senseless. (*Pause.*) Do that for me, Willie please, just the little finger, if you are still conscious. (*Pause. Joyful.*) Oh all five, you are a darling today, now I may continue with an easy mind. (*Back front.*) Yes, whatever occurred that did not occur before and yet . . . I wonder, yes, I confess I wonder. (*Pause.*) With the sun blazing so much fiercer down, and hourly fiercer, is it not natural things should go on fire never known to do so, in this way I mean, spontaneous like. (*Pause.*) Shall I myself not melt perhaps in the end, or burn, oh I do not mean necessarily burst into flames, no, just little by little be charred to a black cinder, all this—(*ample gesture of arms*)—visible flesh. (*Pause.*) On the other hand, did I ever know a temperate time? (*Pause.*) No. (*Pause.*) I speak of temperate times and torrid times, they are empty words. (*Pause.*) I speak of when I was not yet caught— in this way—and had my legs and had the use of my legs, and could seek out a shady place, like you, when I was tired of the sun, or a sunny place when I was tired of the shade, like you, and they are all empty words. (*Pause.*) It is no hotter today than yesterday, it will be no hotter tomorrow than today, how could it, and so on back into the far past, forward into the far future. (*Pause.*) And should one day the earth cover my breasts, then I shall never have seen my breasts, no one ever seen my breasts. (*Pause.*) I hope you caught something of that, Willie, I should be sorry to think you had caught nothing of all that, it is not every day I rise to such heights. (*Pause.*) Yes, something seems to have occurred, something has seemed to occur, and nothing has occurred, nothing at all, you are quite right, Willie. (*Pause.*) The sunshade will be there again tomorrow, beside me on this mound, to help me through the day. (*Pause. She takes up mirror.*) I take up this little glass, I shiver it on a stone—(*does so*)—I throw it away—(*does so far behind her*)—it will be in the bag again tomorrow, without a scratch, to help me through the day. (*Pause.*) No, one can do nothing. (*Pause.*) That is what I find so wonderful, the way things . . . (*voice breaks, head down*) . . . things . . . so wonderful. (*Long pause, head down. Finally turns, still bowed, to bag, brings out unidentifiable odds and ends, stuffs them back, fumbles deeper, brings out finally musical-box, winds it up, turns it on, listens for a moment holding it in both hands, huddled over it, turns back front, straightens up*

and listens to tune, holding box to breast with both hands. It plays the Waltz Duet "I love you so" from The Merry Widow. Gradually happy expression. She sways to the rhythm. Music stops. Pause. Brief burst of hoarse song without words—musical-box tune—from* WILLIE. *Increase of happy expression. She lays down box.*) Oh this will have been a happy day! (*She claps hands.*) Again, Willie, again! (*Claps.*) Encore, Willie, please! (*Pause. Happy expression off.*) No? You won't do that for me? (*Pause.*) Well it is very understandable, very understandable. One cannot sing just to please someone, however much one loves them, no, song must come from the heart, that is what I always say, pour out from the inmost, like a thrush. (*Pause.*) How often I have said, in evil hours, Sing now, Winnie, sing your song, there is nothing else for it, and did not. (*Pause.*) Could not. (*Pause.*) No, like the thrush, or the bird of dawning, with no thought of benefit, to oneself or anyone else. (*Pause.*) And now? (*Long pause. Low.*) Strange feeling. (*Pause. Do.*) Strange feeling that someone is looking at me. I am clear, then dim, then gone, then dim again, then clear again, and so on, back and forth, in and out of someone's eye. (*Pause. Do.*) Strange? (*Pause. Do.*) No, here all is strange. (*Pause. Normal voice.*) Something says, Stop talking now, Winnie, for a minute, don't squander all your words for the day, stop talking and do something for a change, will you? (*She raises hands and holds them open before her eyes. Apostrophic.*) Do something! (*She closes hands.*) What claws! (*She turns to bag, rummages in it, brings out finally a nailfile, turns back front and begins to file nails. Files for a time in silence, then the following punctuated by filing.*) There floats up—into my thoughts— a Mr. Shower—a Mr. and perhaps a Mrs. Shower—no—they are holding hands—his fiancée then more likely—or just some—loved one. (*Looks closer at nails.*) Very brittle today. (*Resumes filing.*) Shower—Shower—does the name mean anything—to you, Willie—evoke any reality, I mean—for you, Willie—don't answer if you don't—feel up to it—you have done more—than your bit—already—Shower— Shower. (*Inspects filed nails.*) Bit more like it. (*Raises head, gazes front.*) Keep yourself nice, Winnie, that's what I always say, come what may, keep yourself nice. (*Pause. Resumes filing.*)

Yes—Shower—Shower—(*stops filing, raises head, gazes front, pause*)—or Cooker, perhaps I should say Cooker. (*Turning a little towards* WILLIE.) Cooker, Willie, does Cooker strike a chord? (*Pause. Turns a little further. Louder.*) Cooker, Willie, does Cooker ring a bell, the name Cooker? (*Pause. She cranes back to look at him. Pause.*) Oh really! (*Pause.*) Have you no handkerchief, darling? (*Pause.*) Have you no delicacy? (*Pause.*) Oh, Willie, you're not eating it! Spit it out, dear, spit it out! (*Pause. Back front.*) Ah well, I suppose it's only natural. (*Break in voice.*) Human. (*Pause. Do.*) What *is* one to do? (*Head down. Do.*) All day long. (*Pause. Do.*) Day after day. (*Pause. Head up. Smile. Calm.*) The old style! (*Smile off. Resumes nails.*) No, done him. (*Passes on to next.*) Should have put on my glasses. (*Pause.*) Too late now. (*Finishes left hand, inspects it.*) Bit more human. (*Starts right hand. Following punctuated as before.*) Well anyway—this man Shower—or Cooker—no matter—and the woman—hand in hand—in the other hands bags—kind of big brown grips—standing there gaping at me—and at last this man Shower—or Cooker—ends in er anyway—stake my life on that—What's she doing? he says—What's the idea? he says—stuck up to her diddies in the bleeding ground—coarse fellow—What does it mean? he says—What's it meant to mean?—and so on—lot more stuff like that—usual drivel—Do you hear me? he says—I do, she says, God help me—What do you mean, he says, God help you? (*Stops filing, raises head, gazes front.*) And you, she says, what's the idea of you, she says, what are you meant to mean? It is because you're still on your two flat feet, with your old ditty full of tinned muck and changes of underwear, dragging me up and down this fornicating wilderness, coarse creature, fit mate—(*with sudden violence*)—let go of my hand and drop for God's sake, she says, drop! (*Pause. Resumes filing.*) Why doesn't he dig her out? he says—referring to you, my dear—What good is she to him like that?—What good is he to her like that?—and so on—usual tosh—Good! she says, have a heart for God's sake—Dig her out, he says, dig her out, no sense in her like that—Dig her out with what? she says—I'd dig her out with my bare hands, he says—must have been man and—wife. (*Files in silence.*) Next

thing they're away—hand in hand—and the bags—dim—then gone—last human kind—to stray this way. (*Finishes right hand, inspects it, lays down file, gazes front.*) Strange thing, time like this, drift up into the mind. (*Pause.*) Strange? (*Pause.*) No, here all is strange. (*Pause.*) Thankful for it in any case. (*Voice breaks.*) Most thankful. (*Head down. Pause. Head up. Calm.*) Bow and raise the head, bow and raise, always that. (*Pause.*) And now? (*Long pause. Starts putting things back in bag, toothbrush last. This operation, interrupted by pauses as indicated, punctuates following.*) It is perhaps a little soon—to make ready—for the night—(*stops tidying, head up, smile*)—the old style!—(*smile off, resumes tidying*)—and yet I do—make ready for the night—feeling it at hand—the bell for sleep—saying to myself—Winnie—it will not be long now, Winnie—until the bell for sleep. (*Stops tidying, head up.*) Sometimes I am wrong. (*Smile.*) But not often. (*Smile off.*) Sometimes all is over, for the day, all done, all said, all ready for the night, and the day not over, far from over, the night not ready, far, far from ready. (*Smile.*) But not often. (*Smile off.*) Yes, the bell for sleep, when I feel it at hand, and so make ready for the night—(*gesture*)—in this way, sometimes I am wrong—(*smile*)—but not often. (*Smile off. Resumes tidying.*) I used to think—I say I used to think—that all these things—put back into the bag—if too soon—put back too soon—could be taken out again—if necessary—if needed—and so on—indefinitely—back into the bag—back out of the bag—until the bell—went. (*Stops tidying, head up, smile.*) But no. (*Smile broader.*) No no. (*Smile off. Resumes tidying.*) I suppose this—might seem strange—this—what shall I say—this what I have said—yes—(*she takes up revolver*)—strange—(*she turns to put revolver in bag*)—were it not—(*about to put revolver in bag she arrests gesture and turns back front*)—were it not—(*she lays down revolver to her right, stops tidying, head up*)—that all seems strange. (*Pause.*) Most strange. (*Pause.*) Never any change. (*Pause.*) And more and more strange. (*Pause. She bends to mound again, takes up last object, i.e., toothbrush, and turns to put it in bag when her attention is drawn to disturbance from* WILLIE. *She cranes back and to her right to see. Pause.*) Weary of your hole, dear? (*Pause.*) Well I can understand that. (*Pause.*) Don't forget your straw. (*Pause.*) Not the crawler you were, poor darling. (*Pause.*) No, not the crawler I gave my heart to. (*Pause.*) The hands and knees, love, try the hands and knees. (*Pause.*) The knees! The knees! (*Pause.*) What a curse, mobility! (*She follows with eyes his progress towards her behind mound, i.e. towards place he occupied at beginning of act.*) Another foot, Willie, and you're home. (*Pause as she observes last foot.*) Ah! (*Turns back front laboriously, rubs neck.*) Crick in my neck admiring you. (*Rubs neck.*) But it's worth it, well worth it. (*Turning slightly towards him.*) Do you know what I dream sometimes? (*Pause.*) What I dream sometimes, Willie. (*Pause.*) That you'll come round and live this side where I could see you. (*Pause. Back front.*) I'd be a different woman. (*Pause.*) Unrecognizable. (*Turning slightly towards him.*) Or just now and then, come round this side just every now and then and let me feast on you. (*Back front.*) But you can't, I know. (*Head down.*) I know. (*Pause. Head up.*) Well anyway—(*looks at toothbrush in her hand*)—can't be long now—(*looks at brush*)—until the bell. (*Top back of* WILLIE's *head appears above slope.* WINNIE *looks closer at brush.*) Fully guaranteed . . . (*head up*) . . . what's this it was? (WILLIE's *hand appears with handkerchief, spreads it on skull, disappears.*) Genuine pure . . . fully guaranteed . . . (WILLIE's *hand appears with boater, settles it on head, rakish angle, disappears*) . . . genuine pure . . . ah! hog's setae. (*Pause.*) What is a hog exactly? (*Pause. Turns slightly towards* WILLIE.) What exactly is a hog,

Willie, do you know, I can't remember. (*Pause. Turning a little further, pleading.*) What *is* a hog, Willie, please!

Pause.

WILLIE: Castrated male swine. (*Happy expression appears on* WINNIE's *face.*) Reared for slaughter.

Happy expression increases. WILLIE *opens newspaper, hands invisible. Tops of yellow sheets appear on either side of his head.* WINNIE *gazes before her with happy expression.*

WINNIE: Oh this *is* a happy day! This will have been another happy day! (*Pause.*) After all. (*Pause.*) So far.

Pause. Happy expression off. WILLIE *turns page. Pause. He turns another page. Pause.*

WILLIE: Opening for smart youth.

Pause. WINNIE *takes off hat, turns to put it in bag, arrests gesture, turns back front. Smile.*

WINNIE: No. (*smile broader.*) No no. (*Smile off. Puts on hat again, gazes front, pause.*) And now? (*Pause.*) Sing. (*Pause.*) Sing your song, Winnie. (*Pause.*) No? (*Pause.*) Then pray. (*Pause.*) Pray your prayer, Winnie.

Pause. WILLIE *turns page. Pause.*

WILLIE: Wanted bright boy.

Pause. WINNIE *gazes before her.* WILLIE *turns page. Pause. Newspaper disappears. Long pause.*

WINNIE: Pray your old prayer, Winnie.

Long pause.

CURTAIN

ACT TWO

Scene as before.

WINNIE *imbedded up to neck, hat on head, eyes closed. Her head, which she can no longer turn, nor bow, nor raise, faces front motionless throughout act. Movements of eyes as indicated.*

Bag and parasol as before. Revolver conspicuous to her right on mound.

Long pause.

Bell rings loudly. She opens eyes at once. Bell stops. She gazes front. Long pause.

WINNIE: Hail, holy light. (*Long pause. She closes her eyes. Bell rings loudly. She opens eyes at once. Bell stops. She gazes front. Long smile. Smile off. Long pause.*) Someone is looking at me still. (*Pause.*) Caring for me still. (*Pause.*) That is what I find so wonderful. (*Pause.*) Eyes on my eyes. (*Pause.*) What is that unforgettable line? (*Pause. Eyes right.*) Willie. (*Pause. Louder.*) Willie. (*Pause. Eyes front.*) May one still speak of time? (*Pause.*) Say it is a long time now, Willie, since I saw you. (*Pause.*) Since I heard you. (*Pause.*) May one? (*Pause.*) One does. (*Smile.*) The old style! (*Smile off.*) There is so little one can speak of. (*Pause.*) One speaks of it all. (*Pause.*) All one can. (*Pause.*) I used to think . . . (*pause*) . . . I say I used to think that I would learn to talk alone. (*Pause.*) By that I mean to myself, the wilderness. (*Smile.*) But no. (*Smile broader.*) No no. (*Smile off.*) Ergo you are there. (*Pause.*) Oh no doubt you are dead, like the others, no doubt you have died, or gone away and left me, like the others, it doesn't matter, you are there. (*Pause. Eyes left.*) The bag too is there, the same as ever, I can see it. (*Pause. Eyes right. Louder.*) The bag is there, Willie, as good as ever, the one you gave me that day . . . to go to market. (*Pause. Eyes front.*) That day. (*Pause.*) What day? (*Pause.*) I used to pray. (*Pause.*) I say I used to pray. (*Pause.*) Yes, I must confess I did. (*Smile.*) Not now. (*Smile broader.*) No no. (*Smile off. Pause.*) Then . . . now . . . what difficulties here, for the mind. (*Pause.*) To have been always what I am—and so changed from what I was. (*Pause.*) I am the one, I say the one, then the other. (*Pause.*) Now the one, then the other. (*Pause.*) There is so little one can say, one says it all. (*Pause.*) All one can. (*Pause.*) And no truth in it anywhere. (*Pause.*) My arms. (*Pause.*) My breasts. (*Pause.*) What arms? (*Pause.*) What breasts? (*Pause.*) Willie. (*Pause.*) What Willie? (*Sudden vehement affirmation.*) My Willie! (*Eyes right, calling.*) Willie! (*Pause. Louder.*) Willie! (*Pause. Eyes front.*) Ah well, not to know, not to know for sure, great mercy, all I ask. (*Pause.*) Ah yes . . . then . . . now . . . beechen green . . . this . . . Charlie . . . kisses . . . this . . . all that . . . deep trouble for the mind. (*Pause.*) But it does not trouble mine. (*Smile.*) Not now. (*Smile broader.*) No no. (*Smile off. Long pause. She closes eyes. Bell rings loudly. She opens eyes. Pause.*) Eyes float up that seem to close in peace . . . to see . . . in peace. (*Pause.*) Not mine. (*Smile.*) Not now. (*Smile broader.*) No no. (*Smile off. Long pause.*) Willie. (*Pause.*) Do you think the earth has lost its atmosphere, Willie? (*Pause.*) Do you, Willie? (*Pause.*) You have no opinion? (*Pause.*) Well that is like you, you never had any opinion about anything. (*Pause.*) It's understandable. (*Pause.*) Most. (*Pause.*) The earthball. (*Pause.*) I sometimes wonder. (*Pause.*) Perhaps not quite all. (*Pause.*) There always remains something. (*Pause.*) Of everything. (*Pause.*) Some remains. (*Pause.*) If the mind were to go. (*Pause.*) It won't of course. (*Pause.*) Not quite. (*Pause.*) Not mine. (*Smile.*) Not now. (*Smile broader.*) No no. (*Smile off. Long pause.*) It might be the eternal cold. (*Pause.*) Everlasting perishing cold. (*Pause.*) Just chance, I take it, happy chance. (*Pause.*) Oh yes, great mercies, great mercies. (*Pause.*) And now? (*Long pause.*) The face. (*Pause.*) The nose. (*She squints down.*) I can see it . . . (*squinting down*) . . . the tip . . . the nostrils . . . breath of life . . . that curve you so admired . . . (*pouts*) . . . a hint of lip . . . (*pouts again*) . . . if I pout them out . . . (*sticks out tongue*) . . . the tongue of course . . . you so admired . . . if I stick it out . . . (*sticks it out again*) . . . the tip . . . (*eyes up*) . . . suspicion of brow . . . eyebrow . . . imagination possibly . . . (*eyes left*) . . . cheek . . . no . . . (*eyes right*) . . . no . . . (*distends cheeks*) . . . even if I puff them out . . . (*eyes left, distends cheeks again*) . . . no . . . no damask. (*Eyes front.*)

That is all. (*Pause.*) The bag of course . . . (*eyes left*) . . . a little blurred perhaps . . . but the bag. (*Eyes front. Offhand.*) The earth of course and sky. (*Eyes right.*) The sunshade you gave me . . . that day . . . (*pause*) . . . that day . . . the lake . . . the reeds. (*Eyes front. Pause.*) What day? (*Pause.*) What reeds? (*Long pause. Eyes close. Bell rings loudly. Eyes open. Pause. Eyes right.*) Brownie of course. (*Pause.*) You remember Brownie, Willie, I can see him. (*Pause.*) Brownie is there, Willie, beside me. (*Pause. Loud.*) Brownie is there, Willie. (*Pause. Eyes front.*) That is all. (*Pause.*) What would I do without them? (*Pause.*) What would I do without them, when words fail? (*Pause.*) Gaze before me, with compressed lips. (*Long pause while she does so.*) I cannot. (*Pause.*) Ah yes, great mercies, great mercies. (*Long pause. Low.*) Sometimes I hear sounds. (*Listening expression. Normal voice.*) But not often. (*Pause.*) They are a boon, sounds are a boon, they help me . . . through the day. (*Smile.*) The old style! (*Smile off.*) Yes, those are happy days, when there are sounds. (*Pause.*) When I hear sounds. (*Pause.*) I used to think . . . (*pause*) . . . I say I used to think they were in my head. (*Smile.*) But no. (*Smile broader.*) No no. (*Smile off.*) That was just logic. (*Pause.*) Reason. (*Pause.*) I have not lost my reason. (*Pause.*) Not yet. (*Pause.*) Not all. (*Pause.*) Some remains. (*Pause.*) Sounds. (*Pause.*) Like little . . . sunderings, little falls . . . apart. (*Pause. Low.*) It's things, Willie. (*Pause. Normal voice.*) In the bag, outside the bag. (*Pause.*) Ah yes, things have their life, that is what I always say, *things* have a life. (*Pause.*) Take my looking-glass, it doesn't need me. (*Pause.*) The bell. (*Pause.*) It hurts like a knife. (*Pause.*) A gouge. (*Pause.*) One cannot ignore it. (*Pause.*) How often . . . (*pause*) . . . I say how often I have said, Ignore it, Winnie, ignore the bell, pay no heed, just sleep and wake, sleep and wake, as you please, open and close the eyes, as you please, or in the way you find most helpful. (*Pause.*) Open and close the eyes, Winnie, open and close, always that. (*Pause.*) But no. (*Smile.*) Not now. (*Smile broader.*) No no. (*Smile off. Pause.*) What now? (*Pause.*) What now, Willie? (*Long pause.*) There is my story of course, when all else fails. (*Pause.*) A life. (*Smile.*) A long life. (*Smile off.*)

Beginning in the womb, where life used to begin, Mildred has memories, she will have memories, of the womb, before she dies, the mother's womb. (*Pause.*) She is now four or five already and has recently been given a big waxen dolly. (*Pause.*) Fully clothed, complete outfit. (*Pause.*) Shoes, socks, undies, complete set, frilly frock, gloves. (*Pause.*) White mesh. (*Pause.*) A little white straw hat with a chin elastic. (*Pause.*) Pearly necklet. (*Pause.*) A little picture-book with legends in real print to go under her arm when she takes her walk. (*Pause.*) China blue eyes that open and shut. (*Pause. Narrative.*) The sun was not well up when Milly rose, descended the steep . . . (*pause*) . . . slipped on her nightgown, descended all alone the steep wooden stairs, backwards on all fours, though she had been forbidden to do so, entered the . . . (*pause*) . . . tiptoed down the silent passage, entered the nursery and began to undress Dolly. (*Pause.*) Crept under the table and began to undress Dolly. (*Pause.*) Scolding her . . . the while. (*Pause.*) Suddenly a mouse—(*Long pause.*) Gently, Winnie. (*Long pause. Calling.*) Willie! (*Pause. Louder.*) Willie! (*Pause. Mild reproach.*) I sometimes find your attitude a little strange, Willie, all this time, it is not like you to be wantonly cruel. (*Pause.*) Strange? (*Pause.*) No. (*Smile.*) Not here. (*Smile broader.*) Not now. (*Smile off.*) And yet . . . (*Suddenly anxious.*) I do hope nothing is amiss. (*Eyes right, loud.*) Is all well, dear? (*Pause. Eyes front. To herself.*) God grant he did not go in head foremost! (*Eyes right, loud.*) You're not stuck, Willie? (*Pause. Do.*) You're not jammed, Willie? (*Eyes front, distressed.*) Perhaps he is crying out for help all this time and I do not hear him! (*Pause.*) I do of course hear cries. (*Pause.*) But they are in my head surely. (*Pause.*) Is it possible that . . . (*Pause. With finality.*) No no, my head was always full of cries. (*Pause.*) Faint confused cries. (*Pause.*) They come. (*Pause.*) Then go. (*Pause.*) As on a wind. (*Pause.*) That is what I find so wonderful. (*Pause.*) They cease. (*Pause.*) Ah yes, great mercies, great mercies. (*Pause.*) The day is now well advanced. (*Smile. Smile off.*) And yet it is perhaps a little soon for my song. (*Pause.*) To sing too soon is fatal, I always find. (*Pause.*) On the other hand it is possible to leave it too late. (*Pause.*) The bell goes for sleep and one has not sung. (*Pause.*) The whole day has flown—(*smile, smile off*)—flown by, quite by, and no song of any class, kind or description. (*Pause.*) There is a problem here. (*Pause.*) One cannot sing . . . just like that, no. (*Pause.*) It bubbles up, for some unknown reason, the time is ill chosen, one chokes it back. (*Pause.*) One says, Now is the time, it is now or never, and one cannot. (*Pause.*) Simply cannot sing. (*Pause.*) Not a note. (*Pause.*) Another thing, Willie, while we are on this subject. (*Pause.*) The sadness after song. (*Pause.*) Have you run across that, Willie? (*Pause.*) In the course of your experience. (*Pause.*) No? (*Pause.*) Sadness after intimate sexual intercourse one is familiar with of course. (*Pause.*) You would concur with Aristotle there, Willie, I fancy. (*Pause.*) Yes, that one knows and is prepared to face. (*Pause.*) But after song . . . (*Pause.*) It does not last of course. (*Pause.*) That is what I find so wonderful. (*Pause.*) It wears away. (*Pause.*) What are those exquisite lines? (*Pause.*) Go forget me why should something o'er that something shadow fling . . . go forget me . . . why should sorrow . . . brightly smile . . . go forget me . . . never hear me . . . sweetly smile . . . brightly sing . . . (*Pause. With a sigh.*) One loses one's classics. (*Pause.*) Oh not all. (*Pause.*) A part. (*Pause.*) A part remains. (*Pause.*) That is what I find so wonderful, a part remains, of one's classics, to help one through the day. (*Pause.*) Oh yes, many mercies, many mercies. (*Pause.*) And now? (*Pause.*) And now, Willie? (*Long pause.*) I call to the eye of the mind . . . Mr. Shower—or Cooker. (*She closes her eyes. Bell rings loudly. She opens her eyes. Pause.*) Hand in hand, in the other hands bags. (*Pause.*) Getting on . . . in life. (*Pause.*) No longer young, not yet old. (*Pause.*) Standing there gaping at me. (*Pause.*) Can't have been a bad bosom, he says, in its day. (*Pause.*) Seen worse shoulders, he says, in my time. (*Pause.*) Does she feel her legs? he says. (*Pause.*) Is there any life in her legs? he says (*Pause.*) Has she anything on underneath? he says. (*Pause.*) Ask her, he says, I'm shy. (*Pause.*) Ask her what? she says. (*Pause.*) Is there any life in her legs. (*Pause.*) Has she anything on underneath. (*Pause.*) Ask her yourself, she says. (*Pause. With sudden violence.*) Let go

of me for Christ sake and drop! (*Pause. Do.*) Drop dead! (*Smile.*) But no. (*Smile broader.*) No no. (*Smile off.*) I watch them recede. (*Pause.*) Hand in hand—and the bags. (*Pause.*) Dim. (*Pause.*) Then gone. (*Pause.*) Last human kind—to stray this way. (*Pause.*) Up to date. (*Pause.*) And now? (*Pause. Low.*) Help. (*Pause. Do.*) Help, Willie. (*Pause. Do.*) No? (*Long pause. Narrative.*) Suddenly a mouse . . . (*Pause.*) Suddenly a mouse ran up her little thigh and Mildred, dropping Dolly in her fright, began to scream—(WINNIE *gives a sudden piercing scream*)—and screamed and screamed—(WINNIE *screams twice*)—screamed and screamed and screamed and screamed till all came running, in their night attire, papa, mamma, Bibby and . . . old Annie, to see what was the matter . . . (*pause*) . . . what on earth could possibly be the matter. (*Pause.*) Too late. (*Pause.*) Too late. (*Long pause. Just audible.*) Willie. (*Pause. Normal voice.*) Ah well, not long now, Winnie, can't be long now, until the bell for sleep. (*Pause.*) Then you may close your eyes, then you *must* close your eyes—and keep them closed. (*Pause.*) Why say that again? (*Pause.*) I used to think . . . (*pause*) . . . I say I used to think there was no difference between one fraction of a second and the next. (*Pause.*) I used to say . . . (*pause*) . . . I say I used to say, Winnie, you are changeless, there is never any difference between one fraction of a second and the next. (*Pause.*) Why bring that up again? (*Pause.*) There is so little one can bring up, one brings up all. (*Pause.*) All one can. (*Pause.*) My neck is hurting me. (*Pause. With sudden violence.*) My neck is hurting me. (*Pause.*) Ah that's better. (*With mild irritation.*) Everything within reason. (*Long pause.*) I can do no more. (*Pause.*) Say no more. (*Pause.*) But I must say more. (*Pause.*) Problem here. (*Pause.*) No, something must move, in the world, I can't any more. (*Pause.*) A zephyr. (*Pause.*) A breath. (*Pause.*) What are those immortal lines? (*Pause.*) It might be the eternal dark. (*Pause.*) Black night without end. (*Pause.*) Just chance, I take it, happy chance. (*Pause.*) Oh yes, abounding mercies. (*Long pause.*) And now? (*Pause.*) And now, Willie? (*Long pause.*) That day. (*Pause.*) The pink fizz. (*Pause.*) The flute glasses. (*Pause.*) The last guest gone. (*Pause.*) The last bumper with the bodies nearly touching. (*Pause.*) The look. (*Long pause.*) What day? (*Long pause.*) What look? (*Long pause.*) I hear cries. (*Pause.*) Sing. (*Pause.*) Sing your old song, Winnie.

Long pause. Suddenly alert expression. Eyes switch right. WILLIE's *head appears to her right round corner of mound. He is on all fours, dressed to kill—top hat, morning coat, striped trousers, etc., white gloves in hand. Very long bushy white Battle of Britain moustache. He halts, gazes front, smooths moustache. He emerges completely from behind mound, turns to his left, halts, looks up at* WINNIE. *He advances on all fours towards centre, halts, turns head front, gazes front, strokes moustache, straightens tie, adjusts hat, advances a little further, halts, takes off hat and looks up at* WINNIE. *He is now not far from centre and within her field of vision. Unable to sustain effort of looking up he sinks head to ground.*

WINNIE (*mondaine*): Well this is an unexpected pleasure! (*Pause.*) Reminds me of the day you came whining for my hand. (*Pause.*) I worship you, Winnie, be mine. (*He looks up.*) Life a mockery without Win. (*She goes off into a giggle.*) What a get up, you do look a sight! (*Giggles.*) Where are the flowers? (*Pause.*) That smile today. (WILLIE *sinks head.*) What's that on your neck, an anthrax? (*Pause.*) Want to watch that, Willie, before it gets a hold on you. (*Pause.*) Where were you all this time? (*Pause.*) What were you doing all this time? (*Pause.*) Changing? (*Pause.*) Did you not hear me screaming for you? (*Pause.*) Did you get stuck in your hole? (*Pause. He looks up.*) That's right, Willie, look at me. (*Pause.*) Feast your old eyes, Willie. (*Pause.*) Does anything remain? (*Pause.*) Any remains? (*Pause.*) No? (*Pause.*) I haven't been able to look after it, you know. (*He sinks his head.*) You are still recognizable, in a way. (*Pause.*) Are you thinking of coming to live this side now . . . for a bit maybe? (*Pause.*) No? (*Pause.*) Just a brief call? (*Pause.*) Have you gone deaf, Willie? (*Pause.*) Dumb? (*Pause.*) Oh I know you were never one to talk, I worship you Winnie be mine and then nothing from that day forth only titbits from Reynolds' News. (*Eyes front. Pause.*) Ah well, what matter, that's what I always say, it will have been a happy day, after all, another happy day. (*Pause.*) Not long now, Winnie. (*Pause.*) I hear cries. (*Pause.*) Do you ever hear cries, Willie? (*Pause.*) No? (*Eyes back on* WILLIE.) Willie. (*Pause.*) Look at me again, Willie. (*Pause.*) Once more, Willie. (*He looks up. Happily.*) Ah! (*Pause. Shocked.*) What ails you, Willie, I never saw such an expression! (*Pause.*) Put on your hat, dear, it's the sun, don't stand on ceremony, I won't mind. (*He drops hat and gloves and starts to crawl up mound towards her. Gleeful.*) Oh I say, this is terrific! (*He halts, clinging to mound with one hand, reaching up with the other.*) Come on, dear, put a big of jizz into it, I'll cheer you on. (*Pause.*) Is it me you're after, Willie . . . or is it something else? (*Pause.*) Do you want to touch my face . . . again? (*Pause.*) Is it a kiss you're after, Willie . . . or is it something else? (*Pause.*) There was a time when I could have given you a hand. (*Pause.*) And then a time before that again when I did give you a hand. (*Pause.*) You were always in dire need of a hand, Willie. (*He slithers back to foot of mound and lies with face to ground.*) Brrum! (*Pause. He rises to hands and knees, raises his face towards her.*) Have another go, Willie, I'll cheer you on. (*Pause.*) Don't look at me like that! (*Pause. Vehement.*) Don't look at me like that! (*Pause. Low.*) Have you gone off your head, Willie? (*Pause. Do.*) Out of your poor old wits, Willie?

Pause.

WILLIE (*just audible*): Win.

Pause. WINNIE's *eyes front. Happy expression appears, grows.*

WINNIE: Win! (*Pause.*) Oh this *is* a happy day, this will have been another happy day! (*Pause.*) After all. (*Pause.*) So far.

Pause. She hums tentatively beginning of song, then sings softly, musical-box tune.

> Though I say not
> What I may not
> Let you hear,
> Yet the swaying
> Dance is saying,
> Love me dear!
> Every touch of fingers
> Tells me what I know,
> Says for you,

It's true, it's true,
You love me so!

Pause. Happy expression off. She closes her eyes. Bell rings loudly. She opens her eyes. She smiles, gazing front. She turns her eyes, smiling, to WILLIE, *still on his hands and knees looking up at her. Smile off. They look at each other. Long pause.*

CURTAIN

8 FOOL FOR LOVE

Sam Shepard

1983

Although to this date he has not had a play performed on Broadway, Sam Shepard (1943—) is certainly America's most significant dramatic writer of the 1980s. His absence from Broadway says a great deal both about Shepard and about Broadway.

Shepard was born (as Samuel Shepard Rogers, nicknamed "Steve") in Illinois. His military-based family moved often in his youth; during his adolescence they settled in South Pasadena, California, where the young "Steve Rogers" tended animals on a horse ranch, joined the 4-H Club, played and listened to rock and jazz music, and acted with an amateur religious theatre company. Upon the completion by this theatre company of a tour of New York City, Shepard, by then nineteen, remained behind there. He assumed his present name, and found a job bussing dishes in Greenwich Village, then the center of a newly emerging "Off-Off Broadway" theatre movement. Within months he was acting and writing plays for experimental theatres, which were soon to become as well known as he would himself: the Café Cino, the Café La Mama, the Judson Poets' Theatre, Theatre Genesis, and the American Place Theatre. The early Shepard plays—many of which he has now renounced—are fascinating, rambling, hugely evocative works; they are for the most part short and hastily written, syncopated "raps" more than conventional plays, wildly imaginative, sexy, and allusive. In these early plays Shepard drew heavily on his middle-American and Californian background, his "urban cowboy" persona, and the seeming rootlessness of his young life. He was also deeply influenced by the jazz and rock musicians with whom he regularly socialized and frequently performed: Bob Dylan and the Rolling Stones became his occasional collaborators during these and later years.

Despite the influence of New York, Shepard's major dramatic works emerged after he left that city. First came the explosive *The Tooth of Crime*, written and first staged in London in 1972 (the play deals with rival rock singers engaged in a surrealistic war of survival), and then a stunning series of full-length plays premiered at the Magic Theatre of San Francisco—a theatre at which Shepard served as playwright-in-residence under a Rockefeller Foundation grant beginning in 1974. His Californian works of this period include the full-length plays *Curse of the Starving Class*, *Buried Child*, *True West*, and *Fool for Love*. All four of these plays—as well as the 1986 *A Lie of the Mind*, which he staged off-Broadway in New York—are closely concerned with American family life, particularly as it is lived on the outskirts

254

of society: in the motels, mobile homes, and decaying farmhouses outside the mainstream of American prosperity. These are his most accessible plays, each with a clearly recognizable plot, well-defined characters, and a powerful sense of ending; with these plays Shepard moved into the mainstream of American dramatic literature, and in 1979 he was awarded the Pulitzer Prize for Drama for *Buried Child*.

Shepard has managed to avoid Broadway and the commercialism of the American theatre; his dramatic work has, so far, been linked either to the experimental Off-Off Broadway movement, or to the adventurous wing of the American regional theatre. He has also developed a major film-acting career and is probably best known to the American public as a leading character in, among other films, *The Right Stuff* and *Country*, as well as in the film of his own play, *Fool for Love*.

Fool for Love is Shepard's first serious treatment of a man-woman relationship. The play's themes typify what is becoming known as "pure Shepard"; they include the loneliness and romance of the American highway, the emasculation of the Ameri-can man, the wanton faithlessness of most human relationships, the incestuous intimacy of the nuclear family, the catastrophe of the negligent parent, and the sudden and unexpected eruption of rural violence. There is in this play, as always in Shepard's work, more here than meets the eye; the characters are not just people with a specific set of problems, but symbols of certain fundamental patterns of American behavior. It may not be possible to define just what those patterns are. As with Beckett (with whom he is frequently compared), Shepard seems to create modern myths, myths that touch us deeply without our knowing exactly why. Certainly the rhythms of his dialogue create a powerful resonance in most audiences (and readers), and often this resonance makes us reassess and reevaluate our lives more than any literal narrative would do. *Fool for Love* carries such resonance. The impact of this play comes from its pervasive ambiguity rather than any clearly posited problem and solution, and this impact creates a level of profound audience involvement, which transcends the basic plot of the play as well as the characters in it.

FOOL FOR LOVE

"The proper response of love is to accept it. There is nothing to *do*."
  Archbishop Anthony Bloom

CAST OF CHARACTERS

MAY
EDDIE

MARTIN
THE OLD MAN

This play is to be performed relentlessly without a break

SCENE

SCENE: *Stark, low-rent motel room on the edge of the Mojave Desert. Faded green plaster walls. Dark brown linoleum floor. No rugs. Cast iron four poster single bed, slightly off center favoring stage right, set horizontally to audience. Bed covered with faded blue chenille bedspread. Metal table with well-worn yellow formica top. Two matching metal chairs in the 50s "S" shape design with yellow plastic seats and backs, also well-worn. Table set extreme down left (from actor's p.o.v.). Chairs set upstage and down right of table. Nothing on the table. Faded yellow exterior door in the center of the stage left wall. When this door is opened, a small orange porch light shines into room. Yellow bathroom door up right of the stage right wall. This door slightly ajar to begin with, revealing part of an old style porcelain sink, white*

towels, a general clutter of female belongings and allowing a yellow light to bleed onto stage. Large picture window dead center of upstage wall, framed by dirty, long, dark green plastic curtains. Yellow-orange light from a street lamp shines thru window.

Extreme down left, next to the table and chairs is a small extended platform on the same level as the stage. The floor is black and it's framed by black curtains. The only object on the platform is an old maple rocking chair facing upstage right. A pillow with no slipcover rests on the seat. An old horse blanket with holes is laced to the back of the rocker. The color of the blanket should be subdued—grays and blacks.

Lights fade to black on set. In the dark, Merle Haggard's tune, "Wake Up" from his "The Way I Am" album is heard. Lights begin to rise slowly on stage in the tempo of the song. Volume swells slightly with the lights until they arrive at their mark. The platform remains in darkness with only a slight spill from the stage lights. Three actors are revealed.

CHARACTERS

THE OLD MAN *sits in the rocker facing up right so he's just slightly profile to the audience. A bottle of whiskey sits on the floor beside him. He picks up bottle and pours whiskey into a styrofoam cup and drinks. He has a scraggly red beard, wears an old stained "open-road" Stetson hat (the kind with the short brim), a sun-bleached, dark quilted jacket with the stuffing coming out at the elbows, black and white checkered slacks that are too short in the legs, beat up, dark Western boots, an old vest and a pale green shirt. He exists only in the minds of* MAY *and* EDDIE, *even though they might talk to him directly and acknowledge his physical presence.* THE OLD MAN *treats them as though they all existed in the same time and place.*

MAY *sits on edge of bed facing audience, feet on floor, legs apart, elbows on knees, hands hanging limp and crossed between her knees, head hanging forward, face staring at floor. She is absolutely still and maintains this attitude until she speaks. She wears a blue denim full skirt, baggy white t-shirt and bare feet with a silver ankle bracelet. She's in her early thirties.*

EDDIE *sits in the upstage chair by the table, facing* MAY. *He wears muddy, broken down cowboy boots with silver gaffer's tape wrapped around them at the toe and instep, well-worn, faded, dirty jeans that smell like horse sweat. Brown western shirt with snaps. A pair of spurs dangles from his belt. When he walks, he limps slightly and gives the impression he's rarely off a horse. There's a peculiar broken-down quality about his body in general, as though he's aged long before his time. He's in his late thirties.*

On the floor, between his feet, is a leather bucking strap like bronc riders use. He wears a bucking glove on his right hand and works resin into the glove from a small white bag. He stares at MAY *as he does this and ignores* THE OLD MAN. *As the song nears the end of its fade, he leans over, sticks his gloved hand into the handle of the bucking strap and twists it so that it makes a weird stretching sound from the friction of the resin and leather. The song ends, lights up full. He pulls his hand out and removes gloves.*

EDDIE (*seated, tossing glove on the table.*) (*short pause*): May, look. May? I'm not goin' any-

where. See? I'm right here. I'm not gone. Look (*She won't.*) I don't know why you won't just look at me. You know it's me. Who else do you think it is. (*Pause*) You want some water or somethin'? Huh? (*He gets up slowly, goes cautiously to her, strokes her head softly, she stays still.*) May? Come on. You can't just sit around here like this. How long you been sittin' here anyway? You want me to go outside and get you something? Some potato chips or something? (*She suddenly grabs his closest leg with both arms and holds tight burying her head between his knees.*) I'm not gonna' leave. Don't worry. I'm not gonna' leave. I'm stayin' right here. I already told ya' that. (*She squeezes tighter to his leg, he just stands there, strokes her head softly.*) May? Let go, okay? Honey? I'll put you back in bed. Okay? (*She grabs his other leg and holds on tight to both.*) Come on. I'll put you in bed and make you some hot tea or somethin'. You want some tea? (*She shakes her head violently, keeps holding on.*) With lemon? Some Ovaltine? May, you gotta' let go of me now, okay? (*Pause, then she pushes him away and returns to her original position.*) Now just lay back and try to relax. (*He starts to try to push her back gently on the bed as he pulls back the blankets. She erupts furiously, leaping off bed and lashing out at him with her fists. He backs off. She returns to bed and stares at him wild-eyed and angry, faces him squarely.*)

EDDIE (*after pause*): You want me to go? (*She shakes her head.*)

MAY: No!

EDDIE: Well, what do you want then?

MAY: You smell.

EDDIE: I smell.

MAY: You do.

EDDIE: I been drivin' for days.

MAY: Your fingers smell.

EDDIE: Horses.

MAY: Pussy.

EDDIE: Come on, May.

MAY: They smell like metal.

EDDIE: I'm not gonna' start this shit.

MAY: Rich pussy. Very clean.

EDDIE: Yeah, sure.

MAY: You know it's true.

EDDIE: I came to see if you were all right.

MAY: I don't need you!

EDDIE: Okay. (*turns to go, collects his glove and bucking strap*) Fine.

MAY: Don't go!

EDDIE: I'm goin'.

(*He exits stage left door, slamming it behind him; the door booms.*)

MAY (*agonized scream*): Don't go!!!!

(*She grabs pillow, clutching it to her chest then throws herself face down on bed, moaning and moving from one end of bed to the other on her elbows and knees. EDDIE is heard returning to stage left door outside. She leaps off bed clutching pillow, stands upstage right of bed, facing stage left door. EDDIE enters stage left door, banging it behind him. He's left the glove and bucking strap off stage. They stand there facing each other for a second. He makes a move toward her. MAY retreats to extreme upstage right corner of room clutching pillow to her chest. EDDIE stays against left wall, facing her.*)

EDDIE: What am I gonna' do? Huh? What am I supposed to do?

MAY: You know.

EDDIE: What.

MAY: You're gonna' erase me.

EDDIE: What're you talkin' about?

MAY: You're either gonna' erase me or have me erased.

EDDIE: Why would I want that? Are you kidding?

MAY: Because I'm in the way.

EDDIE: Don't be stupid.

MAY: I'm smarter than you are and you know it. I can smell your thoughts before you even think 'em.

(*EDDIE moves along wall to upstage left corner. MAY holds her ground in opposite corner.*)

EDDIE: May, I'm tryin' to take care of you. All right?

MAY: No, you're not. You're just guilty. Gutless and guilty.

EDDIE: Great.

(*He moves down left to table, sticking close to wall.*)
(*Pause*)

MAY (*quietly, staying in corner*): I'm gonna' kill her ya' know.

EDDIE: Who?

MAY: Who.

EDDIE: Don't talk like that.

(*MAY slowly begins to move down stage right as EDDIE simultaneously moves up left. Both of them press the walls as they move.*)

MAY: I am. I'm gonna' kill her and then I'm gonna' kill you. Systematically. With sharp knives. Two separate knives. One for her and one for you. (*She slams wall with her elbow. Wall resonates.*) So the blood doesn't mix. I'm gonna' torture her first though. Not you. I'm just gonna' let you have it. Probably in the midst of a kiss. Right when you think everything's been healed up. Right in the moment when you're sure you've got me buffaloed. That's when you'll die.

(*She arrives extreme down right at the very limits of the set. EDDIE in the extreme up left corner. Pause*)

EDDIE: You know how many miles I went outa' my way just to come here and see you? You got any idea?

MAY: Nobody asked you to come.

EDDIE: Two thousand, four hundred and eighty.

MAY: Yeah? Where were you, Katmandu or something?

EDDIE: Two thousand, four hundred and eighty miles.

MAY: So what!

(*He drops his head, stares at floor. Pause. She stares at him. He begins to move slowly down left, sticking close to wall as he speaks.*)

EDDIE: I missed you. I did. I missed you more than anything I ever missed in my whole life. I kept thinkin' about you the whole time I was driving. Kept seeing you. Sometimes just a part of you.

MAY: Which part?

EDDIE: Your neck.

MAY: My neck?

EDDIE: Yeah.

MAY: You missed my neck?

EDDIE: I missed all of you but your neck kept coming up for some reason. I kept crying about your neck.

MAY: Crying?

EDDIE (*He stops by stage left door. She stays down right.*): Yeah. Weeping. Like a little baby. Uncontrollable. It would just start up and stop and then start up all over again. For miles. I couldn't stop it. Cars would pass me on the road. People would stare at me. My face was all twisted up. I couldn't stop my face.

MAY: Was this before or after your little fling with the Countess?

EDDIE (*He bangs his head into wall. Wall booms.*): There wasn't any fling with any Countess!

MAY: You're a liar.

EDDIE: I took her out to dinner once, okay?

MAY: Ha!

(*She moves upstage right wall.*)

EDDIE: Twice.

MAY: You were bumping her on a regular basis! Don't gimme that shit.

EDDIE: You can believe whatever you want.

MAY (*she stops by bathroom door, opposite Eddie*) I'll believe the truth! It's less confusing.

(*Pause*)

EDDIE: I'm takin' you back, May.

(*She tosses pillow on bed and moves to upstage right corner.*)

MAY: I'm not going back to that idiot trailer if that's what you think.

EDDIE: I'm movin' it. I got a piece of ground up in Wyoming.

MAY: Wyoming? Are you crazy? I'm not moving to Wyoming. What's up there? Marlboro Men?

EDDIE: You can't stay here.

MAY: Why not? I got a job. I'm a regular citizen here now.

EDDIE: You got a job?

MAY (*she moves back down to head of bed*) Yeah. What'd you think, I was helpless?

EDDIE: No. I mean—it's been a long time since you had a job.

MAY: I'm a cook.

EDDIE: A cook? You can't even flip an egg, can you?

MAY: I'm not talkin' to you anymore!

(*She turns away from him, runs into bathroom, slams door behind her.* EDDIE *goes after her, tries door but she's locked it.*)

EDDIE (*at bathroom door*): May, I got everything worked out. I been thinkin' about this for weeks. I'm gonna' move the trailer. Build a little pipe corral to keep the horses. Have a big vegetable garden. Some chickens maybe.

MAY'S VOICE (*unseen, behind bathroom door*): I hate chickens! I hate horses! I hate all that shit! You know that. You got me confused with somebody else. You keep comin' up here with this lame country dream life with chickens and vegetables and I can't stand any of it. It makes me puke to even think about it.

EDDIE (EDDIE *has crossed stage left during this, stops at table.*): You'll get used to it.

MAY (*enters from bathroom*): You're unbelievable!

(*She slams bathroom door, crosses upstage to window.*)

EDDIE: I'm not lettin' go of you this time, May.

(*He sits in chair upstage of table.*)

MAY: You never had a hold of me to begin with. (*pause*) How many times have you done this to me?

EDDIE: What.

MAY: Suckered me into some dumb little fantasy and then dropped me like a hot rock. How many times has that happened?

EDDIE: It's no fantasy.

MAY: It's all a fantasy.

EDDIE: And I never dropped you either.

MAY: No, you just disappeared!

EDDIE: I'm here now aren't I?

MAY: Well, praise Jesus God!

EDDIE: I'm gonna take care of you, May. I am. I'm gonna' stick with you no matter what. I promise.

MAY: Get outa' here.

(*Pause*)

EDDIE: What'd you have to go and run off for anyway.

MAY: Run off? Me?

EDDIE: Yeah. Why couldn't you just stay put. You knew I was comin' back to get you.

MAY (*crossing down to head of bed*): What do you think it's like sittin' in a tin trailer for weeks on end with the wind ripping through it? Waitin' around for the Butane to arrive. Hiking down to the laundromat in the rain. Do you think that's thrilling or somethin'?

EDDIE (*still sitting*): I bought you all those magazines.

MAY: What magazines?

EDDIE: I bought you a whole stack of those fashion magazines before I left. I thought you liked those. Those French kind.

MAY: Yeah, I especially like the one with the Countess on the cover. That was real cute.

(*Pause*)

EDDIE: All right.

(*He stands*)

MAY: All right, what.

(*He turns to go out stage left door.*)

MAY: Where are you going?

EDDIE: Just to get my stuff outa' the truck. I'll be right back.

MAY: What're you movin' in now or something?

EDDIE: Well, I thought I'd spend the night if that's okay.

MAY: Are you kidding?

EDDIE (*opens door*): Then I'll just leave, I guess.

MAY (*she stands*): Wait.

(*He closes door. They stand there facing each other for a while. She crosses slowly to him. She stops. He takes a few steps toward her. Stops. They both move closer. Stop. Pause as they look at each other. They embrace. Long, tender kiss. They are very soft with each other. She pulls away from him slightly. Smiles. She looks him straight in the eyes, then, suddenly knees him in the groin with tremendous force. EDDIE doubles over and drops like a rock. She stands over him. Pause.*)

MAY: You can take it, right. You're a stuntman.

(*She exits into bathroom, stage right, slams the door behind her. The door is amplified with microphones and a bass drum hidden in the frame so that each time an actor slams it, the door booms loud and long. Same is true for the stage left door. EDDIE remains on the floor holding his stomach in pain. Stage lights drop to half their intensity as a spot rises softly on* THE OLD MAN. *He speaks directly to* EDDIE.)

THE OLD MAN: I thought you were supposed to be a fantasist, right? Isn't that basically the deal with you? You dream things up. Isn't that true?

EDDIE (*stays on floor*): I don't know.

THE OLD MAN: You don't know. Well, if you don't know I don't know who the hell else does. I wanna' show you somethin'. Somethin' real, okay? Somethin' actual.

EDDIE: Sure.

THE OLD MAN: Take a look at that picture on the wall over there. (*He points at wall stage right. There is no picture but* EDDIE *stares at the wall.*) Ya' see that? Take a good look at that. Ya' see it?

EDDIE (*staring at wall*): Yeah.

THE OLD MAN: Ya' know who that is?

EDDIE: I'm not sure.

THE OLD MAN: Barbara Mandrell. That's who that is. Barbara Mandrell. You heard a' her?

EDDIE: Sure.

THE OLD MAN: Well, would you believe me if I told ya' I was married to her?

EDDIE (*pause*): No.

THE OLD MAN: Well, see, now that's the difference right there. That's realism. I am actually married to Barbara Mandrell in my mind. Can you understand that?

EDDIE: Sure.

THE OLD MAN: Good. I'm glad we have an understanding.

(THE OLD MAN *drinks from his cup. Spot slowly fades to black as stage lights come back up full. These light changes are cued to the opening and closing of doors.* MAY *enters from bathroom, closes door quietly. She is carrying a sleek red dress, panty hose, a pair of black high heels, a black shoulder purse and a hair brush. She crosses to foot of bed and throws the clothes on it. Hangs the purse on a bed post, sits on foot of bed her back to* EDDIE *and starts brushing her hair.* EDDIE *remains on floor. She finishes brushing her hair, throws brush on bed, then starts taking off her clothes and changing into the clothes she brought on stage. As she speaks to* EDDIE *and changes into the new clothes, she gradually transforms from her former tough drabness into a very sexy woman. This occurs almost unnoticeably in the course of her speech.*)

MAY (*very cold, quick, almost monotone voice like she's writing him a letter*): I don't understand my feelings. I really don't. I don't understand how I could hate you so much after so much time. How, no matter how much I'd like to not hate you, I hate you even more. It grows. I can't even see you now. All I see is a picture of you. You and her. I don't even know if the picture's real anymore. I don't even care. It's a made-up picture. It invades my head. The two of you. And this picture stings even more than if I'd actually seen you with her. It cuts me. It cuts me so deep I'll never get over it. And I can't get rid of this picture either. It just comes. Uninvited. Kinda' like a little torture. And I blame you more for this little torture than I do for what you did.

EDDIE (*standing slowly*): I'll go.

MAY: You better.

EDDIE: Why?

MAY: You just better.

EDDIE: I thought you wanted me to stay.

MAY: I got somebody coming to get me.

EDDIE (*short pause, on his feet*): Here?

MAY: Yeah, here. Where else?

EDDIE (*makes a move toward her upstage*): You been seeing somebody?

MAY (*she moves quickly down left, crosses right*): When was the last time we were together, Eddie? Huh? Can you remember that far back?

EDDIE: Who've you been seeing?

(*He moves violently toward her.*)

MAY: Don't you touch me! Don't you even think about it.

EDDIE: How long have you been seeing him!

MAY: What difference does it make!

(*Short pause. He stares at her, then turns suddenly and exits out the stage left door and slams it behind him. Door booms.*)

MAY: Eddie! Where are you going? Eddie!

(*Short pause. She looks after EDDIE, then turns fast, moves upstage to window. She parts the Venetian blinds, looks out window, turns back into room. She rushes to upstage side of bed, gets down on hands and knees, pulls a suitcase out from under bed, throws it on top of bed, opens it. She rushes into bathroom, disappears, leaving door open. She comes back on with various items of clothing, throws stuff into suitcase, turns as if to go back into bathroom. Stops. She hears EDDIE off left. She quickly shuts suitcase, slides it under bed again, rushes around to*

downstage side of bed. Sits on bed. Stands again. Rushes back into bathroom, returns with hairbrush, slams bathroom door. Starts brushing her hair as though that's what she's been doing all along. She sits on bed brushing her hair. EDDIE enters stage left, slams door behind him, door booms. He stands there holding a ten gauge shotgun in one hand and a bottle of tequila in the other. He moves toward bed, tosses shotgun on bed beside her.)

MAY (*she stands, moves upstage, stops brushing her hair*): Oh, wonderful. What're you gonna' do with that?

EDDIE: Clean it.

(*He opens the bottle.*)

EDDIE: You got any glasses?

MAY: In the bathroom.

EDDIE: What're they doin' in the bathroom?

(EDDIE *crosses toward bathroom door with bottle.*)

MAY: I keep everything in the bathroom. It's safer.

EDDIE: You want some a' this?

MAY: I'm on the wagon.

EDDIE: Good. 'Bout time.

(*He exits into bathroom.* MAY *moves back to bed, stares at shotgun.*)

MAY: Eddie, this is a very friendly person who's coming over here. He's not malicious in any way. (*pause*) Eddie?

EDDIE'S VOICE (*off right*): Where's the damn glasses?

MAY: In the medicine cabinet!

EDDIE'S VOICE: What the hell're they doin' in the medicine cabinet!

(*Sound of medicine cabinet being opened and slammed shut off right*)

MAY: There's no germs in the medicine cabinet!

EDDIE'S VOICE: Germs.

MAY: Eddie, did you hear me?

(EDDIE *enters with a glass, pouring tequila into it slowly until it's full as he crosses to table down left.*)

MAY: Did you hear what I said, Eddie?

EDDIE: About what?

MAY: About the man who's coming over here.

EDDIE: What man?

MAY: Oh, brother.

(EDDIE *sets bottle of tequila on table then sits in up-stage chair. Takes a long drink from glass. He ignores* THE OLD MAN.)

EDDIE: First off, it can't be very serious.

MAY: Oh, really? And why is that?

EDDIE: Because you call him a "man."

MAY: What am I supposed to call him?

EDDIE: A "guy" or something. If you called him a "guy", I'd be worried about it but since you call him a "man" you give yourself away. You're in a dumb situation with this guy by calling him a "man". You put yourself below him.

MAY: What in the hell do you know about it.

EDDIE: This guy's gotta' be a twerp. He's gotta' be a punk chump in a two dollar suit or somethin'.

MAY: Anybody who doesn't half kill themselves falling off horses or jumping on steers is a twerp in your book.

EDDIE: That's right.

MAY: And what're you supposed to be, a "guy" or a "man"?

(EDDIE *lowers his glass slowly. Stares at her. Pause. He smiles then speaks low and deliberately.*)

EDDIE: I'll tell you what. We'll just wait for this "man" to come over here. The two of us. We'll just set right here and wait. Then I'll let you be the judge.

MAY: Why is everything a big contest with you? He's not competing with you. He doesn't even know you exist.

EDDIE: You can introduce me.

MAY: I'm not introducing you. I am definitely not introducing you. He'd be very embarrassed to find me here with somebody else. Besides, I've only just met him.

EDDIE: Embarrassed?

MAY: Yes! Embarrassed. He's a very gentle person.

EDDIE: Is that right. Well, I'm a very gentle person myself. My feelings get easily damaged.

MAY: What feelings.

(EDDIE *falls silent, takes a drink, then gets up slowly with glass, leaves bottle on table, crosses to bed, sits on bed, sets glass on floor, picks up shotgun and starts dismantling it.* MAY *watches him closely.*)

MAY: You can't keep messing me around like this. It's been going on too long. I can't take it anymore. I get sick everytime you come around. Then I get sick when you leave. You're like a disease to me. Besides, you got no right being jealous of me after all the bullshit I've been through with you.

(*Pause.* EDDIE *keeps his attention on shotgun as he talks to her.*)

EDDIE: We've got a pact.

MAY: Oh, God.

EDDIE: We made a pact.

MAY: There's nothing between us now!

EDDIE: Then what're you so excited about?

MAY: I'm not excited.

EDDIE: You're beside yourself.

MAY: You're driving me crazy. You're driving me totally crazy!

EDDIE: You know we're connected, May. We'll always be connected. That was decided a long time ago.

MAY: Nothing was decided! You made all that up.

EDDIE: You know what happened.

MAY: You promised me that was finished. You can't start that up all over again. You promised me.

EDDIE: A promise can't stop something like that. It happened.

MAY: Nothing happened! Nothing ever happened!

EDDIE: Innocent to the last drop.

MAY (*pause, controlled*): Eddie—will you please leave? Now.

EDDIE: You're gonna' find out one way or the other.

MAY: I want you to leave.

EDDIE: You didn't want me to leave before.

MAY: I want you to leave now. And it's not because of this man. It's just—

EDDIE: What.

MAY: Stupid. You oughta' know that by now.

EDDIE: You think so, huh?

MAY: It'll be the same thing over and over again. We'll be together for a little while and then you'll be gone.

EDDIE: I'll be gone.

MAY: You will. You know it. You just want me now because I'm seeing somebody else. As soon as that's over, you'll be gone again.

EDDIE: I didn't come here because you were seein' somebody else! I don't give a damn who you're seeing! You'll never replace me and you know it!

MAY: Get outa' here!

(*Long silence.* EDDIE *lifts his glass and toasts her, then slowly drinks it dry. He sets glass down softly on floor.*)

EDDIE: (*smiles at her*): All right.

(*He rises slowly, picks up the sections of his shotgun. He stands there looking down at the shotgun pieces for a second.* MAY *moves slightly toward him.*)

MAY: Eddie—

(*His head jerks up and stares at her. She stops cold.*)

EDDIE: You're a traitor.

(*He exits left with shotgun. Slams door. Door booms.* MAY *runs toward door.*)

MAY: Eddie!!

(*She throws herself against stage left door. Her arms reach out and hug the walls. She weeps and slowly begins to move along the stage left wall upstage to the corner, embracing the wall as she moves and weeps.* THE OLD MAN *begins to tell his story as* MAY *moves slowly along the wall. He tells it directly to her as though she's a child.* MAY *remains involved with her emotion of loss and keeps moving clear around the room, hugging the walls during the course of the story until she arrives in the extreme downstage right corner of the room. She sinks to her knees.*)

(*Slowly, in the course of* MAY's *mourning, the spotlight softly rises on* THE OLD MAN *and the stage lights decrease to half again.*)

THE OLD MAN: Ya' know, one thing I'll never forget. I'll never forget this as long as I live—and I don't even know why I remember it exactly. We were drivin' through Southern Utah once, I think it was. Me, you and your mother—in that old Plymouth we had. You remember that Plymouth? Had a white plastic hood ornament on it. Replica of the Mayflower I think it was. Some kind a' ship. Anyway, we'd been drivin' all night and you were sound asleep in the front. And all of a sudden you woke up crying. Just bustin' a gut over somethin'. I don't know what it was. Nightmare or somethin'. Woke your Mom right up and she climbed over the seat in back there with you to try to get you settled down. But you wouldn't shut up for hell or high water. Just kept wailing away. So I stopped the Plymouth by the side of the road. Middle a' nowhere. I can't even remember where it was exactly. Pitch black. I picked you up outa' the back seat there and carried you into this field.

Thought the cold air might quiet you down a little bit. But you just kept on howling away. Then, all of a sudden. I saw somethin' move out there. Somethin' bigger than both of us put together. And it started to move toward us kinda' slow.

(MAY *begins to crawl slowly on her hands and knees from down right corner toward bed. When she reaches bed, she grabs pillow and embraces it. Still on her knees. She rocks back and forth embracing pillow as* OLD MAN *continues.*)

And then it started to get joined up by some other things just like it. Same shape and everything. It was so black out there I could hardly make out my own hand. But these things started to kinda' move in on us from all directions in a big circle. And I stopped dead still and turned back to the car to see if your mother was all right. But I couldn't see the car anymore. So I called out to her. I called her name loud and clear. And she answered me back from outa' the darkness. She yelled back to me. And just then these things started to "moo". They all started "mooing" away.

(*He makes the sound of a cow.*)

And it turns out, there we were, standin' smack in the middle of a goddamn herd of cattle. Well, you never heard a baby pipe down so fast in your life. You never made a peep after that. The whole rest of the trip.

(MAY *stops rocking abruptly. Suddenly* MAY *hears* EDDIE *off left. Stage lights pop back up. Spot on* THE OLD MAN *cuts to black. She leaps to her feet, completely dropping her grief, hesitates a second, then rushes to chair upstage of table and sits. She takes a drink straight from the bottle, slams bottle down on table, leans back in the chair and stares at the bottle as though she's been sitting like that the whole time since he left.* EDDIE *enters fast from stage left door carrying two steer ropes. He slams door. Door booms. He completely ignores* MAY. *She completely ignores him and keeps staring at the bottle. He crosses upstage of bed, throws one of the ropes on bed and starts building a loop in the other rope, feeding it with the left hand so that it makes a snakelike zipping sound as it passes through the honda. Now he begins to pay attention to* MAY *as he continues fooling with the rope. She remains staring at the bottle of tequila.*)

EDDIE: Decided to jump off the wagon, huh?

(*He spins the rope above his head in a flat hornloop, then ropes one of the bedposts, taking up the slack with a sharp snap of the right hand. He takes the loop off the bedpost, rebuilds it, swings and ropes another bedpost. He continues this right around the bed, roping every post and never missing.* MAY *takes another drink and sets bottle down quietly.*)

MAY (*still not looking at him*): What're you doing?

EDDIE: Little practice. Gotta' stay in practice these days. There's kids out there ropin' calves in six seconds dead. Can you believe that? Six and no change. Flyin' off the saddle on the right hand side like a bunch a' Spider Monkeys. I'm tellin' ya', they got it down to a science.

(*He continues roping bedposts, making his way around the bed in a circle*)

MAY (*flatly, staring at bottle*): I thought you were leaving. Didn't you say you were leaving?

EDDIE (*as he ropes*): Well, yeah, I was gonna'. But then it suddenly occurred to me in the middle of the parking lot out there that there probably isn't any man comin' over here at all. There probably isn't any "guy" or any "man" or anybody comin' over here. You just made all that up.

MAY: Why would I do that?

EDDIE: Just to get even.

(*She turns to him slowly in chair, takes a drink, stares at him, then sets bottle on table.*)

MAY: I'll never get even with you.

(*He laughs, crosses to table, takes a deep drink from bottle, cocks his head back, gargles, swallows, then does a back flip across stage and crashes into stage right wall.*)

MAY: So, now we're gonna' get real mean and sloppy, is that it? Just like old times.

EDDIE: Well, I haven't dropped the reins in quite a while ya' know. I've been real good. I have. No hooch. No slammer. No women. No nothin'. I been a pretty boring kind of a guy actually. I figure I owe it to myself. Once a once.

(*He returns to roping the bedposts. She just stares at him from the chair.*)

MAY: Why are you doing this?

EDDIE: I already told ya'. I need the practice.

MAY: I don't mean that.

EDDIE: Well, say what ya' mean then, honey.

MAY: Why are you going through this whole thing again like you're trying to impress me or something. Like we just met. This is the same crap you laid on me in High School.

EDDIE (*still roping*): Well, it's just a little testimony of my love, see baby. I mean if I stopped trying to impress you, that'd mean it was all over, wouldn't it?

MAY: It *is* all over.

EDDIE: You're trying to impress me, too, aren't you?

MAY: You know me inside and out. I got nothing new to show you.

EDDIE: You got this guy comin' over. This new guy. That's very impressive. I woulda' thought you'd be hung out to dry by now.

MAY: Oh, thanks a lot.

EDDIE: What is he, a "younger man" or something?

MAY: It's none of your damn business.

EDDIE: Have you balled him yet?

(*She throws him a mean glare and just pins him with her eyes.*)

EDDIE: Have you? I'm just curious. (*pause*) You don't have to tell me. I already know.

MAY: You're just like a little kid, you know that? A jealous, little snot-nosed kid.

(EDDIE *laughs, spits, makes a 'snot-nosed-kid' face, keeps roping bedposts.*)

EDDIE: I hope this guy comes over. I really hope he does. I wanna' see him walk through that door.

MAY: What're you gonna' do?

(*He stops roping, turns to her. He smiles.*)

EDDIE: I'm gonna nail his ass to the floor. Directly.

(*He suddenly ropes chair downstage, right next to* MAY. *He takes up slack and drags chair violently back toward bed. Pause. They stare at each other.* MAY *suddenly stands, goes to bedpost, grabs her purse, slings it on her shoulder and heads for stage left door.*)

MAY: I'm not sticking around for this.

(*She exits stage left door leaving it open.* EDDIE *runs off stage after her.*)

EDDIE: Where're you goin'?

MAY (*off left*): Take you hands off a' me!

EDDIE (*off left*): Wait a second, wait a second. Just a second, okay?

(MAY *screams.* EDDIE *carries her back on stage screaming and kicking. He sets her down, slams door shut. She walks away from him stage right, straightening her dress.*)

EDDIE: Tell ya' what. I'll back off. I'll be real nice. I will. I promise. I'll be just like a little ole pussy cat, okay? You can introduce me to him as your brother or something. Well—maybe not your brother.

MAY: Maybe not.

EDDIE: Your cousin. Okay? I'll be your cousin. I just wanna' meet him is all. Then I'll leave. Promise.

MAY: Why do you want to meet him? He's just a friend.

EDDIE: Just to see where you stand these days. You can tell a lot about a person by the company they keep.

MAY: Look. I'm going outside. I'm going to the pay phone across the street. I'm calling him up and I'm telling him to forget about the whole thing. Okay?

EDDIE: Good. I'll pack up your stuff while you're gone.

MAY: I'm not going with you Eddie!

(*Suddenly headlights arc across the stage from upstage right, through the window. They slash across the audience, then dissolve off left. These should be two intense beams of piercing white light and not 'realistic' headlights.*)

MAY: Oh, great.

(*She rushes upstage to window, looks out.* EDDIE *laughs, takes a drink.*)

EDDIE: Why don't ya' run on out there. Go ahead. Run on out. Throw yourself into his arms or somethin'. Blow kisses in the moonlight.

(EDDIE *laughs, moves to bed. Pulls a pair of old spurs off his belt. Sits, starts putting spurs on his boots. It's important these spurs look old and used, with small rowels—not cartoon "cowboy" spurs.* MAY *goes into bathroom leaving door open.*)

MAY (*off right*): What're you doing?

EDDIE: Puttin' my hooks on. I wanna; look good for this "man". Give him the right impression. I'm yer cousin after all.

MAY (*entering from bathroom*): If you hurt him, Eddie—

EDDIE: I'm not gonna' hurt him. I'm a nice guy. Very sensitive, too. Very civilized.

MAY: He's just a date, you know. Just an ordinary date.

EDDIE: Yeah? Well, I'm gonna turn him into a fig.

(*He starts laughing so hard at his own joke that he rolls off the bed and crashes to the floor. He goes into a fit of laughter, pounding his fists into the floor.* MAY *makes a move toward the door, then stops and turns to* EDDIE.)

MAY: Eddie! Do me a favor. Just this once, okay?

EDDIE (*laughing hard*): Anything you want honey. Anything you want.

(*He goes on laughing hysterically.*)

MAY (*turning away from him*): Shit.

(*She goes to stage left door and throws it open. Pitch black outside with only the porch light showing. She stands in the doorway, staring out. Pause as* EDDIE *slowly gains control of himself and stops laughing. He stares at* MAY.)

EDDIE (*still on floor*): What're you doing? (*Pause.* MAY *keeps looking out*): May?

MAY (*staring out open door*): It's not him.

EDDIE: It's not, huh?

MAY: No, it's not.

EDDIE: Well, who is it then?

MAY: Somebody else.

EDDIE (*slowly getting up and sitting on bed*): Yeah. It's probably not ever gonna' be "him". What're you tryin' to make me jealous for? I know you've been livin' alone.

MAY: It's a big, huge, extra-long, black Mercedes Benz.

EDDIE (*pause*): Well, this is a motel, isn't it? People are allowed to park in front of a motel if they're stayin' here.

MAY: People who stay here don't drive a big, huge, extra-long, black, Mercedes Benz.

EDDIE: You don't, but somebody else might.

MAY (*still at door*): This is not a black Mercedes Benz type of motel.

EDDIE: Well, close the damn door then and get back inside.

MAY: Somebody's sitting out there in that car looking straight at me.

EDDIE (*stands fast*): What're they doing?

MAY: It's not a "they". It's a "she".

(EDDIE *drops to floor behind bed.*)

EDDIE: Well what's she doing, then?

MAY: Just sitting there. Staring at me.

EDDIE: Get away from the door, May.

MAY (*turning toward him slowly*): You don't know anybody with a black Mercedes Benz by any chance, do you?

EDDIE: Get away from that door!

(*Suddenly the white headlight beams slash across the stage through the open door.* EDDIE *rushes to door, slams it shut and pushes* MAY *aside. Just as he slams the door the sound of a large caliber magnum pistol explodes off left, followed immediately by the sound of shattering glass then a car horn blares and continues on one relentless note.*)

MAY (*yelling over the sound of horn*): Who is that! Who in the hell is that out there!

EDDIE: How should I know.

(EDDIE *flips the light switch off by stage left door. Stage lights go black. Bathroom light stays on.*)

MAY: Eddie!

EDDIE: Just get down will ya'! Get down on the floor!

(EDDIE *grabs her and tries to pull her down on the floor beside the bed.* MAY *struggles in the dark with him. Car horn keeps blaring. Headlights start popping back and forth from high beam to low beam, slashing across stage through the window now.*)

MAY: Who is that? Did you bring her with you! You sonofabitch!

(*She starts lashing out at* EDDIE, *fighting with him as he tries to drag her down on the floor.*)

EDDIE: I didn't bring anybody with me! I don't know who she is! I don't know where she came from! Just get down on the floor will ya'!

MAY: She followed you here! Didn't she! You told her where you were going and she followed you.

EDDIE: I didn't tell anybody where I was going. I didn't know where I was going 'til I got here.

MAY: You are gonna' pay for this! I swear to God. You are gonna' pay.

(EDDIE *finally pulls her down and rolls over on top of her so she can't get up. She slowly gives up struggling as he keeps her pinned to the floor. Car horn sud-*

denly *stops. Headlights snap off. Long pause. They listen in the dark.*)

MAY: What do you think she's doing?

EDDIE: How should I know.

MAY: Don't pretend you don't know her. That's the kind of car a Countess drives. That's the kind of car I always pictured her in. (*She starts struggling again.*)

EDDIE (*holding her down*): Just stay put.

MAY: I'm not gonna' lay here on my back with you on top of me and get shot by some dumb rich twat. Now lemme up, Eddie!

(*Sound of tires burning rubber off left. Headlights arc back across the stage again from left to right. A car drives off. Sound fades.*)

EDDIE: Just stay down!

MAY: I'm down!

(*Long pause in the dark. They listen.*)

MAY: How crazy is this chick anyway?

EDDIE: She's pretty crazy.

MAY: Have you balled her yet? (*pause*)

(EDDIE *gets up slowly, hunched over crosses upstage to window cautiously, parts Venetian blinds and peeks outside.*)

EDDIE (*looking out*): Shit, she's blown the windshield outa' my truck. Goddamnit.

MAY (*still on the floor*): Eddie?

EDDIE (*still looking out window*): What?

MAY: Is she gone?

EDDIE: I don't know. I can't see any headlights. (*pause*) I don't believe it.

MAY (*gets up, crosses to light switch*): Yeah, you shoulda' thought of the consequences before you got in her pants.

(*She switches the lights back on.* EDDIE *whirls around toward her. He stands.*)

EDDIE (*moving toward her*): Turn the lights off! Keep the lights off!

(*He rushes to light switch and turns lights back off. Stage goes back to darkness.* MAY *shoves past him and turns the lights back on again. Stage lit.*)

MAY: This is my place!

EDDIE: Look, she's gonna' come back here. I know she's gonna' come back. We either have to get outa' here now or you have to keep the fuckin' lights off.

MAY: I thought you said you didn't know her!

EDDIE: Get you stuff! We're getting outa' here.

MAY: I'm not leaving! This is your mess, not mine.

EDDIE: I came here to get you! Whatsa' matter with you! I came all this way to get you! Do you think I'd do that if I didn't love you! Huh? That bitch doesn't mean anything to me! Nuthin'. I got no reason to be here but you.

MAY: I'm not goin', Eddie.

(*Pause.* EDDIE *stares at her.*)

(*Spot rises on* OLD MAN. *Stage lights stay the same.* EDDIE *and* MAY *just stand there staring at each other through the duration of* THE OLD MAN'*s words. They are not 'frozen', they just stand there and face each other in a suspended moment of recognition.*)

OLD MAN: Amazing thing is, neither one a' you look a bit familiar to me. Can't figure that one out. I don't recognize myself in either one a' you. Never did. 'Course your mothers both put their stamp on ya'. That's plain to see. But my whole side a' the issue is absent, in my opinion. Totally unrecognizable. You could be anybody's. Probably are. I can't even remember the original circumstances. Been so long. Probably a lot a' things I forgot. Good thing I got out when I did though. Best thing I ever did.

(*Spot fades on* OLD MAN. *Stage lights come back up.* EDDIE *picks up his rope and starts to coil it up.* MAY *watches him.*)

EDDIE: I'm not leavin'. I don't care what you think anymore. I don't care what you feel. None a' that matters. I'm not leavin'. I'm stayin' right here. I don't care if a hundred "dates" walk through that door—I'll take every one of 'em on. I don't care if you hate my guts. I don't care if you can't stand the sight of me or the sound of me or the smell of me. I'm never leavin'. You'll never get rid of me. You'll never escape me either. I'll track you down no matter where you go. I know exactly how your mind works. I've been right every time. Every single time.

MAY: You've gotta' give this up, Eddie.

EDDIE: I'm not giving it up!

(*Pause*)

MAY (*calm*): Okay. Look. I don't understand what you've got in your head anymore. I really don't. I don't get it. *Now*, you desperately need me. *Now*, you can't live without me. NOW, you'll do anything for me. Why should I believe it this time?

EDDIE: Because it's true.

MAY: It was supposed to have been true every time before. Every other time. Now it's true again. You've been jerking me off like this for fifteen years. Fifteen years I've been a yo-yo for you. I've never been split. I've never been two ways about you. I've either loved you or not loved you. And now I just plain don't love you. Understand? Do you understand that? I don't love you. I don't need you. I don't want you. Do you get that? Now if you can still stay then you're either crazy or pathetic.

(*She crosses down left to table, sits in upstage chair facing audience, takes slug of tequila from bottle, slams it down on table. Headlights again come slashing across the stage from up right across audience then disappear off left.* EDDIE *rushes to light switch, flips it off. Stage goes black. Exterior lights shine through.*)

EDDIE (*taking her by shoulder*): Get in the bathroom!

MAY (*pulls away*): I'm not going in the bathroom! I'm not gonna' hide in my own house! I'm gonna' go out there. I'm gonna' go out there and tear her damn head off! I'm gonna' wipe her out!

(*She moves toward stage left door.* EDDIE *stops her. She screams. They struggle as* MAY *yells at stage left door.*)

MAY (*yelling at door*): Come on in here! Come on in here and bring your dumb gun! You hear me? Bring all your weapons and your skinny silly self! I'll eat you alive!

(*Suddenly the stage left door bursts open and* MARTIN *crashes onstage in the darkness. He's in his mid-thirties, solidly built, wears a green plaid shirt, baggy work pants with suspenders, heavy work boots.* MAY *and* EDDIE *pull apart.* MARTIN *tackles* EDDIE *around the waist and the two of them go crashing into the stage right bathroom door. The door booms.* MAY *rushes to light switch, flips it on. Lights come back up on stage.* MARTIN *stands over* EDDIE *who's crumpled up against the wall on the floor.* MARTIN *is about to smash* EDDIE *in the face with his fist.* MAY *stops him with her voice.*)

MAY: Martin, wait!

(*Pause.* MARTIN *turns and looks at* MAY. EDDIE *is dazed, remains on floor.* MAY *goes to* MARTIN *and pulls him away from* EDDIE.)

MAY: It's okay, Martin. It's uh—It's okay. We were just having a kind of an argument. Really. Just take it easy. All right?

(MARTIN *moves back away from* EDDIE. EDDIE *stays on floor. Pause.*)

MARTIN: Oh. I heard you screaming when I drove up and then all the lights went off. I thought somebody was trying to—
MAY: It's okay. This is my uh—cousin. Eddie.
MARTIN (*stares at* EDDIE): Oh. I'm sorry.
EDDIE (*grins at* MARTIN): She's lying.
MARTIN (*looks at* MAY): Oh.
MAY (*moving to table*): Everything's okay, Martin. You want a drink or something? Why don't you have a drink.
MARTIN: Yeah. Sure.
EDDIE (*stays on floor*): She's lying through her teeth.
MAY: I gotta' get some glasses.

(MAY *exits quickly into bathroom, stepping over* EDDIE. MARTIN *stares at* EDDIE. EDDIE *grins back. Pause.*)

EDDIE: She keeps the glasses in the bathroom. Isn't that weird?

(MAY *comes back on with two glasses. She goes to table, pours two drinks from bottle*)

MAY: I was starting to think you weren't going to show up, Martin.
MARTIN: Yeah, I'm sorry. I had to water the football field down at the High School. Forgot all about it.
EDDIE: Forgot all about what?
MARTIN: I mean I forgot all about watering. I was halfway here when I remembered. Had to go back.
EDDIE: Oh, I thought you meant you forgot all about her.
MARTIN: Oh, no.
EDDIE: How far was halfway?
MARTIN: Excuse me?
EDDIE: How far were you when it was halfway here?
MARTIN: Oh—uh—I don't know. I guess a couple miles or so.
EDDIE: Couple miles? That's all? Couple a' lousy little miles? You wann'a know how many miles I came? Huh?
MAY: We've been drinking a little bit, Martin.
EDDIE: She hasn't touched a drop.

(*Pause*)

MAY (*offering drink to* MARTIN): Here.
EDDIE: Yeah, that's my tequila, Martin.
MARTIN: Oh.
EDDIE: I don't care if you drink it. I just want you to know where it comes from.
MARTIN: Thanks.
EDDIE: You don't have to thank me. Thank the Mexicans. They made it.
MARTIN: Oh.
EDDIE: You should thank the entire Mexican nation in fact. We owe everything to Mexico down here. Do you realize that? You probably don't realize that do ya'. We're sittin' on Mexican ground right now. It's only by chance that you and me aren't Mexican ourselves. What kinda' people do you hail from anyway, Martin?
MARTIN: Me? Uh—I don't know. I was adopted.
EDDIE: Oh. You must have a lota' problems then, huh?
MARTIN: Well—not really, no.
EDDIE: No? You orphans are supposed to steal a lot aren't ya'? Shoplifting and stuff. You're also supposed to be the main group responsible for bumping off our Presidents.
MARTIN: Really? I never heard that.
EDDIE: Well, you oughta' read the papers, Martin.

(*Pause*)

MARTIN: I'm really sorry I knocked you over. I mean, I thought she was in trouble or something.
EDDIE: She is in trouble.
MARTIN (*looks at* MAY): Oh.
EDDIE: She's in big trouble.
MARTIN: What's the matter, May?
MAY (*moves to bed with drink, sits*): Nothing.
MARTIN: How come you had the lights off?
MAY: We were uh—just about to go out.
MARTIN: You were?
MAY: Yeah—well, I mean, we were going to come back.

(MARTIN *stands there between them. He looks at* EDDIE, *then back to* MAY. *Pause.*)

EDDIE (*laughs*): No, no, no. That's not what we were gonna' do. Your name's Martin, right?
MARTIN: Yeah, right.
EDDIE: That's not what we were gonna' do, Marty.
MARTIN: Oh.
EDDIE: Could you hand me that bottle, please?
MARTIN (*crossing to bottle at table*): Sure.
EDDIE: Thanks.

(MARTIN *moves back to* EDDIE *with bottle and hands it to him.* EDDIE *drinks.*)

EDDIE (*after drink*): We were actually having an argument about you. That's what we were doin'.

MARTIN: About me?

EDDIE: Yeah. We were actually in the middle of a big huge argument about you. It got so heated up we had to turn the lights off.

MARTIN: What was it about?

EDDIE: It was about whether or not you're actually a man or not. Ya' know? Whether you're a "man" or just a "guy".

(*Pause.* MARTIN *looks at* MAY. MAY *smiles politely.* MARTIN *looks back to* EDDIE.)

EDDIE: See, she says you're a man. That's what she calls you. A "man". Did you know that? That's what she calls you.

MARTIN (*looks back to* MAY): No.

MAY: I never called you a man, Martin. Don't worry about it.

MARTIN: It's okay. I don't mind or anything.

EDDIE: No, but see I uh—told her she was fulla' shit. I mean I told her that way before I even saw you. And now that I see you I can't exactly take it back. Ya' see what I mean, Martin?

(*Pause.* MAY *stands.*)

MAY: Martin, do you want to go to the movies?

MARTIN: Well, yeah—I mean, that's what I thought we were going to do.

MAY: So let's go to the movies.

(*She crosses fast to bathroom, steps over* EDDIE, *goes to bathroom, slams door, door booms. Pause as* MARTIN *stares at bathroom door.* EDDIE *stays on floor, grins at* MARTIN.)

MARTIN: She's not mad or anything is she?

EDDIE: You got me, buddy.

MAY: I didn't mean to make her mad.

(*Pause*)

EDDIE: What're you gonna' go see, Martin?

MARTIN: I can't decide.

EDDIE: What d'ya' mean you can't decide? You're supposed to have all that worked out ahead of time aren't ya?

MARTIN: Yeah, but I'm not sure what she likes.

EDDIE: What's that got to do with it? You're takin' her out to the movies, right?

MARTIN: Yeah.

EDDIE: So you pick the movie, right? The guy picks the movie. The guy's always supposed to pick the movie.

MARTIN: Yeah, but I don't want to take her to see something she doesn't want to see.

EDDIE: How do you know what she wants to see?

MARTIN: I don't. That's the reason I can't decide. I mean what if I take her to something she's already seen before?

EDDIE: You miss the whole point, Martin. The reason you're taking her out to the movies isn't to see something she hasn't seen before.

MARTIN: Oh.

EDDIE: The reason you're taking her out to the movies is because you just want to be with her. Right? You just wanna' be close to her. I mean you could take her just about anywhere.

MARTIN: I guess.

EDDIE: I mean after a while you probably wouldn't have to take her out at all. You could just hang around here.

MARTIN: What would we do here?

EDDIE: Well, you could uh—tell each other stories.

MARTIN: Stories?

EDDIE: Yeah.

MARTIN: I don't know any stories.

EDDIE: Make 'em up.

MARTIN: That's be lying wouldn't it?

EDDIE: No, no. Lying's when you believe it's true. If you already know it's a lie, then it's not lying.

MARTIN (*after pause*): Do you want some help getting up off the floor?

EDDIE: I like it down here. Less tension. You notice how when you're standing up, there's a lot more tension?

MARTIN: Yeah. I've noticed that. A lot of times when I'm working, you know, I'm down on my hands and knees.

EDDIE: What line a' work do you follow, Martin?

MARTIN: Yard work mostly. Maintenance.

EDDIE: Oh, lawns and stuff?

MARTIN: Yeah.

EDDIE: You do lawns on your hands and knees?

MARTIN: Well—edging. You know, trimming around the edges.

EDDIE: Oh.

MARTIN: And weeding around the sprinkler heads. Stuff like that.

EDDIE: I get ya'.

MARTIN: But I've always noticed how much more relaxed I get when I'm down low to the ground like that.

EDDIE: Yeah. Well, you could get down on your hands and knees right now if you want to. I don't mind.

MARTIN (*grins, gets embarrassed, looks at bathroom door*): Naw, I'll stand. Thanks.

EDDIE: Suit yourself. You're just gonna' get more and more tense.

(*Pause*)

MARTIN: You're uh—May's cousin, huh?

EDDIE: See now, right there. Askin' me that. Right there. That's a result of tension. See what I mean?

MARTIN: What?

EDDIE: Askin' me if I'm her cousin. That's because you're tense you're askin' me that. You already know I'm not her cousin.

MARTIN: Well, how could I know that?

EDDIE: Do I look like her cousin.

MARTIN: Well, she said that you were.

EDDIE (*grins*): She's lying.

(*Pause*)

MARTIN: Well—what are you then?

EDDIE (*laughs*): Now you're really gettin' tense, huh?

MARTIN: Look, maybe I should just go or something. I mean—

(MARTIN *makes a move to exit stage left.* EDDIE *rushes to stage left door and beats* MARTIN *to it.* MARTIN *freezes then runs to window upstage, opens it and tries to escape.* EDDIE *runs to him and catches him by the back of the pants, pulls him out of the window, slams him up against stage right wall then pulls him slowly down the wall as he speaks. They arrive at down right corner.*)

EDDIE: No, no. Don't go, Martin. Don't go. You'll just get all blue and lonely out there in the black night. I know. I've wandered around lonely like that myself. Awful. Just eats away at ya'. (*He puts his arm around* MARTIN's *shoulder and leads him to table down left.*) Now just come on over here and sit down and we'll have us a little drink. Okay?

MARTIN (*as he goes with* EDDIE): Uh—do you think she's okay in there?

EDDIE: Sure she's okay. She's always okay. She just likes to take her time. Just to torture you.

MARTIN: Well—we were supposed to go to the movies.

EDDIE: She'll be out. Don't worry about it. She likes the movies.

(*They sit at table, down left.* EDDIE *pulls out the down right chair and seats* MARTIN *in it, then he goes to the upstage chair and sits so that he's now partially facing* THE OLD MAN. *Spot rises softly on* THE OLD MAN *but* MARTIN *does not acknowledge his presence. Stage lights stay the same.* MARTIN *sets his glass on table.* EDDIE *fills it up with the bottle.* THE OLD MAN's *left arm slowly descends and reaches across the table holding out his empty styrofoam cup for a drink.* EDDIE *looks* THE OLD MAN *in the eye for a second then pours him a drink, too. All three of them drink.* EDDIE *takes his from the bottle.*)

MARTIN: What exactly's the matter with her anyway?

EDDIE: She's in a state a' shock.

(THE OLD MAN *chuckles to himself. Drinks.*)

MARTIN: Shock? How come?

EDDIE: Well, we haven't seen each other in a long time. I mean—me and her, we go back quite a ways, see. High School.

MARTIN: Oh. I didn't know that.

EDDIE: Yeah. Lota' miles.

MARTIN: And you're not really cousins?

EDDIE: No. Not really. No.

MARTIN: You're—her husband?

EDDIE: No. She's my sister. (*He and* THE OLD MAN *look at each other then he turns back to* MARTIN.) My half-sister.

(*Pause.* EDDIE *and* OLD MAN *drink.*)

MARTIN: Your sister?

EDDIE: Yeah.

MARTIN: Oh. So—you knew each other even before High School then, huh?

EDDIE: No, see, I never even knew I had a sister until it was too late.

MARTIN: How do you mean?

EDDIE: Well, by the time I found out we'd already—you know—fooled around.

(OLD MAN *shakes his head, drinks. Long pause.* MARTIN *just stares at* EDDIE.)

EDDIE (*grins*): Whatsa' matter, Martin?

MARTIN: You fooled around?

EDDIE: Yeah.

MARTIN: Well—um—that's illegal, isn't it?

EDDIE: I suppose so.

THE OLD MAN (*to* EDDIE): Who is this guy?

MARTIN: I mean—is that true? She's really your sister?

EDDIE: Half. Only half.

MARTIN: Which half?

EDDIE: Top half. In horses we call that the "topside".

THE OLD MAN: Yeah, and the mare's what? The mare's uh—"distaff", isn't it? Isn't that the bottom half? "Distaff." Funny I should remember that.

MARTIN: And you fooled around in High School together?

EDDIE: Yeah. Sure. Everybody fooled around in High School. Didn't you?

MARTIN: No. I never did.

EDDIE: Maybe you should have, Martin.

MARTIN: Well, not with my sister.

EDDIE: No, I wouldn't recommend that.

MARTIN: How could that happen? I mean—

EDDIE: Well, see—(*pause, he stares at* OLD MAN)—our Daddy fell in love twice. That's basically how it happened. Once with my mother and once with her mother.

THE OLD MAN: It was the same love. Just got split in two, that's all.

MARTIN: Well, how come you didn't know each other until High School, then?

EDDIE: He had two separate lives. That's how come. Two completely separate lives. He'd live with me and my mother for a while and then he'd disappear and go live with her and her mother for a while.

THE OLD MAN: Now don't be too hard on me, boy. It can happen to the best of us.

MARTIN: And you never knew what was going on?

EDDIE: Nope. Neither did my mother.

THE OLD MAN: She knew.

EDDIE (*to* MARTIN): She never knew.

MARTIN: She must've suspected something was going on.

EDDIE: Well, if she did she never let on to me. Maybe she was afraid of finding out. Or maybe she just loved him. I don't know. He'd disappear for months at a time and she never once asked him where he went. She was always glad to see him when he came back. The two of us used to go running out of the house to meet him as soon as we saw the Studebaker coming across the field.

THE OLD MAN (*to* EDDIE): That was no Studebaker, that was a Plymouth. I never owned a goddamn Studebaker.

EDDIE: This went on for years. He kept disappearing and reappearing. For years that went on. Then, suddenly, one day it stopped. He stayed home for a while. Just stayed in the house. Never went outside. Just sat in his chair. Staring. Then he started going on these long walks. He'd walk all day. Then he'd walk all night. He'd walk out across the fields. In the dark. I used to watch him from my bedroom window. He'd disappear in the dark with his overcoat on.

MARTIN: Where was he going?

EDDIE: Just walking.

THE OLD MAN: I was making a decision.

(EDDIE *gets* MARTIN *to his feet and takes him on a walk around the entire stage as he tells the story.* MARTIN *is reluctant but* EDDIE *keeps pulling him along.*)

EDDIE: But one night I asked him if I could go with him. And he took me. We walked straight out across the fields together. In the dark. And I remember it was just plowed and our feet sank down in the powder and the dirt came up over the tops of my shoes and weighed me down. I wanted to stop and empty my shoes out but he wouldn't stop. He kept walking straight ahead and I was afraid of losing him in the dark so I just kept up as best I could. And we were completely silent the whole time. Never said a word to each other. We could barely see a foot in front of us, it was so dark. And these white owls kept swooping down out of nowhere, hunting for jackrabbits. Diving right past our heads, then disappearing. And we just kept walking silent like that for miles until we got to town. I could see the drive-in movie way off in the distance. That was the first thing I saw. Just square patches of color shifting. Then vague faces began to appear. And, as we got closer, I could recognize one of the faces. It was Spencer Tracy. Spencer Tracy moving his mouth. Speaking without words. Speaking to a woman in a red dress. Then we stopped at a liquor store and he made me wait outside in the parking lot while he bought a bottle. And there were all these Mexican migrant workers standing around a pick-up truck with red mud all over the tires. They were drinking beer and laughing and I remember being jealous of them and I didn't know why. And I remember seeing the old man through the glass door of the liquor store as he paid for the bottle. And I remember feeling sorry for him and I didn't know why. Then he came outside with the bottle wrapped in a brown paper sack and as soon as he came out, all the Mexican men stopped laughing. They just stared at us as we walked away.

(*During the course of the story the lights shift down very slowly into blues and greens—moonlight.*)

EDDIE: And we walked right through town. Past the donut shop, past the miniature golf course, past the Chevron station. And he opened the bottle up and offered it to me. Before he even took a drink, he offered it to me first. And I took it and drank it and handed it back to him. And we just kept passing it back and forth like that as we walked until we drank the whole thing dry. And we never said a word the whole time. Then, finally, we reached this little white house with a red awning, on the far side of town. I'll never forget the red awning because it flapped in the night breeze and the porch light made it glow. It was a hot, desert breeze and the air smelled like new cut alfalfa. We walked right up to the front porch and he rang the bell and I remember getting real nervous because I wasn't expecting to visit anybody. I thought we were just out for a walk. And then this woman comes to the door. This real pretty woman with red hair. And she throws herself into his arms. And he starts crying. He just breaks down right there in front of me. And she's kissing him all over the face and holding him real tight and he's just crying like a baby. And then through the door-way, behind them both, I see this girl. (*The bathroom door very slowly and silently swings open revealing* MAY, *standing in the door frame back-lit with yellow light in her red dress. She just watches* EDDIE *as he keeps telling story. He and Martin are unaware of her presence.*) She just appears. She's just standing there, staring at me and I'm staring back at her and we can't take our eyes off each other. It was like we knew each other from somewhere but we couldn't place where. But the second we saw each other, that very second, we knew we'd never stop being in love.

(MAY *slams bathroom door behind her. Door booms. Lights bang back up to their previous setting.*)

MAY (*to* EDDIE): Boy, you really are incredible! You're unbelievable! Martin comes over here. He doesn't know you from Adam and you start telling him a story like that. Are you crazy? None of it's true, Martin. He's had this weird, sick idea for years now and it's totally made up. He's nuts. I don't know where he got it from. He's completely nuts.

EDDIE (*to* MARTIN): She's kinda embarrassed about the whole deal, see. You can't blame her really.

MARTIN: I didn't even know you could hear us out here, May. I—

MAY: I heard every word. I followed it very carefully. He's told me that story a thousand times and it always changes.

EDDIE: I never repeat myself.

MAY: You do nothing but repeat yourself. That's all you do. You just go in a big circle.

MARTIN (*standing*): Well, maybe I should leave.

EDDIE: NO! You sit down.

(*Silence.* MARTIN *slowly sits again*)

EDDIE (*silently to* MARTIN, *leaning toward him*): Did you think that was a story, Martin? Did you think I made that whole thing up?

MARTIN: No. I mean, at the time you were telling it, it seemed real.

EDDIE: But now you're doubting it because she says it's a lie?

MARTIN: Well—

EDDIE: She suggests it's a lie to you and all of a sudden you change your mind? Is that it? You go from true to false like that, in a second?

MARTIN: I don't know.

MAY: Let's go to the movies, Martin.

(MARTIN *stands again*)

EDDIE: Sit down!

(MARTIN *sits back down. Long pause*)

MAY: Eddie—

(*Pause*)

EDDIE: What?

MAY: We want to go to the movies. (*Pause.* EDDIE *just stares at her.*) I want to go out to the movies with Martin. Right now.

EDDIE: Nobody's going to the movies. There's not a movie in this town that can match the story I'm gonna tell. I'm gonna finish this story.

MAY: Eddie—

EDDIE: You wanna' hear the rest of the story, don't ya', Martin?

MARTIN (*Pause. He looks at* MAY *then back to* EDDIE): Sure.

MAY: Martin, let's go. Please.

MARTIN: I—

(*Long pause.* EDDIE *and* MARTIN *stare at each other.*)

EDDIE: You what?

MARTIN: I don't mind hearing the rest of it if you want to tell the rest of it.

THE OLD MAN (*to himself*): I'm dyin' to hear it myself.

(EDDIE *leans back in his chair. Grins.*)

MAY (*to* EDDIE): What do you think this is going to do? Do you think this is going to change something?

EDDIE: No.

MAY: Then what's the point?

EDDIE: It's absolutely pointless.

MAY: Then why put everybody through this. Martin doesn't want to hear this bullshit. I don't want to hear it.

EDDIE: I know *you* don't wanna' hear it.

MAY: Don't try to pass it off on me! You got it all turned around, Eddie. You got it all turned around. You don't even know which end is up anymore. Okay. Okay. I don't need either of you. I don't need any of it because I already know the rest of the story. I know the whole rest of the story, see. (*She speaks directly to* EDDIE, *who remains sitting.*) I know it just exactly the way it happened. Without any little tricks added on to it.

(THE OLD MAN *leans over to* EDDIE, *confidentially.*)

THE OLD MAN: What does she know?

EDDIE (*to* OLD MAN): She's lying.

(*Lights begin to shift down again in the course of* MAY's *story. She moves very slowly downstage then crosses toward* OLD MAN *as she tells it.*)

MAY: You want me to finish the story for you, Eddie? Huh? You want me to finish this story? (*Pause as* MARTIN *sits again*) See, my mother—the pretty red-haired woman in the little white house with the red awning, was desperately in love with the old man. Wasn't she, Eddie? You could tell that right away. You could see it in her eyes. She was obsessed with him to the point where she couldn't stand being without him for even a second. She kept hunting for him from town to town. Following little clues that he left behind, like a postcard maybe, or a motel on the back of a matchbook. (*To* MARTIN) He never left her a phone number or an address or anything as simple as that because my mother was his secret, see. She hounded him for years and he kept trying to keep her at a distance because the closer these two separate lives drew together, these two separate women, these two separate kids, the more nervous he got. The more filled with terror that the two lives would find out about each other and devour him whole. That his secret would take him by the throat. But finally she caught up with him. Just by a process of elimination she dogged him down. I remember the day we discovered the town. She was on fire. "This is it!" she kept saying; "this is the place!" Her whole body was trembling as we walked through the streets, looking for the house where he lived. She kept squeezing my hand to the point where I thought she'd crush the bones in my fingers. She was terrified she'd come across him by accident on the street because she knew she was trespassing. She knew she was crossing this forbidden zone, but she couldn't help herself. We walked all day through that stupid hick town. All day long. We went through every neighborhood, peering through every open window, looking in at every dumb family, until finally we found him.

(*Rest*)

It was just exactly supper time and they were all sitting down at the table and they were having fried chicken. That's how close we were to the window. We could see what they were eating. We could hear their voices but we couldn't make out what they were saying. Eddie and his mother were talking but the old man never said a word. Did he, Eddie? Just sat there eating his chicken in silence.

THE OLD MAN (*to* EDDIE): Boy, is she ever off the wall with this one. You gotta' do somethin' about this.

MAY: The funny thing was, that almost as soon as we'd found him—he disappeared. She was only with him about two weeks before he just vanished. Nobody saw him after that. Ever. And my mother—just turned herself inside out. I never could understand that. I kept watching her grieve, as though somebody'd died. She'd pull herself up into a ball and just stare at the floor. And I couldn't understand that because I was feeling the exact opposite feeling. I was in love, see. I'd come home after school, after being with Eddie, and I was filled with this joy and there she'd be—standing in the middle of the kitchen staring at the sink. Her eyes looked like a funeral. And I didn't know what to say. I didn't even feel sorry for her. All I could think of was him.

THE OLD MAN (*to* EDDIE): She's gettin' way outa' line, here.

MAY: And all he could think of was me. Isn't that right, Eddie. We couldn't take a breath without thinking of each other. We couldn't eat if we weren't together. We couldn't sleep. We got sick at night when we were apart. Violently sick. And my mother even took me to see a doctor. And Eddie's mother took him to see the same doctor but the doctor had no idea what was wrong with us. He thought it was the flu or something. And Eddie's mother had no idea what was wrong with him. But my mother— my mother knew exactly what was wrong. She knew it clear down to her bones. She recognized every symptom. And she begged me not to see him but I wouldn't listen. Then she begged Eddie not to see me but he wouldn't listen. Then she went to Eddie's mother and begged her. And Eddie's mother—(*Pause. She looks straight at* EDDIE)—Eddie's mother blew her brains out. Didn't she, Eddie? Blew her brains right out.

THE OLD MAN (*Standing. He moves from the platform onto the stage, between* EDDIE *and* MAY.): Now, wait a second! Wait a second. Just a goddamn second here. This story doesn't hold water. (*To* EDDIE *who stays seated.*) You're not gonna' let her off the hook with that one are ya'? That's the dumbest version I ever heard in my whole life. She never blew her brains out. Nobody ever told me that. Where the hell did that come from? (*To* EDDIE *who remains seated*) Stand up! Get on yer feet now goddamn it! I wanna' hear the male side a' this thing. You gotta' represent me now. Speak on my behalf. There's no one to speak for me now! Stand up!

(EDDIE *stands slowly. Stares at* OLD MAN)

Now tell her. Tell her the way it happened.

We've got a pact. Don't forget that.

EDDIE (*calmly to* OLD MAN): It was your shotgun. Same one we used to duck hunt with. Browning. She never fired a gun before in her life. That was her first time.

THE OLD MAN: Nobody told me any a' that. I was left completely in the dark.

EDDIE: You were gone.

THE OLD MAN: Somebody could've found me! Somebody could've hunted me down. I wasn't that impossible to find.

EDDIE: You were gone.

THE OLD MAN: That's right. I was gone! I was gone. You're right. But I wasn't disconnected. There was nothing cut off in me. Everything went on just the same as though I'd never left. (*to* MAY) But *your* mother—your mother wouldn't give it up, would she?

(THE OLD MAN *moves toward* MAY *and speaks directly to her.* MAY *keeps her eyes on* EDDIE *who very slowly turns toward her in the course of* THE OLD MAN*'s speech. Once their eyes meet they never leave each other's gaze.*)

THE OLD MAN (*to* MAY): She drew me to her. She went out of her way to draw me in. She was a force. I told her I'd never come across for her. I told her that right from the very start. But she opened up to me. She wouldn't listen. She kept opening up her heart to me. How could I turn her down when she loved me like that? How could I turn away from her? We were completely whole.

(EDDIE *and* MAY *just stand there staring at each other.* THE OLD MAN *moves back to* EDDIE. *Speaks to him directly.*)

THE OLD MAN (*to* EDDIE): What're you doin'? Speak to her. Bring her around to our side. You gotta' make her see this thing in a clear light.

(*Very slowly* EDDIE *and* MAY *move toward each other.*)

THE OLD MAN (*to* EDDIE): Stay away from her! What the hell are you doin'! Keep away from her! You two can't come together! You gotta hold up my end a' this deal. I got nobody now! Nobody! You can't betray me! You gotta' represent me now! You're my son!

(EDDIE *and* MAY *come together center stage. They embrace. They kiss each other tenderly. Headlights suddenly arc across stage again from upright, cutting across the stage through window then disappearing off left. Sound of loud collision, shattering glass, an explosion. Bright orange and blue light of a gasoline fire suddenly illuminates upstage window. Then sounds of horses screaming wildly, hooves galloping on pavement, fading, then total silence. Light of gas fire continues now to end of play.* EDDIE *and* MAY *never stop holding each other through all this. Long pause. No one moves. Then* MARTIN *stands and moves upstage to window, peers out through Venetian blinds. Pause.*)

MARTIN (*upstage at window, looking out into flames*): Is that your truck with the horse trailer out there?
EDDIE (*stays with* MAY): Yeah.
MARTIN: It's on fire.
EDDIE: Yeah.
MARTIN: All the horses are loose.
EDDIE (*steps back away from* MAY): Yeah, I figured.
MAY: Eddie—
EDDIE (*to* MAY): I'm just gonna' go out and take a look. I gotta' at least take a look, don't I?
MAY: What difference does it make?
EDDIE: Well. I can't just let her get away with that. What am I supposed to do? (*moves toward stage left door*) I'll just be a second.
MAY: Eddie—
EDDIE: I'm only gonna' be a second. I'll just take a look at it and I'll come right back. Okay?

(EDDIE *exits stage left door.* MAY *stares at door, stays where she is.* MARTIN *stays upstage.* MARTIN *turns slowly from window upstage and looks at* MAY. *Pause.* MAY *moves to bed, pulls suitcase out from underneath, throws it on bed and opens it. She goes into bathroom and comes out with clothes. She packs the clothes in suitcase.* MARTIN *watches her for a while then moves slowly downstage to her as she continues.*)

MARTIN: May—

(MAY *goes back into bathroom and comes back out with more clothes. She packs them.*)

MARTIN: Do you need some help or anything? I got a car. I could drive you somewhere if you want. (*Pause.* MAY *just keeps packing her clothes.*) Are you going to go with him?

(*She stops. Straightens up. Stares at* MARTIN. *Pause.*)

MAY: He's gone.
MARTIN: He said he'd be back in a second.
MAY (*Pause*): He's gone.

(MAY *exits with suitcase out stage left door. She leaves the door open behind her.* MARTIN *just stands there staring at open door for a while.* THE OLD MAN *looks stage left at his rocking chair then a little above it, in blank space. Pause.* OLD MAN *starts moving slowly back to platform.*)

THE OLD MAN (*pointing into space, stage left*): Ya' see that picture over there? Ya' see that? Ya' know who that is? That's the woman of my dreams. That's who that is. And she's mine. She's all mine. Forever.

(*He reaches rocking chair, sits, but keeps staring at imaginary picture. He begins to rock very slowly in the chair. After* OLD MAN *sits in rocker, Merle Haggard's "I'm the One Who Loves You" starts playing as lights begin a very slow fade.* MARTIN *moves slowly upstage to window and stops. He stares out with his back to audience. The fire glows through window as stage lights fade.* OLD MAN *keeps rocking slowly. Stage lights keep fading slowly to black. Fire glows for a while in the dark then cuts to black. Song continues in dark and swells in volume.*)

CURTAIN